Barbara Leaming is the author of *Orson Welles: A Biography* and *Polanski: A Biography*. She lives in Connecticut.

If This Was Happiness

A Biography of Rita Hayworth

BARBARA LEAMING

SPHERE BOOKS LIMITED

A SPHERE Book

First published in Great Britain by
George Weidenfeld & Nicolson Limited 1989
Published by Sphere Books Limited 1990
Copyright © Barbara Leaming 1990

Typeset by Fleet Graphics, Enfield, Middlesex

Printed in Great Britain by
BPCC Hazell Books Ltd
Member of BPCC Ltd
Aylesbury, Bucks, England

ISBN 0 7474 0716 9

A Division of
Macdonald & Co (Publishers) Ltd
Orbit House
1 New Fetter Lane
London EC4A 1AR

A member of Maxwell Macmillan Pergamon Publishing Corporation

'*I*f this was happiness, imagine what the rest of her life had been.'

– *Orson Welles*

List of illustrations

Margarita Cansino (Rita Hayworth) with her father
  Eduardo Cansino (*UPI/Bettmann Newsphotos*)
Eduardo Cansino and his elder sister Elisa (*Lincoln Center
  for the Performing Arts*)
Baby Margarita was born in Brooklyn in 1918 (*Pictorial
  Parade*)
The Cansino children in New York City (*Pictorial Parade*)
Volga Cansino with her children in Los Angeles
  (*UPI/Bettmann Newsphotos*)
Margarita at 12 (*The Academy of Motion Picture Arts and
  Sciences*)
Margarita at 9 in costume for a Japanese dance (*Pictorial
  Parade*)
Margarita and Eduardo, the Dancing Cansinos (*Lincoln
  Center Library for the Performing Arts*)
Rita Cansino during her first film contract at Fox
  (*The Academy of Motion Picture Arts and Sciences*)
Rita and her first husband Eddie Judson (*UPI/Bettmann
  Newsphotos*)
Rita Hayworth at the time of *Blood and Sand* (*Tanguay
  Collection*)
Rita and Eddie Judson in 1941 (*UPI/Bettmann Newsphotos*)
Rita and Fred Astaire (*Tanguay Collection*)
Orson Welles as Mr Rochester in *Jane Eyre* (*Shifra Haran*)
Orson Welles and Rita at the Stork Club (*UPI/Bettmann
  Newsphotos*)
Orson Welles and Rita at their wedding (*UPI/Bettmann
  Newsphotos*)

Rita and her mother Volga Cansino (*UPI/Bettmann Newsphotos*)

Rita singing 'Put the Blame on Mame' in *Gilda* (*Tanguay Collection*)

Poster for *Gilda* (*Tanguay Collection*)

Sequence in Orson Welles's *The Lady from Shanghai* (*Tanguay Collection*)

Poster for *The Lady from Shanghai* (*Tanguay Collection*)

Aly and a pregnant Rita marry in May 1949 (*UPI/Bettmann Newsphotos*)

The invitation to Rita's third wedding (*Wide World Photos*)

Aly holds Princess Yasmin (*Wide World Photos*)

Rita and 3-year-old Princess Yasmin leave court after the divorce from Aly Khan (*UPI/Bettmann Newsphotos*)

Dick Haymes and Princess Yasmin in Las Vegas (*UPI/Bettmann Newsphotos*)

Rita marries Dick Haymes in Las Vegas (*UPI)Bettmann Newsphotos*)

Armed guards protect Rita in Las Vegas (*UPI/Bettmann Newsphotos*)

Rebecca Welles is led out of court after child neglect hearing (*Wide World Photos*)

An exultant Aly Kkan reunited with Yasmin after the long custody battle (*UPI/Bettmann Newsphotos*)

Princess Yasmin reunited with her grandfather (*UPI/Bettmann Newsphotos*)

Rita Hayworth at London's Heathrow Airport (*UPI/Bettmann Newsphotos and Wide World Photos*)

Rita dances with her dear friend Hermes Pan (*UPI/Bettmann Newsphotos*)

Rita and Mac Krim in 1979 (*Pictorial Parade*)

Rita Hayworth with Rouben Mamoulian in 1980 (*UPI/Bettmann Newsphotos*)

Rita with Yasmin (*UPI/Bettmann Newsphotos*)

Chapter One

*I*n February 1917 a vaudeville comic was doing his turn at the Orpheum Theatre in Duluth, Minnesota. Martin Beck's Orpheum circuit, which controlled theaters from Chicago to California, was known as the Vaudeville big time, so the pressure to succeed was enormous. As all vaudevillians quickly learned, routines that played well in one town might fall flat in others, and with no more than fifteen minutes to get his audience, a comic had to be ready to improvise. If not, the booking agent in New York always had thousands of other acts vying to take his place.

That day in Duluth, the audience was enthusiastic, laughing appreciatively at the funnyman's jokes, but standing in the wings was a grim-faced young couple in evening clothes who never once cracked a smile. Although Eduardo and Elisa Cansino had been in the United States for four years and were a celebrated and highly paid vaudeville dance team, the raven-haired brother and sister from Madrid simply did not yet know enough English to understand him. As one observer noted at the time, the jokes of all the comedians in the show were 'to them but sounds which fret the air.' While they waited to make their entrance, Eduardo, twenty-one, and Elisa, twenty-three, presented to the observer 'rather a lonely, pathetic picture,' until suddenly, at the sound of their music cue, the Dancing Cansinos sprang to life.

So spectacular was their customary repertoire of Spanish dances, typically concluding with an American Whirlwind

9

Trot to show versatility, that they were the show's featured performers, or headliners, the act with the greatest proven box-office appeal. But even onstage, where airy fingers, flashing eyes, and stamping heels allowed them to communicate eloquently without words, it seemed to Eduardo that somehow they weren't really connecting with American audiences. No matter how enthusiastic the applause following each turn, he felt let down, disappointed. To a reporter from a local Duluth paper, Eduardo lamented that by contrast with Spanish audiences Americans seemed apathetic. When the reporter pointed out 'that American audiences as fully appreciate but demonstrate differently, Eduardo was unconvinced.' 'CANSINOS WANT "BRAVOS", NOT HAND-CLAPPING' read the headline in the *Duluth Herald* the next day. Indeed, to Eduardo and Elisa the relative proprieties of American vaudeville seemed a world apart from the lusty *tabernas* of Seville, Barcelona, and Madrid, where they had first danced the gypsy flamenco to encouraging cries of *Olé, Elé,* and *Guapa.*

Their father, Antonio Cansino, or Padre, as they called him, had been the first of the family to dance for a living. Born in 1865, Padre was the son of Joaquin Avecilla and Rosario Montero. Although in America Eduardo liked to claim that his father was descended from the Moorish kings of Granada, in Spain others called Padre a gypsy. At the age of fourteen Padre made his flamenco debut in Seville, and in the ensuing years he would dance his way across Europe and back. His wife, Carmine Reina, a Sevillian who, like Prosper Merimée's Carmen, had worked in a cigarette factory before marriage, gave Padre eight sons and three daughters. Padre saw no need to send his children to school: as far as he was concerned, learning to dance was the only education they required. As soon as they were ready, the sisters – Gracia, Carmellia, and Elisa – joined Padre's act. But on tour in Latin America, the two eldest, Gracia and Carmellia, contracted a fever and died. When he returned brokenhearted to Spain, Padre retired from the stage to teach dance, first in Barcelona and later in

10

Madrid. Meanwhile, Elisa was paired in a new act with the eldest son, Eduardo.

Although at first he bitterly protested that he wanted to be a bull-fighter, not a dancer, before long it was evident that Eduardo and Elisa might make the best dancing Cansinos yet. Their career was interrupted, however, when Elisa became pregnant out of wedlock. In 1911, at the age of seventeen, she gave birth to a son, Gabriel Cansino. Elisa temporarily left her baby in Spain when, in January 1913, she and Eduardo crossed the Atlantic to perform in the United States.

When the S.S. *Prinze Friedrich Wilhelm* docked in New York harbor, after a ten-day voyage from Cherbourg, France, Eduardo was seventeen and Elisa nineteen. The customs officer noted that Eduardo was five feet six inches tall, and Elisa was five-feet-five; and both had black hair and eyes. Through an interpreter they indicated that this would be their first visit to the United States, that they were both unmarried, and that between them they had the equivalent of only twenty dollars.

In the beginning they danced at Crossways, the Newport, Rhode Island mansion of leading society hostess Mrs Stuyvesant Fish, whose husband was the son of Ulysses S. Grant's Secretary of State and a descendant of the Livingston, Schuyler, DePeyster, Beekman, and Stuyvesant families. Mamie Fish liked to entertain in the grand style and was constantly on the lookout for new and exotic acts to amuse and startle her guests. Her insatiable appetite for the unusual had led her to engage a long list of assorted clairvoyants, Oriental dancers, opera divas, a monkey billed as Prince del Drago – and now the Dancing Cansinos, with whom she hoped to rekindle some of the excitement that the Spanish dancers Carmencita and Caroline Otero had brought to America before the turn of the century.

Eduardo and Elisa's triumphant private performances at Crossways quickly led to a series of vaudeville bookings in New York, where they perfected a brisk, precisely timed, eight-minute act consisting of three sinewy Spanish dances

11

plus the surprise or 'wow' finish of a fast-paced American number. With an eye toward their prospective audience, they also shrewdly Americanized their look by adopting costumes that were closer to evening clothes than to the traditional dancers' garb they had brought with them from Spain.

Although silent films were already beginning to encroach on its appeal, vaudeville clearly dominated American entertainment during the first quarter of the twentieth century. Modern vaudeville had its roots in the beer-hall bawdy shows popular with American men in cities and frontier settlements prior to the Civil War. But by the 1880s, through the efforts of the first vaudeville impresario, Tony Pastor, who banished coarseness and vulgarity in favor of wholesome family entertainment, the 'straight, clean variety show' – consisting of eight to fifteen short, contrasting acts – had caught on wildly with the American public. The Dancing Cansinos arrived in America just in time to cash in on Vaudeville's halcyon days, when as many as 2,000 vaudeville theaters dotted the continent and the biggest box-office draws commanded top salaries like Lillian Russell's weekly $3,150 or Al Jolson's $2,000.

Despite their recent success in fashionable Newport, as newcomers Eduardo and Elisa were inevitably relegated to perform the opening act – the 'doormat of vaudeville' – which Fred Astaire later called 'the most dreaded spot on the bill' because of the grating distractions of late arrivals. By the time all the latecomers had found their seats and the audience had finally settled in, the brief opening number might be over, which was why the first spot was so often filled with wordless or 'dumb' acts: acrobats, jugglers, trained animals, or dancers.

Such, initially, was the fate of the Dancing Cansinos; but contrary to audience expectations that – as the least prestigious of acts – the opener might be pretty bad, the graceful Spaniards made a powerful impression from the first. 'For an opening number Eduardo and Elisa Cansino more than made good,' noted an early review in 1914 when they did their turn at the Alhambra Theatre in Harlem.

'All of their dances were finely executed and in a later spot on any bill this act ought to prove a cleanup.'

And clean up they did when, in 1915, the impresario Martin Beck engaged them as vaudeville headliners, the most important act on the bill, at a weekly salary of $1,500. Living out of traveling trunks in far-flung cities across America, they appeared with the motley likes of Toots Paka and her troupe of native Hawaiian singers and instrumentalists ('a world-renowned act staged upon a magnificent scale'); the Australian Woodchoppers ('champion axmen of the world'); and the Meyako Sisters, tiny Japanese girls who performed feats of hand balancing and contortion while singing ragtime in broken English. But invariably it was the Dancing Cansinos who enjoyed the greatest success with audiences and critics alike. 'They offer a series of native, classical, and ultramodern dances in the execution of which they have swept American audiences off their feet,' said the *Houston Post* in 1915.

And in Los Angeles the *Examiner* noted that 'both have to the last degree the Spanish wickedness of grace and lithe sensuousness of expression.'

'The pair dances with the abandon of the race,' declared the *Toledo Blade*, 'but there is poetic grace in their every movement.' Whenever they danced, the Spanish youngsters exuded confidence, and their brashness soon became a popular part of the act.

At Hammerstein's Victoria, in New York, which George Jessel would call 'the most glamorous vaudeville theater in all the world,' Eduardo and Elisa delighted audiences with a dramatic and well-rehearsed challenge in English to any modern ballroom or fancy dancers, the famous Castles and Marvelous Millers included, who might be so bold as to try to top them.

Offstage, however, Eduardo knew how to make himself well liked by fellow performers such as Fred and Adele Astaire. While the Dancing Cansinos were headliners, the Astaires were, as Fred recalled, 'only a minor act on the bill and occupied the number-two spot.' But as was typical of his gregarious personality, Eduardo went out of his way to flatter and encourage them.

Vaudevillians knew that they had it made when they were invited to take a flier into Broadway musical comedy. The often loosely structured musicals of the day enabled leading vaudevillians to do their customary turns while accruing the considerable prestige of appearing in a Broadway show. Thus, by 1916, the Dancing Cansinos were making their musical comedy debut in *Follow Me*, starring Anna Held, at the Shubert Brothers' Casino Theatre. Billed as 'Dancers to the Spanish Court,' they made a stunning guest appearance in act one. For twenty-one-year-old Eduardo, *Follow Me* would represent far more than just a professional breakthrough. During rehearsals he became seriously involved with one of the musical's show girls, a tall, striking nineteen-year-old named Volga Hayworth.

Although she had no particular talent or theatrical training, at the age of sixteen Volga had run away from her parents' home on North Capitol Street, in Washington, D.C., to pursue a stage career in New York City. Her father, Allyn Duran Hayworth, was a native of Terre Haute, Indiana, but had moved to Washington, D.C., where he established a printing business and married the former Maggie O'Hare, a native Washingtonian. Volga was Allyn and Maggie's third child, and from the first she had been an outgoing, extroverted girl with a mind and will of her own. Allyn expected that someday his daughter would meet a nice local boy and settle down, but Volga had other ideas. When without warning she slipped off to 'New York, where she appeared briefly as a show girl in the Ziegfeld Follies, the Hayworths were appalled. But for Allyn Hayworth the worst news was yet to come.

Volga quickly decided that she was in love with Eduardo, whose still sparse English only added to the air of foreign mystery that so entirely distinguished him from the humdrum boys she had known in Washington. Stagestruck as she was, she idolized Eduardo for his vaudeville fame and wealth of performing experience. And like many a rebellious teenager before and after, she was by no means discouraged by the certainty of what her father's reaction to Eduardo might be.

Early in 1917 when the Dancing Cansinos hit the vaudeville circuit again, Volga Hayworth went with them. Not long afterward, when Volga suddenly contacted her family to announce that she and Eduardo had gotten married, Allyn Hayworth bitterly told his daughter that he didn't want to see or speak to her again.

Although she was traveling with Eduardo, Volga had to deal with his sister as well. Eduardo and Elisa had been touring together in a foreign country for several years, so it was only natural that their relationship was exceptionally close. When they spoke Spanish to each other, Volga was the outsider who couldn't understand. Whatever Volga's theatrical aspirations may have been, there clearly was no place for her in their dance act. Still, she worshipped Eduardo and made herself useful to him by taking over the innumerable small details of the tour that he and Elisa had always found so vexing. There were hotel accommodations and sleeper jumps or train connections to be overseen, monies from house managers to be collected, and stagehands to be tipped lest they sabotage the act by deliberately misplacing trunks or botching cues. If an act failed to tip properly or at all, disgruntled stagehands made secret chalk marks on their trunks so that the stage crew at the next stop on the circuit could take appropriate revenge.

At this point the greatest difficulty for Volga must have been the discovery that people sometimes mistook Eduardo and Elisa for husband and wife. Strangely enough, the Cansinos were not averse to encouraging this confusion if it suited their purposes. For Elisa the fiction that Eduardo was her husband came in handy when she went before a New York court in August 1917 to arrange for the adoption of her six-year-old son, Gabriel, who had joined her in America. Nathaniel A. Jackolo, a Romanian-born theatrical manager in his thirties, with whom Elisa had begun a romance, had agreed to adopt Gabriel as his own. When, accompanied by Jackolo, Elisa and Gabriel appeared at the adoption hearing, through her attorney she declared that ever since the death of her husband she had been worried about what their son's fate might be if an accident befell her on tour. According to Elisa, these anxieties had begun to hinder her ability to work and the court's approval of the adoption would greatly add to her peace of mind. As to the identity of her late husband, because of the awkward circumstance that her son's last name was Cansino, and because she had never really been married, it was convenient for Elisa to say that her dancing partner, Eduardo Cansino, had been Gabriel's father.

Elisa's statement in court notwithstanding, Eduardo was very much alive and would soon be anticipating the birth of his first child with Volga. He wanted Volga to give him a son, the start of a new generation of Dancing Cansinos, of which he would be the patriarch like his father before him. So when Volga gave birth to a girl on 17 October 1918, in Brooklyn, New York, Eduardo felt a pang of disappointment upon his first glimpse of the baby. 'I had wanted a boy,' he later told an interviewer. 'What could I do with a girl?' Soon Volga and he disagreed over the selection of their daughter's name. Volga wanted to call the child Maggie, after her mother, but Eduardo favored Carmen, after his. Since the Hayworths had refused to accept him into the family, he was certainly in no mood to honor them. But headstrong Volga insisted, and at length a compromise was reached. They would call the baby Margarita, a Spanish version of Maggie. And for her middle name they chose Carmen – the pet name by which Eduardo stubbornly persisted in calling his daughter for years to come.

For twenty-one-year-old Volga the birth of Margarita meant the end of all hopes for a stage career. Scarcely had Volga given birth to her first child than she was pregnant again. In the past when Volga had gone on the road with the Cansinos, even if she wasn't working, she could still cling to her identity as a show girl who had recently appeared in the Ziegfeld Follies and in Broadway musical comedy. But now, with one Cansino baby in tow and another already on the way, her identity was clearly what the vaudevillians liked to call excess baggage: a non-professional wife who traveled the circuit with her husband.

And no sooner had Volga's theatrical dreams evaporated than Eduardo and Elisa most triumphantly realized theirs when the Dancing Cansinos played the Palace, in New York City. For a vaudeville act a booking at the Palace signified the ultimate in professional achievement. The 'Mecca of every vaudevillian', or 'show-business nirvana', as it has been called, the Palace was where performers faced an audience of illustrious fellow-professionals. All vaudevillians longed to play there, but few actually made it. To considerable acclaim Eduardo and Elisa danced at the Palace the weeks of 19 May 1919, and 23 February 1920.

Thus, in the first years of Margarita's life, Eduardo was at the glorious pinnacle of his career, while Volga routinely handled all her husband's practical business so that he could devote himself fully to his art. Already Volga's air of self-sacrifice and efficiency concealed a gnawing frustration: without an outlet for the strong mind and will of her own that had led Volga to run away at sixteen, as well as to take up with Eduardo in the first place, she was often moody and started to drink. The drinking wasn't a big problem as yet, but definitely the beginning of one. In later years her children would euphemistically refer to Volga's debilitating alcoholism as her 'illness'.

After Margarita, Volga would have two more children: Eduardo, Jr, or Sonny, as they nicknamed him, born 13 October 1919, and Vernon, born on 21 May 1922. Although by his own admission Eduardo had been disappointed when his firstborn was a girl, only Margarita among his children seemed to have inherited his dancing talent.

Unlike her mother, who had been a headstrong rebel from the first, Margarita was a quiet, obedient child. By the time she was four (the age at which, according to Eduardo, Elisa had first been paid the equivalent of five dollars to dance in public), Eduardo had enrolled

17

Margarita in the dancing school that his younger brother, Angel, had opened in New York's Carnegie Hall since joining his siblings in America. As she would recall long afterwards, Margarita had had no say in the matter. Padre had been unconcerned whether young Eduardo wanted to dance (he hadn't), and so it was with Margarita.

For her part, Margarita would much rather have been allowed to play with other children than to undertake the grueling routine of dance classes. But because Eduardo was not a demonstrative parent, winning signs of affection from him was difficult, so she invariably worked as hard as she could to please him. In all things Eduardo was the center of the family universe. And Volga was not alone in taking it upon herself to make things easy for him. At the theatrical hotel in New York where they were living at the time, four-year-old Margarita made it her habit to run the bath water for her father.

In January 1923, ten years after he and Elisa had arrived in America, Eduardo filed papers declaring his intention to become an American citizen. He gave his address as 480 Central Park West in New York City, but in fact the family of five had yet to settle down. Although he and Elisa tried to spend as much time as possible in New York, appearing in revues like the *Greenwich Village Follies*, more often than not they were in transit, and Volga's family frequently had to be split up.

Elisa had been married briefly to Nathaniel Jackolo, but he divorced her the following year, after several love letters she had written to a fellow vaudevillian came into her husband's possession. Eduardo and his sister had always seemed to thrive on a vagabond's existence, but by now Volga was anxious to forsake theatrical hotels and put down roots. Life constantly on the road had isolated her and the children by making it hard to establish more than the most fleeting acquaintances. Besides, Margarita was ready for school, and while Eduardo – who was illiterate and had never gone to school himself – saw no good reason to send his daughter, Volga insisted. Finally, in 1925, the Cansinos moved to a modest three-family, red-brick house

18

at 6420 Thirty-fifth Avenue in Woodside, Queens, where Volga promptly registered six-year-old Margarita in public school in nearby Jackson Heights. Hardly had he settled his family into their new life than Eduardo found himself participating in developments that, unbeknownst to him at the time, would again uproot them before long.

It was a measure of his and Elisa's eminence as dancers that in 1926 Warner Bros. engaged them to appear on screen with featured performers from the Metropolitan Opera and the New York Philharmonic Orchestra as part of a gala exhibition of its new sound-on-disc Vitaphone system. The distinguished hour-long program of music and dance would be followed by the premiere of the film *Don Juan*, starring John Barrymore, and featuring sound effects such as the clanging of swords and an orchestral score recorded on disc. The experimental program not only helped revolutionize moviemaking by introducing to a popular audience the element of sound, but – ironically for the Dancing Cansinos – it also signaled the impending demise of vaudeville, much of whose audience would eventually be lost to talking pictures.

As early as 1915 a writer for *Theater Magazine* called the then silent cinema 'the snowball of the amusement world, rolling over the country and growing bigger and bigger as it annexes theaters, managers, actors, and authors.' But all that was nothing compared to what occurred in the entertainment industry after 1927 when the Vitaphone film *The Jazz Singer*, starring Al Jolson and featuring snippets of improvised talk, aroused in the American public an appetite for synchronized dialogue that quickly led to the triumph of the talkies.

Before long a good many of the most gifted vaudevillians were turning up on screen: Fred Allen, Jack Benny, George Burns and Gracie Allen, and Bert Lahr among them. But now, when Eduardo Cansino announced that he was taking his family to Hollywood, his decision was based on more than just a premonition that the halcyon days of vaudeville were drawing to a close. It had already been several years since he and Elisa had reached the heights of professional achievement in vaudeville, so that making the leap to a new medium was a logical next move. To Eduardo, Warner Bros.' having chosen the Dancing Cansinos to appear in the historical Vitaphone demonstration certainly seemed to suggest that an exciting new career lay ahead in the movies. And why shouldn't he have been so confident? Why shouldn't a leading artist of the vaudeville stage assume that an equal and perhaps greater stardom awaited in Hollywood?

The family was at this point well settled into the most stable way of life it had ever known. Margarita was an average student but she enjoyed school, and despite her persistent shyness ('She was always pulled in,' as her brother Vernon described her), she had even made a best friend named Mary. Living in one place among people who had nothing to do with the theater was much more comfortable than the erratic existence they had known before. Nevertheless, as always in the past, Eduardo's needs unquestionably came first now. In his family's eyes he was most than just the breadwinner, he was a great artist, and his artistic fulfillment was worth making whatever sacrifices were necessary. Although he and Elisa had shot their Vitaphone segment in Brooklyn, if it was a career in the movies that he wanted, then they would all have to relocate in California. But not Elisa. Evidently she did not share Eduardo's dreams of a film career, and for the first time Eduardo faced life without the older sister to whom he had been anchored since youth.

Chapter Two

*T*o finance the trip west in 1927, Eduardo lined up engagements in theaters between New York City and the Pacific Ocean. Meanwhile, he hauled his family and possessions cross-country in a dilapidated truck whose lack of heat or springs made the journey exceedingly uncomfortable. Once in Los Angeles, although his dreams of film stardom did not materialize, for a time he did free-lance work as a choreographer at such studios at Warner's and MGM, and by 1929 he had emulated his father by opening a dancing school, on Sunset Boulevard. But he was restless, dissatisfied. As most people would be in his position, he missed the admiration and acclaim that he had enjoyed throughout more than a decade in the limelight.

The dynamics at home never changed, however. As his son Vernon recalled, 'He was the artist,' while Volga attended to the mundane details of living that 'he just didn't bother with.' No matter how much his family continued to pamper and idolize him, Hollywood did not quite appreciate Eduardo as he had anticipated.

The reason was simple. Unlike Fred Astaire or James Cagney, who had both known and admired him in vaudeville and would themselves brilliantly make the transition to Hollywood stardom, Eduardo was hampered by an inability to speak English properly: a fatal flaw in the era of the talkies. He could dance beautifully, yes, but there was nothing graceful about his broken speech.

To make matters worse, scarcely had Eduardo opened

his dancing school in 1929 than the stock market crashed, heralding America's Great Depression. In a time of bread-lines and bank closings, a dancing school was unlikely to flourish. Still Eduardo kept his doors open in hopes of eking out a living from what students there were.

His personal setbacks notwithstanding, in class Eduardo was by all accounts a stern taskmaster, quick to criticize, but not to praise. After class, however, he became once again the gregarious, engaging personality – the nice guy – whom his students seemed invariably to have liked person-ally as much as they admired him professionally.

As in New York, Eduardo excused his sons from studying dance, for which, disappointingly, they showed no aptitude, but he expected great things of Margarita – although she was a bit chubby and as taciturn as ever – and he required her to attend his dance classes religiously after school. Her teacher as well as her father, he spent much more time with her than with his sons. Eduardo had singled her out as the only one in the family who shared his artistic talent, but as a consequence he placed a great burden of responsibility on her that her two brothers happily escaped.

Before long that responsibility would entail a good deal more than any child should have to bear. Soon it was no longer just a question of dancing simply to carry on a family tradition, but to help support them as well. Like many others in the Depression, Eduardo lost his savings in what turned out to be bad investments. 'It got very, very rough monetarily,' recalled Vernon Cansino of the Depression years. 'And this is why Rita was pressed into dancing with him.'

As Eduardo himself would later tell it, he first envisioned reviving the Dancing Cansinos in the spring of 1931, when he saw Margarita perform onstage in the Carthay Circle Theater in Los Angeles with Elisa's twenty-year-old son, Gabriel Cansino. One way Eduardo earned extra money in this period was by choreographing the live stage shows that preceded feature films in movie theaters. This time the film was *Back Street*, and Eduardo was staging a dance number to be performed by Gabriel and a young woman.

The day before the show opened, Gabriel's partner injured her ankle and a very apprehensive Margarita found herself drafted to fill in. Whatever her trepidations, as in all things Margarita did as her father commanded. He may have become a has-been, but to his children, and especially to Margarita, he was clearly still the powerful authority figure he had been at the pinnacle of his career.

A photograph from 1931 shows Margarita striking a pose in her stage costume – 'a roly-poly little girl' (as her school principal aptly described her), whose garish grown-up attire and slash of dark lipstick make her appear to be playing dress-up in her mother's laughably incongruous clothes. But this is by no means the image Eduardo would call to mind when, a decade later, he described to interviewers what it was he saw that made him want to dance with her himself. 'All of a sudden I wake up,' he would say. 'Jesus! She has a figure! She ain't no baby anymore! We can't wait around here, I think.' He decided, as he put it, that the time had come to 'start her off.'

By striking contrast with the sweetly smiling child in the photograph who would have been only twelve in the spring of 1931, subsequent press accounts of her Carthay Circle debut, as in the famous 1947 *Life* profile of Rita Hayworth, would describe 'a buxom . . . sultry-looking girl of four-teen.' The disparity suggests a subtext of profound discomfort with how very young Margarita actually was when her thirty-six-year-old father decided to take her as his partner. But even if the child were two years older, 'buxom,' and 'sultry-looking,' important questions would still need to be asked about the course that her father charted for her.

Clearly Eduardo's motivation for reviving the old act was not strictly financial. With his daughter's help perhaps he could retrieve some of the acclaim – the bravos – that had so stubbornly eluded him in recent years. Thus, in addition to helping him support his family, it would fall upon Margarita somehow to save her father from the devastating ego blows he had suffered since coming to California.

The social isolation that had characterized so much of her experience in the past was nothing compared to the life that faced her now. In school, although the principal noted that Margarita was 'one of the kindest, most motherly girls I ever knew,' her classwork was another matter: 'She did the best she could, which wasn't too good. She was a good C student, but she wasn't very apt at something that required thought.' And now, on account of Eduardo's big plans for his daughter, there would be less time than ever for studying. School became quite secondary to rehearsing with her father, and eventually he would pull her out of classes altogether, even going so far as to lie about her age so that the state would not require her to attend.

While Volga remained behind in Los Angeles with the boys, Eduardo and Margarita worked the floating casinos anchored off the California coast. Beyond the three-mile limit, laws against gambling and alcohol could be blissfully forgotten. (Prohibtion was in effect in the United States from 1920 through 1933). Although Margarita in one sense regarded it as a privilege and an adventure to be going off alone as her father's partner, she soon learned that, in Volga's absence, she was expected to take care of Eduardo's every need – and faced physical violence if she didn't. In later years she recalled for her secretary, Shifra Haran, and others, how, between rows, after Eduardo had drunk and gambled away their earnings, he would send her out to catch fish for dinner. If, as often happened, she returned empty-handed, he punished her with his fists – always scrupulously careful, however, not to leave any marks for the audience to see. Unlike Volga, whose mood swings and fondness for the bottle would lead others to describe her as erratic and even a bit frightening, Eduardo had the ability to conceal his drinking and the violence that often accompanied it from most people outside the family.

Just across the Mexican border was Tijuana, which America's Prohibition had transformed into a noisy boom-town, a sensual paradise crowded with free-spending U.S. citizens in search of pleasure. Besides gambling and alcohol there was rampant prostitution that would cause Tijuana to be dubbed 'Sin City'. When the Dancing Cansinos secured an engagement at the popular Tijuana night spot called the Foreign Club, Eduardo uprooted his family once again, this time to a rented house in the quiet California border town of Chula Vista, then about twenty minutes by car from the Mexican casinos.

Soon after they arrived in Chula Vista, Volga registered the boys, Vernon and Sonny, in school, but Eduardo would not allow her to do the same with Margarita. Although Eduardo undoubtedly would have been furious if he knew that his sons were routinely carrying family secrets outside the house, Vernon and Sonny revealed to classmates that their parents had lied about Margarita's age to keep her out of school.

Gone were the two long pigtails that hung down Margarita's back when she was allowed to attend school. She wore her dyed black hair parted severely in the center and pulled back into a knot at the nape of her neck. Unlike her brothers, she had scant opportunity to talk to anyone, neither in Chula Vista, where she wasn't permitted to have friends, nor in Tijuana, where she was habitually so silent that Americans often assumed she didn't speak English. In 1913, when Eduardo and Elisa arrived in the United States, they had wasted no time in Americanizing their costumes - but now Eduardo dressed Margarita as a Spanish girl so that the audience would perceive them to be a local couple.

Many years later Rita Hayworth would recall that her thirteenth birthday found her crossing the border to Tijuana. Not infrequently men presumed that, like many another young girl in the casinos of Tijuana, Margarita could be purchased for an evening's pleasure. In years to come Eduardo would always make much ado about how vigilant and protective of Margarita he had been in Tijuana. Invariably he would portray himself as a strict and old-fashioned parent at pains to keep the child from harm's way. While Margarita did indeed need to be closely guarded there, the question remains: What sort of parent, strict or otherwise, would keep his thirteen-year-old daughter out of school to dance in casinos in a town like Tijuana in the first place? If, as Vernon suggested, it was money the family needed, surely Eduardo could have discovered a more suitable partner among his students. Eduardo seemed to have relished a bit too much the need to shield his daughter from others in Tijuana, to restrict her activities by confining her to a dressing room much of the time.

Sad to say, the person Margarita most desperately needed protection from in Tijuana was her own father. For there was another, far more terrible dimension to Eduardo Cansino's relationship with Margarita. Some years later she would reveal to her second husband, Orson Welles: During this period her father had repeatedly engaged in sexual relations with her.

The charge shocks, appalls. And yet there is no denying that circumstances were present in the Cansino household that, studies show, frequently give rise to incestuous abuse. Fathers who abuse their daughters tend to be 'narcissists' – men who exhibit an unhealthy dependence on the adulation of others. When some crisis occurs that cuts off the worshipful admiration on which the incestuous father's self-esteem so entirely depends, he turns to his daughter for comfort. However traumatic the ego blows he may have suffered among adults, to the child he remains a figure of unquestionable power and command. Significantly, professional setbacks are one of the major crises known to trigger incestuous episodes: the traumatized parent seeks solace from his daughter for disappointments in the world of work.

In his family the incestuous father is typically the center of attention. He is a 'perfect patriarch' whose needs and demands come first. As befits his narcissistic craving for admiration, family members will describe him in glowing terms: he is greater, more gifted, intelligent, or artistic than other men. But all too often the world outside somehow fails to recognize his superiority, so that it is up to those closest to him, his family, to make sacrifices on his behalf, to 'save' him.

26

The 'incest mother,' however, is generally described by her family as suffering from a mysterious illness that often, as in Volga's case, turns out to be alcoholism. Since the father's abundant requirements must be met at any cost, his wife's disability compels the eldest daughter to take her place. The father accords his daughter a special position as 'the preferred child.' He may tell her that she is the one in the family who is most like he is – she alone shares his specialness, his talent. But invariably she also has responsibilities that the others don't. She must make sacrifices for him, while her brothers, and boys in general, are 'freer to be children.'

This in every detail was the case with Margarita. Not only does the portrait that emerges of the 'incest family' bear a marked resemblance to the family dynamics of her girlhood, but even more important, as we shall see, many of the hitherto disparate, puzzling, and seemingly inexplicable details of her adult life suddenly make sense as never before in light of her claim of early victimization. Of all forms of incest, that between parent and child is thought to do the most damage; by abusing his power over the child who trusts and depends on him, the incestuous parent commits 'the ultimate betrayal,' psychologically scarring the victim for life. As has been the experience of countless others who had suffered comparable abuse, for many years thereafter the destructive effects of that victimization would define both Rita's self-image and her all-too-often troubled relationships with husbands, lovers, other women, even her children.

Love, sex, motherhood: in each of these key areas of Margarita's life the memory of childhood abuse would have a clear and disastrous impact. For all that, even if one were still inclined to doubt Margarita's disclosure to her husband about what her father had done to her in private, there can be no question whatsoever of the very public exploitation to which Eduardo subjected his daughter. Removed even from the possibility of a normal childhood among others her own age, Margarita passed as Eduardo's wife (he forbade her to call him 'Father' in public) in the

27

raucous offshore gambling ships and Mexican casinos where she danced from the age of twelve on. Her father groomed her to be sexually provocative onstage, while off-stage she remained the same shy, withdrawn child she had always been. Had an incestuous relationship not taught the child, as it so often does, to use sex to get and hold attention, the sexually provocative role that her father encouraged her to play onstage would have done the same.

When Eduardo and Margarita's engagement at the Foreign Club was over, the Cansinos moved back to Los Angeles, where Eduardo briefly returned to free-lancing as a dance director in film. There he ran into one of his former students, Grace Poggi, who offered to put in a good word for him with her wealthy new friend and benefactor, Joe Schenck, co-founder with Darryl F. Zanuck of Twentieth Century Films and a major stockholder in the opulent Tijuana resort Agua Caliente. Known as the Monte Carlo of the West, Agua Caliente was frequented by many of the most powerful film-industry figures of the day: precisely the sort of people the Dancing Cansinos would do well to expose themselves to. Thus, scarcely had they returned to Los Angeles when Eduardo carted his family back to Chula Vista again, where they rented the white-frame, three-bedroom house in which they would remain for two years.

In due course Margarita's highly unusual existence made her a figure of immense fascination to the neighborhood children in Chula Vista. Because Eduardo and Volga kept strictly to themselves and refrained from making friends, adults in town didn't know much about them. The local children, however, were most curious about the mysterious goings-on in the Cansino household, and they succeeded in observing and finding out things that the grown-ups didn't.

Loretta Parkin, who was about eleven at the time, had known Vernon in school during the Cansinos' previous stay in Chula Vista. Now they were neighbors, and Loretta and her older brother came to play ball with Vernon and Sonny Cansino almost every day.

Strange, silent Margarita, however, never joined in their

games, although she often sat on the front porch staring silently ahead or seeming to watch as they played. 'She was so shy,' Parkin recalled. 'I felt sorry for her because all her recreation was just sitting on the front porch. That was all she did. See, I had a sister the same age and my sister was going out with boys and had girlfriends and went to school. Well, Rita wasn't allowed to go to school because she had to work to support the family. Vernon and Eduardo, the younger boys, told us that their parents had lied to keep her out because she was the family income. For Rita there was no life, no school, no friends, no girlfriends. She was never allowed to. Just sitting, sitting, sitting. Till it was time to go to Tijuana.'

'Why doesn't she talk?' Loretta asked Vernon one day.

'Oh, she talks,' he replied, 'but when you're not here.'

When the children occasionally tried to speak to Margarita, she answered in monosyllables only. 'We talked to her a little bit,' said Parkin. 'She'd watch when we'd be playing, and I'd say, "Hi, how are you doing?" or, "You want to play?" and she'd just answer "yes" or "no." Once in a while my brother made her laugh a little bit, but even then she would just hardly speak.' Although Loretta Parkin's brother was only twelve or thirteen at the time, whenever he talked to Margarita, Volga or Eduardo would instantly find some pretext to call her into the house.

At one point Margarita finally had some company on the porch: Eduardo's father, Padre, had come from Spain for a visit, but even his presence didn't seem to make her any more talkative or animated.

'They'd both sit there and he'd be carving castanets for her to use,' Parkin recalled, 'but she'd just keep looking straight ahead.'

On those afternoons when Margarita went inside to rehearse new dance steps with Eduardo, the children would stop playing and spy on her through the living-room window.

'Sometimes in the afternoons they practised their routines,' Parkin explained. 'We'd watch through the window while she and her father danced. He'd scream and

29

holler at her, ''Don't do that! Don't be so stupid! Don't do that!'' Just *screaming* at her. He was kind of a small man, like a little banty rooster.' Throughout these sessions Margarita remained ever the docile pupil, anxious to please, no matter how much Eduardo badgered her. 'When she made a mistake, he would shout at her – I never heard her answer him back, not ever. She would simply do the routine again, until he was satisfied. She was always quiet, sweet, obedient.'

Since his vaudeville days Eduardo had been consistently well liked by other adults. But Loretta Parkin's memory of him as 'a little petty tyrant' suggests that, spying on him through the living-room window, the children may have glimpsed a side of Eduardo's personality that, like his drinking, he didn't often show outside the family. People are frequently stunned to the point of disbelief when a man who has always impressed them as 'a nice guy' is said to have committed incestuous abuse. Many such fathers, however, are quite skilled at masking their private brutalities behind an eminently likeable public persona. Indeed, the very same narcissistic craving for admiration that causes them to have sex with a child also drives them always to work extra hard at making themselves so well liked by others.

After these rehearsals, the neighborhood children watched in wonder as Margarita prepared to leave for the gambling casino. Although by day she looked her age in the simple dresses or skirts and blouses she wore to sit on the porch, the distinctly mature clothes she changed into – 'high heels, a dress or a suit, and a hat' – made her look suddenly 'much older,' as Parkin recalled. 'They'd come out about four o'clock and get in the car – mother and dad in front and Rita in the back seat – and off they'd go to work. We all thought it was so exotic and strange!'

By now Volga had taken to accompanying them regularly to Mexico, although, much to her consternation, that meant leaving the boys alone until long past midnight.

'You could tell she just hated leaving those kids,' Parkin explained. 'Even as little as I was, I could feel that. She'd kiss the younger boy, Vernon, and then she'd tell him, "Now when it gets dark, you go in the house. Dinner's on the stove for you." And sometimes she'd say, "You look dirty. Be sure you take a bath before you go to bed." She was a good mother.' As to why Volga found it necessary to leave her sons alone every night, although in the past she had certainly allowed her husband and daughter to travel without her: 'The boys would tell us things,' Parkin recalled. 'Their mother had to go because he'd get drunk and not take care of Rita.' Vernon and Sonny seem to have heard quite a bit at home about how 'the men down at Caliente were always after Rita,' which also helped explain why Volga was needed for protection.

But even when the Cansinos would return to Chula Vista early the next morning, Volga mysteriously continued to keep her daughter close to her, as if she still required protection. And once again it was from Vernon and Sonny that the other children learned about the family's unusual sleeping arrangements.

'That was another thing that was odd,' said Parkin. 'There were three bedrooms in the house, and the father had the front bedroom, the boys had another, and in the third Rita slept with her mother in a double bed. What a strange thing! I have no idea whether they just didn't get along or whether she just wanted to be with Rita. All I know is, that's what the boys told us.'

Indeed, the Cansino boys seem to have enjoyed a certain status among the other children on account of the tantalizing scraps of family gossip they regularly conveyed outside the household. By contrast with their sphinxlike older sister, who invariably refrained from speaking lest she say or reveal something she shouldn't, the boys were only too eager to tell all about anything that struck them as curious or singular at home, even if, as with the family's sleeping arrangements, they may not have fully grasped what it meant. Or did they?

That the boys included the family's sleeping arrangements in their catalogue of oddities indicates that they had been thinking about it and knew it made their family

31

different from others. But did Margarita's brothers consciously suspect the incestuous abuse that she would later report? Did they sense that their father was among the 'men' in Agua Caliente from whom Volga felt the need to protect her daughter? In families where incest occurs, although family members tend to be at least 'intuitively' aware of the abuse, there frequently exists a tacit agreement not to speak openly of it. They perceive the daughter (and she may even perceive herself) as 'holding the family together' by prematurely exchanging childhood for adult responsibilities, whatever this might mean.

To judge by what Vernon and Sonny told the other children in Chula Vista, the boys were only too aware that their sister had to make sacrifices, to be sacrificed – her role as 'the family income' precluded going to school or having friends and dates like other girls her age. In light of what we now know about the Cansino family dynamics, an interview with Vernon, tape-recorded not long before his death and preserved by his widow, Susan, suggests that an awareness of his sister's plight was just beneath the surface, unspoken but constantly in his thoughts. It comes up in the most peculiar digressions and comparisons. 'You ask me, I didn't even think she was pretty,' says Vernon, discussing the war years when Rita Hayworth was at the height of her fame as a sex symbol. Then he blurts out, 'I was her brother! I'm not an admirer. It's family. I mean, it's like looking at your mother. It's the same relation. I don't know how else to say it.' This is not the inconsequential digression one might at first take it to be. On the contrary, it penetrates to the very heart of what he is thinking about just now but cannot say and must instantly deny. Why possibly mention Volga here, or that his own feelings toward his parent were appropriate? Because what he is probably really thinking about and is most anxious not to mention is the *in*appropriate sexual feeling between parent and child that existed in his family: not between mother and son, however, but between father and daughter. After all, Margarita's sex appeal was what he'd been talking about, when this business about his mother suddenly came up. It is a common psychological mechanism we observe here: the impulse to deny the thought, to put it out of consciousness, causes him to blurt out its opposite – that in the Cansino family the relationship between mother and son was quite as it should have been.

Then, moments after he has taken the trouble to indicate that family members weren't about to respond to Margarita's allure, suddenly the inadvertent suggestion slips out that this may not have been the case with Eduardo. Vernon has been talking about how closely Eduardo always guarded his daughter, when the interviewer breaks in: 'Being European, he didn't trust men.'

'Being Latin?' Vernon shoots back in a skeptical tone, then sharply corrects the interviewer. 'No, being a *man* himself, he didn't trust men. I mean, let's face it . . . ' But then, instead of completing the thought, Vernon thinks better of it and laughs nervously. Has he inadvertently gone too far, said too much about Eduardo's attraction to Margarita? It is the sort of laughter we use to cover supreme discomfort, to cope with the feelings and subjects we find most threatening.

Vernon's remarks also shed important light on his mother's enigmatic role in the family. Volga's attempts to protect Margarita, both by accompanying her nightly to Agua Caliente (although that meant leaving her other children alone) and by faithfully sleeping in a double bed with her daughter at home, strongly suggest that she had become aware of Eduardo's pattern of abuse and was anxious to check it. But if she understood what was happening to her daughter, why didn't she put a stop to it altogether? Volga did, after all, continue to go along with the child's being kept isolated and out of school so that she could dance in Tijuana to support the family. And obviously, Volga couldn't keep tabs on her husband and daughter twenty-four hours a day; working closely together and living under the same roof, Eduardo had only to wait until he was alone with Margarita.

Here once again Vernon's remarks prove unexpectedly revealing. He is talking about the loyalty he feels toward his sister when suddenly he alludes to Volga's comparable devotion to Eduardo: 'It's the same relationship, I think, that my mother had for her family and especially my father – and that is loyalty,' he says. 'I don't think she could explain it, nor could I, but I do know this: Rita could cut my leg off, and if she called tomorrow, I'd be there, and she knows I'd be there.'

Indeed, Margarita may have known the extent of her brother's loyalty, but in view of the tellingly violent image he uses here (a severed leg), she also would have known something else – that no matter what violence Eduardo committed or pain inflicted within the family, Volga would remain ('especially') loyal to her husband.

Not all incest mothers do as much as Volga to try to halt the abuse – but a great many, and this includes Volga, remain divided in their loyalties between husband and daughter (with the husband almost always coming first). Concerned as she may be about her daughter's plight, keeping marriage and family intact is the mother's main priority. Without her husband, how would she and her children survive? Who would support them? Alcoholic, powerless, economically dependent, Volga was typical of the incest mother for whom there can never really be any question of altogether removing the child from her father's reach by walking out on him. Nor in Volga's case would she have dared to jeopardize the family income by breaking up the Dancing Cansinos.

The quiet, bashful girl who would sit staring straight ahead all afternoon on her parents' porch in Chula Vista was nightly transformed into a fiery and sensual stage presence at Agua Caliente. But the intensely adult sexuality, which by all accounts she projected in performance, was a facade, for no sooner was she finished dancing than paralyzing shyness overcame her again.

After a performance, when the Dancing Cansinos were routinely invited to the tables of the Hollywood film-industry bigwigs who frequented their friend Joe Schenck's pleasure palace, the bold and provocative entertainer turned back into the timid fourteen- or fifteen-year-old she really was. Anxious as she may have been to please her father, who desperately wanted her to make a good impression on any potential benefactors from Hollywood, she timidly avoided eye contact, and when she spoke at all, as Louella Parsons would attest, 'her voice was so low it could barely be heard' (the shy, self-conscious manner and barely audible voice often discovered in incest victims).

Her agonies of shyness notwithstanding, Margarita was photographed at tables with the likes of producers Carl Laemmle, Jr, and Hunt Stromberg, and displayed at private parties given by Joe Schenck. However protective of Margarita he would later claim to have been, Eduardo evidently had no compunction about using his daughter's looks to gain entrée to film-industry inner circles. More and more he began to pin his hopes on somehow acquiring a film contract for Margarita that could also mean new opportunities as a dancer and choreographer for him.

Since he had always said that Margarita had inherited his talent, pushing her forward posed no particular problem for his ego (like many a narcissistic father with incestuous tendencies, Eduardo seemed to have regarded his daughter as little more than 'an extension of his own ego'). Before long, as Eduardo had hoped would happen, Warner Bros.' casting director, Max Arno, summoned the nervous fifteen-year-old for a Hollywood screen test. The results proved disappointing, and the anticipated film contract did not materialize. This failure could hardly have been easy to bear for a child who had been conditioned to believe that her family depended on her, and whose father had been known to punish her both physically and verbally when she didn't do as he expected.

For the time being, the only motion-picture work that could be obtained for Margarita was as an extra in films being shot south of the border, in which, as so often happened, she passed for a Mexican.

Indeed, in 1934 when Fox production chief Winfield Sheehan spotted Margarita in Tijuana, he assumed she was a local girl, but his host, Joe Schenck, promptly enlightened him. The fifty-one-year-old Sheehan had begun his film career in 1914 as personal secretary to the company's founder, William Fox. After Fox's ousting in 1929, Sheehan became kingpin at the studio. In Agua Caliente, as he watched the Dancing Cansinos perform, it seemed to him that Margarita might have film potential as a Latin type. However wildly exciting she had seemed on-stage, afterward, when he summoned her to his table, where he had been dining with Louella Parsons and several other companions, Sheehan could see that the 'painfully shy' fifteen-year-old obviously wasn't ready for anything substantial. Still, she definitely had something – at least she did onstage – and on the spot he offered to test her imme-diately at Fox.

After the disappointment of Margarita's first screen test, there was considerable pressure on her not to fail this time. As it happened, when the Cansinos drove up from Chula Vista to Fox Studios, on Western Avenue in Westwood, Margarita had the abundant good luck to be assigned a cameraman who instantly perceived what could be done with her. Newly arrived in America, Polish-born cinema-tographer Rudolph Maté had made his name working for such great directors as Carl Dreyer, Fritz Lang, and René Clair. His dazzling camerawork in Dreyer's *The Passion of Joan of Arc*, in which he masterfully explored what one critic called 'the spiritual dimension of facial expression,' would in itself have earned Maté an important place in film history. If any cameraman was supremely well qualified to discover the cinematic promise that lurked in the timid, slightly overweight Margarita, it was he.

Nobody expected a first screen test to reveal a finished product. It was quite enough to show that the aspirant brought with her the necessary raw material for the studio to develop into something marketable. Margarita's screen test was in two parts. The first registered how she would sound on screen (Sheehan had only naturally assumed that her voice would need extensive training), while the second explored how she looked. The latter part, of course, was where Maté's expert eye confirmed Sheehan's hunch that

Margarita might possess that ineffable quality known as screen presence.

As a result of the successful test, Margarita was given her first significant opportunity on screen: a 'decidedly sensuous' dance sequence set on a gambling ship in Spencer Tracy's last picture at Fox, *Dante's Inferno*, which – a nervous Margarita was relieved to learn – her new friend Maté would also be shooting. Eduardo received a bonus as well – he was engaged to choreograph his daughter's appearance with a new dancing partner: handsome, broad-shouldered Gary Leon.

Shortly after work began on the film early in December 1934, Leon sprained an ankle and shooting of Margarita's sequence could not resume for more than two weeks, during which she and Eduardo continued to appear at Agua Caliente. When her work with Leon was satisfactorily completed, Fox offered Margarita a six-month contract, with a standard renewal option. Her engagement at Agua Caliente was due to end on 9 February 1935. Two days after that she would begin work at Fox.

Chapter Three

'It won't come to anything. She isn't good-looking enough,' pronounced Loretta Parkin's mother after Vernon Cansino excitedly informed his friends in Chula Vista about Margarita's big movie contract and the family's imminent move to Los Angeles. Indeed, for most of the difficult year she spent at Fox, Margarita seemed to have felt much the same way.

But it wasn't her physical appearance that worried Margarita so much as her complete lack of acting experience. Dancing was one thing – she knew all about that, as her splendid performance in *Dante's Inferno* clearly demonstrated. Speaking was another matter entirely. The need to project her voice, to make herself heard as she had never done before, often left her in tears of embarrassment and frustration. By her own account, on the set of the first film in which she had a small speaking role, *Under the Pampas Moon*, she was so 'terrified' when it came time to utter a few words to actor Warner Baxter that she 'couldn't stop stuttering.'

By now the studio had abbreviated her first name to Rita, enrolled her in acting, dancing, and riding classes, and encouraged her to slim down through a regimen of diet and exercise. Press releases billed her as a 'beautiful sixteen-year-old Spanish-Irish dancer who has circled the globe a dozen times' and emphasized that she came from an eminent family of Spanish dancers. Despite all the buildup, she remained anxious, insecure. There were times she could not restrain herself from crying openly in front of directors and co-workers. 'Such bewilderment I have not seen in a long time,' said a writer sent to interview Rita Cansino for the *Milwaukee Journal* in 1935. 'She just didn't know what it was all about.'

After she portrayed an Argentinian girl called Carmen in *Under the Pampas Moon*, Rita was assigned yet another fledgling role as Nayda, the Egyptian girl, in *Charlie Chan in Egypt*. All this was to groom her for the vastly more substantial part for which Winfield Sheehan began testing her: the lead in a Technicolor remake of *Ramona*, based on Helen Hunt Jackson's immensely popular nineteenth-century novel about old California. Sheehan hoped the title role of the illegitimate half-Indian orphan would establish Rita as the new Dolores Del Rio (the Mexican-born star of the silent original).

In the meantime, Eduardo's work as a dance director at Fox – with which he supplemented his income from teaching dance – allowed him to continue to keep tabs on his daughter: 'He's closely watching Rita's every move,' reported the *Milwaukee Journal*, 'guiding her as he did when she was a child.' His supervision was not limited to her film career. Unlike other girls her age in Chula Vista, she had never dated or even talked to boys; Eduardo had been the only man in her life.

At sixteen, however, she met and was much taken with a young man who attended Loyola University, but their attempts at friendship and romance proved abortive. Although Volga warmly approved of her daughter's young suitor, Eduardo all too quickly put an end to the relationship. 'He and Rita could never get together in any serious way because my dad interfered,' Vernon recalled. 'She was sixteen!'

Still, Eduardo could not cut Rita off from the other men altogether: from a callow young student, perhaps, but not from the older, far more sophisticated men ('producers', as they inevitably described themselves, even when they really weren't) whom Rita met on and around the Fox lot, and who promised to boost her career in exchange for the usual sexual favors. When she sought the advice of Pinky Tomlin, a kindly actor who had befriended her during the making of her next picture at Fox, *Paddy O'Day* (in which she played her most substantial role to date, as the Russian Tamara Petrovitch), he urged her to turn down any such offers. That she had even considered these offers indicates something important about her. At sixteen she was already seriously thinking it might be necessary to turn herself over to an older protector.

For this Eduardo had only himself to blame. Women who have been sexually victimized in childhood often fail to develop 'normal adult mechanisms of self-protection' and time and time again feel that they must turn to overpowering father figures to run their lives. In their relations with men they exhibit what Freud called the 'repetition compulsion' – the tendency to recapitulate childhood experiences and feelings (however painful) throughout one's adult years. As Rita's life story amply demonstrates, the powerful protectors they habitually seek all too often turn out to be every bit as exploitative and abusive as their fathers had been.

One older man who had his eye on Rita throughout this period was a shady figure named Eddie Judson, a thirty-nine-year-old self-described 'oil man' with a salesman's easy charm and slick way with words. He could talk circles around almost anyone. But behind the flirtatious banter, the surface friendliness, was a shrewdly concealed secret past. 'He was always mysterious,' said publicist Henry C. Rogers, who regularly played poker with Judson in the forties. 'Nobody ever really knew who he was.' No one, even those who counted themselves his friends, knew anything concrete about Judson, especially not about his finances.

'Nobody really knew what Judson did,' said Roz Rogers, Henry's wife.

Eddie always dressed impeccably, and he seemed to have more than ample funds to make the rounds of fashionable night spots like the Trocadero and Ciro's, and those who glimpsed him only in passing typically described him as 'wealthy,' but, in fact, before he hooked up with Rita, he made do on a scant $400 a month. As late as 1942, when writer Adela Rogers St John described him as 'a very successful businessman, with oil and real-estate offices and companies with holdings,' she was merely repeating one of the many spurious stories Judson had put into circulation about himself. And if she had even improved a bit on Judson's original version, he would have been the very last to complain. The more prosaic truth was that, from the day he had turned up in Hollywood, Judson had been skating on thin financial ice. But by spending his money on the right things – stylish clothes and good tables at the hot nightclubs of the moment – he quickly created a very different image for himself. It was a technique that, somewhat later, he would repeat – brilliantly – on Rita's behalf.

Despite the air of mystery with which he persistently surrounded himself, it is possible to trace significant details of his life prior to his meeting Rita. Edward Charles Judson was born in San Jose, California, in 1896 to an American father, born in Portugal, and a Canadian mother. In 1921 he married a nineteen-year-old Chicagoan named Dorothy Oliver in Waukegan, Illinois, but deserted her three years later. She divorced him on grounds of abandonment in 1926.

By then he had turned up in New York City, where he sold swank Isotta Fraschinis (the extravagant vehicle in which Gloria Swanson is driven about in *Sunset Boulevard*). In 1929 in Mamaroneck, New York, Judson took a second wife, the nineteen-year-old show girl Hazel Forbes, who had been appearing in Flo Ziegfeld's *Whoopee*, starring Eddie Cantor, at the New Amsterdam Theater. Before even a year had passed, however, the marriage ended abruptly when, much to Eddie's chagrin, the beautiful Hazel was the purported cause of a fistfight between Jack Dempsey and another fellow. But Eddie's agitation and resentment were far greater when, shortly after the divorce, Hazel married Paul Owen Richmond, the forty-seven-year-old head of a multimillion-dollar Cleveland tooth-powder and hair-pomade concern – and was promptly

41

made a widow when the bridegroom died of double pneumonia, leaving a great fortune (estimated as high as $15,000,000) to Hazel.

At about the same time Margarita Cansino came to Hollywood at Winfield Sheehan's invitation, the 'tooth-powder heiress' (as the press had dubbed her) arrived there as well, but to considerably more fanfare, on account of her millions. And like Rita, Hazel embarked on a film career, although she attracted further publicity by donating her earnings at RKO Pictures to less fortunate players.

Meanwhile, Eddie Judson had married and divorced again, for a third time, but now, in search of his fortune, he headed for Hollywood, where Hazel was said to be living in grand style. Before long Hazel received two extortion letters, threatening her with death if she didn't turn over first $5,000, then $2,500. Instead, she turned over both pencil-written notes to federal authorities and promptly left Hollywood with no intention of returning in the near future. Although she said that she was heading east to take care of business matters, the real reason for her sudden departure was that she was terrified.

During this time, Eddie had been raising money in Hollywood on behalf of an oil-lease deal being put together by a Texas promoter. Judson had gone to Fox to see an executive about the oil deal when at the last minute his appointment was canceled. Instead of going home, quite by chance Eddie wandered into a screening of the tests for *Ramona*. Afterward, whatever salesmanship he did get to use that afternoon was limited to persuading a studio underling to tell him whatever he knew about the sixteen-year-old Cansino girl. The word around the studio was that Winfield Sheehan planned to make her a big star in *Ramona*; but before long the predictions for her future were suddenly very different indeed. Unbeknownst to Rita, dramatic changes were just then taking place at Fox that would alter entirely the course of her career.

When he summoned her to Hollywood, Winfield Sheehan had been Rita's – and, in effect, Eduardo's – benefactor. Since then, it had simply never occurred to the

Cansinos that the seemingly all-powerful studio production head was himself vulnerable, capable of being toppled virtually overnight. Yet it was no secret in the industry that Fox Film Corporation was ailing financially. In 1935 Fox merged with Twentieth Century, whose aggressive leaders, Joe Schenck (the Dancing Cansinos's former employer in Agua Caliente) and Darryl F. Zanuck, quickly took total control of the new joint entity now known as Twentieth Century-Fox. Not surprisingly, Winfield Sheehan lost his job to Zanuck, the former Warner production head who, as is customary in such shifts in command, cast a dubious eye on the projects of his predecessor.

Unfortunately, as Sheehan's protégée, Rita would be among the first to go. After warily studying the tests she had made for *Ramona*, Zanuck declared her all wrong for the part and replaced her with Loretta Young. As if losing *Ramona* were not bad enough, once she had finished the two additional films Sheehan had scheduled for her by way of preparation for *Ramona* – George Marshall's *Message to Garcia*, from which her performance was subsequently cut, and Allan Dwan's *Human Cargo* – Zanuck dropped the option on her contract.

It was this profound crisis in the Cansino family fortunes that gave Eddie Judson the opening he needed. Before that Eduardo would never have let Judson anywhere near his daughter. With the loss of the Fox contract, however, Eduardo had reason to listen attentively when the smooth-talking salesman approached him with an offer to intercede for Rita with major film-industry figures, in whose select inner circles he purported to be welcome. In fact, as Henry Rogers recalled of Judson: 'Nobody in the movie industry knew him. He didn't have contacts.' But Eduardo Cansino didn't know that, and with nowhere else to turn at the moment, he accepted Judson's proposal to promote Rita.

Suddenly, with Eduardo's unprecedented approval, the seventeen-year-old found herself being regularly squired about town by a man her father's age, whose tall stature, flashy clothing, and supremely confident manner all pleased her immensely. There was, however, one tiny physical flaw that could not escape her attention: a missing finger, which evidently had been lopped off, leaving a stump in its place.

Still, it was Rita's flaws, not Judson's, that they discussed on their first evening together at the Trocadero. Among other criticisms, he declared that her outfit was an embarrassment, but reassured her that she could be a 'knockout' if only she would allow *him* to choose her clothes. Many women would be put off or insulted by remarks like these, but from the first Rita seemed to welcome them and readily allowed Eddie to take over every aspect of her life, to dictate her smallest and most personal decisions.

Their strange relationship frequently puzzled observers. 'I couldn't understand what she was doing with him to begin with,' said Rita's friend Roz Rogers. 'The more we knew him the more we hated him, because Rita seemed so defenseless with him. He was like a father figure to her. He told her what to do.'

But that was precisely what Rita liked about him. 'Eddie Judson was like a father to her,' recalled Rita's longtime hairdresser, Helen Hunt. Indeed, she regarded him as a parent who, at least in the beginning, seemed to nurture and care for her as her own parents had not.

After what Vernon would describe as the 'traumatic' experience of losing both *Ramona* and the Fox contract – a grave setback that seemed only to confirm her own worst insecurities – Rita's frail ego was shored up by Eddie Judson's single-minded interest and attention. His constantly telling her what to do and say made her feel not so much dominated as comforted and protected. Like a great many incest victims who seek to escape their fathers by running off with powerful, older men, Rita saw in Judson a protector capable – as the Loyola boy had not been – of freeing her from Eduardo. Thus, when he struck a deal with Judson, Eduardo himself had unwittingly provided his daughter with exactly the way out he had hoped to keep Rita from finding. In the meantime, Eduardo failed to perceive that soon his daughter's relationship with Judson would by no means be strictly limited to business.

Much as he had promised Eduardo he would, Judson very quickly managed to set up a number of free-lance jobs for Rita that paid an average of $200 per film. The one-time automobile salesman's often unconventional agenting techniques included securing discount car prices for any producer who would give his client a role. In addition to playing a tiny role in Columbia's *Meet Nero Wolfe*, Rita appeared in a pair of Tom Keene Westerns for small-fry Crescent Pictures, *Rebellion* and *Old Louisiana*, and in Republic's *Hit the Saddle*, with a popular cowboy trio known as The Three Mesquiteers.

But the real payoff for Eddie's efforts on Rita's behalf came when Columbia Pictures offered her a starlet's seven-year contract – which meant that she wouldn't have to kick around as a free-lancer anymore. As was typical of such contracts, however, it didn't exactly guarantee that she would be employed for seven years, only that the studio could choose to keep her. If she didn't pan out, they could always decide not to pick up the option, which was what had happened when Twentieth Century-Fox dismissed her. The typical Hollywood contract chiefly protected the employer's investment in a starlet like Rita, but did nothing to protect the poor employee.

Still, Eduardo wasn't complaining. No sooner had his daughter arrived at Columbia than they had her on camera doing some of the fiery Spanish dancing at which she excelled, in a picture titled *Criminals of the Air*. Even a small part like this could develop into something big, since Columbia was very actively seeking a potential star or two among the starlets it had under contract.

Incorporated in 1924, Columbia Pictures had begun as a minor production company, but by the thirties, under the strong hand of Harry Cohn, and thanks to the financial and critical success of Frank Capra's *It Happened One Night* (1934), the studio acquired major status. Its one short-coming, a perpetual thorn in the side of Harry Cohn, was its lack of stars under exclusive contract. A major film studio needed stars of its own for two important reasons. Before they put money into films, the eastern bankers liked to see the names of stars associated with the project as a guarantee of their investment. And before they paid for tickets, audiences wanted to know which stars were in the film as a guarantee that they were going to be entertained. Without stars under contract, Harry Cohn had to borrow them from other studios, and generally paid not only the star's salary, but an additional seventy-five percent or so to the rival studio.

Known as a penny-pincher who detested waste to the point of personally turning out any lights studio employees had left burning at the end of the day, Cohn was desperately unhappy about paying extra for loan-outs. Also, when he calculated how much other studios were making from loan-outs, he wanted to get in on the act. Not surprisingly, he was ever on the alert for fresh talent, and as Helen Hunt, the head of Columbia's hairdressing department in those days, recalled, Rita was one of 'a group of girls that Harry Cohn wanted to try out and see if they would amount to anything.' This he did in what Hunt characterized as 'an awful picture' called *Girls Can Play*, in which Rita and the other starlets portrayed an all-female softball team, thereby affording Cohn the opportunity to give them the once-over on screen. Several of the girls were promptly struck out. Cohn 'didn't want to see them again,' said Helen Hunt. Although Rita was not one of the girls dismissed, after *Girls Can Play* Cohn pretty much dismissed her from his thoughts.

The mogul had been heard to make one passing remark about the Cansino girl, however. He declared that she really ought to change her name. *Cansino* was too . . . well . . . Spanish-sounding. At Fox, Sheehan had expresssly wanted to cultivate Rita as a Latin type: a new Dolores Del Rio. Now Cohn was suggesting another possibility, and Judson took his advice to heart. Whence Rita Cansino became Rita Hayworth, by adopting her mother's maiden name. For his part, Eduardo wasn't thrilled about Rita's shedding his name, but it seemed like a necessary evil.

46

Meanwhile, Rita had been quietly planning to abandon more than just her father's name. In May 1937, less than four months after she had landed the Columbia contract, she and Eddie Judson eloped.

Preventing Eduardo from trying to break up her first affair may not have been the only reason for keeping it a secret. Besides drawing them to overpowering father figures such as Judson, the repetition compulsion leads many women who had been sexually victimized in youth to try to recapitulate in their affairs with men the air of secrecy, of 'specialness,' associated with the incestuous relationship.

The day she planned to run off with Eddie, Rita put in a routine appearance at Columbia to finish up a picture called *Flashing Skates* (released as *The Game That Kills*). She was filled with anxiety that Eduardo might somehow figure out that she was about to elope. The only person in whom Judson and Rita appear to have confided was Helen Hunt, whom they ran into at lunch in a popular restaurant across the street from the studio.

Confiding in her was a calculated move. As Judson would have known only too well, Helen Hunt had the ear of Harry Cohn, and Judson was especially keen to cultivate her potentially quite useful friendship. Telling her their big secret was likely to draw her closer to them. They begged her to tell no one else lest Rita's parents get wind of their secret plans.

When Rita ostensibly went out for a routine meeting with Judson that evening, she asked her father to wake her up early the next morning because she had to shoot retakes for *Flashing Skates* - or so she said. Instead, she and Judson left immediately for Yuma, Arizona, where the next morning they dispatched a telegram to Eduardo and Volga announcing their happy new marital status.

Chapter Four

*M*uch as Rita knew it would, all hell broke loose in the Cansino bungalow on Stearns Drive in Los Angeles when the news of her elopement with Judson arrived. Eduardo wasn't the only one distraught, for the news drove Volga nearly frantic. The marriage, Vernon recalled, was 'a real blow.' When some reporters got wind of the elopement of one of Columbia's starlets, at first the family had to admit that they were 'upset' about being deceived, but on second thought, they offered to forgive the Judsons and give them 'their blessing' when they returned from Coronado and Ensenada, where eighteen-year-old Rita and her forty-one-year-old bridegroom were said to be honeymooning.

The reunion was by no means a happy one, however. Nor were the abortive attempts at reconciliation that followed. More than once Vernon witnessed his mother physically lash out at Judson: 'She slapped him on several occasions, in my presence,' said Vernon. It was not a shrewd strategy on Volga's part. The next development was a series of sadistic visits in which, or so it seemed to fourteen-year-old Vernon, Judson would 'come over just to torment my mother.'

Considering the terrible life that Volga had guiltily allowed her daughter to lead since the age of twelve, there was plenty to 'torment' her with at this point. Judson didn't spare Eduardo, either. Scarcely had he and Rita returned from their honeymoon when he began badgering his new father-in-law with demands to pay him back all the money Rita had earned for the family. As far as Judson was concerned, of course, any cash that could be squeezed out of the Cansinos was to have been a mere stopgap until Rita became a big star at Columbia and more substantial funds began rolling in.

Indeed, shortly after they married, Eddie had been heard to brag that Rita was a 'dead cinch for stardom.' Now, even as he commiserated with Rita about her father's exploitation of her, he was already pocketing her entire paycheck every week. 'He didn't work,' Henry Rogers said of Judson. 'He didn't have any apparent means of support.' Except for Rita.

'I married him for love, but he married me for an investment,' she would say later. 'From the beginning he took charge, and for five years he treated me as if I had no mind or soul of my own.'

This was clearly not her view at the outset, however, when, as Henry Rogers recalled, 'she was Trilby to his Svengali.'

In the past it had been Eduardo who had regarded Margarita as his creation, an extension of his ego. Now, as the first stage of Eddie Judson's program to invent Rita Hayworth, the new husband laid down rules for her behavior, and her malleable, submissive nature made her an apt pupil. If she was going to attract the right attention, she would have to look and walk and talk precisely as Eddie imagined her. He complained that she was too fat, so she promptly lost more weight. He said that her voice was too high, so she struggled to lower it.

Never having developed a proper degree of self-regard, and dependent as she was on Eddie's approval and affirmation, Rita learned to see and judge herself through his eyes: a persistent theme in her relations with husbands and lovers for years to come when – as her longtime friend, the makeup man Bob Schiffer, explained – 'She reflected what the men wanted. Unfortunately, that's the way she thought it should be.' Which may be why, more often than not, the women who were close to her, such as Roz Rogers, did not perceive her as an especially sexual being, and were frequently surprised at the intensely sexual response she elicited from men.

Another of these women was the studio hairdresser, Helen Hunt, to whom Eddie had strategically endeared himself. 'I didn't think she had the material,' Hunt said of Rita. 'She didn't quite have the looks. I didn't pay too much attention to her.'

Hunt had glanced at Rita in *Girls Can Play* and, like Harry Cohn, she hadn't been impressed. But Judson implored her to take a second look. Whether Judson knew for a fact that Harry Cohn had lost interest in Rita is not clear, but at the very least he had begun to suspect that things weren't quite working out at Columbia, and he feared that when the time came to renew her contract Rita might be dropped, as she had been at Fox. Just looking at her himself, he could see that something was wrong with her appearance. Even after the arduous program of exercise and dieting, and lessons in voice and deportment that he had prescribed, Rita still fell short of his fantasy of her. His gaze kept alighting on her hairline, which struck him as much too low and seemed somehow to diminish what should have been the impact of her immense, luminous brown eyes. Whereupon a visit to Helen Hunt was scheduled, and although at first the hairdresser wasn't exactly impressed by Rita's looks or enthusiastic about her potential, her suggestions that day were ultimately responsible for Rita's metamorphosis into one of the greatest screen beauties Hollywood has ever known.

'She looked just like a Spanish dancer,' said Helen Hunt of how Rita appeared to her that first day. 'Her hair was just nothing at all. She had plenty of hair, but the edges around the front were so bad!' Eddie enquired whether anything could be done to alter Rita's hairline, which he described as 'terrible.' 'There was something very impersonal about their relationship,' Henry Rogers recalled. They hadn't been married for long, but already he lacked a newlywed's passion. Actually, in Judson's life there could be only one ruling passion: the advancement of Rita's career.

Rita sat quietly as Judson and the hairdresser discussed what was to be done with her. 'She'll never do much in pictures the way she's looking now,' he lamented. Helen Hunt had an exploratory photograph taken in which Rita's hair was 'skinned straight back,' and they examined this image carefully to see what she might eventually be made to look like if the hairline were moved back at the temples and the widow's peak were accentuated. Afterward they visited a nearby electrolysis studio on Sunset Boulevard, where Helen Hunt knew the chief electrologist and where a whole series of appointments was scheduled.

Hunt instructed Rita to report to her every month for more photographs to gauge her progress. In electrolysis an electric current is used to destroy the hair roots; the process can be a long and painful one. Although Rita acquiesced and, as always, did as she was told by Eddie, she desperately wanted to avoid the agonizing treatments. But Judson had made up his mind and there was to be no backing out, no matter how much of an ordeal it might be for her. 'She hated to go there worse than anything,' Helen Hunt recalled of Rita's many months with the electrologist. 'Eddie Judson made her go. He was the one who decided it should be done.'

Less objectionable to Rita, but certainly no less important to her new image, was the lightening of her hair from her natural dark brown to a striking auburn. Rita had already done away with the midnight black that her hair had been dyed earlier, but eventually this new auburn hue was to become her trademark.

Although his funds were very low, Judson paid for all of this out of his own pocket – or, more precisely, out of the money he was pocketing every week from Rita. But the results were clearly well worth the investment. The photographs Helen Hunt periodically had made showed a distinct metamorphosis. 'We'd turn her every which way, and made a nice indentation where the widow's peak would be, then brought it back away from her face, then brought it forward again,' said Hunt. 'A lot of work was done, but more needed to be.' Judson was eager to bring Rita's new look to Harry Cohn's attention, but he decided to delay the plunge until the electrologist finished her handiwork.

In the meantime he launched the second part of his program to invent Rita Hayworth. Although her physical transformation was still under way, Judson began in earnest to try to get Rita seen by the right people in Hollywood. Thrusting her into the spotlight became something of an obsession with him. Before she broke through in 1939 in Howard Hawk's *Only Angels Have Wings*, Rita worked on a dozen B pictures under her Columbia contract. She had to get up at five every morning to get to the studio on time, and in the late afternoon and early evening she was expected to devote herself to exercise, lessons, and treatments, but her nights were a round of fashionable nightclubs with Eddie.

'He would go out and rent a beautiful dress,' said Helen Hunt. 'Then he would make a reservation at one of the better ballrooms. And he'd have her sit on the edge of the dance floor, so that she'd be seen while people were dancing by. Oh, the things he'd do to try to get her noticed!'

As a minor starlet Rita was still really a nobody, so the truly important people in Hollywood were likely to pay her little attention. Therefore, Judson hit upon the strategy of focusing his and Rita's attentions on the press photographers who haunted the nightclubs. Key figures in the movie business may have been regularly seated a few feet away, but only if they were barraged with Rita's picture in the papers in the morning would they be apt to look with any interest in her direction at night. In the hope of cultivating the photographers Rita needed to establish her existence, Judson would invite them over to their table and buy them drinks. It was a good investment, but it was also agony for Rita, who had never gotten over her painful shyness. Still, she had had years of experience in making sacrifices, doing things she didn't want to do. It was part of her job, her responsibilities – and it became part of what she owed Eddie for all he had done for her. At evening's end, if Eddie complained that his investment in a ringside table hadn't paid off because no one important had taken note of Rita, she would often go to bed in tears for fear of having let him down.

The real test of whether all their efforts had paid off would be if somehow they could rekindle Harry Cohn's interest in Rita. Judson had merely been biding his time. With Rita very nearly ready, Eddie knew perfectly well that he couldn't turn up at Cohn's office on his own. 'Harry Cohn would have said no if Eddie Judson had gone to him,' said Helen Hunt, the one person Judson knew who did in fact have the entrée to Cohn that he needed. Eddie's slender resources were rapidly evaporating and it seemed to him only fair that at this point the studio begin to pick up the tab for Rita's electrolysis treatments. Had he asked Helen Hunt to speak to Cohn about this in the beginning, she probably would have balked, since initially, she hadn't seen much potential in Rita. But the months of electrolysis had changed Hunt's mind about her.

As part of his pitch to Helen Hunt, Judson suggested that because she knew Harry Cohn so well and because Cohn liked her so much, perhaps she could approach him on Rita's behalf. It would be a hard sell, of course.

'He hadn't even looked at her after the baseball film,' said Helen Hunt of Harry Cohn. But when she showed him the photographs of Rita they had taken of late, the movie mogul was stunned. 'Those pictures kind of made him wake up,' said Helen Hunt. 'He said, "Look at this!" ' Cohn wanted a new test made at once, but Helen Hunt wisely suggested a three-month postponement, until Rita was absolutely perfect. After he had agreed to pick up the tab for the remaining electrolysis treatments, Cohn instructed Hunt to inform him immediately when she thought Hayworth was ready. He did not regret the wait.

There are numerous apocryphal tales in circulation about how Rita was cast in Howard Hawks's classic *Only Angels Have Wings*. But the real explanation is very simple. Columbia was desperate for stars of its own, and Harry Cohn figured that if he couldn't get them in any other way, he'd have to create them himself. When Helen Hunt showed him the photographs of the new Rita, bells went off in his head. Perhaps the star he was looking for had been right under his nose all along.

Rita Hayworth was about to be created – *again*.

Chapter Five

*A*n opportunity to use Rita presented itself when director Howard Hawks showed Harry Cohn some tentative notes about a new picture he wanted to make: a drama about a pilot who had bailed out of an airplane and left his partner to die. The salty, rough-hewn Hawks had already directed such classics as *Scarface, Twentieth Century*, and *Bringing Up Baby* when he visited Frank Capra one day at Columbia. Cohn heard Hawks was on the lot and summoned him to his office.

Cohn needed a vehicle for Cary Grant and Jean Arthur and asked if Hawks had anything. He left Cohn's office with a deal to direct *Only Angels Have Wings*. Cary Grant and Jean Arthur were the celebrated names on Cohn's lips that day, but he also distinctly had it in mind to plug the as yet obscure Rita Hayworth somewhere into the picture.

'*Only Angels Have Wings*, that was her first big picture,' said Henry Rogers. 'That was when she really broke through.' However important a turning point it may have been in Rita's career, working with Hawks was definitely not a happy experience for her.

After many months of working in basically mediocre films, she had the opportunity to be directed by one of the cinema's finest storytellers. Still, if she had hoped to learn something about acting from him, she could only have been sadly disappointed. To Hawks, Rita seemed terrified when she appeared on the set to play the small but substantial role of the wife of the disgraced pilot (portrayed by Richard

55

Barthelmess). In his typically pungent fashion, Hawks ascribed her nervous agitation to being a newcomer: 'The reason why stars are good, they walk through the door and they think "Everyone wants to lay me!" Some poor little girl who's getting her first part, scared stiff, doesn't know what the hell to do.'

It certainly didn't help that, when he directed Rita, Hawks – by his own admission – sought mainly to spotlight her sexuality. In front of everyone he told her that he didn't really expect her to act – all she needed to do was show the camera her figure. In a scene in which Rita was supposed to be drunk, Hawks despaired of getting a satisfactory performance out of her and ordered Cary Grant (playing Rita's ex-lover) to spill a water pitcher filled with ice over her head. All Hawks really wanted was her natural reaction. There was no question of her doing any acting in the scene; the director even switched and gave Cary Grant the lines she was originally supposed to speak since Rita seemed unable to handle them.

'She got quite a credit for playing a drunk scene and doing it well,' Hawks recalled. 'But if we'd tried to make her *play* a drunk scene . . .'

Although Hawks would later report to Harry Cohn that Rita's ego needed to be built up, his condescending attitude toward her during filming had had very much the opposite effect. Rita would recall *Only Angels Have Wings* with considerable bitterness (Hawks, she would say, had treated her as if she lacked either a mind or emotions of her own), but there was no denying that the film was everything Harry Cohn had hoped for. 'Once Harry Cohn began to see what she had, he became very much involved with her,' said Henry Rogers. Oddly enough, however, Eddie Judson didn't quite realize what had happened and became desperately afraid that Rita's option wasn't going to be picked up. Obviously he wasn't huddling with Harry Cohn, as the legends portray, or he would have known that the mogul had big plans for her and that there was no reason to worry.

But worry he did – and soon Eddie came to the conclusion that for Rita's career really to take off she needed far-reaching national publicity, of a magnitude well beyond anything he was capable of acquiring on his own. He wanted to put into mass circulation images of the beautiful face and lush red mane of hair he had created. And when people read or heard that name, he wanted them to connect it instantly with that face. There had to be a better way than buying drinks for a few photographers, but he couldn't figure out what it was.

Perhaps Henry Rogers *could*. Rogers was a fledgling publicity man and likely to work for a minimal sum. At the poker game they both frequented the men brought their wives, but Rita didn't display much flair for poker. 'She didn't know what she was doing,' said Rogers. 'She was just being a good little wife.' He also noted that she rarely said much at their get-togethers: 'She was quiet and shy. If she hadn't been so beautiful, she would have been a wall-flower.'

Judson kept after Rogers to go to work on Rita's behalf, but Rogers's wife, Roz, who also played poker with them, wasn't so certain of Rita's potential. Not that she disliked Rita – far from it. Roz just didn't know whether it would be profitable to promote Rita as the sex symbol Eddie wanted her to be. As Roz Rogers recalled, 'I said to Henry, "I think she's adorable and lovely and whatnot, but I don't think she's glamorous." I just saw her in a completely different light: a very sweet, adorable homebody.'

His wife's reservations notwithstanding, Rogers agreed to take on the new client, but more out of friendship than anything else. In lieu of a regular fee, he would take five percent of Rita's gross income. Since she was by then earning $300 a week, Rogers got $15.

Although Judson was wrong to think that Cohn had any intention of dropping Rita at this point, his decision to hire a publicist for her was astute. From the inception of the Hollywood star system, starmaking and publicity had gone hand in hand. The star system was born in 1910 when producer Carl Laemmle planted a false story in the *St Louis Post-Dispatch* saying that actress Florence Lawrence had lost her life in a trolley car accident. The next day Laemmle was loudly proclaiming in indignant advertisements that the story had been a lie, and that Florence was very much alive and soon to appear in his latest film, *The Broken Oath*. There followed something unprecedented in the early history of the movies: a big interview with Florence Lawrence in the *Post-Dispatch*, accompanied by a photospread of her. All this publicity naturally generated a great deal of interest in Miss Lawrence, so that when Laemmle arranged a public appearance for her in St Louis, a near riot was reported to have occurred at the train station.

Before Laemmle's publicity coup, the public did not know film actors and actresses by name. Early producers figured that if actors became too well known, they would ask for larger salaries. Laemmle, however, shrewdly perceived that the filmgoing public wanted to know about the people they saw and admired on screen. Not that he wanted to pay higher salaries to actors any more than the other producers did, but he wanted to give his pictures an edge at the box office, and he did this by attracting interest in the names and personalities of Florence Lawrence and others. Laemmle wasn't just selling movies, he was selling star personalities. One way a starlet became a star was by actively attracting interest to herself in the press. Hence the vital role a publicist could play in the buildup of this latest of Florence Lawrence's 'daughters': Rita Hayworth.

The three-year contract Rita signed with him in 1939 afforded Rogers and his wife an intimate view into the private lives of the Judsons. Although Henry had been hired to publicize Rita, his dealings and conversations were invariably with Judson. 'I don't remember *ever* having had any kind of personal conversation with her in which she expressed her views about life or anything. The ability to speak, the ability to do interviews, must have come later in life, because during the three years that I was with her I don't remember her saying three words.' (Interestingly, Loretta Parkin, the little girl who had observed Margarita back in Chula Vista, would say of Rita: 'In a movie, when I'd see her with all this dialogue, it just seemed so *strange*

58

coming out of her mouth, because I had never really heard more than two or three words strung together from her.') When Rogers had to talk about the publicity campaign with the Judsons, if Rita showed up at all, she sat quietly while Eddie did the talking. 'He never let her make up her mind about anything,' said Roz Rogers. 'He treated her like a child.' If a question were posed to Rita, her husband quickly answered on her behalf, without giving her time to formulate a response. Roz told him, 'Let her make up her own mind! For God's sake, don't answer right away!'

Judson calmly replied that, without him, 'Rita wouldn't know what to do.'

Even stranger was her husband's crisp, businesslike attitude toward her. 'Here was a conniving person intent on making his wife a star,' said Henry Rogers of Judson. 'He was the Svengali pulling the strings. He was the one telling her what to do. *Do this, call this one, go and see this one.* He stayed very much in the background. He was never loving, as such, but very attentive and caring. *Fix your hair here* and *This bow doesn't look good.* I never saw him put his arms around her and kiss her. It was always business. If I had been her husband, I wouldn't have been able to keep my hands off her. She was gorgeous! Judson, I always imagined, had a sense of power, and a sense of wanting to make her powerful so that he could bask in the glory of her power.'

As Rita's friend, Roz Rogers had a good deal more success than did her husband in penetrating to her private feelings. 'She was open with me then,' said Roz Rogers of the shopping expeditions Eddie would send the two women on together. He was still complaining that Rita had no taste in clothes, and asked Roz to help dress her properly. Inadvertently, in doing so, he gave Rita a rare chance to relax a bit with Roz, although even in private it went against the grain of her basically acquiescent disposition to complain. 'She was much more open and free, talking and laughing,' said Roz Rogers of their times alone together. No sooner was she back with Eddie, however, than Rita clammed up again. 'She was always afraid of what she would say in front of him, that she wouldn't say the right thing,' recalled her friend.

Rita's publicity campaign was launched with a spurious story about her that, in the Laemmle tradition, had been entirely made up by Henry Rogers. The publicity man had approached *Look* magazine with a unique story angle about Rita. He knew it was unlikely that they would have heard of her at the magazine, so he quickly described her as the Hollywood actress who spent every penny of her $15,000 yearly salary on clothing. She had the best wardrobe in all of Hollywood, he confidently assured them, far more elaborate than the wardrobes of even the biggest stars. Not only that, but recently she had been voted the year's best-dressed offscreen actress by the Fashion Couturiers' Association of America (who at the same time had named Carole Lombard best-dressed onscreen actress, so Rita was in pretty good company). Rogers showed *Look* a telegram addressed to Rita announcing the award, signed by the organization's president, Jackson Carberry. The magazine was intrigued by the story and assigned a photographer, apparently never once suspecting what Rogers himself would reveal many years later – that he had made up the whole thing. The fabulous wardrobe, the Couturiers' Association, even Jackson Carberry – all had been fabricated. It was Rogers who had sent the telegram to Rita at the studio. The award to Carole Lombard he had tossed in for verisimilitude. Once he had lured a major magazine photographer into the Judson's modest bungalow on Veteran Avenue in Westwood, Rogers knew they had better quickly come up with the fabulous wardrobe for which Rita was supposed to have spent all her money. Since Judson certainly didn't have the cash to buy the expensive garments Rita needed for the shoot, they all dashed around town borrowing clothes for her. Rogers understood that the public's interest in stars extended far beyond their film roles; people wanted to know – or think they knew – every last detail about the stars, down to the exact contents of their clothes closets.

Six weeks later Rita was on the cover of *Look*, as the focal point for a spectacular layout inside. But that was only the start of the vast and ceaseless press coverage of the Rita Hayworth phenomenon. Thenceforth scarcely a day went by that the influential columnists and movie magazines of the moment didn't receive items about Rita dreamed up by Rogers. Even better, many of the items about Rita that began to appear in the papers hadn't even been planted by him. 'Once the ball got rolling,' said Henry Rogers, 'it accelerated by itself, it was self-generating.'

Before long Rita was known among the movieland press corps as 'the most cooperative girl in Hollywood,' which meant that she never turned down an interview or a photo session. There may not have been much of substance to write about her yet, but at least she was beautiful and always available – an important consideration for editors with space to fill. The press even began running stories about Rita's publicity campaign, for, in the years since Florence Lawrence, star-making had become an intensely self-conscious process; the steps a starlet took to become a full-fledged star were part of what the public wanted to know about her.

Eager to satisfy the public's hunger for intimacy, Judson happily opened his and Rita's home to the press seven days a week. After all, stars were expected to make their private lives public – or at least to give the illusion of doing so. To Rita the psychic cost of all this constant exposure was immense. 'She was basically *very* shy,' said Roz Rogers. 'She was never terribly comfortable with people looking at her.'

There began a curious phenomenon that would be observed repeatedly throughout her career: while silently and obediently taking orders, doing exactly as she was told, Rita would seem somehow to blank out, to withdraw deeply inside herself. Thus, in a telling metaphor, Henry Rogers would recall that, at photo sessions, she typically 'just went through the motions, almost *robotlike*.'

'I owe everything to Ed,' she would tell reporters. 'I could never have made the grade in Hollywood without him. I was just too backward. My whole career was his idea.'

Not surprisingly, however, Judson himself was responsible for many of the lines attributed to Rita in interviews and feature articles of the day. Not only had he created her look, but eventually he was, in effect, speaking the words that came out of her mouth. As she would reveal later, in private, Eddie constantly reminded her that she couldn't think for herself, that she was – as he put it – 'irresponsible.'

Having once passed for the wife of her father, Eduardo, with whom her behavior onstage was often electrically sexual, with her real husband, Eddie, her outward behavior was strangely childlike. Not only did the disparity between their ages make her seem almost like Judson's daughter, but she acted the role as well. In a tiny, hesitant voice, she would seek Eddie's approval about the smallest aspect of clothing and makeup. Only when he nodded and said that it was all right would she turn to the others in the room. 'He told her when to talk,' remarked longtime Columbia Vice-President Jonie Taps.

As Rita soon discovered, as far as her husband was concerned, there was really no end to *how* cooperative with others Rita should be, as long as it helped her career. To Roz Rogers, Eddie Judson was 'a monster.' 'He was trying to push her to have affairs with people if it was going to do some good,' recalled Roz of this appalling, but perhaps not surprising, development in Rita's first marriage. The man who had rescued her from Eduardo – or so she had perceived it at the time – did not hesitate to suggest that she sleep with other men if, in exchange, they could give her career a push. Nor, as her husband, did he seem to care – as long as *he* chose with whom she slept.

'It seemed to me that Eddie would have sold his wife to the highest bidder if it would have enhanced her career,' recalled Henry Rogers.

It is not uncommon for the husband-rescuer, such as Judson, subsequently to submit his wife to exploitation no less terrible than what she suffered at the hands of her father. Anxious as she may have been to escape her father, and grateful to her husband for having taken her away, there may also be a sense in which, based on what she has seen happen both to her mother and herself, she actually expects to be abused and exploited again – an expectation that, tragically, dooms her to a life of 'repeated victimization.'

'It's the saddest story in the world,' Orson Welles would say of Rita. 'She had the terrible thing with her father. And the *continuation* of that in one form or another. Her first husband was a pimp. Literally a pimp. So you see what she was. *All* her life was pain.'

If Rita was inclined to believe, as Judson insisted, that she should do virtually anything to further herself, it was partly because her film career inexplicably seemed to have stalled again. Notwithstanding Harry Cohn's immense enthusiasm about the potential she had shown in *Only Angels Have Wings*, Columbia had a good deal of trouble figuring out quite how to use her to maximum advantage. For many months nobody seemed able to dream up the right vehicle for her. In 1940 she turned up in five pictures, but not one caught on with the general public, which was undoubtedly more aware of Rita from her bombastic publicity than from her relatively quiet film work to date.

Working so hard with so little success could not have been easy on Rita. Dreadful mistakes like *Music in My Heart* (a musical co-starring Tony Martin) and *Blondie on a Budget* (the latest in the Dagwood and Blondie series) did nothing whatsoever for her image. Nor did better pictures such as George Cukor's *Susan and God* (MGM's adaptation of Rachel Crothers's sophisticated stage play) or Charles Vidor's *The Lady in Question* (a remake of the French film *Gribouille*) spark the public's imagination anywhere near so much as the abundant press coverage of Rita had.

Still, whatever the troubling disparity between the star image that was daily being created for her in newspapers and magazines and the less-than-dazzling film work she was actually doing, Rita continued to drive herself at a relentless pace. After *The Lady in Question*, she had only a single day off before plunging into yet another picture, Ben

Hecht's *Angels Over Broadway*. Unfortunately, while Columbia had pinned great hopes on Hecht's witty script, and while Harry Cohn had shown his continued confidence in Rita by starring her in it, at length *Angels Over Broadway* turned out to be the unhappy fifth in a succession of misfires in her career.

Then at long last came the big role that changed everything. After the Hecht film, Rita and Eddie had gone to Tucson, Arizona, for a brief recuperative vacation, when Warner Bros. requested her for a loan-out to replace Ann Sheridan, who had entered into a contract dispute with the studio, in Raoul Walsh's *The Strawberry Blonde*. For his part, Harry Cohn was thrilled to find that Rita was becoming a valuable property whom other studios sought to borrow for major projects like *The Strawberry Blonde*. Afterward, if Rita came back to Columbia from her loan-out with a bigger name and a greater following among moviegoers than when she left, the value of Cohn's investment in her would be even greater than before, and in the meantime, he would be collecting a surcharge on her salary at the other studio.

Set in the Gay Nineties, *The Strawberry Blonde* is the story of an earnest young dentist (James Cagney) who falls for a gorgeous heartbreaker (Rita Hayworth) but marries a plainer, more down-to-earth girl (Olivia de Havilland). Lighthearted and frivolous as the overall tone of the film may be, at least where Rita's fascinating performance is concerned there is something dark and disturbing beneath the surface. Rita's cruel character wears an icy, impenetrable mask. It is impossible for the innocent played by Cagney to fathom anything of what is going on behind her perpetually frozen smile. She has the curious knack of distancing herself psychologically (Rita would have learned to do this in childhood) in order to make herself unreachable. In *The Strawberry Blonde*, Cagney describes Rita as his 'ideal,' and as such establishes what will be the classic Rita Hayworth image as the girl of men's dreams and fantasies: physically accessible, perhaps, but *not* psychologically. This fantasy sexuality would emerge in a variety of incarnations in the key film roles to follow – *Blood and Sand, Gilda,* and *The Lady from Shanghai* – as well as in Rita's immensely popular wartime pinup, in each of which, as much as she seems to give her body to the camera, she nonetheless keeps her *self* in mysterious reserve.

As in youth, when she had been taught to become another person onstage, Rita would now project a bold eroticism for the camera; but the moment she was off camera, by all accounts, she turned back into her shy, silent self again. Indeed, she may have seemed to come alive during shooting, but invariably afterward, as James Cagney described it, she would just 'go back to her chair and sit there and not communicate.'

Following Rita's triumph in *The Strawberry Blonde*, the whirlwind of national publicity about her picked up even greater momentum. The public seemed utterly enthralled by the idea that a star could be created through publicity. Although Rita obviously possessed an innate and distinctive quality that enabled her to light up the movie screen in *The Strawberry Blonde*, readers of movie magazines engaged in the delightful fantasy that, with the right coaching and publicity, they, too, could be magically transformed into stars. For Rita the knowledge that she had been in large part *created* would remain a source of immense anxiety; did she really have any acting talent, or was it all a publicist's hype? Ironically, for the public this was from the first a big part of her appeal. By contrast with the otherworldly likes of Greta Garbo or Marlene Dietrich, Rita Hayworth was someone with whom moviemagazine readers could identify.

After remaining on loan to Warner Bros., where she was cast in an abortive comedy titled *Affectionately Yours*, Rita returned to Twentieth Century-Fox, of all places – again on loan-out from her home studio, Columbia – to make *Blood and Sand* for her old nemesis Darryl F. Zanuck. Only five years before, when he took charge at Fox in 1936, Zanuck had turned up his nose at the little 'Spanish' dancing girl whose contract he scornfully refused to renew. She had seemed hopeless to him then. But in 1941 she had metamorphosed into something else entirely, and suddenly Fox could not do without her. Before, Zanuck had had her under contract for pennies; now the director Rouben Mamoulian insisted on Rita for his new film, Zanuck would have to ransom her from Harry Cohn. Rita must have gotten some grim satisfaction from Zanuck's comeuppance when she returned in triumph to Fox.

Having spent several years being transformed into an all-American glamour girl, Rita had been summoned back to play a Spaniard – precisely what Judson and others complained she looked too much like before the transformation. For the role of the Spanish femme fatale Doña Sol, Mamoulian had initially had the exotic Maria Montez in mind, but on inspection he had found her screen test disappointing. At length, after considering several other actresses, the urbane Russian-born Mamoulian – who had been romantically involved with Greta Garbo and rumored to be close to marriage with her at the time he directed her in *Queen Christina* – discovered in Rita Hayworth something of Garbo's sphinxlike mystery. At their first meeting he was fascinated by Rita's languid, sensual way of walking, which he told her reminded him of a great cat. In *Blood and Sand* Mamoulian's sensitive direction would vastly intensify the enigmatic quality she had already demonstrated in Walsh's *The Strawberry Blonde*.

In this, however, he had a most capable partner in the incomparable Hermes Pan, who was called in to work with Rita for the film. Celebrated for his brilliant choreography for Fred Astaire, Pan also had an immense, if less well-known, impact on Rita's career, for it was he who liberated the raw kinetic energy within her that no one had hitherto been quite able to tap, and that, thanks to him, made its first dazzling appearance on screen in *Blood and Sand*.

Hermes Pan would also soon become one of the great friends of her life. 'She was so simple and down to earth,' he recalled of their first meeting to discuss the Mamoulian picture. 'I liked her right away. We became very friendly, and it remained over the years. She would sort of confide in me. I guess she knew that I wasn't after anything and that

66

she could talk to me without me talking to other people. She was always a little suspicious of people. We became very close because she trusted me.'

It was by no means in conversation that the two communicated most eloquently. By all accounts Rita was no more talkative at this point than she had been as a girl in Chula Vista. As a choreographer Pan was tuned in to her nonverbal mode of self-expression. He understood her code.

'She always reminded me of a gypsy,' he recalled. 'Her moods, you know. She would suddenly get up and start to dance. You'd talk to her, but she wouldn't answer, she'd just *dance*. But it was beautiful!' Even when Rita wasn't literally dancing, he was acutely sensitive to her every gesture. 'She would never *say* what she thought much,' he recalled. 'But you could tell. I knew her well enough to know whether she liked somebody or didn't like him, or whether she resented a question or something you might say.' When he brought up the sensitive subject of her father, Pan perceived at once that 'she didn't like him. I could tell there was a strain there. She would just shrug her shoulders and say, "Well, I don't know." '

Thankful for a friend with whom she could communicate almost wordlessly, Rita became a frequent visitor to Pan's home, where he cooked spaghetti dinners for the two of them.

Already the mood swings that were to become prevalent later in life manifested themselves, and her good friend respected these melancholic silences. 'I have seen her switch moods very quickly,' said Pan. 'Even then I had seen indications of mood changes. Suddenly from being sort of *up*, she would just get *down*. You could tell that maybe she was preoccupied about something. Then it would pass and she would be herself.'

Although *Blood and Sand* was a serious drama and *The Strawberry Blonde* had been a lighthearted comedy, Rita's Doña Sol bears a significant resemblance to her role in the earlier film. Once again Rita was called upon to transform herself into an icy heartbreaker. The sexual triangle of *The*

Strawberry Blonde reappears here as well, although in a much darker form. This time it is Tyrone Power, as a Spanish bullfighter, who becomes obsessed with her to the point of self-destruction. As in *The Strawberry Blonde*, there is a kind, down-to-earth woman, represented here by Linda Darnell as the bullfighter's loving wife, whose sensitive face provides a stark contrast to Rita's once again impenetrable, masklike beauty. This time, gloriously liberated from the confining whalebone corset and tightly pinned-up hair that went with the Gay Nineties setting of *The Strawberry Blonde*, Rita burst forth as the great erotic icon of the forties. There in lurid Technicolor is the signature auburn hair, tumbling down to her astonishingly broad, sensuous shoulders. Indeed, those shoulders in themselves play an indispensable role in the film when Rita seduces Power by moving them hypnotically as she plays the guitar and sings to him. The voice with which Doña Sol sings is not Rita's own – but no matter. The seduction is enacted almost entirely with those dancing, undulating shoulders, assisted by what Hermes Pan called 'the most beautiful hands I think I've ever seen,' long slender fingers tapping rhythmically on the guitar. For that matter, virtually *all* of Rita's performance in the film is carried by the richly expressive movement Pan helped her to create, rather than by her line readings, which, in a misguided attempt to seem refined, are more often than not stilted and even slightly absurd.

'That picture is the thing that zoomed her,' said Pan of *Blood and Sand*. 'There's that one close-up, the one up in the balcony. And *that* did it.' The close-up in question shows Doña Sol fixing her gaze on the handsome bullfighter. But it isn't her beauty alone that makes this image so arresting. It is the intense sexual desire that every inch of her conveys: the fact that, thenceforth, Doña Sol will be the desiring subject, the sexual aggressor, the callous seducer.

Although they are not, strictly speaking, dance sequences, Pan worked with Rita both on the remarkable scene in which she seduces Power, and a later scene in which, in a thinly veiled sadomasochistic charade, she pretends to be a bullfighter and Power the bull.

All this had little to do with the Rita Hermes Pan had come to know off screen. 'A whole different personality came out for the camera,' he explained. In private, Rita was antithetical to the provocative characters she played in films like *Blood and Sand*. 'She always reminded me of a little girl,' said Pan. 'She would giggle or she would do little things that little girls do. People would think of her as the glamorous Love Goddess, and yet she was just a little eight-year-old girl. It was an amazing transformation – or, rather, an amazing *combination*. You couldn't believe the two were the same person!' Indeed, the very same Rita who so successfully incarnated the ruthless Doña Sol on screen was meanwhile playing a very different role at home with Eddie.

After Rita's triumph in *Blood and Sand*, her option at Columbia was about to come up, and Judson – always looking for an angle to exploit – wanted Harry Cohn to be pleased with her. He and Rita had been invited to spend the weekend with Cohn on his yacht, but Judson had a different idea. He told Henry Rogers that at the last minute he would claim to be sick, so that Rita could go off alone with the mogul. Rogers was appalled. It was perfectly obvious that at this stage in her career Rita didn't have to go to bed with Harry Cohn. She had done well enough of late for him to have happily renewed her contract without Judson's pimping. But Judson was adamant. 'She didn't want to go,' said Roz Rogers, 'and he insisted she go.' Cowering in fear of her husband's outrageous demands, Rita was no Doña Sol. 'It was almost like her father saying, "You've got to go," ' said Roz Rogers. 'She was afraid of him. She was desperate, I'll tell you that. She *had* to get out of it.'

Chapter Six

*A*t this point Rita made an important decision, one that she stuck with for all the years she was at Columbia. Although she was accustomed to doing whatever her husband told her to do, she refused to offer herself sexually to Harry Cohn. If Eddie conspired to send her off in intimate circumstances with the notoriously crude movie mogul, she had no choice but to go on the boat, as ordered. But she decided that she didn't have to sleep with Cohn.

Cohn, however, developed an obsession with getting Rita into bed that was more than just sexually motivated; he had what Orson Welles called 'a tremendous proprietary sense for Rita.' It had taken Cohn so long to get a star under contract to him alone that he wanted to possess her in all ways. As time went by he would become preoccupied with keeping other men out of her life, including her own husband and any other men who might come between Rita and the studio.

There was also the added complication of Cohn's wounded ego. As Orson Welles pointed out, Eddie Judson had become known around Hollywood as a 'pimp.' Rita's steadfast refusal to sleep with Harry Cohn, even when her own husband ordered her to, seemed only to get the mogul's juices going, to make him more obsessed with her than ever. It created a good deal of tension between them that was to last for all the years of their temptestuous working relationship. As Columbia makeup man Bob Schiffer explained, 'All Harry Cohn wanted to do was get even because he'd never had any sexual encounter of any kind with Rita, which annoyed the hell out of him.'

'Harry Cohn always had a yen for her,' recalled dancer and musical-comedy star Ann Miller. 'Her big problem on the lot was trying to get away from him because he was really mad for her.'

Even if Cohn couldn't possess Rita sexually, like a jealous lover he insisted on knowing her every move, and went so far as to put hidden microphones in her dressing room to listen in on her private conversations. 'He had spies everywhere,' said Shifra Haran. 'Miss Hayworth couldn't go to the toilet, he knew where she was, what she was doing.'

Rita's resistance to Cohn was perhaps the first really independent action she had undertaken, and it was an important first step toward breaking loose from Eddie. 'She was stronger than we all thought,' said Roz Rogers. 'She was so young. As she got older she got a little more guts. Underneath she grew. She got stronger and stronger, and was able to survive.'

Before long Rita's instincts were proven correct. Columbia renewed her contract even though she hadn't slept with the boss. For his part, Cohn was far too shrewd a businessman to let sexual rejection get in the way of using Rita in the next picture he had in mind for her. It was a mark of how highly Columbia thought of Rita's box-office appeal at this point that they brought her back to the studio as Fred Astaire's new partner in *You'll Never Get Rich*, dancing to the music of Cole Porter. Fred and his elder sister, Adele, had once reigned as the American theater's most important dance team, and later, paired with Ginger Rogers, he had similarly dominated the American cinema. Thus, finding herself appointed the great Astaire's latest teammate was a major new triumph for Rita.

Still, on her return to Columbia after her emergence as a star, Rita didn't exactly get star treatment. From the first, Harry Cohn treated her with unabashed rudeness, and others at the studio followed suit. 'They were always demeaning to her,' recalled Bob Schiffer. When she was in

Cohn's office the mogul would get up to use the bathroom and leave the door wide open. This was an act of contempt, as if he wanted to show her that no matter how successful she might be on screen, as far as he was concerned she was still nothing. Her own husband's having offered her sexually to other men seemed to have cheapened Rita in Cohn's eyes, and his attitude toward her never really changed.

'He gave her a hard time,' recalled Ann Miller, who didn't have the same trouble with Cohn, and explained why. 'He had a temper and he cursed a lot. I think he offended a lot of people with his language, but basically Harry Cohn was a very tough, gruff, good businessman. You always knew where you stood with him. There was never any pussy-footing around. I never had any problem with him because I had a very strict, very strong mother. I was very young when I was at Columbia. I was seventeen, and I have to tell you, this man respected me and my mother, and if anybody cursed me when I was in the office, if anybody said something, he called them down. He had great respect for me, so therefore I never saw him the way a lot of the girls probably did that he didn't think were quite that nice. My mother brought me up very strict and I worked very hard, and he respected that. I had a very nice relationship with him. He was my boss and that was it. He never tried to chase me. But he was really enamoured of Rita. Her whole life was running from him.'

Despite problems at home with Eddie, who responded angrily to Rita's challenge to his authority, and on the job with Harry Cohn, during the filming of *You'll Never Get Rich* nothing in Rita's behavior even remotely suggested that anything was wrong. Their unhappy personal circumstances notwithstanding, women who, like Rita, have been exploited in youth often exhibit unusual diligence and dedication on the job: the adult responsibilities with which they were burdened in childhood have prepared them for a life of disciplined labor and self-sacrifice – although all too frequently, as in youth, their labors ultimately afford them little in the way of satisfaction. It is a profile that quite perfectly describes much of Rita's film career, in which an almost compulsive discipline on the job would often stand out in marked contrast to the chaos of her personal life.

For his part, Fred Astaire was delighted by his hardworking partner, whom he called a 'born dancer': 'She learned steps faster than anyone I've ever known,' he would say. 'I'd show her a routine before lunch. She'd be back right after lunch and have it down to perfection. She apparently figured it out in her mind while she was eating.'

In their first number together, a rumba, 'So Near and Yet So Far', although Astaire anticipated the usual ten days to prepare it for the camera, with Rita it was ready in four. 'I'd see Fred every few days,' Hermes Pan recalled, 'and he said, "I'm working with Rita. She's really remarkable. She'll just do anything."'

While Astaire would give his all in rehearsals, Rita would seem to hold back until they were actually on camera.

'In rehearsal she would sort of walk through it,' Hermes Pan explained. 'And you would say, 'I wonder if she is going to do more.' And then when the cameras turned on she was larger than life, she was all over the place!'

Naturally the prospect of working with a great dancer like Astaire filled Rita with daily anxiety. When Ginger Rogers had partnered Astaire they seemed to have been made to dance together. (Coincidentally, Ginger Rogers was distantly related to Rita. Volga's brother Vinton was married to the sister of Ginger's mother.) Plagued by her usual insecurities, Rita desperately feared that Astaire would not like her as a partner. The last thing she wanted was to disappoint him. 'She was nervous at the start of working with him, he being such a perfectionist,' recalled Earl Bellamy, assistant director of *You Were Never Lovelier*, the second, and last, picture Rita did with Astaire. 'But Fred had a way of relaxing her and just calming her down. The first thing you knew, it was like they'd been dancing all their lives together.'

Astaire's efforts notwithstanding, for Rita shooting *You'll Never Get Rich* proved physically and emotionally draining. Although she was careful never to show her exhaustion to Astaire on the set, afterward was another matter. 'Fred used to make her cry every day, he worked her so incredibly hard,' said Orson Welles of what would happen when Rita went home after endless hours of rehearsal. Unfortunately, she didn't get much opportunity to rest or recuperate at night. No sooner would she come in the door she would find herself confronted by Eddie, who seemed to have been waiting for her all day. Although she just wanted to relax quietly, he badgered her endlessly with questions and insinuations. He demanded a detailed account of everything that had gone on that day. How else could he know if Columbia was going to let her go? Judson's fears about her losing her job had become totally out of touch with reality. She knew that she was getting along beautifully with Fred Astaire and that *You'll Never Get Rich* was Columbia's most prestigious production of the moment.

Eddie's paranoid rantings made her feel sick. Night after night she left the food on her plate untouched. Unable to eat supper, she would try to go to bed, but still Eddie would trail after her, this time to insist that she go out night-clubbing with him. It would help her career to be photographed there with him, or so he told her. Did he really believe it? Was he so deluded that he didn't see how far her career had progressed? Or was he just trying to get her back in line, to make her see that she still needed him? She didn't know, nor did she really care anymore. Nevertheless, the incessant fights with Eddie gave her sleepless nights. At five o'clock the next morning the cycle would begin again when she got up to go to the studio, but somehow, perhaps because she was only twenty-three, the camera did not register her acute exhaustion.

While Rita worked to support him, Eddie used his abundant free time to conduct affairs with other women, such as the wife of a cosmetics multimillionaire, a South American former singer whom Judson had met while Rita was being interviewed on a radio program, and who later described him to a friend as 'a terrific lover.'

Even before this there had been talk in Hollywood that

all was not well in Rita's marriage. These rumors were the result of a peculiar real-estate transaction in which Judson used Rita's earnings to build a fourteen-room house, only to sell it a few weeks after the couple had moved in. As always, all money and financial decisions were strictly in Judson's hands; he took care of everything for Rita, most especially her paycheck. Nor had Judson allowed Rita to enjoy much privacy in the new house. Although they hadn't had time to furnish it during their few weeks of residence there, Judson had managed to fill it with the reporters and photographers whose friendship he cultivated, and for whom he ran perpetual open house. A movie star's having lived in the now much-photographed house had dramatically increased its value. The startling announcement that Eddie had sold the place before the couple was properly settled in aroused suspicion even among his cronies in the press – were he and Rita having marital difficulties? – but Rita was quick to deny any discord. These were still the days when Rita was heard to say only good things about Eddie, and she publicly attributed the swift sale of the house to her brilliant husband's business acumen. Indeed, he had profited from the sale of the house, although as usual Rita had no idea of the deal's specifics, especially not where the money went.

Despite her denials to the press, Rita did finally broach the subject of a separation with Eddie. The further she advanced in the movie business, the less omnipotent he seemed to her. Like Eduardo before him, Eddie had lost his initial power over Rita – however desperately he struggled to reassert it.

'I know the situation became impossible,' said Roz Rogers. 'It took a lot of guts to get out of it. She was really afraid of him.' And Rita had good reason to be afraid. When she brought up the possibility of a separation, he angrily threatened to toss acid in her face, to destroy the moneymaking beauty that he took credit for having created. If he wasn't going to profit from Rita's success, he would make sure nobody else did.

When Eddie wasn't terrorizing her with threats of

75

disfigurement and mutilation, he played on her innate sweetness by describing himself as 'an old man going downhill' just when his young wife's career had taken a dramatic turn upward. These self-pitying tirades were supposed to make her feel sorry for him. At other times he couldn't resist hurting her by saying that he had only married her as an investment, and that he intended to collect on that investment. While Rita had been aware of his previous marriage to Hazel Forbes, he suddenly revealed to her that Hazel had been only one of his previous three wives. He warned her that being divorced three times before had given him plenty of experience at getting precisely what he wanted from his ex-wives.

Somehow Rita was not deterred by all he said and threatened, but she did make one major mistake at this point – she failed to hire a lawyer to represent her. Since Eddie controlled all their finances, she didn't really know what they had in the way of savings or investments. When Eddie took her to a lawyer to have a property settlement drawn up, she came out having agreed to a reconciliation instead. Only later would she have the good sense to secure the services of an attorney to look out for her interests alone – but for the time being things were right back to where they were before, with her despotic husband in complete financial control.

Still, she had made a significant stab at thinking and acting independently, which showed considerable development on her part. Rita had begun to create a personal support system: caring friends of her own, such as Hermes Pan and Bob Schiffer, who valued her for herself. And yet, for all the public affirmation that the professional successes of recent months had provided, Rita remained fundamentally unsure of herself. 'In the beginning she was terribly insecure,' said Bob Schiffer of this difficult period in her life, when he did her makeup for the first time. 'I thought she was one of the most beautiful women in the world, with a face that was structurally perfect. But I don't think she felt beautiful. There was an insecurity way down.'

Able as always to mask private problems, to conceal what she was feeling, Rita certainly did not give any hint of being insecure about her looks when she struck the sultry pose for *Life* photographer Bob Landry that was to become a principal fantasy photo for millions of GIs during the war. *Life* magazine often played an important role in Hollywood star buildups; besides the glossy publicity shots issued by the studios, they also ran plenty of evocative pictures of their own. Dressed in a satin-and-lace nightgown for her most famous photo, Rita was posed kneeling seductively on a bed, her head turned to look over her left shoulder directly into the eye of the camera. She may have longed to be valued for her acting, but there is no question that every bit as much as her best film roles, the Landry photograph crystallized the public's growing fascination with her when it appeared in *Life*'s 11 August 1941 issue.

There followed a massive new wave of Rita Hayworth publicity, this time engineered by Columbia to launch *You'll Never Get Rich*, set to open in New York City that September at Radio City Music Hall. Columbia sent Rita on a lavish press junket to New York that signaled the studio's major commitment to her career. Although relations were exceedingly tense between her and Judson, she traveled with him in tow. *The New York Times* reported somewhat mysteriously that Judson 'only comes out at night' and was otherwise being 'held incommunicado by press representatives.'

On the subject of her husband, Rita told another New York paper: 'Sometimes you are bound to be a little edgy after a hard day's work. Edward seems to understand. In fact, he's the most understanding man imaginable.'

Not long afterward, when she filed for divorce, Rita would tell a very different story – but for the moment she had no choice but to try to keep Eddie from causing trouble in front of the press. She even joined him in yet another quest in search of his millionaire ex-wife Hazel Forbes. Since inheriting the tooth-powder fortune from her second husband, Hazel had married and divorced a third, Harry Richman, the singer and noted ladies' man. Richman was then singing at Ben Marden's Riviera, and Judson had heard that, their divorce notwithstanding, Hazel often showed up there to see him. Unfortunately for Eddie, the night he and his movie-star wife attended, Hazel was nowhere in sight.

Later that fall it was evident that Rita had had good reason to pacify Eddie during the press junket. In the past he had worked hard to cultivate the Hollywood press, many of whom owed their Rita Hayworth stories and photo opportunities to him. Were there to be a public falling-out with Rita, their natural sympathies might be with their pal Judson. It could prove immensely embarrassing to Rita – and to Columbia, which was pouring an enormous amount of effort into promoting her. So it was that by November Eddie was sounding off in *Photoplay* magazine that Rita didn't want to go nightclubbing with him anymore. He complained to *Photoplay*'s Ruth Waterbury that since Rita's successes in *The Strawberry Blonde* and *Blood and Sand*, she seemed more concerned with her acting career than with having fun with him. Judson's concerns may have seemed relatively innocuous – but there was a definite subtext. Nightclubbing with Eddie meant making herself available to the Hollywood press corps, while turning away from him was construed as rejecting them. Not surprisingly, the article was distinctly favorable to Eddie, who was described as 'more poised' than Rita: 'He it is who originally counseled Rita to be always friendly and cooperative to publicity people, reporters, and photographers. To Rita's credit be it said that she has lived up to his good advice.' Furthermore, declared Ruth Waterbury: 'Personally, I think she is smart enough to realize that she is primarily a publicity-made star.' On the one hand Rita was being warned that she had better not get so highfalutin as to forget that the real source of her fame had been the publicity Eddie had helped her to secure. But he also seemed to be sending out the message that, just as publicity had made her, *bad* publicity could undo her. It was Rita's first indication, borne out by later events, that her husband would threaten to use the press against her should she try again for independence.

The suggestion that Rita was shying away from publicity was way off base. As the New York press junket demonstrated, Rita was just then the subject of a major publicity campaign, with which she was cooperating to the hilt (the same month Judson's complaints appeared in *Photoplay*, Rita was on the cover of *Time* magazine) – although it wasn't Eddie Judson masterminding her campaign anymore, but Columbia. In a way Harry Cohn was pushing him out, taking his place. Rita, whose earnings had escalated to $800 a week, had spent her whole life being controlled by others. First Eduardo Cansino had guided her destiny, then Eddie Judson. While Rita certainly wasn't anxious to put herself in Harry Cohn's hands, eventually Columbia's taking charge of Rita's career would make it much easier for her to break free from her husband.

Harry Cohn loaned her out to do two other pictures. At Paramount she appeared with the Gallic heartthrob Charles Boyer in a segment of Sam Spiegel's *Tales of Manhattan*. Boyer may have enjoyed a reputation as a great screen lover, but Rita certainly didn't respond to him that way. Said Orson Welles: 'They went a day over because every time Boyer gave her the *ooh, ooh* look, she broke up. *Broke up*! The thing that all the women were panting for struck her as funny. And poor Boyer, a very sweet fellow, didn't know what he was doing wrong. He would just talk with his French accent, and away she'd go!'

By contrast Rita had no difficulty getting into a romantic mood while filming *My Gal Sal* for Twentieth Century-Fox, but this time her love interest in Victor Mature – Hollywood wags called him 'the poor man's Charles Boyer' – went a good deal beyond acting. In one love scene on camera, their kiss reportedly went on for much too long and had to be reshot. He was certainly handsome enough, with thick black curls, a strong nose, a sensual mouth, as well as a powerful physique. Mature's first small acting roles had been in the movies, but he'd made his name on Broadway, playing the male lead in *Lady in the Dark*, opposite the great Gertrude Lawrence. Of the sexy character Mature portrayed, another character in the play said,

'When he talks his voice goes through you like a pound of cocaine! Oh, what a beautiful hunk of a man.'

The tag stuck – forever after, Hollywood publicity dubbed him the 'beautiful hunk of a man.'

'He was sort of hammy,' recalled Hermes Pan, who staged dances for *My Gal Sal*. 'He's come in with loud shirts that said ''The Genius.'' It was a gag, trying to be funny.'

But to Rita silly gags like the shirt were a welcome relief from the agonies she had to put up with at home. A muscleman's telling people to pay attention to his brains was a kind of self-mocking humor she wasn't accustomed to hearing. She longed to have some fun for a change, with someone her own age. 'He's very funny in life,' recalled Orson Welles of his former rival for Rita's affections, 'and that amused her.'

Mature wooed Rita by turning up outside her dressing room during a break in shooting and making her laugh with an old minstrel routine. There followed a romantic dinner at Mature's apartment, a late-night drive along the beach at Santa Monica, and a first gift: a gold bracelet with a dangling heart. She responded to his sweet and solicitous nature. Rita said that unlike Judson, Mature never told her what to do; he asked her. Before long it was no great secret in Hollywood that they were involved, and not everyone approved.

Unfortunately, like Rita, Mature was still legally married to someone else at the time. (He and a New York socialite had married at the close of his Broadway run, but they split up shortly thereafter.) Nevertheless, Rita's burgeoning romance with him did a world of good for her, and may even have given her the courage to stand up to Eddie once and for all. Before Rita and Vic had completed *My Gal Sal*, she had given Judson notice that her marriage to him was finally over.

Chapter Seven

Rita Hayworth's year of triumph ended that December of 1941, when the Japanese bombed Pearl Harbor and America entered World War II. While Eddie Judson dashed about town desperately hiding Rita's earnings from her in dummy corporations, bank accounts under fake names, and with friends, America mobilized for war. Tension was exceptionally high in Los Angeles, where many people feared the city would be Japan's next target. During the war years that followed, Rita Hayworth was to play an important role in the American imagination. But she devoted the early part of 1942 to her own private life with Eddie Judson, who had renewed his threats of violence and disfigurement.

Once a divorce was set in motion the California community-property laws would protect Rita from being cleaned out financially, so Eddie had to move quickly. He had the distinct advantage, however, since Rita had no clear idea of their finances. When he took $25,000 in cash from their safe-deposit boxes, he bragged about it to Rita in front of her secretary, Patricia Biddle. The secretary also heard him threaten Rita with physical violence.

'She needed help,' said Roz Rogers of Rita's plight. 'She wouldn't have known how to get out of this without some sort of help. She was miserable.'

Eight months before, Rita had tried to go it alone in breaking free from her husband, but this time she knew better. Back in June 1941 she had allowed herself to be dragged to a lawyer by Judson, but now she made the first move by turning to a Los Angeles attorney, Don Marlin, who provided the shrewd legal guidance and personal support she needed to get through the painful episode.

Judson had left Rita without cash when he emptied their safe-deposit boxes and checked into the Beverly Hills Hotel – then, as now, the epitome of Hollywood glamour. His choice of hotel suggested that Eddie planned to live it up, on her earnings. It was clear that he wasn't waiting for an equitable settlement of their property; he wanted it all. Besides his threat of physical harm, Judson warned Rita that he had it in his power to destroy her motion-picture career.

Press accounts of the day speculated that Eddie knew certain embarrassing information about her, and although her consistently terrified reactions to his threats clearly suggested that he did indeed have something on her, no one ever knew quite what it was. The answer to the mystery has lain hidden all these years in Rita's secret FBI file, which records Judson's claim to possess an 'obscene letter written by Hayworth which he was using to extort various sums.' In this 'obscene letter,' Rita was said to have 'set out various intimacies with other men.' Ironically, then, it was Rita herself who had given Judson the ammunition that he was using against her. But why?

If on a conscious level Rita had written to Judson to punish him for pushing her to sleep with other men, her letter actually had quite the opposite effect – it made *her* suffer, not Eddie. Rita's letter reveals quite a bit about the unconscious self-destructive impulses that all too often dictated her actions. By the time she wrote the letter she obviously knew the kind of man her husband was and the lengths he would go to to get what he wanted. Could it possibly be unintentional that she had put such a harmful document in Judson's hands? Her expression of anger had taken the form of an action that, in effect, would punish no one but herself. Saddest of all, it was a punishment for crimes perpetrated against her – as if it were she who was somehow guilty and had to pay for what another had forced her to do.

No sooner had Judson decamped for the Beverly Hills Hotel than Rita's lawyer, Don Marlin, sprang into action. On 24 February 1942, seventy-two hours after her husband had moved out, Margarita C. Judson filed for divorce from him in the Superior Court of Los Angeles on the grounds of 'great and grievous mental and physical cruelty and suffering.' She furthermore charged that Judson had 'injured and undermined [her] health and mental well-being.' Marlin asked that Rita be awarded the couple's accumulated property. Since Judson had hidden all of these assets from Rita, Marlin asked the court to issue a restraining order to prevent him from dispensing the money.

Rita's lawyer was buying time to try to figure out precisely how much money and property Judson would have had access to; for her part, Rita had no idea. Marlin also noted that because Judson had 'threatened plaintiff with physical violence,' Rita feared for her safety. Whereupon the court acted swiftly to protect her by warning Judson not to molest or interfere with Rita in any manner. The belligerent husband who had vowed to 'disfigure' her was not to visit Rita at the studio, nor was he to show up at her home, or to communicate with her by other means. As for the money he had taken from bank accounts and safe-deposit boxes, he was forbidden to dispose of it, or to destroy any documents or records pertaining to the couple's finances.

This was an anxious time for Rita, professionally as well as personally. Although stars generally received a greater volume of fan letters when going through a divorce, Eddie's threats to besmirch Rita's reputation could potentially be quite damaging to her at the studio. Harry Cohn would not be amused if her husband acted to tear down her reputation at the very moment that Columbia was going to such great lengths to build it up. The studio had a substantial investment in Rita, and any damaging publicity was most unwelcome since there was no telling how the fickle public would react. It was always possible that unsympathetic press coverage could cause her fans to turn on her. Rita represented an important form of capital to the studio; her loan-outs alone were bringing in substantial revenue. In its expectation that Rita should keep her personal life from jeopardizing her popularity in any way, Columbia was no different from any other film studio that routinely expected stars to keep out of trouble.

Harry Cohn certainly couldn't punish Eddie Judson at this point, so Rita was the one who stood to suffer all round. If Rita found herself unable to keep Judson from dragging her through the mud, Cohn could always cut his losses and abandon her. Thus, it was not surprising that, while she had been quite candid about Judson's brutality in her formal complaint against him in court, Rita also took great pains in her initial statements to the press to downplay the sensational aspects of her plight. Eddie was volatile; he could explode at any moment and bring her down with him. (But Harry Cohn was volatile, too – so Rita was caught in the middle.) When Eddie read what she had said about him in the press, she didn't want him to feel provoked.

'Due to the fact that Mr Judson's business takes him to Texas and Oklahoma so much of the time and that my career is in Hollywood, we just came to the parting of the ways,' Rita told the press in a carefully prepared statement. 'There is no one else in either of our lives, and I certainly wish him a world of happiness. Eddie is a grand fellow.' The statement was another mask. Not long afterwards, Rita admitted publicly that one of the big problems in the marriage had been her husband's not having held down a job for a long time; but for the moment it seemed prudent to pacify the man who had threatened to toss acid in her face by calling him 'a grand fellow.' Perhaps he would act like one – and disappear.

But Eddie had no intention of disappearing; unlike Rita, he had nothing to lose from a brouhaha in the press, and potentially a lot to gain. For the moment he was biding his time, toying with her. To judge by his statements to the powerful filmland journalist Louella Parsons, his strategy at this point was to patronize Rita in public, to make her decision to divorce him seem a bit irrational: 'I can only say that she is a wonderful girl and that she is completely exhausted, and I feel any trouble we may have is a result of her highly nervous condition.' In the guise of showing solicitude toward her, he was implicitly calling into question her state of mind. For the 'highly nervous condition' that had caused their breakup, he blamed not himself but Columbia, which would hardly be thrilled about the bad publicity. Said Judson: 'She has been having a discussion with Columbia over her contract, and this, along with the many pictures she has made, has caused our matrimonial trouble.' Unlike Rita in her statement, Eddie said he still hoped to patch things up: an ominous sign.

That Eddie wasn't about to slink off quietly became clear to Rita when, despite the court's warning to stay away, he began following her. Since Judson had cleaned her out financially, she sometimes found herself without the money to pay for food, and she and her secertary would go to Hermes Pan's house to eat. Outside Rita's, Judson would be waiting, and Hermes Pan recalled the car chases that ensued: 'She didn't have a penny. She'd get on the phone and say, "Have you got anything to eat? We haven't got any money." And I'd say, "Sure, come on over." She'd say, "Well, if I can ditch this *so and so*." Judson used to get a car and try to follow her. They'd go all around blocks losing him, and finally end up in the Valley and come to my house. I'd cook some spaghetti and we would have a nice time.' Following Rita was part of Judson's campaign of terror and harassment, but it is also likely that he was hoping to dig up more scandal to use against her later if he had to.

In the press Eddie may have been talking of patching things up with Rita, but in court his lawyer, Charles Beardsley, filed a demurrer, challenging Rita to cite specific instances of mental and physical cruelty. Eddie seemed to be trying to smoke her out on the assumption that she would hesitate to go into too much embarrassing detail lest the press pick it up.

To make matters worse, Judson also informed Rita that

he planned to countercharge her, which meant that the husband who in the past had pushed her into having sex with other men if it would help her career – and line *his* pockets – was now going to cry adultery. Desperate to keep all this out of the papers, Rita petitioned the court to seal testimony and files in the case, on the grounds that as a movie star her professional standing in the film industry would be injured by scandalous publicity. Her petition stated her belief that the cross-complaint Judson threatened to file would bring her 'into public contempt, ridicule, and obloquy.'

Her fears were not limited to Judson's countercharges. Judson had challenged her to be more specific in her charges against him, and she pleaded with the court to seal from the eyes of the press her own, more detailed account of his brutalities. Rita was plunged into a fit of agitation when she learned that the court had refused to seal the proceedings.

When the morning papers appeared on 22 March 1942, her worst fears were instantly confirmed, as reporters had a field day with the amended complaint she had filed, as well as with her secretary's affidavit supporting her claims. Everyone learned that her husband had told her he had married her 'as an investment' and 'for the purpose of exploiting her'; that he had always expected her to 'pan out' for him; that he intended to be paid for the time they had been married; and that he didn't care what happened to Rita as long as he got his money.

All in all, printed in black and white like this, the sordid details would be enough to make almost anyone feel humiliated, especially a desperately insecure individual like Rita, who had long been accustomed to masking her most embarrassing secrets from others. Much as she had warned the court would happen, overnight the star looked a good deal less glamorous. Worst of all, it was Rita's own testimony that had done it to her. Judson had not yet even filed the threatened countercharges.

In the face of further embarrassing revelations, a quick divorce settlement would be best for Rita. As yet Judson had no reason to refrain from dragging out the painful process, so Rita's lawyer moved to give him one. Because Judson had left Rita penniless, Don Marlin asked the court to appoint a receiver – an official to take charge of the couple's assets until they reached a settlement. For his part, a shady wheeler-dealer like Judson was most unlikely to want a court-appointed official nosing around in his finances. Almost instantly Marlin's tactic worked; Judson's new lawyer, Harry Sadicoff, informed Marlin that Eddie agreed to start settlement talks on the condition that they call off the receiver.

Because Rita didn't want Eddie to file the much-dreaded cross-complaint, she made it clear that she was very anxious to settle. Sensing her fear and weakness, Judson's side quickly saw its advantage, and before long Rita had agreed to give him everything but her car – community assets estimated in court papers at $75,000 – as long as he promised to stop harassing her and to get out of her life. Whatever it cost in money, it was worth it to be rid of him. On balance, she stood to lose a great deal more than money in the future if the scandalous publicity didn't stop and the studio began to shy away from her.

Not only did Judson come out of the marriage with all the couple's cash and stocks, but with a promise of an additional $12,000, to be paid in $500 monthly installments. He, in turn, agreed not to answer her complaint with one of his own.

On 20 May Rita filed a second amended complaint saying that there was no community property and she wanted only her freedom from Eddie, nothing else. Two days later, accompanied by her mother and her secretary, Rita appeared before Superior Court Judge John Gee Clark. Her tailored suit and floppy picture hat were both funereal black, and she carried herself in a manner that was dignified and restrained. 'My husband was always finding fault with me,' Rita told Judge Clark, as she crushed a tiny handkerchief in her palm. 'He was extremely jealous and quarrelsome.' Eddie did not, however, find fault with anything Rita said against him now. As agreed, he steered clear of the court, allowing Rita a decree by default. And Rita lived up to her part of the bargain by saying that she didn't want alimony, and that the property settlement they had worked out in advance was 'fair and just' – although it left her with only a car in which to drive away.

'She wasn't sure of herself after that,' said Roz Rogers of the period following the split with Judson. 'It must have been very hard for her to function without somebody telling her what to do. So this came as her growing period. I'm sure that, as part of being shy and part of being unsure of herself, if she made some mistakes it was during that period of growing up and wanting to make sure she was loved.'

Her personal problems aside, Rita's professional life seemed in high gear. At Columbia she successfully teamed with Fred Astaire again, this time in the delightful musical comedy *You Were Never Lovelier*. Partnering Astaire in dance numbers like the 'Shorty George' and 'I'm Old-Fashioned', Rita reached new heights of style and sophistication, quite unlike anything she had done on screen before. After they finished their second film together, however, Astaire decided that it would have to be their last. Rita had worked out beautifully as Astaire's newest teammate, but for his part, after Adele Astaire and Ginger Rogers, Fred simply didn't want to be permanently linked again in the public mind with a single partner.

Meanwhile, Victor Mature had stuck by Rita through her recent troubles, and by the fall of 1942, when he was ordered east to a coast guard station in Boston, they were talking about a future together. Her divorce from Eddie would not be final until the following spring. She met with Vic again briefly in New York, where she attended the premiere of *You Were Never Lovelier*, but scarcely was Rita back in Hollywood than she came under the influence of the brilliant, deep-voiced, hypnotic man who, long afterward, she would call 'the great love of my life.'

His name was Orson Welles.

Chapter Eight

*A*lthough Orson Welles was only in his late twenties when he encountered Rita, he already had more artistic achievements to his credit than most men can hope to accomplish in a lifetime. Besides the pair of magisterial films he had made thus far in Hollywood, *Citizen Kane* and *The Magnificent Ambersons*, back in New York City Welles had repeatedly made history both in theater and radio. On the air he had introduced major innovations in the art of radio drama, including the notorious *War of the Worlds* broadcast that had thousands of listeners convinced that Martians had landed on Earth, while onstage his dazzling productions both for the Federal Theater Project and his own Mercury Theater were already legendary. Welles was regarded by many as a great artist, perhaps even an authentic genius.

At the time he met Rita, however, although she seemed not to have realized it at first, Welles was in the throes of a major career crisis. His problems had begun as early as *Citizen Kane*. Welles's scathing fictional portrait of William Randolph Hearst had brought the press lord's wrath down on Hollywood, and, fearful of the power of the press to make or break movies, the film industry resented Welles for making trouble. If Rita was known as 'the most cooperative girl in Hollywood' in 1941, Welles had been a bad boy, its rebel. Before long he acquired a reputation as a director whose storytelling techniques were too difficult, too experimental to attract a mass audience. Accordingly,

RKO had taken his controversial second film, *The Magnificent Ambersons*, away from him, to be recut and finished by others in hopes of making it more palatable to the general public. An even worse fate was to befall the movie he had just been shooting in Brazil, *It's All True*. The new regime at RKO would abandon the footage altogether, which meant not only that Welles's many months of work had been for nothing, but also that, with two strikes already against him – *The Magnificent Ambersons* and *It's All True* – his future as a Hollywood director was in serious jeopardy.

Welles was shooting *It's All True* in Brazil when he received word that *The Magnificent Ambersons* had been wrested from his control. The news only intensified the acute panic that he was already feeling about his stubborn inability to discover the proper artistic form for his South American film. Significantly, it was in the midst of this atmosphere of crisis that Orson happened upon the famous Bob Landry photo of Rita Hayworth in a back issue of *Life* magazine.

'I saw that fabulous still in *Life* magazine,' Welles recalled, 'where she's on her knees on a bed. And that's when I decided: when I come back [from South America] *that's* what I'm going to do!' Rita's kneeling pose projected a sense of sexual accessibility that instantly soothed him in his time of trouble – much as it did the countless wartime GIs who became similarly obsessed with it.

Orson had never even met Rita, but already he started telling associates such as Jackson Leighter that when he returned to Hollywood he planned to make her his second wife. (His first marriage, to Chicago socialite Virginia Nicolson, had ended in divorce, and although in Hollywood he had briefly been set to marry Dolores Del Rio, she had broken off the engagement.) 'He said that he was coming back to America to marry Rita Hayworth,' Leighter recalled. 'He made a great point of it, oh, yes. That was before he had even met her. In fact, the first thing he wanted to do when he got back was to find her.'

Upon his return to America, in addition to accepting various radio assignments, Welles threw himself into the important role of the dashing and darkly romantic Mr Rochester in Robert Stevenson's film version of *Jane Eyre*. But Orson had not been back in Hollywood for long when Rita heard that he was talking about his plans to marry her, and as she would explain to him later, she was definitely not amused. Acutely insecure about her lack of education, Rita feared that the reputed 'genius' was mocking her with all this ridiculous talk. Even if she agreed just to meet him, what would she possibly have to say to an intellectual and brilliant conversationalist like Welles when she feared talking to *anyone*? She figured that, like the numerous other men who had started to badger her for dates after Victor Mature had departed, Welles was obviously after only one thing anyway. Finally 'he arranged a party to meet her,' recalled Welles's secretary Shifra Haran.

But the Rita Hayworth he met there came as a complete surprise to him. Although she was every bit as dazzlingly beautiful as he had hoped, he perceived at once that Rita was also very different from the Circean temptress he had been led to expect. 'The whole wicked Gilda figure was absolutely false,' said Welles of the image Rita had embodied in the public mind since *The Strawberry Blonde* and *Blood and Sand*. 'It was a *total* impersonation – like Lon Chaney or something. Nothing to do with her. Because she didn't have *that* kind of sex appeal at all. She carried it off because of her gypsy blood. But her *essential* quality was sweetness. There was a richness of texture about her that was *very* interesting and *very* unlike a movie star.'

More than ever she fascinated him. But Rita had not changed her mind about him and refused to take his calls following the party.

'She wouldn't answer the phone, she wouldn't talk to me. Nothing!' Welles recalled. 'She was sick of being chased around by Hollywood guys – and she was quite right. But I just wouldn't give up. And that's the only way I made it. I really persevered with Rita.'

Instead of discouraging him, Rita's persistent refusal to take his calls seemed only to intrigue Welles.

'I am like Casanova,' he explained. 'Not as a sexual

acrobat – because I'm not. But because I am willing to wait under the window until four-thirty in the morning. I'm that kind of romantic fellow, you see. I go the distance in the chase. It took me five weeks to get Rita to answer the phone, but once she did we were out that night.'

There followed a series of discreet dinners – Rita didn't want the press to report that she was seeing someone else in Vic's absence – at which, more and more, Orson drew her out with an old mind-reading trick he often used on dates with show girls. Rita was by nature shy and taciturn, so to get her talking he would pretend to peer into her thoughts. If by chance he guessed what she was actually thinking, good enough; perhaps she would fill in some additional details. But if he was mistaken, she would correct him, and in this way she gradually began to talk about herself as perhaps she had never done before.

At first they talked mostly about the movie business; and to Orson's amazement his bitterness about the fate of his last two pictures was nothing compared to the rage she expressed towards Hollywood. 'She had been propelled into a position that gave her no joy,' said Orson. 'She hated being a movie star so! She never got a moment's pleasure out of being a famous movie star. It gave her nothing. Nothing! She didn't like being "Rita Hayworth." She didn't believe in it. She had that dark gypsy pessimism about it. It was just work. She was just a laborer going to her job as she had from the age of twelve. And I'd say to her, "Since you're a star, get some fun out of it." But she'd say, "Oh, it's a lot of nonsense. The moment I have a flop, I'll be nobody again." It wasn't an attitude, it was absolutely genuine. She wanted to escape from "Rita Hayworth." But she couldn't walk out yet, she had to earn a living.'

Exciting and glamorous as it may have seemed to other people, her Hollywood career was to Rita simply an extension of her labors dancing in the gambling ships and Mexican casinos of her youth. If it wasn't Eduardo Cansino sending her out to catch fish for supper, it was Eddie Judson or Harry Cohn, each of them working her as hard – and with as little personal satisfaction for Rita – as her father had.

Indeed, Welles could see that Rita had grown as morbidly preoccupied with Harry Cohn as he evidently was with her. After *You'll Never Get Rich*, when she had balked at a script he wanted her to do that she thought wasn't right for her, Cohn put Rita on suspension from the studio, an act that plunged her into a fit of agitation. To Rita, Harry Cohn represented all the tyrants in her life, and she was determined somehow to take revenge.

'She wanted to get back at Cohn,' Welles recalled. 'She was so *obsessed* with him, it was just awful!'

Rita and Orson spent their first night together at Welles's rented house on Woodrow Wilson Drive. Orson's previous lady love, Dolores Del Rio, had always been impeccably made up and coiffed, even in the bedroom. But Rita was different: more natural and relaxed. She didn't care if her nightclothes were wrinkled, or her hair mussed up. Dolores would rush out of bed in the morning to put herself together for the day, but Rita didn't need to.

'She didn't wear much makeup even, except for work – and she was much prettier without makeup,' Welles recalled. 'Her sexiness was *womanly* rather than girlish. A shy *woman*, but not a shy girl.'

In the nights of lovemaking that ensued, Welles soon discovered that in bed with a man Rita seemed to experience the affirmation and security that she lacked so entirely at other times. Although he didn't know it yet, this was one of the tragic legacies of her past: 'Miss Hayworth was someone who would only believe that someone loved her if they were making love to her,' said Shifra Haran, who also observed Rita during her relationship with Prince Aly Khan. 'Her only security was knowing that someone would go to bed with her. That's the only thing that meant security to her.'

'For all her fame and beauty, Rita was very insecure,' recalled the writer Jim Bacon, who knew both Rita and Orson throughout the years. 'She was in awe of Orson's genius and found it hard to believe that one of the great talents in the movies could actually fall in love with her.'

Although Welles was by no means out to exploit Rita as her father and first husband had, as his friend Roger Hill would aptly put it, 'Orson, too, was a father figure. But this time a protective one.' Rita may have been rid of her real father, and of the equally exploitative first husband who had taken his place, but in Welles she discovered a new overpowering male to look up to.

'Welles was a *very* strong figure and Rita was in awe of him,' observed Hermes Pan.

According to Bob Schiffer, 'She respected Orson tremendously and was actually a bit frightened of him.'

Welles's entourage discovered that his Rita Hayworth fantasy had come true when he brought her to a rehearsal of his weekly radio show on CBS. He seemed so proud to have her there, and she in turn watched him quietly with a mixture of awe and affection. She didn't take her eyes off him and every so often he turned away from his work to flash a boyish smile at her. They were obviously very deeply involved by then, which came as a surprise to anyone who had been following the press accounts of her supposedly ongoing relationship with Victor Mature. But as Shifra Haran recalled: 'When she was with one man I never knew her to play around with another man. During the time of the relationship, that was it. She did not cat around.' When Rita began to sleep with Welles, it meant that her prior relationship was over. Before long she had moved into Orson's house on Woodrow Wilson Drive. 'She had just broken off with Victor Mature,' said Shifra Haran, 'and I had to go to her apartment – she lived one block off Wilshire – and take away all the things with the initials V.M. He was *out.*'

The public remained largely unaware of Rita's new love affair. Even when she had agreed to move in with Orson, she preferred not to go out much and to spend most of her free time at home with him. Much as Miss Haran had removed Victor Mature's possessions from Rita's apartment when the romance with Welles began, now she transported some of Rita's clothes to Woodrow Wilson

Drive – but not all. At the last minute, in a flash of insecurity, Rita suddenly decided that the bulk of her wardrobe would displease Orson, so she instructed Miss Haran to give away all of her gaudier outfits lest Orson think her tasteless.

Any fears Rita may have had about life with Orson were quickly dispelled. 'She was very happy in the beginning,' recalled Shifra Haran of the period just after Rita had moved in with Welles. 'He was lovely with her. He never talked down to her. He always treated her as if she understood everything. I never saw him make her feel more insecurity than she already felt. Women used to say, "What does he see in her? She's pretty but she doesn't have any brains!" People liked to downgrade her. They said she was so dumb. But she never had a chance! She didn't have much education, thanks to her father. And she was very aware of it. She wanted so to learn, to read, to *listen*.'

Perhaps at another more typically busy time in Welles's life, the relationship might not have thrived. But this was one of the rare interludes when he was not frantically juggling too many diverse projects all at once. Orson had the time to give Rita the attention she needed to be certain that he really cared for her. 'I don't think she was used to having someone really love her,' said another Welles assistant, Elisabeth Rubino. 'Since she was a beautiful woman she naturally was admired by a lot of men, but I don't believe that she had ever been loved for herself before.'

Rita quickly caught on to the things that gave Orson sexual pleasure. With Dolores Del Rio, he had acquired a passion for the flimsy lace-edged slips and gossamer embroidered nightgowns that she favored. With Rita, Orson ran up enormous bills at the exclusive Juel Parks lingerie store, where Dolores had shopped. Rita knew that although she might have spent the afternoon in rolled-up jeans, a rumpled old blouse, and a face pack, at night it was time to change into the sexy lingerie that excited him so. She learned, too, that nothing thrilled him more than to watch her undress.

Even as early as this Welles noticed the first signs of Rita's grave insecurities. 'When it came to the man in her life, she had to have *all* his attention,' said Elisabeth Rubino. Although Orson was absolutely devoted to Rita, suddenly for no apparent reason she would angrily accuse him of flirting with other women.

'She was terribly jealous,' Welles recalled, 'and she was always telling me I was looking at girls when I didn't even *see* them because I wasn't thinking about them.' He knew relatively little of Rita's background as yet, and it did not occur to him that her fits of irrational jealousy betokened something more serious. 'I didn't know she was sick then. This was before we were married, early in our - awful word - *relationship*. Later I began to know, but I didn't at the very beginning because I was being super virtuous and she had *absolutely* no reason to be jealous. I wasn't smart enough to know that it was neurotic. I just thought it was gypsy, and I said, "This is that gypsy kick and I've got to cure her of that."'

In a restaurant where they were dining, Orson made his first stab at curing Rita's irrational jealousy. 'I sat in a restaurant with her, and I looked across her and acted as though I had seen the most beautiful girl who ever lived and that I was returning her looks. Rita dropped her napkin in order to take a look - and there was *nobody* there. The restaurant was empty. I was so tired of jealous scenes when there was no reason for them. I'd had an awful lot of jealousy, totally undeserved. And this was a joke to show her she had nothing to fear. She wasn't humiliated because nobody saw her. I didn't say a word, I just went on looking like that.'

The best medicine for Rita's insecurity was the sense of belonging that she seemed to feel for the first time in her life as part of Orson's extended theatrical family. Welles had landed in Hollywood followed by a close-knit group of performers such as Agnes Moorehead and Joseph Cotten from his acclaimed Mercury Theater in New York. They had appeared in his films, *Citizen Kane* and *The Magnificent Ambersons*, and on radio with him, and now - to Rita's immense delight – they were cooking up a tent show: a magical extravaganza for the GIs waiting to be shipped out of Los Angeles to the war in the Pacific.

Had Welles and company been preparing something from Shakespeare or one of the other theatrical classics for which the Mercury was famous, Rita probably would have felt out of her element. Although she was one of Hollywood's most popular stars of the moment, she remained painfully self-conscious about her lack of formal training as an actress. But with her background in vaudeville and casinos, a tent show was familiar ground.

Since the outbreak of war, Hollywood had gone all out to entertain visiting men in uniform. Like other top stars, Rita had done her part at the Hollywood Canteen, where GIs got to dance with their favorite screen goddesses, and on USO tours. As for the *Mercury Wonder Show*, Welles had conceived of it after his draft board declared him 4F on account of asthma, flat feet, and a bad back. 'It started because he felt bad that he didn't go into the service,' recalled Shifra Haran.

And Welles himself confirmed: 'I felt guilty about the war. I was guilt-ridden by my civilian status.' The tent show for the GIs was supposed to assuage his guilt for remaining at home when at least twelve percent of his fellow employees in the film industry had joined the military.

The *Mercury Wonder Show* harked back to Orson's romantic memories of the tent shows he had visited as a youth with his beloved eccentric father, Dick Welles, whose passion for magic and vaudeville Orson inherited. For Rita, joining the tent show was a way of entering Orson's world, of working closely with him at something she could do well. But it also represented something more: the lonely little girl who had watched the other children from her parents' porch in Chula Vista was finally being allowed to come down and play. And it was as if she had been waiting all her life to heed their call.

Suddenly everywhere Rita turned in the house on Woodrow Wilson Drive there was magic equipment:

swords, trunks, ropes, top hats. In the ensuing months Orson shared the arcane secrets of magical illusion with her. In one trick in the show, Orson would descend into the audience to ask the GIs to scratch numbers on a slate; then Rita would miraculously cry out the sum of the figures from her perch opposite. The more she practised the easier it was to bring off the seemingly impossible. In another of the tricks they worked on, Orson locked Rita in a trunk, then seemed to hack her to pieces within, only to open the trunk afterward and reveal that, incredibly, she was still in one piece. As he demonstrated this famous old trick to Rita, Orson showed her that in his competent hands she had nothing to be afraid of.

Perhaps it was so in her life, as well. Determined to put past fears out of her mind, she had ceased the monthly $500 payments to Eddie Judson that she had agreed to at the time of her divorce. After she had made the first few payments, her suspension from the studio had given her lawyer, Don Marlin, an excuse to stall Judson, but on Orson's advice, she said she did not merely want to *stall*, and she refused to pay altogether. With Orson, Eddie's threats seemed very far away. She was protected within a magic circle and there didn't seem to be anything that Judson could do to her anymore.

The *Mercury Wonder Show* was scheduled to open officially in August 1943 in a tent on Cahuenga Boulevard in Hollywood. First there would be previews, to begin in June at the Playtime Theater in Hollywood, and it was on the gala first night of these previews that, suddenly, Rita found herself brutally confronted again with her past. It happened as she and Orson prepared to leave the theater. The evening's performance had gone entirely as planned. The magic tricks had come off beautifully, and the audience was delighted. Then, as she and Orson left by the stage door, Rita spotted someone moving toward her through the crowd of autograph seekers. Before she could pull back or alert Orson, the process server had thrust into her hands the legal papers that announced Judson's lawsuit.

At that moment Eddie had successfully broken into the

magic circle that she had been sure would protect her. It was as if he wouldn't leave her alone to be happy in her new life. Just when she had begun to put it out of her thoughts, her ugly past was back with a vengeance. Afterward she grew hysterical, but Orson managed to calm her down.

The month before, in May, Rita's final divorce decree had been granted. But Eddie wasn't about to disappear without the $10,000 she still owed him, according to their original settlement. At Orson's urging Rita instructed her lawyer to inform the court that she had signed the outrageous property settlement the year before solely because she was afraid of Judson. Eddie had come out of their marriage with nearly everything she had earned. But that was before. Now that he had decided to take her to court to collect the rest, she in turn would ask that the court set aside the original property settlement and force Eddie to give everything back that was rightfully hers. She wasn't alone this time. Orson told her that she was a different person from the one who had signed the original settlement. This time she would show Eddie that the terrified little girl he remembered didn't exist anymore.

Judson wasn't the only one out to destroy Rita's happiness. Harry Cohn resented her participation in the *Mercury Wonder Show* even though it in no way interfered with her commitments to Columbia. 'He didn't like her being in Mr Welles's magic show one bit,' recalled Shifra Haran. 'Harry Cohn was such a son-of-a-bitch, if I may say so. Oh, he was terrible to Miss Hayworth. He put her in a very tough position.'

That summer, by day Rita had been working on *Cover Girl*, her major new picture co-starring Gene Kelly, and moonlighting in previews for the *Mercury Wonder Show*, which toured various military camps in anticipation of opening officially in August. The hectic pace seemed only to invigorate her. Co-workers on the set of *Cover Girl* noted how unusually happy she appeared.

Then, the day before the tent show's long-awaited premiere, Harry Cohn suddenly forbade Rita to participate in Orson's extravaganza on the grounds that all her energy should be devoted to *Cover Girl*. He was paying her to act in his movie, not in her boyfriend's magic show. She pleaded with him, but to no avail. He had her under contract, and no matter how it irked her, she had no choice but to accept his ruling. When she checked with her lawyer, he confirmed that Harry Cohn did indeed have a legal right to pull her out of the magic show.

That night, at home on Woodrow Wilson Drive, Rita went wild with anger. She wept that she had never wanted to be a movie star anyway. What better moment than this to give it all up? Let Harry Cohn sue her, as he threatened to do if she went on opening night of the *Mercury Wonder Show*. She vowed that she would be at the premiere with Orson and the others, no matter what the consequences. Orson saw things differently, however. Much as she wanted to go on, he told her that he couldn't let her jeopardize her whole career like that. Cohn's choice of the eve of the premiere had been revealingly cruel and sadistic; there was no telling to what lengths he was capable of going to punish Rita if she provoked him further.

Orson assured Rita that although he would have to replace her with someone else, she was still part of the company. She shouldn't feel left out; they all still loved her. To his horror, he noticed that when he mentioned replacing her with someone else she acted as if he had said he was going to leave her. For perhaps the first time in his life, Orson felt himself overwhelmed by the impulse to *protect* another; she seemed so 'fragile' to him, he wanted only to shield her from the world.

There was one way to make her feel better – to give her back the growing sense of security that Harry Cohn had just snatched away. 'That's why I married her,' Welles recalled. 'I adored her. It *had* to be done for her.'

If Harry Cohn had intended to strike a blow against Rita's involvement with Welles, removing her from the *Mercury Wonder Show* had precisely the opposite effect: Orson nervously proposed marriage and Rita said yes, confident at last that she was not going to be abandoned. 'She had this phobia about being left,' said Shifra Haran.

'She couldn't trust anybody because she'd been played around with. She had been so used by men. She was like an innocent child. She *had* to have Orson there for her – someone who loved her for herself.'

Unfortunately, the feeling that in childhood their mother *abandoned* them and their father *betrayed* them leads many incest victims to exhibit fears of abandonment and betrayal for the rest of their lives – no matter what reassurances they are given to the contrary. If for the moment Welles's marriage proposal to Rita had put such fears to rest, this was only temporary, as he was soon to discover.

With Rita out of the show, Orson had to find someone to fill in at the last minute and thought of his friend Marlene Dietrich. Recalled Dietrich: 'I replaced her in the show that Orson Welles erected for the soldiers in California because her boss at Columbia Studios refused to let her stay up at night, as she was making a film at the time.' When he called her at the eleventh hour, Marlene replied, 'Come teach me the tricks and I do it.' Welles taught Marlene a telepathy stunt, which she performed in a form-fitting skin-toned gown that was covered with sequins.

Every night one of the GIs in the audience was recruited to participate in Dietrich's mind-reading routine. 'Those guys practically peed in their pants on the stage,' said Shifra Haran. 'Those kids were just devastated to be in her presence.'

Orson himself wasn't any less dazzled by Marlene. 'She was so much larger than life,' Welles recalled. 'We forget. Now there are *no* larger-than-life people left, but Marlene really was the last dinosaur.'

The ruggedly handsome French movie actor Jean Gabin was Dietrich's beloved in this period, and in order to keep an eye on her he toiled as the prop man in the *Mercury Wonder Show*. Gabin's relationship with Marlene fascinated Orson, who noticed that, alone with her man, Marlene deliberately transformed herself into a German hausfrau: an image entirely opposite that of the glamour she projected on stage and on screen.

'Marlene was the most *untouchably* glamorous and strange

101

creature that walked the face of the earth,' Welles said. 'For *that* woman to put on an apron and cook a great meal was an absolute thunderbolt!'

Yet Gabin didn't seem to *notice* that a thunderbolt had struck. Marlene cooked and prepared for Gabin with the utmost tenderness, but she confessed to Orson that she was disappointed with the unvarying result. Instead of responding with the passion she had hoped for, he turned into a typical French peasant, silently puffing his cigarette, reading the newspaper, and waiting for his food to be put on the table in front of him. What was she doing wrong? She wanted him to pay more loving attention to her, to show greater ardor.

Orson told her that her big mistake was so entirely discarding her glamour image for Gabin. With Rita, Orson was indeed happiest when she was her shy, sweet self – but all men didn't want that. Perhaps Marlene would do better to stop playing the hausfrau with Gabin and to remain 'Marlene Dietrich,' the glamorous screen star to whom he had been drawn.

Chapter Nine

*T*he *Mercury Wonder Show* was still going strong when, on 7 September 1943, Orson and Rita were married. That morning Rita had her usual early call for *Cover Girl*. At the studio she appeared especially exuberant, and before long her co-workers found out why. Just before the lunch break she said matter-of-factly that she hoped no one minded if she was a little late getting back to work, since she and Orson were to be married that afternoon.

Typically news traveled with unusual speed at Columbia, where Harry Cohn had a well-earned reputation for always knowing everything that went on. While he may have been wringing his hands when he heard this particular piece of news ('Harry Cohn didn't like it one damn bit that Welles married her,' said Shifra Haran), no time was wasted in milking the maximum publicity for the wedding of his leading star. Scarcely had Rita disclosed her plans than the publicity office launched full steam into action.

Driven by his hunchbacked dwarf chauffeur, an ex-convict named Shorty, who had attached great blocks of wood to the pedals so that his feet could reach the brakes and gas, Welles picked up his bride at the studio. Orson had on a dark, chalk-striped suit, a pink shirt, and a bow tie; Rita had changed into a tailored tan suit with stylishly padded shoulders and a matching wide-brimmed hat with a tiny veil. In the rush to leave Columbia, she hadn't finished removing her movie makeup, so while she scrubbed away at the yellowy residue, Orson instructed Shorty to stop at a nearby drugstore, where, since they'd be missing lunch, Welles and his chauffeur fortified themselves with ice-cream sodas.

Then it was off to Beverly Hills to pick up another curious member of Welles's entourage: his mentor and surrogate father, Dr Maurice 'Dadda' Bernstein, who, back in 1916, had been the first to proclaim baby Orson – or 'Pookles', as 'Dadda' always called him – a genius. Ever since, Dadda had taken an obsessive interest in Pookles's life and loves; only recently he had expressed violent opposition to his protégé's liaison with Dolores Del Rio, whom he accused of having forged her birth certificate to make herself appear younger. Much to Rita's relief, Dadda had had no such objections to her and heartily approved of the match.

Shorty made stops to pick up the other invited guests: Welles's business manager Jackson Leighter and Mercury cohort Joseph Cotten. Conspicuously absent from the guest list were Rita's parents. Indeed, not only had she failed to invite Eduardo and Volga Cansino, but she hadn't even told them of her plans.

When at last the wedding party arrived at the Bay City Building in Santa Monica, they were thronged by the Hollywood press corps, whom Columbia publicity had tipped off. Orson and Rita were nervous wrecks. At the license bureau on the twelfth floor, the usually dexterous Welles found himself suddenly all thumbs as he filled out the application form ('I dreaded it, you know,' he recalled), then headed absentmindedly out of the office with Rita until the clerk summoned them back. 'This is only the application,' he informed them. 'Wait for the license.'

Moments later another disconcerting mob of press people greeted them outside the chambers of Superior Court Judge Orlando Rhodes, on the fourth floor. In front of the judge, Rita could barely get her words out straight, and Orson was evidently no calmer. He fumbled extracting the wedding ring from its box, then couldn't seem to slip it on her finger. 'Hold her finger with your other hand,' Judge Rhodes suggested. No sooner was the ring on her finger than Rita burst into happy tears. Orson kissed the bride, wiped the lipstick from his face, and dashed off with her to the waiting car.

When a newsman inquired about honeymoon plans, Rita answered that they had none. 'I gotta get back to the studio,' she was reported to have said as Shorty drove off.

Once the press was safely out of sight, the newlyweds calmed down considerably. 'I never saw a happier, more tickled, delighted, adorable couple in the world,' said Shifra Haran, whom they had summoned to join them within an hour of the wedding. 'Oh, she was *radiant!*'

Back on the set of *Cover Girl* Rita was fêted with an impromptu cast party before everyone wound up the day's work. Meanwhile, at Eduardo Cansino's dance studio the phone was ringing incessantly with reporters asking for comments. This occasioned some awkwardness, since Rita's family had to admit that it was the first they had heard of the wedding. 'Goodness, I wish she'd let me know,' an embarrassed Volga Cansino told the press. 'I was supposed to have dinner with her tonight.'

That night after work Rita headed for the *Mercury Wonder Show*. Harry Cohn might have forbidden her to join Orson onstage, but there was nothing to stop her from waiting in the wings for him. When a radio reporter asked for a comment on the surprise wedding of the year, Rita said a few shy, giggly, hesitant words into the microphone before Marlene Dietrich rescued her by taking over the interview.

There was nothing hesitant about Eddie Judson's reaction to the news. Throughout the summer Rita had dragged her heels about giving a deposition in court regarding Eddie's financial claims; her excuse was the hectic shooting schedule for *Cover Girl*. Whereas part of her wanted to face him and to demand that he return all he had taken from her, another part continued to fear the immense embarrassment he was capable of causing her should he produce the obscene letter she had written, and it was this latter impulse that motivated her repeatedly to ask for post-ponements of their courtroom encounter; she wanted nothing to intrude on her happiness.

Judson had been angry enough about the postponements, but her wedding to Welles send the belligerent ex-husband flying to his lawyer to urge immediate action. Thus, two days after the wedding, Judson's lawyers filed an indignant affidavit to the court, objecting to any further postponements. Eddie wanted Rita in court on 11 September. In an attempt to win the court's sympathy, he painted himself as the little man at the mercy of the arrogant movie star. Judson's attorney argued that Rita 'believes that because she is a motion-picture performer that she is above the law and above the courts and that she is entitled to continuances of any legal proceedings, in which she is a party, at her whim, and that the legal rights of others are secondary to her wishes or convenience.' The court, however, sided with Rita, who postponed her deposition until October. Things seemed to be going her way for a change.

The *Mercury Wonder Show* closed on 9 September and the next day Rita and Orson flew to Chicago, where he was scheduled to speak at the Mass Rally to Win the Peace at Chicago Stadium. In recent months his frustrating problems in the film industry had led Welles to investigate other career possibilities. The studios simply weren't interested in backing the kinds of artistically challenging films that Welles wanted to make, and he was not ready to compromise by doing more standard commercial work. Under the tutelage of his friend, the brilliant and enigmatic Romanian emigré Louis Dolivet, who headed the International Free World Association, Orson had seriously begun to consider politics as his next route. The aim of Dolivet's organization was to further a lasting world peace, and although he had already successfully attracted a good many prominent international political figures into its ranks, as his ex-wife, the Academy Award-winning actress Beatrice Straight, pointed out, he wanted badly to draw top movie stars into the fold for the glamour and publicity they would bring to his activities. For this purpose Orson Welles – and, soon, Rita Hayworth – quite perfectly fit the bill. Best of all, in Orson Dolivet discovered 'the combination of

106

actor and orator' that would prove a major asset should Welles run for public office – with his friend Dolivet as the power behind the scenes, of course. Was it too much for Orson to dream, as Dolivet had encouraged him to do, that in a period of charismatic political leaders like Roosevelt and Churchill, the equally dynamic Welles might make a successful politician? 'Imagine the great orator he would have made in the Senate!' said Louis Dolivet decades later.

Now that Orson was newly married, a future in politics held another potential attraction: a way out of Hollywood for Rita. 'I didn't want the responsibility of having her walk out until I had a program for my life that made sense,' Welles explained, 'and then, I asked her how she would feel about it and she just lit up with joy! When I decided to quit as an actor and go into politics she was thrilled. She was ready to give it up. Delighted. Would have gone with *great* pleasure. Would never have regretted it for a minute.'

Something else that happened on the Chicago trip gave Rita hope that life with her new husband might provide the way out of Hollywood for which she had been longing. In Chicago she met Welles's dearest friends, Roger and Hortense Hill, whose loving, mutually supportive relationship showed Rita what a successful and happy marriage could be.

In Orson's mind, although the political speech was the official reason for going to Chicago, far more important was presenting Rita to the Hills, whom he had known and loved since boyhood, when Roger – or 'Skipper' as Orson affectionately called him – had been his teacher at the Todd School for Boys in Woodstock, Illinois. When *Citizen Kane* had its Chicago premiere, Orson had brought Dolores Del Rio there to meet the Hills, but on that visit he had been constantly uneasy that they were a bit too simple and old-fashioned for the worldly and sophisticated Dolores. It seemed to Orson that she was distinctly out of place in their company, and he regretted having brought her there. The awkwardness had been no one's fault, but Dolores and the Hills did, in fact, represent the two very different, seemingly irreconcilable worlds that Orson inhabited: one filled with Hollywood glamour and elegance, and the other with homespun midwestern simplicity. By contrast, Orson could bring Rita out to meet Skipper and Horty and know in advance that, although she was one of Hollywood's biggest stars, she would immediately fit right in with them, and that they would adore her.

At first Rita's usual insecurity made her desperately nervous in anticipation of meeting two such important people in her husband's life; but they opened their hearts to her, and she was charmed. Said Shifra Haran: 'Miss Hayworth was very bashful and shy but the Hills succeeded in setting her at ease about them. They were real folksy, easy people to be around.' Years of running the Todd School had taught Skipper and Horty how to make even the shyest newcomer feel right at home. At last Rita had found the real family about which she had dreamed but never actually experienced: warm, unpretentious, and - most of all - loving.

Watching Orson with Skipper, suddenly she saw her husband in a whole new light. With his old schoolmaster Orson turned back into a little boy, the two of them talking endlessly and enthusiastically of ideas and of the myriad projects they hoped to pursue together.

'She loved to sit there and just enjoy the conversation that was going on,' said Shifra Haran.

While most of his conversation was with Orson, Skipper did not fail to turn a keen eye on Rita, who struck him as a 'frustrating dichotomy': On the one hand, there was her 'glamour image,' the film star whose 'face and form adorned every soldier's barracks and sailor's bunk,' while on the other hand there was what Hill perceived as the reality: 'a sweet, shy, unlettered, fearful, beautiful child' whose 'whole life was a tragedy.' Skipper knew only too well that 'the role of father figure was a new one for Welles. But he assumed it, perforce, for this new wife.'

Indeed, by his own admission Welles had never been much of a father to the daughter he had from his first marriage; the role went against the grain of his fundamentally egocentric personality, so that his assuming it now for Rita suggested how much he cared for her.

It struck Skipper as ironic that in Orson's magic act Rita had allowed herself to be sawed in half: 'Until that time, the girl had experienced real, not fake, torture from every man in her life. First it came from a father. Next from an early husband-manager who packaged and sold his 'property' to the cruelest of them all, Harry Cohn, that bully of Gower Street. Then came a new husband, and with him, at long last, kindness.' To Skipper, who probably knew Welles better than anyone, the years with Rita were 'Orson's finest hour in the saga of his marriages.'

For her part, Rita quickly grew very fond of Skipper, who had so many marvelous stories about Orson's boyhood to tell her. But from the first she was especially drawn to Hortense, who seemed to be everything her own mother had not been. Said Welles: 'Until she met Hortense, there was nobody, no woman that she could *believe*, you know.'

And as Roger Hill observed, in Hortense Rita discovered a 'mother-figure.' By contrast with Volga, Hortense seemed so strong and in control. She had three happy, healthy children and a husband who adored her, and with whom she continued to enjoy a passionate sex life. To Rita, she seemed to hold the secrets of a happy, contented existence.

There followed periodic visits between Rita and Hortense. When the elder woman underwent several operations she convalesced at the Welles household in Los Angeles, where, as Roger Hill observed: 'The weeks would prove equally therapeutic for her devoted nurse, Rita Hayworth, even then a troubled girl.'

Rita felt at peace when she and Orson spent time with Horty and Skipper, whose happy home she hoped somehow to emulate, but even in their company she could be suddenly, brutally reminded of a part of her life that she hated and wanted only to forget. This occurred one night when she and Orson were dining with the Hills on the terrace of Chicago's Tavern Club. In the water beneath them Skipper saw the ship *Theodore Roosevelt* and a poster advertising a moonlight sail, and he proposed that they go: 'An unfortunate impulse considering the nature of our guests,' as Hill was to realize only too late. 'Rita was at the height of her fame: sex goddess to a nation, pinup girl to an army.' The happy foursome had boarded the ship expecting a pleasant evening together, but once the crowds spotted Rita this was impossible. 'Our efforts at protection proved futile,' Hill recalled. 'A state-room key was in my pocket and maneuvered towards its door. Once behind it, a frustrated crowd's adulation turned to anger. We cowered inside for a frightening two hours.'

Back in Hollywood after meeting the Hills, Rita seemed more determined than ever to abandon her film career. After much discussion she and Orson decided to give up the rented house on Woodrow Wilson Drive and to put their things in storage in Westwood so that Orson might continue political speechmaking in the East on behalf of the Free World Association. In the meantime Orson had also been negotiating with producer Alexander Korda to direct a film adaptation of *War and Peace* in England. Wartime travel was no simple matter, of course, and he wired Korda for help in obtaining a passport for Rita and passage to Europe. Welles hoped that the money for directing *War and Peace* would sustain them when they returned to the States to pursue his political ambitions.

Before they left Los Angeles, however, something would have to be done about Judson's lawsuit. The affadavit his lawyer had filed showed that Eddie was steaming. Past experience made it clear to Rita that Judson would hesitate at nothing if he failed to get what he wanted. Now that she was a married woman, she wasn't the only one Eddie was capable of harming. A scandal of any kind could be poisonous to her new husband's political ambitions. As the October deposition date approached, Rita could no longer simply deny Eddie's existence in hopes that he would just disappear. Still, the pressure of facing Eddie, of dredging up all those painful memories and associations, was too much to bear.

Only a few months before, Orson had urged Rita to go

head to head with Judson, but now he saw that that would be far too immense a strain for her. He immediately took charge, instructing his lawyers, the firm of Wright and Millikan, to negotiate a rapid out-of-court settlement with Rita's ex-husband. Pay him what he wanted, but let him not torture Rita for one second more.

As Orson and Rita left for the East Coast nothing whatsoever had been resolved. The abundant social pressures that awaited Rita in the international political circles in which she and Orson would be traveling in New York made her anxious enough, but far worse was the knowledge that Eddie might strike at any moment. Orson was scheduled to deliver his most important speech yet at the Free World Congress in October, which was to be attended by a host of eminent political figures from around the world. Judson probably knew all about it already, for there had been a good deal of advance publicity for Orson's address on international cooperation at the Free World dinner at the Hotel Pennsylvania, where the other speakers included Harold Butler, the British Minister to the U.S.; Wei Tao Ming, the Chinese Ambassador to the U.S., and J. Alvarez Del Vayo, the Minister of Foreign Affairs of the Spanish Republic. Dolivet was particularly keen on displaying Rita prominently at the banquet's main table, where her presence would lend a touch of Hollywood glitter to the proceedings. What if Judson chose precisely this moment to humiliate her publicly with the obscene letter she had written? How could she ever forgive herself for having embarrassed Orson like that?

In New York her anxieties over Judson brought her nearly to the breaking point. She was 'very, very upset,' recalled Beatrice Straight, and at the eleventh hour hesitated to appear on Orson's arm at the Free World dinner. Most unfortunately, the threat of being exposed and humiliated by Judson played on her worst insecurities as a victim of childhood sexual trauma. Like many such victims, never having developed a normal and healthy degree of self-esteem, Rita went through life secretly believing herself a fraud; no matter what her accomplish-

111

ments, she was tormented by the nagging fear that at any moment she would be exposed and everyone would know the terrible truth about her inadequacies and unworthiness.

Such was Rita's torment as the hour of the Free World dinner approached. Nor was her anxiety about Judson kept secret from the organizers of the conference, to whom it was 'particularly important,' as Beatrice Straight pointed out, that Rita make her promised appearance. There was considerable excitement among the assorted international political figures set to attend the dinner that Rita Hayworth would be sitting up on the dais, and Louis Dolivet did not want to disappoint them. In many ways, since Rita was the far bigger star, her presence at the dinner was widely deemed a good deal more important even than Orson's. Thus, until virtually the last minute, the conference organizers were all 'very nervous' that Rita would back out.

But as always throughout her life, Rita went ahead and forced herself to do what she did not want to do: a legacy of her childhood conditioning in self-sacrifice. If it was important to Orson that she attend the much-dreaded event, she would put herself through it. Ironically, Orson's political career was supposed to have liberated her from being placed on display yet again. But now this was exactly what she found herself being asked to do once more, as she brilliantly concealed all that she was thinking and feeling behind the familiar 'Rita Hayworth' mask.

Whatever her fears and insecurities about mingling with people of culture and education, by now she knew every trick in the book for not revealing them in public. 'When she didn't know something, she pretended she wasn't paying attention,' said Libby (Mrs Everett) Sloane of Rita's typical social strategy. 'She was smart enough not to get involved in things that she didn't understand. She was – why don't we call it – *streetwise*. That kind of mentality. No learned intellect, she. She was not going to be the head of the class in the history department, if you know what I mean. But she really knew how to work it. She always had an air like she knew what she was doing when she really didn't. She would either say it was time to leave, or she would raise her head and look over in the other direction – and everybody would look to see where she was looking. But it didn't meant anything! She just came by it from necessity.'

During the Welleses' stay in New York they were ensconced in a suite of rooms at Applegreen, Beatrice Straight's family estate in Old Westbury, Long Island, where Louis Dolivet had taken up residence since his advantageous marriage to the beautiful Whitney heiress. When Orson first arrived with his famous bride, Rita was not at all what Beatrice Straight had been expecting. The glamorous movie star turned out to be a 'sweet, shy, undemanding young girl,' who also seemed 'rather dull.' Beatrice Straight couldn't figure out what Orson was doing with Rita. Nor did Welles seem to treat Rita very well, at least not in front of Beatrice, who was surprised by Rita's failure ever to protest at her husband's brusqueness and lack of courtesy. So persistently docile and uncomplaining was she that it seemed to Beatrice as if 'that was the way Rita expected to be treated.'

Orson wasn't scoring any points for courtesy with the household staff, either. He typically slept until three in the afternoon, at which time he expected special meals to be prepared for him immediately, and exploded angrily if his demands weren't met right away. By contrast with her husband, who very quickly 'drove the staff mad,' Rita 'never asked for anything' from the servants. The entire staff – most especially Beatrice's father's butler – was absolutely thrilled to have Rita Hayworth as a guest; although they were quite accustomed to tending to prominent political figures from around the world, Rita was their first movie star and it was considered a special occasion to have her living at Applegreen.

When Orson and Louis discussed politics, the two wives were expected to listen silently and attentively: a role that came easily to Rita, who followed her husband's line on all topics. 'If he believed in it, she believed in it,' as Shifra Haran observed. Most of the time, however, Welles and Dolivet were off on political business, so Rita and Beatrice were left to their own resources at Applegreen. Although the two women often had tea together, Rita never seemed to get over her shyness. She would just sit there quietly, reacting sweetly and politely to things her hostess said, but never initiating conversation or talking about herself.

None of this social pressure was easy for Rita, who was constantly afraid of somehow embarrassing her husband. It certainly didn't help matters that the Hollywood press had dubbed the Welleses 'Beauty and the Brain.'

'It was so *easy* to make fun of Miss Hayworth,' said Shifra Haran. 'She was so easily hurt.' Hardly a night went by that Rita didn't ask Orson if she had made some mistake that day. He would reassure her that she had done just fine and that he was very proud of her. Then they would make love and, as always, she would feel confident and secure again. How could Orson possibly explain to her what he understood very well indeed? Louis Dolivet and the other brilliant men she wanted so to impress were themselves anxious to be 'well thought of by a famous sex symbol.' No, that was something Rita would definitely not want to hear.

That November, two days before Welles was scheduled to deliver another important address, this time to the Soviet-American Congress, good news arrived from Los Angeles, where Judson had agreed to the out-of-court settlement Orson's lawyers had negotiated. This put Rita's mind at rest. Without actually having to face him in court, she was rid of one of the ghosts that had haunted her. Once again her life seemed to have taken a positive new turn. Her husband's talks on international cooperation were being generally very well received, and more than ever their plans to leave Hollywood permanently appeared likely to come to fruition.

But once again, too, her happiness was only temporary. The fates wouldn't seem to let up on her. In Los Angeles Superior Court Rita's latest settlement with Judson was being filed when, purely as a matter of routine, their 1942 agreement was unsealed. The press hadn't seen it before. At the time of the divorce proceedings, they *had* seen Rita's detailed charges against Judson, and she had been mortified when these charges were made public. But at the time the divorce was granted no one had known that she had given Eddie virtually everything plus the promise of $12,000 more *expressly in exchange for his future silence and discretion.* Among other explicit promises that the press had not known about, he had agreed not to imply that she had 'conducted herself in any manner which would cause her to be held in scorn, or which would damage her career.' Nor would he 'sell, publish, or circulate any slanderous, libelous, or defamatory matter concerning her.'

Now, suddenly, in the very midst of her new husband's political speechmaking in New York, the press disclosed that Rita had 'bought her former husband's silence about her personal affairs.' It wasn't Eddie's threats to besmirch her reputation that generated so much current interest, but the fact that she had agreed to give him virtually everything she had and more if only he would shut up about her.

The implication seemed clear: she did indeed have something to hide – but what? Why, after all, had she been so anxious to buy his silence? No woman in her right mind would have signed such a ridiculous settlement if Eddie didn't have something on her. Just at the moment when Rita was working so hard to be an asset to her husband, to be someone he could be proud of, there in the press for all to see was clause after clause from the divorce settlement in which Eddie agreed not to embarrass her. Eddie hadn't taken her obscene letter to the press, as he had threatened to do; he had not uttered one word against her. He had been paid off and he had backed down. Still, Rita had been punished. Merely the innuendo that she had something to hide, and her apparent willingness to buy his silence, had been enough to bring her down.

In private Rita kept bursting into tears. Her husband was more clear-headed, however. It seemed to Orson that the ugly situation would only get worse if they didn't take control immediately. In consultation with lawyers, Rita and Orson went over her every option. Finally they decided to call a press conference to deny that Rita had bought

Judson's silence. Although Rita agreed to put in an appearance, she was much too distraught to face reporters' questions. Her husband and an attorney would do that. She did sign a written statement in which she contended that Judson's promises not to besmirch her reputation were nothing more than standard clauses in the divorce settlement. Rita's written statement concluded: 'Other than this I have no comment, since that would violate my agreement not to discuss matters.'

The press conference began when an angry Welles strode into the room alone. He seemed barely able to contain his rage. When one reporter asked him how all this made him feel, Welles shot back, 'I've just married the girl. How would any husband feel?' Soon Rita joined him, but uttered not a word. Welles explained that her eyes were red because she had been crying all day. Dressed in a tailored gray suit, Rita tried to hold herself erect as the photographers' flashbulbs exploded all around her. 'It will be all right, baby,' Orson reassured her – and so, in a way, it was.

'RITA TALKS JUST A LITTLE ABOUT SECRET' read one headline – but the press appeared satisfied that she had faced up to the speculation. After the press conference, to Rita's great relief, the newspapers dropped the matter. Unbeknownst to Rita and Orson, who probably never subsequently found out about it, just as the press decided to pursue the matter no further, the FBI launched a secret investigation of its own. Word had reached federal authorities that Judson had extorted sums of money from Rita on the basis of her obscene letter.

Accordingly, the FBI moved to determine whether any federal violations were involved, 'particularly of the Extortion statute, as well as transmission of obscene matter through the mail.' Although Judson was the target of the investigation, it was most fortunate for Rita that the FBI could never get its hands on the 'mysterious letter' in order to establish its existence in court. Not only would such a court case have heaped additional scorn on her, but it also could have involved criminal charges. Eddie may have

116

been using the letter to extort money, but it had been Rita, who had mailed the letter to him in the first place, thereby, ironically, implicating her in the 'transmission of obscene matter through the mail.'

However successful the press conference had been in quieting the public speculation about her, the tension of the past few days had taken its toll on both Rita and Orson. Even before that, Welles's bad back had flared up again, as it was wont to do in stressful circumstances. He had been born with anomalies of the spine that gave him lifelong agony, but stress invariably exacerbated his condition. When the pain was almost too excruciating to bear, he had himself strapped into a heavy metal brace that he wore under his clothes, and which Rita helped him put on and take off. In New York several doctors had recommended surgery, but Welles claimed that he was too busy. He and Rita planned to leave for England any day, as soon as Alexander Korda was ready for them.

Suddenly, while out in Old Westbury with Beatrice and Louis Dolivet, Welles was stricken with hepatitis. The Dolivets had a houseful of other guests, but Orson was far too ill to do anything but stay in his rooms, attended by Rita and his secretary, Elisabeth Rubino, who had been summoned from New York City. Orson demanded that a doctor be sent for immediately, and when Beatrice Straight was unable to provide one swiftly enough, he roared with anger. 'He was very difficult when he was sick,' his hostess declared. And although, as she recalled, everyone 'walked around on tiptoes' lest Orson be disturbed, it was he who caused a great 'commotion' in the household with his litany of demands and complaints.

With Orson confined to bed, Rita was left to cope with her shyness in the face of a group of intimidating strangers. When Beatrice came up to ask Rita to take a break from nursing Orson and join the others downstairs, even though Orson urged her to go, Rita was afraid to appear without her husband. 'She was worried that he would send her down,' said Elisabeth Rubino. 'She felt that she wasn't good enough for these people mentally.'

117

It was winter and the snow was falling in New York, and when Orson was finally a bit stronger, friends advised a very worried Rita to take her husband to Florida for some sun. A sojourn in Florida – just the two of them – seemed like a perfect idea to Rita and she talked Orson into it, although he was really too weak from his illness to put up a fight. Besides, laughed Shifra Haran, who knew Orson's inclinations backward and forward in this regard, 'He probably *enjoyed* being sick, being waited on a lot.' As soon as he could make the trip, Rita and Orson headed south.

Things went much more smoothly once the Welleses reached Florida. Without the customary fanfare, Rita and Orson ushered in the new year of 1944 at the Roney Plaza, in Miami Beach, where she lovingly nursed him back to health. 'I sat in Florida hardly able to move,' Welles remembered. 'The hepatitis had almost killed me. I was very sick. And poor Rita stayed with me, taking *wonderful* care of me.' Having the man in her life all to herself for a change, and knowing that in his infirmity he needed and depended on her, had a profound healing effect on Rita. The two weeks they spent in Florida marked a significant new phase in their relationship. Although his illness had drastically diminished their sex life, it seemed to Orson that for once Rita felt loved and secure just being alone with him.

Before long Orson's vigor had begun to return, but his back continued to torment him, so that by 7 January the Welleses had resigned themselves to returning to Hollywood. There Dadda Bernstein, whose medical speciality was orthopedics, would be able to treat him without surgery, as well as monitor his further recovery from the bout with hepatitis. Dadda prescribed a high-protein diet, sunshine, and plenty of rest. As late as March, a doctor from the Johns Hopkins Hospital was writing to Orson to urge him to undergo surgery for a herniated disc, but Welles preferred Dadda's less drastic approach.

Rita and Orson regarded the return to Hollywood as only temporary, until he was well enough to go to England for *War and Peace*. Still, they were not without trepidation about going back to a town – and a life – that in their hearts they had hoped to leave behind. Rita seemed confident enough in their love to sustain this temporary setback. In Orson's weakened condition the five-and-a-half-day train trip west was, as he said, 'pretty rough,' but Rita was by his side the whole way to soothe him. In Los Angeles Jackson Leighter had reserved a suite at the Beverly Hills Hotel until a small rented house was ready for occupancy.

Back in Hollywood, Rita had to face Harry Cohn again. Not without reason, Cohn perceived Orson as having interfered with the studio's big plans for her. To Cohn the undeniably brilliant *enfant terrible* Welles was obviously a far more formidable adversary than Rita's first husband had been. Orson had wired Alexander Korda in London to say that Harry Cohn was giving Rita trouble about leaving town for *War and Peace*. Cohn had a new film that he wanted her to make at Columbia: *Tonight and Every Night*.

As much as Rita had tried to block it from her thoughts, she was still under contract to Columbia and obliged to do as Harry Cohn instructed. When initially she didn't want to go back to work, Cohn blamed it on her husband's bad influence. 'He imagined that I decided these things for her, but I didn't,' said Welles. 'I left it entirely to her. She made those decisions entirely herself.'

In large part Rita was disinclined to return to film work because she had decided that she wanted something very different out of life and finally had a chance to get it.

Said Welles, to illustrate what it was she wanted and needed: 'There was a young *torero*, a Mexican boy, that I had discoverd and was supporting while he was becoming a *novillero*. Rita and I were down in Mexico to watch him take his *alternativa* and he was very badly gored. We went to the hospital, where Rita joined his mother and sisters and stayed with them for two or three days. I'll never forget it: you saw her with them and you saw her *absolutely at home*. Absolutely relaxed and at home. And you saw how *happy* she would be to be one of those simple people.'

When Orson and Rita had settled into a cozy new house on Fordyce Road, they resumed the vigorous sex life that they had enjoyed before his illness. Sometimes it was as if they were making up for lost time. One such night, in March, they couldn't wait to get to the bedroom and made love on the sofa. It was a night they would have occasion to remember when, not long afterward, Rita learned that she was pregnant. The news made her 'deliciously happy,' as Shifra Haran recalled. A baby would complete Rita's sense of having the real family for which she had always longed.

She told Orson that she wanted her baby's life to be completely different from what hers had been. Above all, she hoped to be a more responsible parent than her own mother had been to her. The first important step, she said, was to give the baby a happy childhood. When her pregnancy was more advanced she would ask her friend Horty Hill to stay with her, to help her through the rough spots.

As for Orson, although he was thrilled to see Rita so happy, he already had one daughter with whom he didn't care to spend much time anyway. Fatherhood 'wasn't his thing,' explained Shifra Haran. 'To expect him to have been otherwise would have been your mistake. You can't expect of people what they're not *capable* of giving.'

More than once, as he passed through the living room, Miss Haran heard him grumble under his breath, 'That's the couch where I lost control!'

According to Louis Dolivet, during this period Rita began to worry about Orson's drinking. Dadda Bernstein asked Dolivet, who had a good deal of influence on Welles, to keep an eye on Orson's fondness for the bottle. The hepatitis had weakened his liver and alcohol could prove destructive. Finally Rita made Orson promise that, at least until the baby was born, he would refrain from drinking.

Rita was two months pregnant when she began fittings for *Tonight and Every Night*, a musical set in London during the Blitz. Having the birth of her baby to look forward to had considerably altered Rita's attitude both to working and to living in Los Angeles. Orson, who was already doing a radio show and working on the staging of a play for Billy Rose, said that the house on Fordyce Road was much too small for a family with a baby, so they went

120

house-hunting and soon rented a considerably larger and more dramatic place on Carmelina Drive, in Brentwood.

The new house boasted ten rooms, fabulous grounds, and a swimming pool in the center of which was a tiny island with a palm tree. The rent was also fabulous for the period: $1,500 a month. Before they moved in, Orson ordered the construction of a special roofless solarium so Rita could sunbathe in the nude. This was hardly the 'simple' life Welles perceived that Rita wanted. Still, regardless of its grand size and lavish appointments, the house in Brentwood represented something very special to Rita: in a town where she had almost always been unhappy, it was an oasis, a *home*. 'It was the familiar, comfortable place that she could always come to,' recalled Shifra Haran, who had an office in the new house, as well. 'That to me was the finest hour in her life, and maybe in his, too. Comfort and contentment! Neither of them had had it before. Didn't last all that long. But she had it with him then, and that's what she wanted!'

Years later Rita told actress June Allyson: 'Maybe I tried hardest to be a good wife in my second marriage. I really wanted to be everything Orson wanted of me.'

Welles had always been a voracious reader, and in an effort to please her husband, Rita struggled to become one, too. Wherever Orson was, inevitably there were great stacks of books all about. When she thought that nobody was watching, Rita would get out his books and secretly try to read them. If anyone came into the room, she would quickly hide the books and pretend to be doing something else. One volume that she read with particular fascination that summer of 1944 was Sir Walter Scott's *Ivanhoe*, in which she found herself powerfully drawn to the beautiful name of one of the female characters: Rebecca. She told Orson that if they had a little girl, this would be her name.

Despite her program of furtive reading, Rita remained painfully insecure about her intellectual capacities. When the Hills visited Carmelina Drive that summer, Rita lay in her bathrobe on the couch, peacefully listening to, but not daring to participate in, the complicated word games

Orson and Skipper loved to play. 'She would be just so thrilled!' said Shifra Haran. 'But she didn't try to participate because she felt she wasn't smart enough, and she didn't want to embarrass herself.'

For her husband's sake she did, however, manage to overcome her innate shyness – or *seemed* to – when for the first time she opened her home and acted as hostess to a lavish party for more than a hundred of his friends and associates. Rita was five months pregnant. With great pride she personally supervised everything: the guest list, the invitations, the food, and the staff. It was her way of celebrating their happiness together and their impending parenthood. The evening of the party Rita was the picture of contentment, deeply tanned and breathtakingly beautiful in her simple long white dress.

Not long after the party, as the fall approached, Orson was scheduled to campaign on behalf of President Franklin Delano Roosevelt's reelection. As Orson's departure drew near, Rita's old anxieties about being abandoned began to plague her again. She couldn't get it out of her mind that somehow she was going to lose him. Before he left, she broke down in tears and told him that she knew he was going to betray her while he was away. Why couldn't he leave the presidential campaign to others and stay with her in California until the baby was born? Orson insisted that she was being silly – betraying her was not something he would ever consider doing. Before very long the campaign would be over and Roosevelt reelected, and they would be together again. Rita listened and, for the moment at least, was soothed.

Even Harry Cohn had to agree that there was no question of Rita's making another film soon after *Tonight and Every Other Night*. Rita would remain at home until the birth of her baby. To keep her company while Orson was away, Dadda Bernstein gave her an adorable white-and-gold cocker spaniel called Pookles, which was also Dadda's pet name for Orson. Hortense Hill came out from Illinois for an extended stay. Before Orson's departure, the Welleses had pooled their money to buy a tumbledown

122

hideaway house in Big Sur, on the beautiful rugged northern California coast. Miss Haran had been dispatched to take measurements, and Rita occupied herself with sewing curtains.

Yet all was not well with Rita. Naturally she wanted her husband home during these last months of her pregnancy, but he was in New York, operating out of a suite at the Waldorf Towers; she could barely keep track of him as he crisscrossed the nation doing radio broadcasts and speeches for Roosevelt. 'The only way she knew that someone loved her was if they were in bed with her. She couldn't accept that someone could love her two thousand miles away,' said Shifra Haran, who, as Welles's secretary traveled with him and often tried to comfort and reassure Rita on the telephone when the frantic wife had tracked down her husband's whereabouts to farflung cities and towns.

For Orson, no matter how desperately lonely and unhappy his pregnant wife might be, taking a break from the campaign, as she longed for him to do, was out of the question.

Still, 'I really think he loved her as far as he was capable,' said Shifra Haran. '*As far as he was capable* – you had to give him that limitation. He *had* to have his freedom now to go away. He *had* to do those things. And that was hard for her. She didn't like it one damn bit. She always had to have that assurance that somebody loved her. Of course, if I had been able to stay behind and be with her, I could have tried to convince her it was all right. But I had to go with him.'

To make matters worse, no sooner had Welles departed than a number of hangers-on from the film studios, the beauticians and wardrobe personnel with whom Rita felt distinctly more comfortable than with her ostensible peers, began showing up regularly at Carmelina Drive to drink beer with her and swap studio gossip. With them Rita became another person; she didn't have to put on an act or pretend to understand things she really didn't. Their language was frequently down and dirty, and so, in their company, was hers.

'Those were the kind of girlfriends you *don't* need,' said Shifra Haran. 'They're your worst enemies instead of your best friends.' Because he perceived them as troublemakers who only brought Rita down, Welles had frowned upon their attempts to visit in the past, and now they took their revenge on him by talking constantly to Rita about how awful it was that he had gone away and left her. That was the last thing she needed to hear in her already anxious state of mind.

If Orson wouldn't come to see her, Rita decided that she would have to go to him in New York. Being with her husband again at Applegreen, on Long Island, may have temporarily put Rita's anxieties to rest; however, it was at this very moment that he proceeded to betray her, much as she feared he would. When they had stayed at Beatrice Straight's family estate in Old Westbury in the past, Rita had grown accustomed to Orson's frequent absences with Louis Dolivet. So there was nothing odd when Orson left his pregnant wife at Applegreen and went off to dine at '21', in Manhattan, where he caught a glimpse of lovely young Gloria Vanderbilt at a table with her husband and several other people.

'Something happened when our eyes met,' recalled Gloria Vanderbilt about what occurred when Orson joined her group, 'and later under the table he kept touching my knee and soon we were holding hands.' At a party afterward Orson and the young heiress found themselves alone in a narrow corridor, where they embraced and kissed. Welles's exciting presence made her feel 'alive every second,' but Gloria knew that his pregnant wife, Rita, was with him on Long Island, and this kept things from proceeding any further, however much she continued to 'think about him all the time' in the days that followed.

Back in California that October, Rita was seven months pregnant when she received word from New York that Orson had fallen gravely ill with a 104-degree fever. Roosevelt wired his best wishes for a speedy recovery, but it looked as if Welles was out of commission at least until after the election. There were even persistent rumors that Orson might be dying. Rita told Miss Haran that she felt terribly guilty: was this what her premonition about losing him had really meant? There was little that Rita could do to help except urge him to come home as soon as he was well enough to travel. When he had partially recovered by the end of October, however, instead of returning to Carmelina Drive he promptly went back on the road for Roosevelt, against the advice of his doctors. Rita did not rest easy until two days after Roosevelt's reelection, when at last Orson and Miss Haran boarded a plane for California.

Chapter Ten

Orson arrived home with great plans. He kept talking excitedly about how, suddenly, it all seemed possible now: he might be president one day and Rita the First Lady! Roosevelt had declared that it was time for young Welles to start thinking seriously about seeking public office. The president advised Orson that if he hoped someday to make a bid for the White House he should start by running for the Senate.

It affords a fascinating perspective on the curious contradictions in American political life of the period that even as Franklin Delano Roosevelt was warmly encouraging Welles's political ambitions, other elements in Washington were clearly a good deal less enthusiastic about Orson's activities. Just days before Roosevelt's reelection that November, the Los Angeles office of the FBI had prepared an extensive secret report on Welles and the question of his possible membership of the Communist Party. In addition, because at Orson's instigation Rita had lent her famous name to various left-wing political causes, she, too, would be subject to secret FBI scrutiny. The 1944 report on Orson would also find its way into Rita's own FBI file, which includes the notation that although an FBI informant 'whose reliability is well established' had scrutinized the records of the Northwest Section of the Los Angeles Communist Political Association and been 'unable to find any record of Welles's membership . . . an examination of Welles's activities and his membership in various organizations reflects that he has consistently followed the

Communist Party line and has been active in numerous ''front'' organizations.' Henceforth, the Los Angeles Field Division of the FBI would 'follow and report Subject's current activities.' Accordingly, because she followed her husband's lead in all things, Rita's FBI file would catalogue an assortment of left-wing groups and causes with which her name was associated, such as the Council of Hollywood Guilds and Unions; the National Council of American-Soviet Friendship; and the Joint Anti-Fascist Refugee Committee. Her activity in these causes was basically limited to lending them the prestige of her stardom, but her FBI dossier would come back to haunt her in Hollywood long after her marriage to Welles was over.

Tantalizing as Orson's visions of their future together in Washington undeniably were, Rita's principal concern at the moment was that he be with her in Los Angeles when she gave birth. Welles used the time to begin work on a new daily political column to be syndicated by the *New York Post* that he hoped would provide a forum to test his ideas in print. In the final weeks of Rita's pregnancy Welles often spent day and night working frantically in the seclusion of the pool house, but at least she knew he was nearby. Meanwhile, Rita set up a nursery on the second floor of their home and hired a nanny.

On 15 December 1944, she entered St John's Hospital, in Santa Monica, known for the privacy it afforded celebrities, and two days later she gave birth by Caesarean section to a healthy seven-pound girl who, from the first, looked remarkably like her father. Orson drew a picture of the stars in the sky on the night his daughter was born and sent copies to friends. Rebecca, or Becky, as they called her, came home to Brentwood on Christmas Eve. Congratulations poured in from around the world, but the missive Orson read most keenly was from the White House. Eleanor Roosevelt dispatched kind words on the birth of Rebecca, as well as an invitation to Orson and Rita to attend an inauguration luncheon and to come back afterward for a private visit with Franklin and herself. Another note came from Vice-President Harry S. Truman, who

127

predicted a splendid future for the golden couple's daughter: 'Congratulations on the arrival of Miss Rebecca,' wrote Truman. 'I know she can't help having a grand career with the support she will have from her parents.'

Rita planned to attend the inauguration with her husband, but at the last minute she realized she was not yet strong enough to make the trip. (Air travel was a good deal more arduous during the war than it is today.) If she had assumed that Orson would stay behind with her, she was wrong. He remembered later that she had seemed terribly depressed when he left for Washington, but he told himself that, with a baby to take care of, she would feel less lonely in his absence. Rita was especially bitter about her husband's departure because after the inauguration he was scheduled to give a series of lectures on fascism in New York, Baltimore, and Washington, D.C. Wasn't he interested in spending time with his new daughter? Not according to Shifra Haran, who observed that he was 'not all that interested' in Becky. 'I don't really think Mr Welles ever paid any attention to her – just not in the cards.'

Once more Rita found herself left behind indefinitely. She was supposed to be making plans to fix up the old house in Big Sur, but with Orson away again there didn't seem to be much point to it. The hideaway was supposed to have been for the two of them; Rita certainly didn't want to go there alone. Left empty and forlorn, the tumbledown place in Big Sur loomed as a reminder of all her unrealized hopes. One afternoon, in a fit of disappointed anger, she threw away the curtains she had sewn. Her loneliness and resentment, coupled with a weakened physical condition, made it all the more difficult for Rita to cope with the unanticipated adversity that faced her next.

Precisely at the moment that Rita became a mother, full of great plans for being a better parent to little Rebecca than she considered her own mother to have been to her, Volga Cansino fell gravely ill. One of the consequences of Rita's tragic youth was that she had mixed emotions about a mother who had ultimately failed to protect her from

Eduardo's exploitation. Rita's sense of Volga's having let her down had made her own impending motherhood all the more anxiety-provoking. Like Volga, would she, too, prove inadequate to the task of raising a child? Indeed, it is common among women with histories comparable to Rita's to be plagued by desperate fears that, no matter how hard they try to be good parents, they will inevitably fail at motherhood as miserably as their own mothers did.

During her marriage to Orson, Rita's contacts with both her parents had been perfunctory. Although she hadn't even invited the Cansinos to her wedding, superficial appearances were kept up to avoid gossip; but a glance at the Welleses' Christmas list for the first year of their marriage suggests a subtext of hostility – next to the presents that an assistant had innocently proposed for Volga and Eduardo, the usually munificent Orson had written 'Too Much.' (Welles's attitude also evidently extended to Rita's brothers. 'Somebody always *wanted* something from her – her father, her brothers,' recalled Shifra Haran. 'People would say to both of the brothers, "You're Rita Hayworth's brother. What's she doing for you?' And she was so docile that she exerted herself to do what they asked.' Elisabeth Rubino came into the drawing room one day to find Rita in a clearly agitated state. 'Is there something I can do?' asked the secretary. 'No,' Rita replied. 'I just got a telephone call from my brother and he wants five thousand dollars. Please don't tell Orson.' 'Of course I won't tell him,' Miss Rubino comforted her.)

Welles had just arrived in New York after the inauguration when Rita called him about Volga. What should she do? When at Welles's request Dadda Bernstein examined Mrs Cansino, the doctor said that she was suffering from appendicitis, and immediately had her admitted to the same hospital where Rita had given birth just weeks before. There it was determined that Volga's appendix had ruptured. Efforts to help her were in vain. She seemed to grow weaker by the hour. For a forty-seven-year-old woman she was in very poor general physical condition. She might have passed for someone in her sixties.

Obviously the years of heavy drinking had taken their toll. Volga died at 9.30 in the evening on 25 January 1945, with Rita at her side. On her death certificate, Dadda Bernstein listed the immediate cause of her demise as 'generalized peritonitis' due to 'ruptured appendix.'

Coming as it did only a month after the birth of Rita's own child, Volga's death triggered an emotional crisis. Later Rita would tell Orson that although she had long resented Volga, she had begun to wonder whether she hadn't simply been insensitive to her mother's plight with Eduardo. The early death of her mother made Rita horribly guilty about the bad feelings she had secretly harboured toward her all those years.

Rita said none of this when Welles called her as soon as Dadda Bernstein had notified him of Volga's death. She was too distraught to say much of anything at all. On the telephone she seemed to agree – or Orson *wanted* her to agree – that there was no need for him to cut short his lecture tour and come home. Still, he should have sensed how difficult a time this would be for Rita. Years later, even he had to admit that he had made a dreadful mistake in failing to fly to Los Angeles for Volga's funeral.

When Orson finally returned home from the lecture tour, he promptly took Rita to Mexico for a vacation with the Hills. The new baby was left behind in a nurse's care. Across the border, Rita went from abysmal depression to what seemed like high spirits. They resumed their love life with a vengeance. Rita appeared to Miss Haran to feel comforted and secure as she had not been in months. Around midnight one night in Mexico City, when suddenly he ran out of condoms, Orson summoned Miss Haran, whom he dispatched to go out at once and purchase some more: a most awkward assignment for a maiden lady alone in a strange city late at night, but he considered this an emergency. Orson wanted to take no chances with Rita's becoming pregnant again.

Back in Los Angeles after their Mexican holiday, Rita was confronted with a new crisis: her father's attempts to visit her now that Volga was dead. Orson almost always

130

managed to head him off. 'He was a terrible man,' Welles recalled. 'And she really hated him. She couldn't deal with him at all.' At times like these Rita felt so safe with Orson. Once again she appeared confident that Orson was soon going to take her and Becky away from Hollywood – but by now, unfortunately, although he certainly didn't say anything about it to her, Orson was no longer so sure that that was going to happen.

No matter how diligently he struggled to make his new column a success, he found himself consistently unable to discover his authentic voice as a political commentator. Orson had counted on the *Post* column to launch him as a force in American politics, but there was growing reason to fear that he wasn't going to pull it off. He did not talk to Rita about his professional problems – he was hesitant to admit even to himself his evident failure to attract the widespread readership he had hoped for – but it was inevitable that he would seem increasingly preoccupied and withdrawn to her. She couldn't help but notice that something had changed.

To make matters worse, Orson had accepted an acting assignment in the film *Tomorrow Is Forever*, co-starring Claudette Colbert. He said that he would have to act in one movie a year until he actually began earning a living at politics, but Rita didn't see it that way. Having come to the conclusion that his withdrawn behavior had to do with the time he was spending at the film studio, she became convinced that he must be cheating on her. There were angry scenes and accusations. 'Every night I would come home, and I would find her in tears,' Welles recalled. 'She said, "I know what goes on in the studio!" Oh, it was terrible!'

Rita's nightly crying fits and recriminations only drove her husband further away. 'For him to be confronted with this gorgeous creature collapsing was devastating,' recalled Shifra Haran of this stormy period. Much as he had once turned to Rita to shore up his ego in the midst of an earlier career crisis, now he embarked on a string of affairs with various other women. Nothing serious, but they soothed his wounded vanity. 'I think if you take ego and vanity out of sex,' Welles would explain, 'you would find that the actual amount of sexual activity would be reduced drastically. I'm thinking of men, particularly, more than women. A man is to a great extent operating on other juices than the sexual ones when he's chasing around.'

Chief among the extramarital affairs Orson conducted in this period was with Judy Garland. It was Welles's custom to bring Judy great bouquets of white flowers, but one night when he returned home from his rendezvous the flowers were still in his car. He had somehow forgotten to give them to her. When Rita spotted the beautiful bouquets in the back seat, she only naturally assumed they were a gift for her. But before Rita could get to them, Miss Haran rushed out and discreetly removed the card that she knew only too well would be addressed to Judy. This wasn't simply a case of covering up for her boss. By now Miss Haran was every bit as loyal to Rita as to Orson, but after much debate, she and Shorty had decided that there was really no good reason for Mrs Welles to discover things that would only agitate her further.

Rita's girlfriends from the studio apparently didn't see it that way. They fed Rita the rumors they had heard about her husband – and unfortunately there was plenty to hear. Welles had been seen about town with this one or that one; he was known to visit so-and-so's apartment. Perhaps they believed they were helping her by telling her all this; or perhaps they were just being malicious. 'She was at the mercy of those rotters,' said Shifra Haran. 'They *enjoyed* bringing dirt to her that would only make her unhappy. They wanted to bring her down and to see the marriage break up. You really don't have a chance in hell in that rotten environment.'

Although years later Orson himself did not deny having *repeatedly* betrayed his wife in this period, still he shuddered at the thought of how devastated Rita must have been when she heard about his infidelities. 'We're such a *cruel* race of people,' groaned Welles, with reference to those who told Rita about his transgressions, but also, undoubtedly, to himself, to what *he* had done to her.

Like her mother before her, Rita began to drink. And when she drank there were further scenes with her husband. Then she would insist on going out driving. Suddenly in the midst of an argument, she would storm out of the house and head for the car. Nothing he said could stop her. Fearful that she was going to kill herself, Orson would accompany her. He would never be able to forgive himself if she died like this. Sometimes it seemed to him that she actually wanted to kill herself as she careened at top speed along the perilous winding roads high in the Hollywood Hills. His guilt was intensified by memories of his own father's death from alcoholism. As a boy Orson had stopped seeing his father on account of his heavy drinking, and when Dick Welles died not long afterward, Orson was overwhelmed with guilt at having abandoned him. These same emotions tormented him when he saw what his actions were doing to Rita. As he had done with his beloved father, he was turning away from Rita precisely when she needed him most. And he knew it was even worse in this situation because as an adult he was fully responsible for his own actions.

If, indeed, he felt *that* guilty about hurting Rita, why didn't he just stop? No one was forcing him to dally with Judy Garland and the others. The answer has to do with his horror that Rita's rages weren't 'just gypsy,' as he had presumed early in their relationship. It seemed to him that she was far more deeply troubled than he had imagined. Only now was he stuck by the fact that her rages 'seemed so out of character' – it was as if another self had taken over. This was beyond anything he felt himself capable of managing. The wild rages, the violent mood swings, the sudden losses of emotional control – these were among the long-term repercussions of Rita's history of childhood abuse.

Again, why, if he loved her – as he insisted he *still* did even on the very night he died – did he turn away from her? His explanation was blunt, but accurate: 'If I hadn't been a person obsessed with his work, I could have stayed with her,' he said. Sadly for Rita, she was married to a man

133

whose career came first, not his love for her. In the beginning he had turned to Rita in the midst of a career crisis, and her sweetness and beauty had sustained him. As time passed she was in no condition to do that. By his own admission, he began spending time with prostitutes at the home of producer Sam Spiegel: *they* made no emotional demands on him, and for the moment that was the way he liked it.

Before long, Rita's feelings of rejection began to explode in public, as in the New York hotel suite where Orson was working with a group of writers in the living room when suddenly Rita's weeping could be heard issuing from the bedroom. 'Rita seemed to want attention,' recalled Elisabeth Rubino, who was there taking dictation. Anxious to get on with his work, Welles instructed one of his associates to take Rita to Elizabeth Arden to get her hair done. 'Now I can concentrate!' Welles said once Rita was gone.

Several hours passed and Rita came back to discover Orson still immersed in his work. 'She had her hair piled up on her head and it was absolutely gorgeous,' Elisabeth Rubino recalled. 'She thought she would come in and make an entrance. But he didn't even look up! I felt like kicking him! She sat on a chair near the door, and she just stared and stared. Then she went into a tantrum.' Only then did Orson look up at her, and when she rushed off into the bedroom, he followed her. 'I think we'd better go home,' said one of the writers. 'It'll be a while now.' When Orson closeted himself with Rita at such tense moments in their relationship, it was always a very long time before he came back out.

Perhaps it was inevitable that with the breakdown of their marriage, *both* Orson and Rita were soon making exactly the kinds of professional decisions that they had been hoping to escape together: he signed up to direct *The Stranger*, a conventional, straightforward film that would be deliberately unlike the exciting experimental work he had insisted on doing before (his hitherto stubborn resistance to telling a standard conventional story had been one of the reasons he'd wanted to leave Hollywood in the first place);

and she took the title role in *Gilda* – a film that would forever after identify her with the sex-symbol image that marriage to Orson was to have allowed her to put behind her. *The Stranger* and *Gilda*: each in its way was a confession of defeat, a sign that the dreams they had shared had not come to fruition.

Chapter Eleven

'*M*iss Hayworth herself said she was two people,' recalled Shifra Haran. 'She was the movie star on the screen, and she was the person. People expected things of her that she wasn't as a person.' Indeed, more than any of her other film roles, that of the sultry, provocative Gilda was responsible for the expecations that people – men especially – would forever after have of her. Or as Rita herself would later put it, with evident bitterness: 'Men go to bed with Gilda, but wake up with me.'

Directed by Charles Vidor and produced by Virginia Van Upp, Rita's signature film is the extravagant and sometimes rather farfetched story of the sexual temptress (Hayworth) who marries the mysterious Ballin Mundson (George Macready), the proprietor of an illegal South American gambling casino. The fireworks start when Mundson introduces his new bride to his right-hand man at the casino, Johnny Farrell (Glenn Ford). Unbeknownst to Mundson, Gilda and Johnny once had a passionate affair that ended badly – and now she will do anything to arouse her former lover's jealousy. Rita's extraordinary presence and performance made *Gilda* a major box-office hit for Columbia, particularly with returning American soldiers who flocked to the film to see their wartime pinup come-to-life.

And come to life she did in erotically charged scenes like the legendary 'Put the Blame on Mame' song-and-dance number (dubbed by Anita Ellis), in which a drunken Gilda tortures Johnny by doing a mock striptease for the delighted casino audience. Dressed in a strapless black satin gown that the designer Jean Louis modeled on the costume worn by Madame X in John Singer Sargent's famous painting, Rita ultimately peels off only her long black gloves, but her swinging hips and bold glances, her brilliant embodiment of sheer sensual abandon, make the scene a masterpiece of illicit innuendo. While, according to Jonie Taps, 'Rita never considered herself or tried to be a sex symbol,' thenceforth she was inevitably identified with Gilda: an image she would spend much of the rest of her life struggling unsuccessfully to escape.

Although at the time she made *Gilda* Rita still briefly held out hope for somehow recapturing her dreams with Orson, it soon became apparent that that was most unlikely to happen. By the time of *Gilda* and *The Stranger*, Welles's secretary, Miss Haran, had resigned, so there was no one left to shield Rita from hearing about her husband's infidelities. While she was filming at Columbia, the gossip in her dressing room centered on Orson's philandering over at Goldwyn, where he was directing and starring in *The Stranger* for International Pictures. The news must have hurt all the more because it was Rita who had actually made it possible for Orson to do *The Stranger* in the first place; on account of Orson's reputation for being difficult and unreliable, International Pictures had required that she co-sign his contract, promising to indemnify them if he failed to finish the picture according to their specifications. Considering how abominably he'd been treating her of late, asking for her help now was most awkward – but if he wanted to work he had no choice. In addition, Orson owed her approximately $30,000, which he had borrowed in the course of their marriage.

Unfortunately, his gratitude to Rita for bailing him out again didn't stop Orson from spending much of his time in an apartment on the Goldwyn lot, which he used as a trysting place. At night, more often than not Rita found herself at home alone with the baby. 'He had a few extra-legal affairs with girls that would drop by in the afternoon and evening,' recalled production manager Jim Pratt. Her knowledge of these affairs notwithstanding, Rita frequently came to the set to talk to Orson. But if she had hoped for some sign that he was coming home to her, this was not to be. 'He impressed me as being very much in love with her,' recalled film editor Ernest Nims, who lunched with Rita and Orson several times at Goldwyn. 'But I guess that that suite of rooms at the studio may have developed into a problem.'

Nor did Orson come home after finishing work on *The Stranger*. Rita's visits to the Goldwyn lot had failed to lure him back to wife and daughter. Instead, on 30 November 1945, Orson flew to New York to talk to Cole Porter about a stage production of *Around the World in Eighty Days*. Welles had decided that his dreams of a future in politics were probably not going to come true. Even if he did eventually manage to win a Senate seat, he wondered whether Rita was up to the role of senator's wife: 'She didn't like to be left alone, and I knew that a junior senator or congressman doesn't have much home life.' Besides: 'Rita was very unhappy, and I didn't believe that she was going to stay with me,' he said. 'I didn't see it coming soon, but I thought that she was somebody who would finally break down in one way or another' – and a divorce or a breakdown would definitely put an end to his presidential aspirations.

Rita surprised him, however. No sooner had he left for New York than she decided to divorce him. The sexual betrayals, the long absences, the excessive preoccupation with his work at the expense of a home life – Rita couldn't take these anymore. Much as she continued to love him, his departure was the final blow. She decided that once she finished *Gilda* she would take a much-needed rest in Palm Springs, while her attorneys worked out details of the divorce.

They hadn't talked about anything like this before he left for New York, so Welles was startled by Rita's sudden decision. Of course he knew perfectly well that their marriage had gone awry, but still he had not expected this of her. Much as he had done to hurt her of late, he was brokenhearted, but also strangely relieved that *she* had been the one to put an end to the difficult marriage. 'I could have patched it up in a day,' he recalled, 'but I had reached the end of my capacity to feel such a total failure with her. I had done *everything* I could think of and I didn't seem to be able to bring her anything but agony. I really thought that maybe somebody else could make her happy, because I could see that there was no way I could, except to give her some moments of joy during the week. I was going to come home every night for the rest of my life to a woman in tears. I felt so *guilty* – and I adored her!'

Rita did not hear from Orson after she publicly announced that she was divorcing him. Even when he got back to Los Angeles to put some finishing touches on *The Stranger*, still he didn't contact her. (Without a word he quietly slipped off to Mexico, to spend the holidays in solitude). Two years before, Rita had spent New Year's Eve patiently nursing Orson back to health in Florida. Everything had seemed possible for them then. They had been alone and in love, and she had been very, very happy. All that was changed. Little Becky wasn't even a year old and already her daddy was gone.

This New Year's Eve Rita shed 'lonely tears' with actress Shelley Winters on their way to the big annual party at Sam Spiegel's house. (Did Rita know about the prostitutes Orson had frequently sported with there?) In the limousine Rita told Shelley Winters that she hated holidays because they were 'the lonesomest time of the year.' At the crowded party Winters lost track of Rita. Later when she asked actress Ava Gardner if she had seen her, Ava pointed to a bed where Rita lay fast asleep beneath a pile of fur coats. She had been 'so lonely and bored' that she had dozed off, and Ava Gardner had draped the fur coats over her. When Shelley Winters came close to Rita to make sure she was all right, she could see that 'her hair and her face were a mess. She'd been weeping.' Ava Gardner proposed that when Rita woke up the three of them should sneak out of Spiegel's house together and find a limo to take them home. But it didn't happen that way at all. When Rita opened her eyes and pulled off the fur coats, she didn't leave the party, but fixed her hair and makeup, then headed for the dance floor. Suddenly she was dancing with singer Tony Martin, who had appeared with her in *Music in My Heart* in 1940.

Martin didn't know with whom she had come to the party, so when a Hollywood wag butted in to tell Rita to call him whenever she was ready to leave, Martin assumed that the fellow was her date and was surprised to hear her respond, 'Oh, Tony's taking me home.' And take her home he did, in a hastily borrowed car. For several weeks thereafter, Rita and Tony Martin were an item, seen and photographed about town – until Rita broke off the affair as abruptly as it had begun. She said mysteriously that she and Orson were getting back together.

Actually, when Welles heard about the affair with Tony Martin, he felt absolved of responsibility for Rita. As far as Welles was concerned, she was in another man's hands – perhaps he could make her happy as Orson could not. When he talked on the telephone to her from New York for the first time since she had moved for divorce, he made every effort to be solicitous. Perhaps she misinterpreted this as a desire to get back together, when in fact he was just relieved that she was already seeing someone else. He had no intention of coming home. Far from it.

Although there was no question of Rita's asking for alimony, she did insist that he return the $30,000 she had loaned him in the course of the marriage – or at least agree to a schedule of payments. Since Orson was just then embarking on a costly new stage production (*Around the World*) and was reluctant to part with any cash, Rita agreed to take an extra $30,000 from the sale of the hideaway in Big Sur that they owned fifty-fifty. Rita also wanted Orson to adjust his life insurance to provide future protection for her and little Becky, as well as a guarantee that he would provide for them in the event that Rita found herself unemployed, which was most unlikely after *Gilda*. Finally, her lawyer argued that Rita had a community interest in

Welles's profits from *The Stranger*, as well as in the potential profits from the stories to which he had purchased film rights in the course of their marriage. After some haggling between their representatives, Rita agreed to relinquish her interests in *The Stranger* in exchange for a promise of half of Welles's profits from *Around the World*.

There was nothing here of the bitter, acrimonious dealings with Judson. Neither party was out to take financial advantage of the other. Everything was swiftly settled – but then something odd happened. Rita hesitated to make the agreement final. Although she had been the one who initiated the proceedings, she suddenly backed off. She kept postponing signing the papers. It was as if she wanted to hang on to the marriage for a while longer. And immersed as he was in mounting *Around the World*, Welles did nothing to encourage her to bring matters to a conclusion.

With Orson gone for good, the house on Carmelina Drive was much too large for just Rita and the baby. Besides, the owners wanted it back for themselves. So Rita and Becky moved to a considerably smaller and more manageable place in Bel-Air. The rental was a temporary measure, however, until Rita found a house she wanted to buy. Much as she had longed to abandon Hollywood, and still did, there was no way out for her at the moment. It was the last place in the world that she wanted to put down roots – but it was the *one* place where she could earn a living to support herself and her daughter.

After the immense box-office success of *Gilda*, her agent, Johnny Hyde, demanded that Harry Cohn give her a share in the profits from her films. As might have been expected, Harry Cohn immediately balked at the proposal. But the agent wasn't finished. When Cohn adamantly refused, Hyde only pretended to have been licked. Scarcely had Rita begun her next film for Columbia, an expensive production titled *Down to Earth*, than suddenly she was sick. Without its star the production ground to a virtual halt. Costs mounted. Harry Cohn knew that this was all Hyde's doing. The agent had put Rita up to feigning illness. He also encouraged her to refuse a pet script of Cohn's in which Rita would co-star with Humphrey Bogart, on loan to Columbia. Cohn knew when he'd been beaten. He reluctantly agreed that after one more film made strictly under salary, Rita's newly formed Beckworth Corporation – a combination of Becky's name and hers – would rake in twenty-five percent of the net profits from her films. People in the industry were saying that with this amazing deal Rita was soon going to be one of Hollywood's richest women. In light of the financial problems Welles was reportedly experiencing in New York, the joke going around the film studios was that he had picked the wrong time to break up with Rita.

Sad to say, Orson wasn't there to hear little Becky's first word, but Dr Bernstein was: 'The other day she spoke her first word,' he wrote to Orson in New York. 'It was "Pookles."'

Another day, when her nanny showed her Orson's photograph: 'She looked at it very seriously for a moment, then smiled broadly and said "Dadda,"' reported a Welles secretary who was there to see Rita on business. And in case Orson was interested, the secretary reported on another occasion that his daughter was a joy to behold: 'She would far rather run than walk. She is one of the most beautiful and graceful children I have ever seen. Her sturdy little legs are as straight as pins.'

Welles, however, was entirely preoccupied with other matters at the moment. His backer, Mike Todd, pulled out of his monstrously expensive stage production of *Around the World*, and Orson frantically called just about everyone he could think of for cash – even Harry Cohn, who promptly loaned him $25,000 on the condition that Welles direct a picture for him. Delighted to have Orson out of Rita's life at last, Cohn was ready to let bygones be bygones if it meant getting a Welles film on the cheap. *The Stranger* had amply demonstrated Orson's ability to play by the rules: to make a conventional Hollywood thriller without his usual violent disagreements with the studio. How was Harry Cohn to know that Rita had been secretly hesitating to finalize the divorce agreement, and that with her husband back in town she would leap at the chance to reconcile with him?

Although Orson had in mind a beautiful French actress named Barbara Laage to star in the low-budget thriller he was going to make for Columbia, Harry Cohn figured that putting Welles's estranged wife in the picture would be a magnificent publicity coup. However, Rita's motives for wanting the part were quite different. Once before she had worked closely with Orson, in his magic show, and it had been one of their best periods together. Perhaps now, too, working with Orson, sharing in his labors, would result in that same sort of emotional intimacy.

When she heard that Orson wanted another actress for the film, Rita decided to campaign actively for the part – but also for a good deal more than that: she wanted him to move in with her and Becky at the new home she had bought in Brentwood. The house had just been decorated by Wilbur Menefee, a Columbia set director, whose services Harry Cohn – who had been only too happy to see Rita living alone – had provided as a bonus. When Rita told Menefee that her husband would soon be staying with her in the master bedroom and that something would have to be done about the bed to accommodate him, the decorator installed two box springs and two mattresses to make a single 'huge' bed for them.

Welles knew nothing about any of this. Upon arrival in Los Angeles, he checked into the Bel-Air Hotel. A dinner invitation from Rita brought him to the house, where, Orson recalled: 'In the course of talking me into having her in the movie, she talked me into moving in. And that's what brought us back together.'

When Rita told him, 'You know, the only happiness I've ever had in my life has been with you,' Welles was over-whelmed with guilt about how badly he had treated her and with sadness at the perspective this gave him on her life.

'If this was happiness,' he would say of their marriage long afterward, 'imagine what the rest of her life had been.'

Shortly before their reconciliation Rita had been devastated to learn that American soldiers had affixed her pinup to the nuclear test bomb exploded on Bikini atoll. The GIs had nicknamed the bomb 'Gilda,' after Rita's most famous role. Instead of being flattered, Rita felt horribly violated. 'Rita used to fly into terrible rages all the time,' Welles recalled, 'but the angriest was when she found out that they'd put her on the atom bomb. Rita almost went *insane*, she was so angry. She was so shocked by it! Rita was the kind of person that kind of thing would hurt more than anybody. She wanted to go to Washington to hold a press conference, but Harry Cohn wouldn't let her because it would be *unpatriotic*.'

On the phone with Orson, Rita insisted that Cohn had himself been responsible for the Gilda-bomb, as a sick publicity stunt, but Orson tried to persuade her that it probably wasn't so. Quite simply, for American military men Rita Hayworth incarnated perfect female sexuality: putting her picture on the bomb had been their innocent homage to her.

But now Rita was determined to take her long-awaited revenge on Harry Cohn by shocking him with the news that she and Orson were back together. With Welles directing her, she would give the first *serious* performance of her acting career. Then, her lucrative new profit-sharing deal at Columbia notwithstanding, she and Becky would follow Orson to Europe, where he was set to do a number of films (to include *Carmen* and *Salome*) for Alexander Korda, who, like Cohn, had invested in the ill-fated *Around the World*. Thus, the day before Orson applied to the Secretary of State for a passport to go to England, 'Margarita Carmen Cansino Welles' filed a separate application, stating her intention to discuss film projects with various independent English producers.

Chapter Twelve

While Orson had initially conceived of *The Lady from Shanghai* – an adaptation of Sherwood King's novel *If I Die Before I Wake* – as a low-budget quickie to be shot in New York, of necessity his conception changed drastically once Rita was in the picture. Now that it was a vehicle for Columbia's biggest star, a much grander production would be necessary; he would work to deepen Rita's part, making it ever richer and more complex. Much as Welles's other films would often be laced with autobiographical allusions, so it was now with *The Lady from Shanghai*, which evolved slowly into Orson's guilt-ridden artistic meditation on the failure of his and Rita's relationship.

On the surface, however, the melodramatic plot of *The Lady from Shanghai* doesn't seem terribly serious at all. Welles portrays an idealistic young Irish sailor named Michael O'Hara who rescues the beautiful Elsa Bannister (Rita) from a band of thugs in New York's Central Park late one night. Shortly thereafter, Elsa's much older husband, the wealthy criminal lawyer Arthur Bannister (Everett Sloane), hires Michael as a crew member on his yacht. As the vessel sails from New York to San Francisco, at times it seems as if the crippled Bannister actually wants Michael to have the secret love affair with his wife that ensues. Desperately unhappy with a loathsome and sadistic husband who holds her with threats of exposing her lurid past, Elsa looks to Michael as her rescuer. At length, however, Michael actually plays a very different role: the fall guy in the murder of Bannister's law partner, George

Grisby (Glenn Anders). Tried for the murder, with his nemesis Bannister ostensibly defending him but all the while doing him in, Michael suddenly makes a dramatic escape from the courtroom. Finally, he winds up in the crazy house of a deserted amusement park, where he watches as Elsa and her husband shoot it out – the violence ingeniously depicted in the myriad reflections of a hall of mirrors.

Although the famous hall-of-mirrors sequence is often taken for a mere baroque exercise in visual pyrotechnics, in fact it represents Welles's appalled vision of a self split asunder: the multiple fragments of personality at war with one another in a battle that he feared would eventually do Rita in. If in the end of *The Lady from Shanghai* she dies in the hall of mirrors, it is precisely because *he* has abandoned her – hence, the theme of guilt with which the entire film is shot through.

Welles's cinematic confession of failure begins on a very different note: a scene in which Orson shows himself *saving* Rita (which, at the start of their relationship, he had hoped to do.) Significantly, before the censor at the Hays Office got his hands on an early version of the script, *The Lady from Shanghai* was to have opened with an attempted rape. 'There should be no indication of an attempted rape in the scene with the girl and the men,' wrote the censor Joseph I. Breen to Harry Cohn. Thus, in the finished film, the thugs who attack Rita are said to be robbers, although their intentions remain visually obvious. But even in its present censored form, the opening scene vividly establishes the film's central conflict: Welles's desire to save Rita from the violence – specifically, the *sexual* violence – perpetrated by other men. With its air of unreality, the opening functions for Welles as a dreamlike wish-fulfillment. As, of course, he could *not* in life (because it happened long before he met her), here he is indeed able to rescue her from being raped.

In numerous important ways, the character Rita portrays in Welles's film echoes her own. She is a 'poor child' (as one of the other characters describes her), married to a much older father figure who, like Eddie

Judson, threatens her with dark secrets about her past. There is even talk of a mysterious letter (although penned by the husband) that reveals things about her that, if made known, would bring her down. And like Judson, the older husband sets her up with another man on a yacht and perversely encourages their liaison.

But it is in her relationship with the character Welles wrote for himself that the most poignant echoes can be heard. 'Stop cryin'. I can't stand for you to cry,' he tells her, reminding us of the description Welles would feel over Rita's frequent tears. And as Welles himself often did, he promises to take her away with him, to help her escape circumstances she despises. 'I'm gonna take you where there aren't any spies,' he says (these 'spies,' an allusion to Harry Cohn and his obsessive monitoring of Rita).

But later, much as Welles eventually would do, the pro-tagonist appears to have second thoughts: 'Do you still want to take me away with you?' she asks desperately.

Only after a long painful pause does he reply. 'Why do you ask me that?' he says, obviously still in love with her, but frightened and hesitant now. 'Stop tormenting me . . . '

At one point, however, she actually seems to realize why he (like Welles) couldn't possibly save her, no matter how much he might want to: 'You just don't know how to take care of yourself,' she says disappointedly. 'So how could you take care of me?'

Overwhelmed as he was by his own personal crises, Welles had seen himself as having no choice but to turn away from Rita – but in doing so he recapitulated his own turning away from his alcoholic father after a traumatic journey to China, a betrayal that would rack the son with guilt for the rest of his life. Now again with Rita, in order to save himself he was pulling back from someone he loved: abandoning her to struggle alone with her own demons, much as he had done to his father. That he linked the two betrayals in his thoughts is strongly suggested in the film by his locating her tormented past not in Mexico (where it really occurred), but in China: the locale that only naturally he associated with his father's dissolution.

To betray her, to leave her to die in the hall of mirrors, made Orson guiltily think of himself as the latest of the men who had brought about her destruction – and so in the crucial scene in which he and a tearful Rita dance together in a Mexican dive, he symbolically gave *himself* the role of Eduardo Cansino: the first of her partner-destroyers.

Orson may have saved her from a rape in the opening scene, but in the film's final moments the ultimate destruction wrought by the father cannot be undone. Thus: 'Killing you is killing myself,' the father-husband tells her as they shoot at each other in the maddening maze of reflections (Welles rightly saw Judson as a 'continuation' of Eduardo, hence the condensation of the two figures here). In the hall-of-mirrors sequence, when Rita confronts the multiple fragments of her divided self, no matter where she turns she also unavoidably sees the father-husband's reflection staring back at her, trying to destroy her. For the incest victim this vision of the destroyer in the mirror, in oneself, may be the ultimate horror.

With this startling series of visual images, Welles, the artist, crystallized his deep understanding of the enigma of Rita's personality as no one else could possibly have done.

To signal to all the world that he was going to show them a Rita Hayworth they had never seen before, Welles made the drastic decision to cut off her trademark auburn tresses for the film. Rita's luxuriant, long hair was one of her most instantly identifiable characteristics. Hence the audacity of Welles's proposal to chop it off, then to dye the rest topaz blond. However, as Earl Bellamy noted: 'When Rita worked with Orson she was enthralled by him. Almost like she was hypnotized. She could do no wrong because she would do anything he said.' Sixteen photographers were called in to record Rita's spectacular metamorphosis: an explosive publicity stunt if ever there was one.

Nevertheless, when Harry Cohn heard what Rita had agreed to do without consulting the studio, 'He went mad!' recalled Bob Schiffer.

And of the general reaction at Columbia, Earl Bellamy said: 'Everybody practically had a stroke!'

With Orson's help, Rita was happily thumbing her nose at Cohn and company, who evidently suffered far more from the loss of her locks than she did; to them it wasn't just hair, it was a studio asset, a valuable piece of property.

After some initial shooting to be completed at Columbia Pictures, Welles planned to move cast and crew to Mexico for location work. The first scene, to be shot in Hollywood, was the attempted rape, in which Orson saves Rita from a band of thugs who drag her from a hansom cab in Central Park. Dressed in a flowing cape, Welles was first to arrive on the set, where Shorty dashed about after him with a bowl of water on a tray so that the director could shave without wasting time. Rita arrived somewhat later, having been made up by her friend, Bob Schiffer, who had recently returned from the armed forces and gone back to work at Columbia. The shot called for twenty-five to thirty fake trees pushed about on rollers to give the illusion that the hansom cab was actually travelling through the park. A number of the men pushing the trees were quite old and the exertion left them badly winded. Much to Orson's chagrin, Rita was unable to repress her laughter at the sight of the panting men and she spoiled the first take. 'The first time they did it, Rita got to laughing so hard that they had to stop shooting for about a half hour so she could compose herself,' said Earl Bellamy.

What happened next, however, did not strike Rita as a laughing matter. '*Makeup!*' Orson bellowed at Bob Schiffer. 'Put a red nose on the cab driver!' Schiffer resented not being called by his name. To be haughtily addressed as 'makeup' struck him as demeaning. In spite of the urgency with which Welles had summoned him, Schiffer deliberately walked ever so slowly . . . 'Faster! Faster!' boomed the enraged director. 'Run! Run!' But Orson's commands seemed only to have the opposite effect.

The more he would yell, the *slower* I walked,' recalled Schiffer, who finally became so annoyed that he stopped walking altogether. 'Listen, goddammit!' he told Orson. 'I've been running for the last three and a half years. *No one* is ever going to tell me to run again.'

At which audacity Orson went totally wild. 'Fire that man! Get him off the lot!' he roared.

When Rita learned that Orson had fired her makeup man, she was more upset. Still it is curiously revealing about her relations with Orson that she did not complain directly to him. At home she said not a word about it to the husband with whom she was struggling to rebuild a marriage. But early the next morning she informed the Columbia production manager that she would not report to work unless Schiffer was promptly brought back. She would not allow anyone else to do her makeup.

When the studio told Schiffer about Rita's ultimatum, he shot back, 'Well, she's sleeping with the fellow. Tell her to roll over and tell him what the situation is.'

That Rita was unwilling to do; but she would work with Schiffer on the sly. Eventually it was decided that there was no need to tell her husband about Schiffer's rehiring. Thenceforth Bob Schiffer did Rita's makeup in secret, then dispatched an assistant to work with her on the set in Welles's presence. The setup worked to everyone's satisfaction, especially Rita's – *until* the company moved to Mexico for location shooting.

When Columbia informed Schiffer that he would be flying down on the same plane as Mr and Mrs Welles, he asked whether Orson knew about it and was assured that there would be no problem. He would be carefully concealed on the aircraft from his nemesis, Welles. The charter flight was scheduled to leave at midnight. Rita always experienced intense anxiety before flying (a problem that plagued her throughout her life), so Orson had tried to keep the flight a secret from the press. The presence of reporters and photographers would only heighten her nervousness.

But as Bob Schiffer recalled: 'At that time Rita and Orson were *really* big news. The press wanted to know everything about them. They knew they were going on location and they wanted photographs of their departure.'

Still, no one in the press knew exactly when or where the flight was scheduled. A few hours before takeoff, Schiffer wandered into a bar called The Cock and Bull, where a good many reporters hung out, and when they spotted him they began plying him with drinks in hopes that he would tell them what they wanted to know. (Schiffer was known to be a friend of Rita's.)

Eventually, 'I would have told them where my grandmother was buried!' Schiffer recalled. 'By that time I was falling off the barstool. They said, "Look, Bob, don't drive. We'll take you to the plane." ' At the airport the studio people took over, concealing Schiffer 'way in the back, where I immediately fell asleep.' When, shortly before midnight, the Welleses arrived, they were greeted by precisely the flashing cameras and shouted questions that Orson had hoped to avoid.

Neither Rita nor Orson was in a particularly tranquil mood when at length the plane took off. Rita had finally fallen asleep when suddenly the plane hit terrible turbulence. Orson rushed down the aisle to the cockpit, where, intending to yell at the incompetent pilot, he threw open the door to see . . . Bob Schiffer! By coincidence the pilot had been an old wartime buddy of Schiffer's, and had invited him into the cockpit. Just before the turbulence, the pilot had stepped out of the cockpit, leaving Schiffer alone and the aircraft on automatic pilot. But Schiffer didn't have a chance to explain any of this to Welles, who went frantically charging back up the aisle to tell Rita that her makeup man was trying to kill them all! Orson was convinced that this was Schiffer's revenge for being fired. Moments later, Rita was in the cockpit, pleading with Bob, 'Jesus Christ! Get out of here! Orson's tearing up the airplane!'

In Acapulco, Orson threw a twenty-eighth birthday party for his wife at the Hotel de las Americas. An orchestra and two singers entertained the eighteen celebrants, who consumed eight bottles of red wine, six bottles of white, and thirteen bottles of champagne. For all the abundant toasts, it was already becoming evident to others that the reconciliation between Rita and Orson wasn't working out quite as Rita had planned. 'They were cute together,' recalled Libby Sloane, 'but they were *not* like lovers. They were polite. They weren't rotten to each other – there was no crying or crankiness. But it was definitely on the wane.'

Another evening, Errol Flynn (on whose yacht the *Zaca* shooting had taken place) gave a lavish party in Orson's honor. 'Everybody got into evening togs, all dolled up,' said Libby Sloane, 'and we were taken out to the *Zaca* on a launch. On deck everything was absolutely right out of a movie: paper lanterns and all that nonsense.' The last to arrive were Rita and Orson, and as they emerged from the launch they made quite an impression: she with her topaz blond hair, and he in a spotless white suit. The partygoers weren't alone in taking notice of them – so apparently did the screeching pet monkey of one of the crew members. Just as the Welleses were making their grand entrance, 'The monkey took a dislike to Orson,' said Libby Sloane. 'He jumped on him and began to shit all over him. It was unbelievable. Everybody was stunned. They didn't know what to do. After all, this was the guest of honor and his wife!'

Upon their return to the States, where Becky had remained with her nanny, Rita seemed generally weak and unwell. Indeed, dysentery, seasickness, and other complaints had been quite common among cast and crew. In Rita's case extreme anxiety was an added factor. Even when she worked a full day, in her weakened condition she was able to do only a half day's worth of labor. Since so many major scenes had been written around her, her ill health posed serious obstacles to finishing the film. Eventually, late in December, she collapsed from exhaustion on the Columbia set and, upon doctor's orders, she remained in bed for more than a week. There she could enjoy the intimate gifts Orson had given her for Christmas; four sheer nightgowns from Saks, a sheer half nightie and a negligée from Juel Parks, a sterling-silver milk jug for her bedside, and an ounce of a very expensive Egyptian perfume.

Because of the money he had lost in *Around the World*,

Orson had to repress his usual holiday generosity with his friends, to whom he sent only the program for the ill-fated show, with the message: 'This is a souvenir of the expensive reason why the (otherwise deliriously happy) O. Welles family cannot this year wish you Merry Christmas with flowers or anything except this.' Did Orson and Rita genuinely believe that they were 'deliriously happy'? Perhaps at Christmastime that was what they were still telling others – and themselves. Indeed, in January they made arrangements to travel abroad once *The Lady from Shanghai* was finished in March. But by that time, a mere two months later, everything had changed between them.

It was the same old story. Now that they weren't working together, Rita was seeing a good deal less of Orson at home. As her director, he had often seemed to focus on her in the single-minded way she needed, but when that attention came to an end, so did their marriage.

The final break came soon after Rita had received a terrible scare: although it was kept quiet at the time, a particularly grotesque and frightening threat of violence to Rita and her daughter had been received at MGM Studios. 'The Scar Never Fails,' began the strange letter mailed in Cleveland, Tennessee, on 2 February 1947. 'This I assure you sis is no crank letter, unless two thousand dollars in cash is sent to me by the tenth of the month, then I assure you that your baby will be snatched from your home, and that your beautiful face will be ruined by having lye thrown into those beautiful eyes of yours.' Rita was instructed to mail the $2,000 in five-, ten-, and twenty-dollar bills to George Welch, General Delivery, San Pedro, California. 'Rest assured,' the extortionist continued, 'the Scar gets what he wants you don't want to look like the Blue Dahlia do you, nor do you want your child to be disturbed from your arms, this is your final warning RITA, ORSON WELLS cannot help you nor can the FBI, for they have been wanting me for some time no one can help you only the money will talk.' The letter was signed 'The Scar.'

Fortunately, before Rita had learned about the threat, the perpetrator, a former naval-yard worker named James

Gibson, was already in FBI custody in Atlanta, Georgia. By mid-February, the FBI had turned him over to the Cleveland, Tennessee, Police Department, to be returned to his home state for trial on extortion and other prior charges. Still, both Rita and Becky had been threatened and the FBI had yet to complete its investigation, so the possibility of accomplices could not have been ruled out.

Astonishingly, this crisis failed to draw the Welleses closer together. By March Orson had fled to a rented beach house in Santa Monica, and Rita had decided to file for divorce. Whereupon she took off for Palm Springs to sort things out for herself.

As it happened, she would not be quite alone in Palm Springs, for there she met her friend, actor David Niven, with whom she embarked on a brief love affair. In the period following the first split with Welles, Rita had regularly visited Niven to console him about the tragic accidental death of his beloved young wife, Primmie. While playing a party game at the home of Tyrone Power, Mrs Niven had fallen down a dark flight of stairs. The mother of two little boys died as a result of head injuries. Only naturally her husband took quite a while to recover from the sudden loss of a woman he adored, and Rita had been one of several Hollywood actresses to offer him comfort. In Palm Springs Rita and David did their best to keep their romance a secret, since, as far as the world was concerned, her reconciliation with Orson was still in effect.

The affair with Niven hardly outlasted the end of March, when Rita publicly announced her intention to file for divorce. But the big news of the split with Welles, coupled with reports of a liaison with Niven, set all Hollywood awhirl with rumors that Rita planned to marry again as soon as she had her freedom. Much to Rita's chagrin, a new star marriage made excellent copy for the movieland press, even if in fact her relationship with Niven had been little more than a pleasant fling.

The passport that Rita had applied for when she and Orson were planning to go to Europe came through and she decided that even without him a trip abroad might be just the thing she needed. Eager to keep Rita calm now that she was evidently back in his control, Harry Cohn offered to pay for the trip. He couldn't use her for anything until her hair grew back anyway. The only condition was that Rita attend the London premiere of *Down to Earth* in July.

Once again little Becky would be left behind in Los Angeles, this time for more than four months. This was a long period in the life of a two-year-old who had already been left behind so much in the past, and against whom violence had so recently been threatened. Rita had an aunt, Frances Rosser, from her mother's side of the family, of whom she was fond. And now, Rita asked Aunt Fanny, as Mrs Rosser was called, to come out from Washington to supervise Becky's nanny.

Meanwhile, the FBI continued its investigation into the threats against Rita and her daughter. In mid-March, an FBI special agent had interviewed James Gibson (alias 'the Scar') in the Cleveland, Tennessee, county jail. Clearly Gibson had been working alone. On 16 April, the Knoxville, Tennessee, FBI prepared a detailed report on the extortion case, a copy of which would be dispatched to Los Angeles so that Rita could be apprised of their findings. Perhaps it would put her mind at rest about the danger to her daughter and herself. She would not be there to receive it, however, for on the very day the report had been written up in Tennessee, Rita and two female traveling companions had sailed from New York for Europe.

There, much to her embarrassment, the rampant speculation about Rita and David Niven persisted. To make matters worse, Niven happened to arrive in London just as Rita was about to leave, and everyone there seemed to expect them to use the occasion to announce their engagement. Whereupon Niven did the gentlemanly thing by publicly denying that he had ever had a romance with Rita in the first place.

Actually, since her arrival in Europe, there was already a new man in Rita's life: the good-looking blond bandleader Teddy Stauffer, whom she had met with Orson and Errol

Flynn while filming *The Lady from Shanghai* in Mexico. Their brief affair soon turned stormy, however, and once again Rita found it impossible to keep her love life entirely quiet. In Paris, when Rita had banished him, Stauffer tried to reconcile with her by climbing up into her window at the elegant Hôtel Lancaster as a crowd of amused Frenchmen gathered below on rue Berri to cheer on loudly and enthusiastically the efforts of the spurned lover.

When Rita returned home to California that September, there was one last matter to be taken care of before she went back to work at Columbia: in October she officially filed for divorce. Not a word of protest came from Welles, who, meanwhile, had been hurriedly shooting a low-budget *Macbeth* at Republic Studios, enjoying a fling with Marilyn Monroe, and preparing to decamp for Italy to star in a film about Cagliostro. By the time of the divorce hearing in November, he was already out of the country.

Chapter Thirteen

*O*n 10 November 1947, in Los Angeles Superior Court, Rita was swiftly granted a divorce (not to become final until the following year) from the man she called the great love of her life. By a grotesque coincidence, the cover of *Life* magazine for that date showed Rita Hayworth with the caption: 'The Love Goddess in America.' Inside, *Life* proclaimed: 'Rita Hayworth is not only a girl, but one of the many embodiments of our most prevalent national myth – the goddess of love.' For Rita, who considered herself to have failed at love, the timing was painful, unfortunate – but the tag stuck. From then on everybody called her the Love Goddess: a label she would always bitterly associate with the sad day of her second divorce.

Her next picture at Columbia, Charles Vidor's *The Loves of Carmen*, based on Prosper Mérimée's classic tale of a wanton gypsy temptress, would be the first Rita Hayworth film under the new Beckworth contract. If, as she hoped, the film was a major success, for the first time in her career Rita stood to make a great deal of money from it. But even now that she was quite safely back at work, 'Harry Cohn was paranoid about finding out what Rita was up to all the time,' recalled Bob Schiffer, who did her makeup for *Carmen*. 'It was terribly uncomfortable.' A maid outside Rita's dressing room reported on exactly who went in and out; and a bug inside picked up Rita's private conversations. Rita had known about the bug for some time, but she also knew that if she tore it out, another would soon take its place. Accordingly, she whispered or omitted intimate details that she would not want Cohn to know. But one thing Rita made no attempt to conceal from Harry Cohn was her contempt for him and his toadies. 'She hated them all,' said Bob Schiffer. 'She didn't pull many punches with Cohn as to what she thought of him.'

Consummate professional that she was, she never showed her anger or resentment on the set. 'She was within herself a great deal,' said assistant director Earl Bellamy.

According to her stand-in, Grace Godino: 'She had the ability to kind of blank out. On the busiest set she could sit there and block it out. Like none of it was happening. She would sit there quietly and no one would disturb her.'

Drifting off into herself like that, she seemed not to mind the long, tedious hours it sometimes took Rudolph Maté to set up the intricate lighting for her close-ups. 'He would spend a couple of hours if he had to, to get a perfect close-up,' recalled Bob Schiffer. 'Then when he was finished I would go in with a little palette and work under her eyes to correct a few things.' One of Rita's eyes was a tiny bit smaller than the other. ('It's like saying, "Gee, you've got lovely legs, especially the right one," ' Schiffer explained), so the resourceful makeup man would slowly, painstakingly even them out.

'There was a lot you couldn't figure out with her,' said Earl Bellamy of the quiet, compliant Rita. 'She kept it to herself.' After work, however, Rita seemed to 'let down her hair' a bit: 'After we'd finished a day's shooting, Bob and I would go back to her house,' Earl Bellamy recalled. 'We'd just sit around the bar. She'd get in back of the bar and pour the drinks. Then you'd have to watch her because she would get a little on the *strong* side, and the first thing you knew you were having a little problem getting out the front door!'

'All the men on the set were like little boys trying to show off before her,' said Grace Godino. 'They were like little kids standing on their hands in front of the girl next door.' As for the men in her life off the set at this point, the Shah of Iran's brother, Mahmud Pahlavi, would often pick her up at the studio after work for an evening of dinner and dancing at the Mocambo.

Rita's serious, if less public, liaison was with the Texas-born tycoon Howard Hughes: a frequent late-night visitor to her home in Brentwood. Backed by the fortune he had inherited as a teenager, the tall, slender Hughes had turned up in Hollywood in 1925, at the age of twenty, and established himself there as a flamboyant producer-director, as well as one of filmdom's leading playboys. Apart from his Hollywood career, Hughes later became legendary for exploits as a daredevil pilot and designer of advanced aircraft, and in 1946 nearly lost his life when a plane he was test-flying crashed.

Rita found Hughes dynamic and fascinating but saw no future in their romance. She intended to break things off with him as soon as she was finished with *The Loves of Carmen* and went abroad for another extended holiday. Before that, however, while the affair with Hughes was still going on, Rita made the shocked discovery that she was pregnant. Shifra Haran, Orson Welles's former secretary, whom Rita had recently hired to work for her, recalled that the secret pregnancy posed problems during filming: 'When they photographed her, her clothes had become so tight that they had to be pinned shut in the back.' For Rita there was no question of having a baby out of wedlock (even if the child would someday be heir to Hughes's mighty fortune) – but to whom could she turn for help? Was there any doctor in Hollywood who could be counted on to be totally discreet? Although Welles was entirely out of the picture, Rita called on his surrogate father, Dr Maurice Bernstein, who quietly arranged for an abortion. Since Orson was violently opposed to the very idea of abortion, Dadda Bernstein was unlikely to tell him about the incident.

Following the abortion, Rita once again left Becky with Aunt Fanny and departed by train for New York, en route to the four-month holiday abroad she had been planning. Shifra Haran had been drafted as Rita's traveling companion. 'Miss Hayworth needed a friendly person near her,' she recalled. 'She was vulnerable as a celebrity, vulnerable as a beautiful woman, and vulnerable because of her own personality. I guess in a way she was as comfortable with me as with anybody because at least she knew I wasn't spying on her. She trusted me because Mr Welles had trusted me. Can you imagine living that way? It's a nightmare.'

During her previous trip abroad, Rita had met President al-Khuri of Lebanon, who had invited her to visit him there. Now, on her way to Lebanon, she planned to stop in Europe, where, it seemed all too obvious to Miss Haran, Rita hoped she might run into Orson again. Having completed her chores on *The Loves of Carmen*, Rita did not have to be back in Hollywood until the fall, when Harry Cohn wanted her to co-star with William Holden in a Western titled *Lona Hanson*: a prospect that dismayed her since she associated Westerns with the dreadful independent pictures that Eddie Judson had arranged for her to make after Fox let her go.

Although her affair with Howard Hughes had ended, after the abortion he was extremely helpful and solicitous of her. 'The Hughes thing was over in terms of *amour*,' said Shifra Haran, 'but he wanted to make her trip as pleasant as he could. He had all these people in place all around the world. As we went across the country Hughes's TWA was in constant contact with us, as though they were shadowing us. They knew *everything* we were doing. It was as if there were a little angel flying over us. Wherever we stopped, Hughes's people would call. *Does Miss Hayworth need anything? Did I want anything?* Whatever I wanted for her, I could have had.'

At a stopover in Kansas City, Rita sent Miss Haran to get an article about her that was supposed to appear in connection with *The Loves of Carmen*. When she read it she was surprised to find her acting praised, not just her beauty or her dancing. Yet strangely enough, instead of making her happy, it seemed only to plunge her into a melancholy mood. 'You know, I always thought that if I ever got good reviews I'd be happy,' she told her traveling companion in a small, sad voice. 'It's so empty. It's never what I wanted, ever. All I wanted was just what everybody else wants, you know – to be loved.'

In New York there were more offers of comfort and assistance from Howard Hughes's representatives. Rita insisted that she didn't want anything from them. She was anxious just to board the ship and set sail for France. Perhaps far out at sea she could rest and take her mind off all the things that were bothering her. Unfortunately, she seemed not to have anticipated the commotion that her presence would cause among the other passengers.

Although by now Rita had lived for years with all eyes on her wherever she went, she remained painfully sensitive to the scrutiny of strangers. The first evening on board ship, when the glamorous movie star and her traveling companion entered the enormous dining room, every head seemed to turn their way. As she and Miss Haran were led toward their assigned table, Rita panicked at the idea of being seated out there with everybody else. Initially the captain's invitation to Rita to dine with him instead seemed as if it might help matters, but when she got to his special table she found that it was elevated slightly above the rest, which made her all the more visible to the other passengers. She was so frightened and upset that she hardly touched her food. Not until she was locked in her cabin did she feel safe. 'We never went back to the dining room because she couldn't stand being looked at,' said Shifra Haran. 'We ate in the room. And then we would go walking when it was darkest and when there weren't too many people around. She was virtually a prisoner in her room.'

Except when she was sent out on an errand, Miss Haran remained with Rita, who didn't want to be left alone. This was how it was to be during all their travels together: 'I never left her alone because I never knew when she might want to talk – although she wasn't a talker. She wasn't someone you'd sit and visit with for hours. But I always felt that I should be there in case she wanted anything. She needed to have a friendly person near her.'

At teatime one day Rita decided to try leaving her cabin.

For tea, unlike the more formal meals on board, there were no assigned tables. Scarcely had she and Miss Haran chosen an obscure spot than they were joined by two top fashion models from New York, one of whom had met Rita during the filming of *Cover Girl*. Evidently they didn't really want to talk to Rita, however – only to be seen with her. They made no effort to include her in their conversation. Indeed, as they talked to each other, they seemed to be subtly making fun of Rita, under the assumption that she didn't understand what they were doing.

'They thought they were talking over her head,' said Shifra Haran. 'They were real bright, sharp New York types who enjoyed feeling they were smarter and better than she was. Miss Hayworth sensed that feeling of superiority and I certainly did. She was very uncomfortable.'

But there was no polite way of stopping it. For what seemed an eternity, the two models just kept talking past her as Rita sat there silently staring straight ahead. Finally she worked up the courage to break things off. 'Well, I think we have to go,' Rita said, meekly excusing herself and Miss Haran.

Rita did make one most useful acquaintance en route to Europe: an elegant playboy from a very old and respected French family. Whenever he caught a glimpse of Rita on board, he rushed up to inquire if he could be of any service to her. 'He was just smitten with her,' said Shifra Haran. Although at first Rita was merely polite in response, eventually she agreed to contact him if she needed anything in Paris.

While Rita might not have seriously thought that she would require the gentleman's help, not long after she arrived in Paris she became gravely ill as a result of complications from the abortion. In Rita's suite at the Lancaster there were only Miss Haran and Angel, the maid, to care for her.

'She was hemorrhaging and had to have a curettage,' recalled Shifra Haran.

Obviously this wasn't something they could deal with

themselves, even if Rita was desperately anxious to avoid scandalous publicity. The Hughes organization had continued to shadow them in Europe, but Rita preferred not to ask for his help in this matter. Whereupon the wealthy Frenchman whom she had met on the ship was contacted and he discreetly arranged for Rita to see two of the best physicians in Paris.

Soon Rita had quietly checked into the American Hospital, in Neuilly. Care was taken to keep her presence there top secret. 'Miss Hayworth was isolated from every-body else in the hospital, in a special wing,' said Shifra Haran. 'There were strict orders that nobody was to sneak in there. Angel and I went every single day to the hospital. I stayed with Miss Hayworth most of the day in case she wanted something and so that she wouldn't be absolutely alone.'

At the hospital Rita secretly underwent a dilation and curettage to check the complications of her recent abortion. The hospital staff did everything they could to make her comfortable.

'The whole hospital just waited on her hand and foot,' said Shifra Haran. 'They just adored her. She was like a queen there, although she never put on any airs and never asked for anything.'

But Rita was in constant fear that reporters would some-how find their way into her hospital room. She felt much too sick to face them. How would she answer their inevitable questions? What would she possibly say she was doing in the hospital?

At first it seemed that her fears were groundless. No one from the press appeared to have picked up her trail. Gradually even Rita seemed somewhat less tense about being found out. She had almost let her guard down and relaxed when, without warning, the door to her hospital room flew open.

'All of a sudden a strange woman came into her room,' said Shifra Haran. 'It was uncalled for to intrude on her! *Horrible!*'

At the sight of the reporter, Rita buried her head in her

163

pillow. 'Who told you I was here?' she said. 'I won't talk to reporters.'

Hovering over Rita's bed, the reporter noted that Rita, who wore no makeup, had 'a yellow complexion like jaundice.'

Meanwhile, Shifra Haran warned that Rita 'might get hysterical' if the intruder didn't leave at once. Then, in hopes that the whole thing might still be kept quiet, Miss Haran told the reporter: 'She doesn't want anything printed about her sickness because she's afraid people in America might worry.'

Her efforts to protect Rita were in vain. Soon the story had been picked up all across America. 'RITA HAYWORTH FOUND ILL IN HOSPITAL NEAR PARIS,' read the headline. While Rita was terribly upset to have been discovered there, she was relieved that at least the reporter had failed to ferret out the real reason for her hospitalization. Rita was reported to be 'suffering from anemia and an unidentified infection. She is receiving blood transfusions and four injections daily. Considerable mystery surrounds Rita's illness and even hospital attendants refuse to admit she is a patient.'

Stress of this sort was obviously not conducive to recovery. And when Rita checked out of the hospital and returned to her hotel suite, she was terrified that similar incidents would occur there. Miss Haran, who slept in an adjoining bedroom, was constantly on guard against intruders. Indeed, one morning when the secretary answered a knock on Rita's door, she was greeted with a blinding light and the pop of a flashbulb. Evidently the photographer had presumed that he'd be getting a picture of the ailing Rita.

At first Rita's trips outside the hotel were confined to regular follow-up visits to the doctor. 'They were very careful with her,' said Shifra Haran.

Although encounters with the press made her over-wrought, as a movie star and an international celebrity she knew that she could not avoid them indefinitely. When she did meet reporters Rita conveyed the impression that she had merely been suffering from exhaustion. She publicly thanked a French municipal fireman who had donated blood for her transfusion. 'Now I've got French blood as well as Irish by my mother and Spanish by my father,' she said.

In private at the Hôtel Lancaster she was lonely, wistful. Going through her recent medical ordeal with only her secretary and her maid to care for her had not been easy. According to Shifra Haran, various men came to dine with Rita in this period, but there was no one serious. When an old friend from the Welles days, the society writer, Elsa Maxwell, visited Rita at the Lancaster during her recuperation, it was evident that in the aftermath of her hospitalization 'her thoughts were with Orson.' Elsa Maxwell informed her that Orson, who was making a new movie in Italy, already had a new girlfriend, a fiery Italian actress with whom he was absolutely enthralled. Still, Rita began to toy with the idea of canceling the trip to Lebanon and going to the Riviera instead, where perhaps Orson could be persuaded to meet with her. Their divorce was not yet final. Once before when they were separated all it had taken was a romantic supper to bring them back together.

In the meantime, Rita was invited to appear at a spectacular charity ball to be held at the Eiffel Tower. Although she had not yet fully regained her health, she agreed to make a tiny speech on behalf of the poor children of Paris. For the occasion Pierre Balmain designed a brocade gown for her, modeled on a costume worn by Françoise de Montespan, mistress to King Louis XIV. When Rita saw the dress she pronounced it excessively revealing. To the designer's horror, she insisted that something be done at once to veil the décolletage. After her recent ordeal, she could not bear to be so exposed.

The morning of the ball Miss Haran dashed about Paris in a cab picking up the many thousands of dollars' worth of jewelry and furs that were being loaned to Rita for the evening. Rita spent the afternoon nervously practising her lines. She worried about how she would sound in French – and, above all, how she would look. As it happened, there had been nothing to fear. Rita's dazzling appearance made it hard to believe that she had just been in the hospital. After she was introduced by Charles Boyer, Rita said a few words in very well rehearsed French. However nervous she may have been inside, her sweet little speech was met with thunderous applause. All the fashionable people of Paris seemed to have fallen in love with her.

Among those intently watching Rita from out in the audience was a handsome, athletic, brown-eyed man she had never met. But he certainly knew who *she* was. In Egypt during the war he had been captivated by his first glimpse of her on screen in *Blood and Sand*, and now, having finally seen her in person, he began to track her whereabouts in Europe. He wanted desperately to meet her and had only to wait for the right circumstances. If an opportunity did not soon present itself, Prince Aly Khan would have to create one.

'Rita, I think, came to Cannes because it is Orson's stomping ground,' Elsa Maxwell speculated in 1949. 'Perhaps she hoped they might patch up their differences.' In the summer of 1949 the French Riviera was suddenly *the* fashionable vacation spot for the Hollywood elite, moguls like Jack Warner and Darryl Zanuck and actors Clark Gable and Tyrone Power, who gathered at the elegant Hôtel du Cap, once the watering-hole of British and Russian aristocracy. The undisputed social arbiter of the visiting American movie crowd was Elsa Maxwell, who regularly gave lavish dinner parties for them at a charming old farmhouse in the village of Auribeau, outside Cannes (where she picked up a good deal of useful inside information for the unusually revealing articles about the rich and famous that she regularly published in America).

When Rita and Miss Haran moved into adjoining bedrooms at the Hôtel du Cap, Orson was due to arrive any day from Rome. His principal reason for coming to the Riviera this time was to raise money from Zanuck for the audacious film version of *Othello* he was working on in Italy. Upon his arrival, however, Welles was surprised to learn that Rita was there, and, much as she had hoped, he went to her at once. He proposed to call for her with a hired cab later that evening to take her to the romantic Fisherman's Restaurant, in La Napoule. Later, in her suite with Miss Haran, Rita was all anticipation. She wondered aloud if somehow she could lure him away from his Italian actress. Yes, Rita had been the one who had filed for divorce in California, but now she said that she had made a terrible mistake. If all went well she might return to Los Angeles with the father of her little girl, the man she still loved more than anything.

The evening out with Orson did not begin in an auspicious manner. On the road to La Napoule, the taxi had a flat tire and was very nearly wrecked as it went off the road. Fortunately no one was hurt, but without a car to take them home later, Orson saw no point in going on to La Napoule. Instead, he negotiated a ride back to Cannes, where they dined at the Pampan restaurant. Afterward in a chic night-club where he had taken Rita to dance into the morning hours, the other patrons burst into applause when at midnight Orson suddenly leaned over and kissed her. 'RITA HAYWORTH AND WELLES RUMORED WED,' announced the headlines back in the States, where, on the basis of that magical night in Cannes, it was widely reported that they were already embarking on a second honeymoon.

Indeed, when Orson left her at the Hôtel du Cap, Rita had convinced herself that he was coming back to her. But in the days that followed, she waited in vain for his call. This time there was nothing Miss Haran or anyone else could do to cheer her up. Rita simply had to face the fact that as soon as he'd had his little talk with Zanuck, Welles had rushed back to his beloved in Rome.

After that, a great many men would pursue Rita, and she consented to dine with the Shah of Iran and King Farouk, among others. 'She was the prize plum!' said Shifra Haran. 'Down at the Riviera all these men were chasing her because they wanted to be seen with her and photographed with her. They *all* wanted to use her.'

When Elsa Maxwell asked her to a small dinner party,

Rita was not particularly anxious to go. She said that she was brokenhearted and upset about Orson. But Elsa was gently persistent. She urged Rita to buy a new dress for the evening, preferably something in white, and to make an entrance by arriving strategically late. Someone special was going to be at the dinner party whom she wanted Rita to meet. He was a Persian prince, she explained, and for at least an evening he would make her forget her troubles.

Chapter Fourteen

*C*asanova, sybarite, gentleman jockey, auto racer, hunter, pilot, horse breeder, soldier, *and* Muslim religious leader: thirty-seven-year-old Aly Salomone Khan was a complex and enigmatic man of many facets. In partnership with his father, the Aga Khan III, Aly operated stud farms that bred some of Europe's finest racehorses. But he was perhaps even better known as a legendary and insatiable lover, a man who was said to have bedded countless women. While his father's illustrious Persian family claimed direct descent from the Prophet Mohammed's daughter, Fatima, Aly's mother, a beautiful former ballet dancer in the Casino at Monte Carlo, had been of humbler Italian origins. Aly spent much of his life in the giant shadow cast by his father, who, as Imam (or Pope) to some 15,000,000 Asian and African Ismaili Muslims, as well as a statesman, sportsman, bon vivant, and multimillionaire of global reputation, was truly one of the most fascinating and colorful figures of his era. He had played an important role in the founding of the All-India Moslem League, and had once served as president of the League of Nations. The Aga Khan's diverse accomplishments notwithstanding, as a father to young Aly he seems to have had his distinct short-comings, and from the first reportedly showed the boy little in the way of warmth and affection. Well into adulthood, Aly, whose mother died when he was fifteen, would appear to be engaged in a desperate struggle for the attention of his demanding and emotionally distant father.

At midnight following Elsa Maxwell's party at the Cannes Summer Casino, Aly had been scheduled to fly his private plane, *The Avenger*, to Ireland, where one of his horses, Attu, was set to run in an important race, but the meeting with Rita made him instantly postpone his departure. He invited her to drive up into the hills with him that night so that they could study the stars. Nor did he leave for Ireland the following day, when Rita had agreed to visit him at his spectacular white seaside villa, the Château de l'Horizon. Although she had readily accepted both of the prince's invitations, at this point Rita took him no more seriously than any of the other playboys she'd met thus far on the Riviera. 'The prince was immediately smitten,' recalled Shifra Haran, 'but Miss Hayworth definitely was *not.*'

After his first evening with Rita, Aly told his chauffeur, Emrys Williams, that he'd never been so excited in his life. He said that he felt as if he were walking on air. Anxious to be able to dance with Rita when she came for tea, Aly dispatched his chauffeur to Nice to purchase a gramophone and popular records. When, at the appointed hour, Williams arrived to pick up Aly's date for the afternoon, he was met instead by Shifra Haran, who informed him that Rita had *also* accepted a lunch invitation with the Argentine millionaire Alberto Dodero. Aly's man would just have to wait - *three hours*, as it happened. Nor when Rita finally turned up did she seem to have dressed very carefully for the occasion. She wore simple shorts, a white blouse, and no makeup.

By the time they arrived at the Château de l'Horizon, the prince was understandably in a dither. Still, before long music was pouring from the gramophone, Rita and Aly were dancing cheek to cheek, and everybody *seemed* happy. But as charming as the prince had been to her, she remained put off by his reputation as a dissolute ladies' man.

Finally Aly could postpone his departure from France no longer, but first he elicited a promise from Rita to wait in her hotel on the afternoon of his return, for he would have a marvelous surprise for her then. In the meantime, dozens and dozens of roses kept arriving in her suite. Miss Haran didn't know where to put them all. Rita, however, wanted no part of waiting for Aly. 'I don't think she wanted to get involved,' said Shifra Haran. 'She wanted to get away from the hotel and not be there when he came back, so she went out on a boating trip with friends. She was gone most of the day.' Thus, Miss Haran was alone in the suite when suddenly she heard a great deal of noise outside the window. 'He was buzzing the hotel with his private plane!' she recalled. 'Dipping the wings and all that. But she wasn't there! He thought she'd be there, but the only person who saw it was me.' Afterward, when the prince called excitedly to see how Rita liked her surprise, he was crestfallen to learn that she had gone out for the day.

Rita began to see a good deal of Aly, but no matter how much fun she seemed to be having, she resisted plunging into a serious love affair with him. Although Aly was officially still married to the mother of his two sons, Joan Yarde-Buller, the prince had largely returned to his bachelor ways. Rita wanted a home, family, security: the antithesis of the kind of rootless, hedonistic existence Aly appeared to lead. Still, the prince seemed to think of everything that would please her: dancing in exotic, out-of-the-way nightclubs; candlelit dinners in small restaurants in the hill towns.

'The prince was *much* more attentive and romantic than Mr Welles,' said Shifra Haran.

The more time Rita spent in Aly's undeniably seductive company, the more she felt herself drawn to him. Nevertheless, he was moving too quickly. While at first she had assumed that he was just toying with her as any playboy might do with a beautiful woman, she began to fear that he sincerely wanted to enter into a long-term relationship with her. She felt she wasn't ready for that.

Finally, the only way out that Rita could think of was to leave Cap d'Antibes immediately. Perhaps then the prince would give up. 'She didn't want him to come around anymore, so she fled from him and we went to Beaulieusur-Mer,' recalled Shifra Haran. Secretly, Rita and Miss Haran checked into the Hôtel La Réserve. There Rita planned to remain in hiding until the prince despaired of finding her.

During her stay at La Réserve she accepted a luncheon invitation with Fletcher Markle (a writer whom Alexander Korda had sent to collaborate on a script with Orson in Mexico during the shooting of *The Lady from Shanghai*) and his wife, actress Mercedes McCambridge. On the telephone with Markle, Rita asked if they could bring an extra man for her. This gave the couple an opening to have a bit of cruel fun at her expense. Rita's date was actually a Basque waiter in a local restaurant, but they implied to her that he was a man of great wealth and property. 'He looked gorgeous,' recalled Mercedes McCambridge of the waiter as he prepared to meet the Love Goddess. 'Wisteria silk shirt, open down to there, brown peek-a-boo body, hairy-ape-type chest framed in wisteria cloth. White duck pants, generous genitalia all but exposed beneath the cloth, which, at long last, had finally reached the perfect state of warp nearly parting from woof! One good rip and away we go!'

The waiter's name was Jean. When Rita met him she swallowed whole everything he said about himself.

According to Mercedes McCambridge: 'Rita kept looking at Jean as though he were a giant Christmas present in Neiman-Marcus wrapping and as if he were two pounds of Godiva chocolates contained in a Fabergé egg. The unexplored package before her was so intriguing that, like any eager child, she could scarcely keep her hands off it!' On the terrace at La Réserve a string trio was playing, and Rita and her young man got up to dance. 'I had seen Rita Hayworth dance on the screen with the best of them,' explained Mercedes McCambridge. 'Fred Astaire, to mention only one, but when she melted into the arms of our boy Jean, I had never seen her in finer form, a form in all its fineness pressing itself against the matching fineness of Jean's form.'

Another of Rita's visitors at La Réserve was a mysterious

Italian-speaking gypsy woman in her late forties who began making inquiries about her at the hotel desk. The woman was insistent that she must see Rita Hayworth, that she had an important message for her. 'How the woman knew we were there was a mystery,' said Shifra Haran, who was called down to talk to the gypsy. 'There was something about her that fascinated me. Normally I would never have told Miss Hayworth about it. But I asked her if she would care to see this lady and she said yes – which surprised me.'

When Rita received the woman upstairs, the gypsy offered to tell her fortune. First, however, as if to prove her powers, she dramatically rattled off trivial details of Rita's past.

'She seemed to know everything you could think of about Miss Hayworth,' said Shifra Haran. The fortune-teller predicted that Rita was about to embark on the greatest romance of her life. He was someone she already knew but whose overtures she had foolishly resisted. Instead – warned the fortune-teller – Rita must relent and give in to him *totally*. Only if she did that would she find happiness at long last.

After their visitor departed, it seemed to Miss Haran that Rita had been strangely convinced by all the fortune-teller had said. While it was likely that Prince Aly himself had been responsible for sending her, there was no way of proving it. And perhaps there was something in Rita that desperately wanted to believe the gypsy woman. Rita told Miss Haran that she couldn't stop thinking about their mysterious visitor. Perhaps it *had* been a terrible mistake to run away from the prince. On the spur of the moment, Rita changed her plans and she and Miss Haran suddenly headed back to Cap d'Antibes, where, before long, she seemed to have given herself over to Aly precisely as the gypsy had urged her to do.

The night of the International Sporting Club Gala, Rita danced every dance cheek to cheek with Aly. The music and dancing went on until three A.M., when waiters appeared with a breakfast of ham and eggs and champagne. Only a few weeks before the patrons of a nearby *boîte* had applauded when Orson kissed Rita in public. But tonight, as the festivities drew to a close, it was the prince who grew passionate with Rita for all to see.

Soon the talk of Cannes was Rita's having moved in with Aly at the château. The prince's three-storey villa included ten sun-filled bedrooms and seven baths. Paintings by Dégas, Renoir, and Utrillo lined the walls throughout. In the living room, where Aly liked to greet guests, were rows of bookcases, a grand piano, and an Aubusson carpet. French doors opened on to an immense terrace with a panoramic view of the Mediterranean. Beneath the terrace sprawled an enormous swimming pool with a slide that led directly to the sea. The prince frequently gave buffet luncheons on the terrace. In the evening guests repaired to the powder-blue dining room, with its enormous Italian marble table, surrounded by antique chairs.

Upstairs in one of the bedrooms was a safe where Aly kept currency of many nations. That way he could fly off in *The Avenger* at any moment to any destination. There were always large sums of cash ready for whichever country he cared to visit. Contrary to rumors that persist to this day, it was by no means the prince's wealth that Rita was after. 'She didn't care about fancy clothes or jewels or anything like that,' said Shifra Haran, who moved into the château with her. 'No, to her the prince was just a big brown-eyed guy! She responded to all the *attention* he gave her, not to *things*. She was never after things. Never. That's not what she wanted out of life. She just wanted someone to love her and her alone!'

Sadly, though, if it was his single-minded attention that she hoped for in the serene privacy of Aly's château, Rita was sorely disappointed. By nature, Aly was gregarious. He moved easily among people and was the sort of man who seemed happiest when his house was full of guests. It simply would not have occurred to him that the intro-duction of a new lady in his life was any reason to change. The very day Rita moved in, Aly had somewhat per-versely scheduled a big party. To make matters worse, a good many of the guests were invited to stay on indefinitely.

Aly's chauffeur noted Rita's annoyance at discovering several other attractive women among the houseguests.

It wasn't jealousy alone, however, that made Rita so acutely agitated. Like the two models who had mocked her on the ship from New York, the catty women in Aly's set seemed only too anxious to put Rita down. 'Those Europeans the prince had as houseguests didn't treat her too well,' said Shifra Haran. 'And she sensed that they didn't. Just imagine being the Love Goddess and having all these women looking at her, not lovingly or admiringly, but *critically*. She wanted to shrink from that.'

To Rita it was a nightmare. Practically all conversation at the château seemed to be carried on in French, and few of the guests made any effort to talk to Rita in English.

'She had a very nice accent in the few French words that she knew,' said Shifra Haran, 'but she was too embarrassed and wouldn't try. She would have experimented with me and with Angel, but not in front of strangers.'

Rita quickly grew restless and uneasy with life at the château.

'It was too overwhelming for her,' recalled Shifra Haran. 'She wasn't the great hostess who could receive people. That just wasn't her personality.' Sensing that she was about to flee again, Aly proposed a two-week motoring trip to Spain and Portugal. Perhaps there she would find the serenity and privacy that she longed for. When Rita accepted, Aly proceeded to make the necessary arrangements. A shiny new Cadillac was ordered from Paris. On his private plane they would fly to Biarritz to pick up the car, and drive on from there. During their little holiday the utmost discretion would be necessary, however, since as a religious leader Aly did not wish to be photographed in compromising circumstances with a woman who was not his wife. If the paparazzi took pictures of Aly and Rita traveling together, his father, the old Aga Khan, would definitely not approve. Although in his day the Aga Khan had been a notorious *coureur* himself, it was no secret that he was most anxious for Aly to tone down his image as an incorrigible ladies' man.

175

Meanwhile, as she and Aly prepared to fly off in *The Avenger*, Rita secretly called Orson in Rome. She had been so desperately unhappy at the château that she made one last attempt to win back her husband. All that she would say to Welles on the telephone was that she needed to see him at once. When a worried Orson agreed to meet with her on the Riviera, they set a date *after* her scheduled departure with Aly. Welles, of course, knew nothing about the impending trip to Spain and Portugal. He had heard on the international social circuit that Rita was supposed to be seeing Aly, but knowing the prince's reputation, and knowing Rita's particular emotional needs, he did not take the relationship seriously.

For her part, Rita had been aware from the first that she and Aly would be gone when Orson arrived. Perhaps the discovery that she was off with the prince would arouse his jealousy. 'Rita, in the beginning, intended her friendship with Prince Aly as a come-on to intrigue Orson Welles,' Elsa Maxwell would write. When he arrived in Cannes, however, it wasn't jealousy Welles felt, but irritation. He told Elsa Maxwell that although he would go anywhere for Rita if she *really* needed him, he was furious that this time he had flown all the way from Rome for nothing.

If leaving for Spain with the prince had not had the effect on Welles that Rita had hoped for, nor did it bring the privacy and tranquillity she and Aly sought. Everything seemed to go smoothly at first. In Biarritz they picked up the new Cadillac without a hitch. Although Aly's chauffeur was along, now and then the prince took the wheel and quickly confirmed all that Rita had heard about his reckless, daredevil driving. In Spain, en route to Madrid, the prince hit a horse-drawn cart, and while he settled with the owner for damages, a curious crowd gathered around. Peering into the windows of the Cadillac, someone spotted Rita.

By the time the lovers had reached Madrid, the Spanish press had been tipped off. A mob of excited newsmen gathered outside the Ritz Hotel, where everyone wanted a picture of Rita and the prince checking into a hotel together. Although obviously they weren't fooling anybody, Rita and Aly registered separately, in adjoining rooms. When they tried to sneak out to attend a dinner party they were chased through Madrid by taxicabs filled with newspeople. The evening was ruined, so they headed back to the Ritz to dine in their rooms instead.

After that they dared not venture outside the hotel, where the press had them cornered. Still it didn't seem to have occurred to Aly to return to Cannes. Instead, when Rita said she wanted to attend a bullfight, Aly made secret arrangements to head south to Toledo, where he hoped they would attract less attention than in Madrid. He thought it best that they leave the hotel separately.

The prince went ahead with the luggage. Rita and the chauffeur would meet him later on the other side of Madrid. As the time drew near for Rita to leave the hotel, she appeared to panic. Aly wasn't with her, only his man. Suddenly she despaired entirely of getting out of there without being accosted by the press. Only at the last minute did she pull herself together for the getaway. Aly's Cadillac screeched up to the staff entrance, she leaped in, and was off before the startled newsmen knew quite what had happened.

Things were certainly no better in Toledo. Any hopes that Rita may have had of attending the bullfights in obsurity were quickly dashed. At the gorgeous sight of her, the band began to play 'Put the Blame on Mame' as the crowd chanted, 'Gilda! Gilda!' To them Rita's presence was a far better spectacle than the actual bullfights. As always Rita was terrified of all the people staring and calling at her. She wanted to flee, but the prince subdued her by holding her arm. A sudden departure might only incur the wrath of the mob. Rita and Aly dared not leave until the end. Even so, the crowds did not let up on her.

When one of the matadors sliced off the bull's ear and tossed it to Rita in a ritualistic tribute to her beauty, the crowd went wild. For that moment, however, the terrified little girl seemed magically transformed in Doña Sol (the character she was playing when Aly saw Rita for the first time in *Blood and Sand*, in Cairo during the war). Instead of being disgusted, she boldly rose to catch the severed ear.

'I am a lover of animals and this incident nauseated me,' Emrys Williams would recall. 'I was sitting next to Rita and had the opportunity of watching her closely at this dramatic moment. Her eyes were shining with a sort of fierce pride. She looked radiant. Her whole body was taut and I could see the muscles quivering in her outstretched neck.'

Moments later Rita turned 'pale with fright' as the excited, shouting spectators rushed en masse toward her across the arena. They meant no harm – but Rita and Aly were clearly in danger of being trampled. Only through the intervention of several policemen did they finally escape the surging mob.

Next the couple headed farther south, to Seville – the birthplace of Eduardo Cansino, and a city filled with Cansino relatives. There, once more, Rita and Aly made a great point of registering separately at the hotel. Before she had even arrived, reporters had already interviewed Rita's grandfather, old Padre Cansino, who had returned to Seville himself on a visit. Relatives piled in to the hotel to see Rita: 'These were really poor people,' noted Emrys Williams,' 'poorer than my own family in Wales.' And they were all clearly thrilled to see the family's famous relative – the American movie star. That she had arrived in Seville on the arm of a prince was a detail that could only have added to their sense of wonder at what had become of Eduardo's little Margarita.

Rita gave a dinner party for Padre and the others in a lovely garden restaurant. The tables surrounded a small space where one by one the Spanish family danced flamenco, as the onlookers responded with the encouraging *Olés* that Eduardo had so missed when he had first come to America. Rita was instantly very much in her element among them. These were the simple people with whom she felt most at home. Finally Padre took the floor, followed by Rita herself.

'She danced like a real Spaniard – not like a film star,'

Aly's chauffeur recalled. 'Her white arms flashed above her head as she clicked her fingers. Her skirt had wings as she spun round and long loose red hair floated above her shoulders.'

That night, as Aly watched the emergence of the bold, flamboyant Rita whom he had previously admired on screen, he made up his mind to get a divorce and marry her.

Rita, however, had other ideas. The summer was almost over, and as far as Rita was concerned, so was her romance with Aly. When she returned to Cannes to pick up Miss Haran for the voyage home, Rita said good-bye to the prince. The necessity of returning to work and to her daughter in California made for a natural conclusion to their romance. She found Aly charming, delightful, perhaps even lovable – but she had no place in his world. So precisely at the moment when Aly considered that their relationship was really only just getting started, Rita began packing for the trip back to the States. Aly wasn't used to rejection. Startled by her resoluteness, he tried to coax her to linger at the château, but to no avail. Not only was she leaving, but even worse, they were ending with a quarrel: the last thing he had expected.

Chapter Fifteen

*O*n her way to Europe four months earlier, Rita had been frightened and depressed, but the trip home proved much better. So much seemed to have happened since her abortion. She felt that she could put that terrible episode completely behind her. When the *Queen Elizabeth* docked in New York harbor Rita was in an unusually lighthearted mood. To avoid being caught in the crush at the customs, she and Miss Haran remained on board while most of the other passengers were getting off. As they waited, Rita and her secretary stuck their heads out the portholes to watch the scene below.

'All of a sudden she and I started to spit,' laughed Shifra Haran. 'It was such a wonderful height! I had one porthole to spit from and she had the other. That's the kind of gal she was!'

The game was cut short when Rita suddenly jerked her head in, shut the porthole, and nervously beckoned Miss Haran to do the same. 'My God!' said Rita. 'The man directly below us just stuck his head out and I think I hit him!' From her porthole Miss Haran could see the angry man looking up in their direction, trying to figure out what had happened.

Four days later when Rita's train pulled into the Pasadena station there was little Becky Welles clutching a bouquet of roses for her mommy. Behind Becky stood stern Aunt Fanny. Rita had not seen the three-year-old for four months. The reporters who also greeted her at the station were a more familiar sight. After giving her daughter a big kiss, Rita answered their questions with equanimity. No, she wasn't reconciling with Orson. No, it wasn't a romance with Prince Aly Khan, just friendship.

Yet scarcely was she home in Brentwood than the phone calls from Aly began – and wouldn't stop. He was terribly upset about how things had ended between them. To his great dismay, the prince discovered that Rita had not changed her mind about him. She was back with her daughter in California and had no intention of returning to Europe in the near future. Nothing he said would sway her – in fact, she even seemed a bit annoyed by his persistence.

Meanwhile, the day after she got off the train in Pasadena, Rita dutifully reported to Columbia only to be told that the script for *Lona Hanson* wasn't ready. A war of nerves had evidently begun. Her new Beckworth contract entitled her to script approval, but Harry Cohn was anxious to overlook this important provision and proceed as in the past – with the studio assigning her projects. Before Rita left for Europe she had told Harry Cohn that she didn't really want to do a Western, but she had finally agreed at least to look at the script upon her return. Now there was no script for her to read and Cohn was acting as if it were her sacred duty to agree to do the picture anyway. All her old hatred of him was quickly revived. Although she stood to make a great deal of money for whatever picture she appeared in now, she was determined to exercise her right to script approval – all the more so because Cohn was already acting as if she had no rights at all.

Aly had despaired of getting Rita even to consider returning to him in Europe. He had taken to secretly calling Miss Haran to see if she could be of any help. She began to feel sorry for the prince, who seemed so genuinely upset that the romance with Rita had ended badly. Although later, in retrospect, she would worry that she had made a serious mistake, she suggested at the time that perhaps she could arrange a compromise. She would try to get Rita to allow the prince to visit her in Hollywood. During the often tempestuous marriage to Orson Welles,

Rita had frequently heeded Miss Haran's advice. When the secretary delicately interceded on Aly's behalf, Rita listened and, finally, agreed. The prince was so grateful to Miss Haran that, shortly thereafter, when she picked him up at the airport, he presented her with a diamond-and-sapphire watch from Van Cleef & Arpels.

As fate would have it, he arrived in Los Angeles at a most opportune moment. Rita was already almost at the breaking point in her exasperating dealings with Harry Cohn, and she welcomed Aly back into her life, but this time in a new role: as the latest of the strong male protectors to whom she repeatedly turned throughout the years.

Although Rita had lived with Aly at the château, there could be no question of his moving into her house in Brentwood. She was certainly not averse to receiving men there – Howard Hughes, after all, had paid frequent amatory visits – but she knew that the prince's staying under the same roof with her would constitute intolerably scandalous behaviour in 1948 America. Thus, Miss Haran had rented a furnished pink-stucco house directly across the way for Aly and his pistol-packing valet, Tutti. Rita and Aly might be sleeping together – but at least they were formally maintaining separate residences. Upon Aly's arrival Rita issued a statement to the press acknowledging that the prince was in town and that she would be going out with him 'frequently'. Anything more than that she denied.

Despite the announcement, Rita and Aly were rarely seen in public, and the Hollywood press was soon thrown into a frenzy. Where were they? Why didn't anyone ever see them? There were even rumors that Rita's announcement had been merely a publicity stunt. Others wondered whether such a person as Prince Aly Khan existed at all! The fact was that no one saw the prince because, with the exception of a rare night at Ciro's, he and Rita were spending most of their time at home together. 'They just stayed in the room and made love,' said Shifra Haran. It was precisely what Rita had been looking for in Europe –

and hadn't found. At the château, and later in Spain, there had been far too many distractions, not enough privacy. This time, determined not to lose her again, Aly made certain that she was completely satisfied. 'I never saw the prince as a sex maniac,' said Shifra Haran. 'It was *Miss Hayworth* who was insatiable in her appetites.'

Aly was by no means the first man with whom Rita had sought security and affirmation in the act of lovemaking. But in him she discovered a lover uniquely capable of spending as much time with her as she wanted and needed. 'In the precise and complex art of love, Aly had no peer,' wrote his biographer, Leonard Slater. 'The woman's satisfaction came first with Aly.' According to Slater, Aly practiced an Eastern art of love known as Imsak, which allowed him to exercise indefinite control in the bedroom. Even after hours of lovemaking he could keep himself from climaxing. Locked away with the prince in her house in Brentwood, Rita seemed happy and serene as she had not been in a very long time.

Another thing that pleased Rita beyond her expectations was how kind Aly was to her three-year-old daughter, whom he was meeting for the first time. 'The prince was wonderful to Rebecca, just wonderful!' said Shifra Haran. 'She needed someone.'

Becky Welles had seen very little of her own father. According to Rita's friend Bob Schiffer, Rita deeply resented Orson's apparent lack of interest in their daughter. She was touched by the bond of affection that quickly formed between Aly and the little girl. Becky called him 'Aly,' and he called her 'my little princess.' Watching him play with her made Rita see the prince in a whole new light. Having known terrible childhood loneliness himself, Aly may have been trying to give another child the attention he had never known. In Europe Rita had written him off because of his notorious reputation. That fall in California she reevaluated him. It seemed to her that perhaps he could give her the secure home and family life she had been dreaming of for such a long time.

Although the press complained of almost never seeing

the prince in public, he did go on a number of shopping expeditions to Beverly Hills with Miss Haran. If the reporters and photographers didn't spot him, it may have been because most Americans didn't yet know what he looked like – but a few months in the spotlight with Rita would certainly change that. Aly was used to being a celebrity in Europe, so his newfound invisibility in America amused him.

'Nobody knew who he was and he enjoyed that,' said Shifra Haran, who escorted him mostly to fashionable men's clothing shops and ice-cream parlors. Aly had a passion for ice cream. 'He enjoyed walking around in Beverly Hills and not being noticed because it gave him a lot of freedom.' (Even when the prince wasn't in town Rita almost never shopped in public for fear of being stared at or even mobbed by the other customers. Instead, she typically dispatched Miss Haran to come back with, say, ten pairs of shoes, from which she chose one and sent the others back.)

While Aly shopped in Beverly Hills, Rita reported to the film studio, where nothing seemed to have changed in the past few weeks. Harry Cohn remained adamant about her doing *Lona Hanson* even though she had yet to see a script. She may have had a new contract befitting a star, but Cohn obviously had no intention of giving her the courtesy and respect that went with it. When he wasn't ordering Rita to shut up and do the picture, he tongue-lashed her for all the nasty publicity her affair with a married man was attracting. Rita had been back in Hollywood for less than two months and already she felt the urge to flee again.

On the spur of the moment, she and the prince flew to Mexico City, accompanied by Miss Haran. Although the tickets had been purchased at the last minute, somehow the press got word of Rita's sudden exit. Aly was already distressed that his father might see a photograph of him with Rita that had been taken one evening at Ciro's, in Los Angeles, and published in the American press. When he spotted the photographers on the airplane, he locked himself in the rest room to avoid them.

It was even worse in Mexico City, where the hotel desk clerk had sold the information about their secret arrival to the local papers. When they saw the press waiting outside the hotel, Rita and Aly did a quick about-face. Miss Haran, who knew the city from her days there with Orson Welles, rapidly led them through obscure back streets to another hotel, the Reforma. There, in hopes of escaping detection, only Rita and Miss Haran signed the register. But before long the press had tracked them there and surrounded the building. One Mexican journalist who examined the guest register saw the secretary's name near Rita's and printed a story the next day announcing the discovery that Prince Aly Khan's real name was Shifra Haran!

Reporters bribed workers in the hotel to give them their uniforms. Soon the elevator operator was a newsman in disguise, as was the maid who knocked on Rita's door to ask if she needed anything. 'Miss Hayworth had no peace of mind,' said Shifra Haran. 'She didn't know who was who anymore. There was no control over it. The reporters just secretly invaded the hotel.'

As in Madrid, Rita and Aly found themselves living under virtual siege conditions.

'This was the big scandal of the year,' recalled Shifra Haran. 'If they wanted to go anywhere, I had to sneak them out through the garbage entrance. It was terrible!' The exasperated hotel manager pleaded with Miss Haran to persuade Rita to give a small press conference. Perhaps if journalists were invited to meet briefly with Rita and take a few pictures, the chaos would stop. There was no question of the prince allowing himself to be photographed in these scandalous circumstances. Although Rita was resistant at first, eventually she agreed to talk to reporters. Aly waited behind in his room while Rita put on her most charming face for the press.

Back in the suite, however, there was no hiding Rita's overwrought state of mind. As if to recapture their days of undisturbed intimacy in Los Angeles, she was constantly pulling Aly into the bedroom. She wanted the prince to stay in bed with her almost all the time, and Miss Haran started to worry that, Aly's legendary sexual stamina notwithstanding, Rita's physical demands might eventually prove too much even for him.

Suddenly there began the explosive jealous tantrums on Rita's part that Miss Haran recalled only too well from the marriage to Orson. Accompanied by Miss Haran, the prince had gone out for a haircut and manicure. When they left the hotel, Rita had seemed perfectly fine. Ninety minutes later they returned to find her plunged into a fit of agitation. Her secretary saw at once that the accumulated stress of recent days had caused her old feelings of abandonment to resurface. It was the legacy of her tormented youth: the deeply ingrained expectation of inevitably finding herself betrayed and abandoned. Rita was screaming and throwing things, and angrily accused Aly of having gone off to meet another woman.

'She couldn't stand not to be reassured *constantly* that he loved her,' explained Shifra Haran. Even when the prince calmly reminded her that her own secretary had been with him the whole time, Rita was not placated. He had never seen this side of Rita before, but instead of being appalled by her tirade, he actually seemed exhilarated. 'Oh, it was *stimulating* to him,' recalled Shifra Haran.

Rita wanted to go next to the coastal resort of Acapulco, which she had last seen during the filming of *The Lady from Shanghai*. For the 249-mile trip south, Miss Haran hired a chauffeur who had driven Rita and Orson when they were married. In Acapulco, Aly made every attempt to help Rita unwind. During the day he patiently went shopping with her for the hot Latin records she adored. As the chauffeur drove them about, Aly instructed Miss Haran to write down any unusual street names they encountered; when Rita asked why, he explained that he was always looking for exotic names for his horses. That night he found an out-of-the-way spot for a blissfully private dinner. This was all much, much better than Mexico City. Still, there had been abundant press coverage of what was to have been a quiet romantic holiday and Rita worried incessantly about the barbs and innuendoes that she would have to face back in the studio.

Anxious to put off her return to Hollywood for a little while longer, Rita suddenly asked the prince to take her to Cuba, whereupon Aly dispatched Miss Haran to the Cuban embassy in Mexico to secure the necessary visas. When the clerk in the embassy learned that she was there on behalf of Rita Hayworth and Aly Khan, he demanded a princely bribe not to stall the paperwork.

On the plane to Havana and in the airport, Rita pretended to be traveling only with Miss Haran. As they went through Cuban immigration, it was as if she and Aly were strangers to each other. For thirty minutes Rita did not so much glance at Aly. As they had come to expect, someone in the Cuban embassy in Mexico had alerted the press. For the benefit of reporters Rita and Aly made a great show of suddenly meeting as if by coincidence. But the Cuban newsmen certainly weren't fooled – in fact, they seemed slightly offended that the prince would think them so gullible. When they hurled questions at the scandalous couple of the year, Aly retorted, 'I'd like to answer your questions, but how can I when they are so embarrassing?'

Rita and the prince were driven into Havana in separate vehicles. At the Hotel Nacional the desk clerk quoted an exorbitant room rate, far in excess of what other guests paid. The prince was used to being cheated like this and paid without protest. But Miss Haran was furious: 'They were such robbers in the hotel!' she said. 'The bill was outrageous. They were fleecing him. They knew he was a wealthy man, so they overcharged him ten times as much as they would anybody else. Someone must have told them, "You've got a couple of suckers coming."'

As was their routine, Rita and Aly were shown to separate accommodations. Once the bellhop was out of sight, they chose whichever room they wanted to stay in together, and Miss Haran quickly rearranged the beds so that the lovers would have a mattress large enough for the two of them.

It quickly became obvious that their feeble attempt to

fool the Cuban press hadn't worked when Rita and Aly found themselves splashed on the front pages of the Havana papers. Carloads of teenage girls began arriving at the Nacional in hopes of meeting their screen idol. Why Rita's fans in Havana seemed to be principally female she had no idea. But great numbers of them poured into the hotel lobby in search of Rita's room. 'Those were trying times!' recalled Shifra Haran. 'I had to keep all these wealthy little girls and their giggly friends away from the room. The hotel was inundated with them. I kept going down to the lobby to ward them off.'

In Havana Aly hired a driver to take them around in search of Cuban records for Rita's growing collection. The next day, accompanied by Miss Haran, they motored out into the Cuban countryside, to magnificent Varadero Beach, where they stayed in an exquisite, jewel-like hotel that afforded Rita and Aly a few precious hours of the total privacy and serenity for which they had been searching.

The return to Los Angeles could be postponed no longer. From Havana they flew to New Orleans. As their plane approached Moisant International Airport, it dropped through a dense cloud bank. The experience threw Rita into a sudden panic. Rita was always frightened on airplanes, but this time she felt almost certain they were going to crash. It didn't help matters that she and Aly had agreed in advance to pretend that they were traveling separately. Miss Haran did her best to calm Rita.

After the difficult landing, Rita was in no mood to face the reporters she knew would be waiting for her. She wanted only to rush to Aly for comfort, but this she could not do in the interests of discretion. It is difficult to comprehend how Rita and Aly could possibly think that standing ten feet away from each other would fool anybody, yet this is the absurd course of action they steadfastly pursued. Before Rita left the plane, Miss Haran helped her on with her mink coat. Rita was still trembling, and trying not to show it, when she found herself deluged with questions about her love life. Aly lingered helplessly five passengers behind her and Miss Haran. 'I really have nothing to say about any romance,' she told reporters. 'I've just been on a six-month vacation and now I'm going back to do a picture.' At last she and Aly slipped into the public limousine to New Orleans, and only then did he reach for her hand.

Although they were scheduled to take a connecting flight to Los Angeles that night, the prince saw that Rita was much too shaken up from the difficult landing to board another plane. Accordingly, he instructed Miss Haran to cancel their reservations; they would proceed by train. Before embarking Aly suggested that he and Rita change into blue jeans, and on the way to California, Rita, Aly, and Miss Haran sat around a small table where they played cards and discussed the passing scenery. This casual fellowship, and Aly's incomparable charm and warm smile, had a calming effect on Rita – before long she seemed to have forgotten all about her bad experience on the plane. But new trials inevitably faced her in Los Angeles.

On 1 December 1948, Superior Court Judge Elmer Doyle made her divorce from Orson final. Rita was free to marry again. The next day she was ordered to Columbia for tests of makeup and costumes for *Lona Hanson*, which was scheduled to begin shooting the following week in Mexico. Since she still hadn't seen a script, she made the bold move of refusing to report for work. Her Beckworth contract specified script approval and she didn't want to let Harry Cohn intimidate her into accepting the role sight unseen. When at last a script materialized, Rita read it and promptly rejected the assignment as unsuitable. It seemed to Rita that the part of a woman who inherited a cattle ranch in Montana had not been properly tailored for her, and therefore would not show her in the best possible light. Saying no to the film was difficult for Rita, who was not aggressive and assertive by nature. 'She didn't have that kind of makeup,' explained Shifra Haran. 'She wasn't like Bette Davis, who you can see fighting back. She wasn't that way at all.'

Incensed by Rita's decision when he had an entire

production all ready to roll, Cohn announced that he would stop paying her $5,000 weekly salary. Rita had been put on suspension before when she balked at projects Cohn wanted her to do, but this time it was a good deal more serious. She had caused an entire costly production to be postponed indefinitely. William Holden, who was to have been her co-star, was released to Paramount to make another film. Similarly, the hundreds of others who were to have worked on the film in some capacity, large or small, had to change their plans.

Rita perceived her dispute to be with Harry Cohn. It had certainly never occurred to her that she was about to incur the wrath of virtually the entire film industry. Cohn quickly put out the word that she had refused to report for work, and this, coupled with her much-publicized exploits of late with an international playboy, badly tarnished her professional image. Although until now Harry Cohn had been fretting about it, the extensive press coverage of Rita's illicit romance with Aly Khan played right into the mogul's hands by causing people to think of her as a globe-trotting good-time girl. When she turned down *Lona Hanson*, the film industry didn't regard her as an employee standing up for her contractual rights; to them she was just a spoiled brat frivolously refusing to report for work. The consensus in Hollywood seemed to be that the fractious star should get in line and show some gratitude for her lucrative profit-sharing contract.

Mindful of the immense damage that was being done to her reputation, Rita issued a public statement defending herself against the studio's allegations:

The statement that I had refused to report to work is not correct. I reported for work on September 12 but no script was ready for me. A script was handed to me last Thursday. The part to be portrayed by me in this script was not adapted to me and was detrimental to me. I so stated to the company and they suspended me.

Her protestations were in vain, however. The financial

health of the film industry was relatively poor at the moment, and the general perception of the film studios was that petty rebellion such as Rita's hurt everybody. Thus, *The New York Times* reported that Rita 'was reminded in no uncertain terms by trade commentators that the present unhappy economic condition of the film industry "obligates everyone concerned in it to exert new effort".'

What hurt Rita most in all of this was being thought somehow lazy, a shirker. She knew that she was the very opposite: someone who had been working hard virtually all her life. Having been forced to give up an important part of her childhood to help support her family, Rita prided herself on her capacity for self-sacrifice. How could anyone possibly think her irresponsible now? Her predicament left her feeling angry and confused.

It is impossible to tell how Rita would have responded to this crisis had Aly Khan *not* been there with her at the time. But he *was* there and he *did* want her to return to Europe with him. She had certainly never intended to go off with him permanently. That was precisely what she had refused to do in the first place, and it was why he had come to see her in America. But suddenly everything had changed. Not only had her divorce given her new freedom – but, un-expectedly, the studio had turned her loose as well. At a moment when almost no one in Hollywood seemed to be on her side, there was Aly, who worshipped her and wanted only to make her happy. Perhaps she could find in a new life with Aly the home and family for which she had always been searching. Her glorious time alone with Aly in Los Angeles and his immeasurable kindness to Becky made Rita think that perhaps he was capable of giving her what she really needed. While he clearly wanted to take care of her, to satisfy her every need and desire, there was one need that he appeared never to have quite understood. As Aly himself would later admit, in the beginning he had fallen 'in love with her beauty and fame.' Indeed, Gilda was the prize he had won in Hollywood – why would he ever possibly want his Rita to be anyone else? Rita's desire to escape Hollywood notwithstanding, the thought of her

191

permanently abandoning her film career was something Aly would never really be able to abide.

But neither Rita nor Aly appeared to have thought of this. When he proposed that she leave her problems behind and run off with him, she said yes. This time not only did Miss Haran get to go along, but also Rita's daughter, Becky Welles. The house in Brentwood was closed and the servants dismissed. Evidently Rita meant to stay abroad a long while.

Chapter Sixteen

*I*n New York City, where Rita's party had taken rooms at the Plaza, the care of her daughter was mostly left to Miss Haran – who, unfortunately, hadn't spent much time around small children before. 'She was very hard for me,' she recalled. 'I wasn't used to being with children, and Rebecca wasn't used to traveling, so it was difficult for Rebecca and difficult for me. A trained nanny would have known much better how to handle her.' The idea that Becky might have a terrible accident while she was watching her preyed on the secretary's mind. 'There were no grilles on the windows,' she said. 'What if she leaned over and fell out? It used to scare the hell out of me. I sure kept those windows locked!' It was only natural that the child seemed terribly disconcerted to be in a strange city, in the care of someone new. At least Miss Haran was a familiar face.

Becky's relations with another secretary appear to have been a good deal worse. Elisabeth Rubino had worked for Orson Welles in New York, and on the advice of Shifra Haran the prince hired her. One morning, she found herself assigned to look after Becky. 'I could have killed her!' laughed Miss Rubino. 'She was a lovely child, but very opinionated for her age. *Definitely* Orson Welles's daughter! I was taking care of her in the hotel room and I gave her some paper to draw on. "Wouldn't that be a nice color to do?" I suggested. And she said, "Don't tell me what color to do!" Then I said to her, "Don't you think you want breakfast?" And she answered, "Don't tell me what breakfast to have! I'll see on the menu!'' Now, whether she could read the menu I don't know, but she certainly ordered what she wanted. She was quite a child!'

The one person who seemed to get along best with Rita's daughter was the prince himself. He would get down on all fours and she would leap onto his back. As he circled the room little Becky would emit cries of delight.

Before leaving for Europe, the prince dispatched Miss Rubino to buy a great many Christmas gifts, principally for the employees at his stud farm in Ireland, where he and Rita would be spending the holiday. On the eve of their departure he handed Miss Rubino an unsealed envelope with some $10,000 in American currency to be deposited the next morning in a bank downtown. Since he and Rita were leaving the United States for a long time he wouldn't be needing so much loose cash in his pocket. 'Don't worry about it,' he reassured Miss Rubino. 'If you lose it, don't worry about it.' Still, when the secretary brought the money home, she and her mother couldn't sleep all night until it was safely out of the house.

A blanket of snow was covering Central Park outside the Plaza on 15 December 1948, the morning Rita and Aly prepared to make a run for their ship, the *Britannic*, which was bound for England. Aly slipped out first, unnoticed by reporters. Then, a little before three P.M., Rita, Becky, and Miss Haran descended in the hotel's freight elevator. Wrapped in her mink coat, and looking tired and harassed, Rita clutched her bewildered daughter's hand as newsmen hurled questions at them. Why wasn't Rita giving interviews? they demanded to know. 'I wanted privacy,' she snapped back, 'but that seems to be impossible with the American press.'

Shortly thereafter, when they arrived by limousine at Pier Fifty-four, more press accosted them. This time their questions were nearly drowned out by the boisterous cheers of about two hundred longshoremen who had lined up for a glimpse of the Love Goddess as she rushed up the gangway. Even as her secretary was calmly insisting to reporters that Miss Hayworth had no idea whether Aly Khan would be traveling on the same vessel, the prince was quietly boarding the *Britannic* with all the other passengers.

The Atlantic crossing took eight days, during which Rita and Aly maintained separate cabins. When, two days before Christmas, several shivering passengers disembarked shortly before midnight at Cobb, Ireland, reporters were waiting there as well. The accents were different but the questions were the same. *Did she plan to marry the prince? Did she love him?* Rita may well have been asking herself similar questions as she was swiftly ushered into one of the cars waiting to take them to his stud farm in County Kildare.

At the entrance to Gilltown Stud loomed an imposing iron gate ornamented with a pair of gargoyles. Behind it, at the end of a winding driveway, lay the massive two-storey beige-and-green farmhouse where little Becky would be spending her first Christmas away from Los Angeles. There was no snow on the ground, but the icy-cold air cut to the bone. Inside, the enormous high-ceilinged rooms were heated only by tiny peat fireplaces – what little warmth there was rose to the bedrooms on the upper floor. When she woke up the next day, to her consternation Rita discovered that once again she was expected to play the gracious hostess, this time to a houseful of Aly's riding friends. Only a few days before Rita had left Hollywood to escape being in a Western, but suddenly there were horses everywhere. A noisy wagon arrived and great numbers of foxhounds poured out, barking, panting, sniffing. When the prince and his friends rode off, Rita was left behind. 'She didn't ride, of course,' Shifra Haran explained. 'She was scared of horses.'

She was also rather afraid of Aly's social set. After her recent troubles in Hollywood, she just wanted to relax – but she found herself thrown in with people who invariably made her feel awkward and uncomfortable. Every encounter with them was a trial. Her secretary observed one such exceedingly painful evening. There were eight guests for dinner: a relatively small group by Aly's standards. The cook had prepared a roast that was attractively displayed on a side table. One had only to cross the room, take a bit of meat, and go back to one's place. Simple, but not for Rita. She was enough of an actress to hide what she was feeling, but someone who knew her as well as Miss Haran could sense the tiniest flash of panic in her eyes, the slightest rigidity in her neck and shoulders. Still seated, she glanced at the side table, apparently gauging what it would be like to cross the room toward it. For a long moment she seemed to hesitate. As always, she knew that everyone would be watching her, sizing her up. Indeed, there had been similar occasions when Rita had chosen not to eat, rather than to get up and serve herself for all to see. But this time something in her allowed Rita to overcome her anxiety, and suddenly she rose confidently and was crossing the room as if it were the simplest thing in the world for her to do. 'She would have normally been too frightened to go up to the sideboard herself,' said Shifra Haran, 'but she did it, and I was very proud of her!'

Still Rita plainly didn't fit in here. 'The affair with the prince may have been a passionate thing for a month or two, but it was ill-conceived from the beginning,' said Shifra Haran. 'Their worlds were too far apart.' Even when Aly's guests tried to be nice to her, she was most often silent. 'She seemed remote, not because she *was* remote, but because she was shy,' explained her secretary. As at the Château de L'Horizon, Rita felt lost in a strange, enormous house where it seemed as if she were on constant display. How was she expected to act? What was she supposed to wear? Was there never any privacy here? 'I think her being with Welles had been a better arrangement than her being with the prince,' said Miss Haran. 'The home with Mr Welles on Carmelina was *her* home. She was the lady of the house and she could go up to her room and put on her bathrobe. Lots of times she would be sitting around in her bathrobe with comfortable people like Roger and Hortense Hill. She was more at ease there. She wasn't living by someone else's rules.'

The prince approached Miss Haran in the hallway to inquire about Rita's puzzling behavior. The secretary had known Rita since her marriage to Welles: if anyone could tell Aly what was going on, she could. Why was Rita so quiet most of the time? Why did she seem to hold herself back from the other guests? For Christmas Rita had given Aly a dart board, and his gift to her was a spectacular diamond bracelet – but she hardly seemed interested in wearing it. Although she had been anxious to get away from Hollywood, the moment they arrived at Gilltown Stud she had turned moody and skittish. What was he to do with her? Embarrassed, Miss Haran shrugged her shoulders and delicately tried to explain to him that perhaps he was expecting too much of Rita. Maybe with time and understanding . . .

Aly's solution as always was to keep moving. Three days after Christmas, the prince, Rita, Becky, and Miss Haran boarded his plane, *The Avenger*. Paris was their destination, but hazardous weather conditions forced them to stop over in London. The usual mob of reporters pursued them into the lobby of the Ritz Hotel, but this time they might have gone too far. Poor Becky was so frightened by all the clicking cameras that she fell down. The prince quickly scooped her up in his arms and carried her to his suite. He said that they would spend the night there, and, weather permitting, fly to Paris the next day.

In the morning Aly thought it best to sneak Rita and Becky out through the empty hotel restaurant, while he diverted the waiting reporters' attention by leaving through the main entrance. According to plan, mother and child proceeded to the basement, then up a flight of service stairs to the restaurant, where the hotel manager awaited. The manager indicated a set of French windows leading to a tiny balcony, from which a narrow twenty-foot plank provided access to the hotel garden. It all seemed terribly precarious, but there was no turning back – Aly had already gone. Grabbing Becky by the hand, Rita led her step by step down the plank, only to discover that an iron fence completely enclosed the garden. In frustration Rita began to kick the iron bars. The noise alerted the very reporters she had been struggling to evade. At last a hotel workman with a crowbar created enough of a space between the bars for Rita and the child to squeeze through and rush to a waiting station wagon.

But this time, what exactly was she heading to? Paris, yes – but what else? Back in New York when she slipped out of the Plaza, she had been heading to a new life with Aly in Europe. Now she had already sampled that life, in Ireland, and it had not made her happy. Still, the reporters were pursuing Rita as doggedly as ever. For them nothing had changed – and she was caught up in the chase. As she fled the Ritz in London she really had no clear idea of what lay ahead. There was still no question of returning to Harry Cohn in Hollywood – but life with Aly? At Gilltown Stud she had been quickly reminded of how little she fit into his world, how agonizing it all was for her. But here she was speeding to the airport, where *The Avenger* was waiting to take her away with him again. To Paris.

There four-year-old Becky Welles was set to be briefly reunited with the father she had never really had a chance to know, and who had flown in from Rome for the occasion. Inevitably, when Miss Haran bundled her up in her rain clothes and accompanied her to Welles's Paris hotel suite, the visit proved a strange and confusing experience for little Becky, already keyed up from the chaos of the trip thus far; in a very short time Aly had become a loving and protective presence in the child's life. Everyone remarked on his excellent rapport with Rita's daughter, who evidently responded eagerly to his abundant warmth and affection. By contrast, the encounter with Orson Welles that followed was strained, to say the least.

In Welles's hotel suite, all three parties – Orson, Miss Haran and little Becky herself – seemed supremely uncomfortable. The secretary was shocked and depressed by Welles's shabby, soiled, unkempt appearance – so unlike the impeccable, immaculate figure she remembered from his glory days in Hollywood. Back then she and Shorty would follow him around with spare shirts in case he wanted to change, which he sometimes did several times a day. But the immense financial and psychological pressures of independently mounting his film production of *Othello* had clearly taken their toll. Undoubtedly he looked even worse simply because he was nervous about seeing his little girl.

Unlike Prince Aly Khan, Orson had never been very good with children, and this time was no exception. Becky took little interest in the presents he had brought her and bawled uncontrollably while Miss Haran undid the child's rain clothes. At Christmastime in Ireland, the prince had already given her more toys than she needed, so the gifts from her real father went unnoticed. A few perfunctory words about old times were exchanged between Welles and his former secretary. After much silence and awkwardness, when it became evident that Orson really had no idea of what to do with his daughter, Miss Haran announced as cheerfully as she could that it was time to leave. The moment she began to dress her, Becky started screaming again. At last Orson threw the cranky child a long, hard look: 'Same as me – no discipline!' he muttered. 'That's my trouble: I never had any either!'

On New Year's Eve, Aly's *Avenger* landed in Geneva, Switzerland. The flight from Paris left Rita feeling ill, and it took her a few extra minutes to compose herself before leaving the plane. At the celebrated Palace Hotel, in Gstaad, she was to meet Aly's beloved sons, Amyn (ten) and Karim (twelve). Aly's wife had wisely decamped the day before so as not to be confronted with his glamorous new mistress, Rita Hayworth. If the headlines and scandalous news coverage were hell for Rita, they could not have been easy for Aly's wife either. From first to last, Joan Yarde-Buller Khan handled herself with admirable grace and dignity.

Rita and her daughter, and Aly and his sons, celebrated the new year of 1949 in seclusion. Although no one saw them at the hotel's festivities, the mysterious presence of Rita and her prince was naturally much talked about at the Palace. On the evening of 1 January, the couple emerged for an hour of drinks and dancing. The hotel manager evidently echoed the sentiments of the other guests when he pronounced Rita 'maddeningly beautiful.' The next morning she took her first skiing lesson alone, while the prince remained behind, ostensibly to look after the children, but also because he still didn't wish to be photographed with her.

Aly had reason to be cautious. Apparently everyone was not prepared to be as gracious and complimentary to Rita as the manager of the Palace Hotel. In some quarters a sense of moral outrage was building against Rita because of her travels with a married man. The following Sunday two British papers pilloried Rita for what one of them, *The People*, called 'extravagant expeditions' with a 'colored prince.' The headline in *The People* proclaimed: 'THIS AFFAIR IS AN INSULT TO ALL DECENT WOMEN.' From then on, the article announced, *The People* would no longer cover the Rita-Aly love affair 'on the grounds of public decency.'

Similarly, 'A VERY SORDID BUSINESS' was the headline in *The Sunday Pictorial*, according to which,

The current behavior of Miss Hayworth and millionaire Prince Aly Khan, if described in a film script, would never get by the censors either here or in America. How would you describe a friendship in which a divorced woman careens across two continents with a married man – coming to a temporary halt in Switzerland, where his wife was already staying with his children? Or do you find a certain charm in the fact that motherly Miss Hayworth continues to drag around her four-year-old daughter on this vulgar joyride?

For the first time – but by no means the last – Rita's fitness as a mother was being publicly questioned. Thus, *The Sunday Pictorial* went on to suggest that if a British mother carried on like this, the courts would probably move to give her daughter to 'somebody who knew the right way' to care for children. And by way of sarcastic comment on Rita's moral character, the paper reminded its readers of the line she had spoken in *Gilda*: 'If I had been a ranch, they would have called me the Bar Nothing.'

Although Aly was by nature a good deal more thick-skinned than Rita, he worried constantly about how his father, the Aga Khan, would react to all the scurrilous stories. And indeed, before long, the Aga sent word to Aly in Switzerland that the scandal was to be contained immediately. In effect, this meant either that Aly terminate his affair with the Love Goddess, or that he marry her. Even if the couple did declare their intention to marry, the Aga might not approve of Rita, or Aly might not be able to get a divorce quickly enough.

Suddenly everything was moving *very* rapidly. A decision – *some* decision – had to be made at once. So it was that, whatever her reservations about what life with him was going to be like, Rita agreed to go with Aly to Cannes to ask for the Aga's approval to marry. It was that or break up with him instantly – there was really no middle ground.

The Aga Khan was installed at the twenty-one room Villa Yakimour, on a hillside in the Cannes suburb of Le Cannet, about four miles from his son's Château de l'Horizon. Everything depended on Rita's audience with him. If she could not manage to win him over, it would probably mean the end of her relationship with Aly. Meanwhile, Becky had come down with the flu, so the child would have to be left behind in Gstaad, at the Palace Hotel. As Rita prepared for the drive to Cannes on 12 January, she could feel herself getting sick. It was the worst possible moment for a cold. She needed all her strength for what faced her. By this time the rumor was rampant in Europe that she was pregnant with Aly's child. This was untrue, but if she arrived at the Villa Yakimour looking pale and haggard, there was no telling what the old potentate might think.

For the trip to Cannes, Rita threw her mink coat over her ski clothes. Icy roads, coupled with the absurdly high speeds at which Aly insisted on driving, would make the trip a perilous one. They were pursued for part of the way by a newsman in a taxi, but by the time they crossed the Swiss border at Perly, Aly had managed to lose him.

When Aly dropped Rita off at the Château de l'Horizon,

she tried to get some rest and nurse her cold. Fortunately she did not have to face the Aga Khan immediately. Aly, however, was expected at the Villa Yakimour, where he endured a tense fifteen-minute preliminary meeting with his father that did not bode well for what Rita would be confronted with. As the Aga Khan later indicated, he had been expecting the worst.

Even in her own country, a public outcry had begun against Rita's morals. That very day in Chicago, the American Federation of Women's Clubs was loudly threatening to boycott any films in which Rita Hayworth might appear in the future. 'I don't believe Miss Hayworth should be given another chance to make other movies unless she improves her conduct,' said a spokeswoman for the organization. The timing of the announcement was hardly auspicious. No matter that Aly was every bit as responsible for the scandal as she – was this an appropriate bride for a Muslim religious leader?

Afterward Rita would tell Elsa Maxwell about how nervous she had been in anticipation of meeting the prince's father. Despite the brief rest she had enjoyed at the château, her flu had only worsened. Nonetheless, as she had done with millions of men before him, she quickly and easily won over her future father-in-law. Aly's valet, Tutti, later reported to Miss Haran that the Aga Khan lit up the moment he caught his first glimpse of Rita. He may have been wringing his hands over her before they met, but days later he was saying publicly of Rita, 'I know of no one who is more quiet or ladylike.'

And she was seen to pat his hand affectionately and call him 'very sweet.'

All that remained was to inform the press that Rita and Aly were getting married – perhaps then the gossip and speculation would be brought to a halt.

Chapter Seventeen

*T*he prince had spent the past few months dodging reporters, so he shocked them by inviting them into the château as his guests. These were some of the very same irritating fellows who had been harassing him at every turn, but there he was warmly shaking hands with each. Rita, he informed them, was ill with flu. As for the reason he had invited them in, perhaps the typed announcement that was suddenly being distributed would answer that. It read:

I have hitherto refrained from making any comment upon the uninformed and often scurrilous and vicious reports which have recently appeared in some sections of the press in connection with my domestic affairs.

I should like it to be made known that by mutual consent my wife and I have lived apart for over three years; that appropriate proceedings have been in progress for nearly a year; and that immediately [after] these proceedings terminate, steps will be taken to remedy the position which appears to have provided material for these press comments complained of.

I am going to marry Miss Hayworth as soon as I am free to do so. In these circumstances I hope that my private affairs will be treated with the consideration which is usually extended to the private affairs of individuals in general.

Another statement, this from Rita, was attached:

I am fully conversant with the statement which Prince Aly Khan has today issued to the press, and am in full agreement with what he says. I have only been waiting to be free to marry him.

As soon as they absorbed all this, the excited reporters had new questions for the prince. He cheerfully explained that no date had been set, that the Aga Khan approved, and that there would be a marriage according to Muslim religion and according to the law of the country in which they happened to have the ceremony. As to whether Rita would have to renounce Roman Catholicism, the prince was prepared to be most liberal, but there was one important stipulation: although he did not expect Rita to change her religion, he said that any children from the marriage would be Muslims.

The air of scandal had not entirely been dispelled. For Rita it remained to be seen how messy the divorce proceedings would be. Since she was *the other woman*, her name might still be dragged through the mud in the French courts. Rita braced herself for the worst – especially when the *Los Angeles Times* reported on 1 February 1949 that the prince's scorned wife, Joan, planned to name her in the divorce petition. But the next day, 2 February, when the *current* Princess Aly Khan arrived at the Seine civil court in Paris, one of her two lawyers announced, 'Miss Hayworth will not be named in the princess's suit. The suit will be drawn up in mild and measured terms in order to protect the couple's children from further scandal.'

Indeed, after the princess and her attorneys had met with Judge Jacques Rousselet, the judge confirmed publicly that Rita's name had come up 'neither in private talk nor in [the princess's] complaint.' The prince was being discreetly charged with having perpetrated a 'grave insult' to his wife, to whom he had 'shown lack of consideration' – nothing nastier, or most specific, than that.

After Aly in turn huddled with the judge, there remained the potentially sticky business of the reconciliation meeting between husband and wife that French law required no matter how much animosity might exist between them. By law the judge had at least to try to help

Aly and Joan overcome their differences and get back together. Once the judge accepted that no reconciliation was possible, it would be just a matter of time before the marriage was dissolved. At first the all-important meeting had to be postponed a few days when the princess took ill in London. But on 19 February, both she and her errant husband appeared in the French court for the pro forma attempt to patch things up between them. This having failed – as everyone assumed and expected it would – Aly was well on his way to becoming a free man.

That the divorce proceedings were going smoothly was all to the good. The Aga Khan was in poor health and had recently been hospitalized in Paris – a forceful reminder that one of the reasons he was so concerned about the prince's public demeanor was the need for Aly to establish his fitness to succeed his father as temporal and spiritual leader of the Ismaili sect. However, if Aly seemed anxious to put an end to the scandal that had pained the Aga Khan so, what he did next was curious behavior, to say the least (especially for someone who prided himself on prodigious control in the bedroom). Although it would be a while before Aly's divorce actually came through and a wedding date could be set, in March 1949 Rita became pregnant. Just as the many months of secrecy and hiding were coming to an end, suddenly Rita had something new to conceal.

On 7 April 1949, more than a month before it was actually expected, Aly's divorce was granted in Paris. The judge blamed the failure of the marriage equally on the prince and the princess. With his wife's consent, Aly was awarded custody of his two sons. All that remained was for the divorce decree to be formally entered in court records – which was likely to take another four to six weeks, although this, too, might be expedited.

By 11 April, Aly and Rita were driving south to Cannes, where the usual houseful of guests awaited them. To Rita's horror and amazement, even the prince didn't seem to know all the people who partook of his lavish hospitality, since those he invited frequently arrived with guests of their own. Almost every afternoon Aly treated his guests to a lavish buffet loaded with caviar, lobster, truffles, and other delicacies. In rare moments of privacy, Rita would angrily refer to all these people as 'freeloaders,' but Aly didn't seem to grasp what she meant. Rita had worked hard since childhood to earn her money, while Aly's money was acquired very differently – hence the inevitable and fundamental difference in their attitudes toward how it was spent. Several times Rita came upon the 'freeloaders' making expensive long-distance calls from the château. Although Aly seemed accustomed to being taken advantage of like this, Rita was enraged, but dared not say anything to them.

The château was soon a hive of activity in anticipation of the royal wedding. For Rita there were interminable fittings with couturier Jacques Fath for her wedding dress and trousseau (complicated by the fact that she was secretly pregnant); and for the prince, guest lists and menus to be prepared, and logistics to be worked out. Even when he stumbled and broke his ankle while playing with the children, Aly did not diminish his pace.

His principal concern of the moment was to keep the wedding private. French law required weddings to be held in public. But it seemed to Aly that Rita had already been subjected to too much unwanted public exposure. The prince knew only too well that journalists from around the world would overrun his and Rita's wedding if it were accessible to them. In hopes of sparing Rita yet another difficult ordeal, Aly applied to the French Ministry of Justice for permission to hold the wedding at home, where reporters and photographers would not be able to get at her. The Duke and Duchess of Windsor had been granted similar permission, so why not Prince Aly Khan? The wedding date of 27 May 1949 had been set, but still no word came from the ministry. Under the reasonable assumption that almost certainly the ministry would act favorably on his request to marry in private, Aly had the wedding invitations sent out, giving the Château de l'Horizon as the location.

While making preparations for his wedding, however, Aly had not abandoned his wandering ways. Although reporters searched in vain for Aly in nightclubs and thereby concluded that he had reformed, in fact the prince regularly slipped out of the château undetected in the wee hours of the morning. Rita's business manager, Lee Ellroy, accompanied the prospective bridegroom on one such after-hours jaunt and soon found himself offered his choice of a pair of good-looking women in the Cannes casino. Ellroy's demurral evidently didn't stop Aly, who went off with one of the women, nonetheless.

For her part, as her wedding day approached, Rita grew more anxious and ambivalent than ever about all that faced her with Aly. While guests and presents had already begun arriving at the château from around the world, and indeed all of Cannes was gearing up for the big event, Rita made a secret decision. She would quietly arrange an assignation with her ex-husband Orson Welles to propose that they run off together and remarry.

Welles was in Rome when he received the unexpected summons from Rita. 'She sent for me and asked me to take her back,' Welles recalled. 'She sent me a telegram in Rome. I couldn't get any plane, so I went, stood up in a cargo plane to Antibes.' Rita was waiting for him there in a hotel. 'There were candles and champagne ready – and Rita in a marvelous negligée,' Welles said. 'And the door closed, and she said, "Here I am. Marry me." ' As to why Rita would have possibly wanted to remarry after all the trouble they had had together, Welles speculated: 'She was marrying the most promiscuous man in Europe, just the worst marriage that ever could have happened. And she *knew* it! It was a *fatal* marriage, the worst thing that could have happened to her. He was charming, attractive, a nice man – I knew him all my life – but the *wrong* husband for her.'

When one considers that Welles hadn't exactly been faithful to Rita either, Rita's last-minute attempt to back out of her wedding suggests enormous trepidation about what life as a princess was going to be like. However much

207

Welles cared for Rita, still he returned to Rome the next morning.

'I was insanely in love at that moment with the least attractive woman I've ever known, who was giving me horns every night!' Welles recalled about why he said no to Rita and rushed back to Italy. Shortly thereafter, when he learned that Rita had indeed married the prince, Welles attributed it to her desire not to have to go back to Holly-wood. 'Aly was her great escape from Hollywood,' Orson explained. 'The real appeal of Aly was that she became somebody that had nothing to do with *Rita Hayworth*. She became the Princess Aly Khan. She could say "screw you" to Hollywood.'

That Rita was indeed trying to tell Hollywood something along these lines is suggested by the fact that one of the people she hated most in the world, Harry Cohn, was among the few guests she personally invited to the royal wedding. He wisely declined; being there at the moment his prize star property became a princess would have been almost as unbearable to the foul-mouthed mogul as having to call her 'Your Highness' afterward.

Following her secret rendezvous with Welles, Rita returned to the château as if nothing had happened – she would be marrying Aly, after all. Then, just forty-eight hours before the wedding, bad news arrived. Rita burst into tears when she learned that the French Ministry of Justice had finally ruled against Aly's request to hold the ceremony behind closed doors. According to French law all it took was the protest of a single individual to force the prince and the Love Goddess to get married in public. That individual turned out to be a shrewd French journalist who simply did not wish to be excluded from the ceremony. Now that the wedding had to be conducted in public, not only the journalist who had protested but the entire press corps would be able to crash what was to have been a private event.

Everything at the château was ready for the Friday ceremony and the reception that was to follow. Entirely new arrangements would have to be made at the last minute. For Rita the pressure of getting married again was obviously bad enough, but this new development keyed her up even more. Annoyed, the prince quickly telephoned both his lawyer in Paris and the Aga Khan to see if either could do anything. When that failed, Aly had no choice but to secure the town hall in Vallauris for the ceremony, and to try somehow to minimize as much as possible Rita's exposure to the press and the inevitable crowds of curious residents and tourists.

Aly's efforts notwithstanding, Paul Derignon, the Communist mayor of Vallauris, clearly relished the spotlight that was suddenly being turned on the quaint little red-roofed village where Picasso made pottery. For two days Mayor Derignon's up-to-the-minute progress reports from Vallauris were echoed around the world. He promptly ordered the town hall whitewashed and redecorated, and the local police force of six was to be augmented by one hundred and twenty officers from Nice. Out of courtesy to Prince Aly, who drove to Vallauris to meet personally with the mayor (and to donate 1,000,000 francs to the town treasury), Derignon agreed to conduct the wedding on the ground floor so that the sickly old Aga Khan wouldn't have to trudge upstairs. But Aly could not have been pleased when the Communist mayor adamantly insisted on throwing open the doors of the town hall to 'let the peasants in.' Seven princes, four princesses, a maharajah, a gaekwar, and an emir may have been among the royal wedding's eighty-five invited guests, but still the major proclaimed: 'We must keep this thing democratic.' For Rita, with her terror of threatening mobs, it was to be a nightmare.

As the wedding drew nearer, nothing seemed to be going quite as Aly had hoped. When the Aga Khan drove out to the château to drop off his wedding gift for Rita, the prince was out playing tennis. Emrys Williams accepted the box, which he gave to Aly upon his return. According to the chauffeur, Aly took the box into his study, but when he opened it he was disappointed to discover only a pair of diamond earrings. Williams recalled: ' "Is that all!" exclaimed the prince, pulling out the stuffing and turning the box upside down. ''Father's getting pretty mean, isn't he?'' I rather fancy he expected a check for a million pounds.'

Rita selected a blue linen dress and white shoes for the buffet lunch the day before the wedding. There some twenty Ismailis dressed in colorful native garb showered her with precious gifts of pearls, ivory, and gold from Africa, India, and the Middle East. Rita had braced herself to act in the sophisticated manner that Aly's Continental friends expected of her, but how was she supposed to respond, what was she supposed to say, when one by one the prince's Ismaili devotees threw themselves on their knees to kiss her feet? Before she could think of something, the Ismailis retreated and once again Rita found herself surrounded by the elegant Europeans with whom she struggled to seem well-bred and refined.

Rita lost a bit of her composure that night, however, as fans pawed and called at her outside the Alexandre Cinéma in Cannes, where the prince had scheduled a private screening of *The Loves of Carmen* in her honor. During the making of that film she had been secretly pregnant from her affair with Howard Hughes, and now, as she watched *Carmen* with the others, she was secretly pregnant again, with the child of yet another fabulously wealthy man. She had hoped that having a baby with Aly would give her a shot at the warm, loving family life she craved. But already, Aly's having arranged this screening of *Carmen* was a bad sign. Clearly the prince saw himself as marrying a *movie star*; he was enraptured by precisely the image of herself from which Rita longed more than anything to escape.

During the private screening the mob outside the theater had grown considerably. Everyone wanted a glimpse of Rita Hayworth. When she finally emerged from the theater, her difficult passage through the crowd to a waiting limousine wasn't enough for them. No sooner had a chauffeur helped her climb inside and shut the door behind her than her fans forced it open again. Even as the limousine pulled away, the well-wishers bustled after it through the streets of Cannes until it disappeared from sight, on its way up into the hills to the lovely old walled village of Mougins, where the prince had .nvited some sixty guests to dine with them at the chic restaurant Les Terrasses.

Si Caddour Ben Ghabrit, the imam of the Paris mosque, called Rita's wedding day the 'biggest Muslim marriage of the century.' Mayor Derignon had declared it a holiday in Vallauris, where more than five hundred villagers gathered in front of the town hall to await the bride's arrival. Early that morning as crowds were just beginning to form along the roads between the château and Vallauris, the prince quickly drove his Alfa Romeo into town to plead with the mayor one last time to exclude reporters and photographers from the ceremony. Aly would look bad in front of his father if he could not at least accomplish that. Somehow this time the prince managed to persuade Mayor Derignon, who immediately ordered seventy-five furious journalists out of the fifty-foot-high room on the ground floor where the ceremony was to take place in an hour.

By eleven A.M. when the Aga Khan's green Rolls-Royce pulled up in front of the town hall, all that could be heard of the journalists were their angry but muffled protests issuing from the staircase that the police had hastily forced them to ascend. Dressed in a voluminous double-breasted white suit with a bright red rose pinned to his lapel, the Aga Khan waved and blew kisses to the cheering crowd. Beside him stood his wife, Aly's stepmother, the Begum, in a magnificent flowing blue sari. Although he would later say that he had been unhappy with the day's circus atmosphere, the Aga Khan concealed his displeasure for the time being.

Next came Rita's new white Cadillac convertible, with a police escort in front and behind, and motorcycles on either side. The luxury automobile had been shipped from America especially for Rita's wedding day, but en route vandals had inscribed greetings to the Love Goddess on the painted surface, so that it had to be entirely resprayed in France.

As the crowds called her name, the mayor dashed out of the town hall to pose with Rita on the front steps. Dressed in an ice-blue, long-sleeved chiffon dress by Jacques Fath and a floppy-brimmed blue picture hat, Rita nervously waved a white handkerchief to the crowds, then turned to join the prince, who was already waiting inside.

Meanwhile, the journalists who had been forced into the staircase bitterly pleaded their case to the mayor. The thirty or so French newsmen sent up especially loud cries of protest. In effect, they said, the prince was being allowed to marry in private after all; keeping newsmen out of the ceremony was undemocratic and illegal. Thus, at the very last minute, when there was nothing Aly could do to stop it, the protesting journalists were allowed to file into the rear of the wedding room, where they promised not to be disruptive.

Rita and Aly were already sitting in upholstered armchairs in the front of the high-ceilinged room as the secretary-general of Vallauris ever so slowly and solemnly proclaimed: 'There have appeared before us Prince Aly Salomone Khan, Croix de Guerre with palm, born in Turin the thirteenth of June 1911, son of His Highness the Aga Khan of Yakimour and of Thérèse Magliano, deceased; divorced from Barbara Joan Yarde-Buller; and Margarita Carmen Cansino, born in New York the seventeenth of October 1918; in the presence of witnesses Georges Catroux, General of the Army of France, Grand Cross of the Legion of Honor, and His Highness Prince Jean D'Orléans Braganza of Rio de Janeiro.'

Next the mayor took over. Seated across a small table from Aly and Rita, he nervously inquired whether they accepted each other as husband and wife.

'*Oui*,' Rita answered, in the faintest of voices.

'*Oui*,' said the prince, more firmly.

Then they exchanged gold wedding bands and the mayor said, 'After your separate and affirmative responses we pronounce that in the name of the law you are united in marriage.' Once the witnesses signed the guest register, Aly held Rita by the waist and kissed her as the royal wedding party applauded. 'Your Highnesses,' interrupted Mayor Derignon.

Your Highness.

It was the first time Rita had heard herself addressed this way.

'It is a sensational event, and at the same time an unhoped-for honor,' the mayor droned on, 'that our little city has been chosen by *Your Highnesses* to unite your destinies. Thanks to you, our industrious little town, in which our workmen fashion celebrated pottery and ceramics and where our peasants harvest orange blossoms, is honored on this day and the name of Vallauris is spread to the ends of the world with that of Prince Aly Khan and the great artist Rita Hayworth.' In the meantime, Aly shifted about uneasily in his chair, while across the room the Aga Khan leaned heavily on his cane, as motionless as an immense sculpture. 'I wish with all my heart,' the mayor was saying, 'and a sincere hope that after the feverish days you have been experiencing, which are the price of glory and success, that you may find in this oasis the happiness that you desire in calm and tranquillity. Prince, Princess, our dearest wish is that you may be happy in our community.'

Eight minutes after the ceremony had begun the royal newlyweds emerged into the sunlight, where the townspeople cheered and showered them with rice. The prince and princess allowed themselves to be photographed for a moment or two, after which the chauffeur helped them through the unusually cooperative crowds to the white Cadillac that took them back to the château along roads lined with hundreds of additional well-wishers.

On the terraces of the château buffet tables piled high with delicacies awaited the wedding guests, as well as an estimated twenty gate-crashers. In the swimming pool overlooking the Mediterranean white carnations formed two enormous interlocking twelve-foot letters: A, for Aly, and M, for Margarita. As Aly read aloud from some of the congratulatory telegrams that were pouring in almost every minute from around the world, the Aga concentrated on devouring prodigious quantities of caviar at the center table, where he perched for much of the reception. Rita's daughter, Becky Welles, had not been to the ceremony at the town hall, but she appeared at the château wearing an adorable organdy party dress and clutching the hand of a governess.

As for the bride herself, she was observed at the reception apparently 'trying to lose herself in the crowd.' And Louella Parsons would sniff that Rita 'didn't seem happy to me.' She *was* pregnant, after all, and the activities of the past few hours had been unusually demanding and exhausting; it would have been only natural for her to want the day over and done. Nonetheless, the festivities at the château dragged on for some six hours, and at length the weary bride made her way to the Aga Khan's table, where he, too, seemed rather fatigued by now. 'Too much caviar, Rita,' he was heard to tell her. 'Too much caviar.'

The day after the wedding a pair of white-robed Muslim priests from the Paris mosque married Rita and Aly in a religious ceremony, at which passages from the Koran were read aloud and the prince and princess were toasted with fruit juice (Muslim law prohibits consumption of alcoholic beverages).

The air of scandal that hung over Rita and Aly was by no means dispelled by their having legitimized their relationship. The Ismailis of Asia and Africa may have been jubilant about their new princess, but the Vatican took a dim view of Rita's wedding.

'The church ignores this marrage,' a Vatican spokesman promptly declared. 'As a Catholic Rita Hayworth should know that her civil marriage has no value in the eyes of the Church. For a Catholic, a religious marriage is obligatory when she marries a non-Catholic.' Since Rita was secretly expecting, the worst part was that, according to the Vatican, any offspring of her union with Aly would have been 'conceived in sin.'

Chapter Eighteen

'She reflected what the men wanted,' said Bob Schiffer of Rita's relations with her husbands and lovers. 'Unfortunately, that's the way she thought it should be.'

And so it was with Aly Khan.

No matter how much fame and success she had achieved in life thus far, the debased self-image and feelings of inferiority that had been among the legacies of her childhood made it seem only natural once again to make her new husband the center of her universe, to struggle to become whatever he expected of her. Her father had cast her as a provocative Spanish dancer, Eddie Judson had made her a star, and with Welles she became the wife of a would-be political figure. Now Aly hired a tutor to train her in the spoken French that she needed to function in the prince's social circles, and another tutor was to instruct her in etiquette and royal protocol. It fell upon a Georgian prince, Gregory Eristoff, to initiate Brooklyn-born Rita into the mysteries of being a princess. She would have to learn how properly to approach various members of royalty, how to address them, and how to seat them at a dinner table. All of this, of course, went very much against the grain of her inherently shy personality, but, at least in the beginning, she forced herself to try to please Aly, to make him proud of her.

Ironically, in the preceding months Rita and Aly had spent an inordinate amount of time fleeing the public spotlight – but now it was precisely into that spotlight that the prince thrust them once more as he showed off his movie-

215

star bride at an endless succession of social and sporting events in England and France.

As in the past, the enormous attention Rita inevitably attracted often proved dangerous – especially for a pregnant woman. Thus, in England when Aly took his princess to Epsom Downs, where he and the Aga Khan had horses running, the day nearly turned disastrous as the overexcited crowd pressed in too tightly around Rita while she and Aly were departing through a rear gate. Police had to be summoned to hold back the surging mob so that the frightened Love Goddess could safely be led to her car.

Twice in France Rita fainted in the face of similar crowd scenes. At the Longchamps racetrack in Paris she collapsed into the arms of the textile magnate Marcel Boussac, who had been standing alongside her. Again, at the Festival of Stars at the Tuileries Gardens, when a mob of autograph hounds closed in on her, she collapsed near Maurice Chevalier, whose tuxedo was splashed by an overturned bottle of champagne. 'My new suit is ruined!' Chevalier was heard to cry out, as others – more gallant than he – rushed to revive the actress with a bit of brandy.

Like other much-publicized members of the international monied set, Rita soon became the target of criminals, such as the gang of thieves who stalked her and Aly outside a Paris nightclub. There followed a car chase through nocturnal Paris, during which Aly's chauffeur-driven Cadillac was pursued by the robbers' Citroën. Petrified, Rita suggested hurling her jewelry out of the window to placate their pursuers, but Aly wouldn't hear of it. Suddenly he produced a gun and prepared to fire, when the chauffeur wisely warned him that if he did, the thieves would likely shoot at them in return. Finally, the fortuitous appearance of a policeman caused the thieves to flee. Aly was glad simply to have the incident over with, but the danger they had just faced left Rita deeply shaken. 'Rita was quite overcome and sobbing hysterically, her face buried in her hands,' recalled chauffeur Emrys Williams. 'She was all bunched up with loose hair hanging down over her knees.'

Margarita Cansino (Rita Hayworth) dancing with her father Eduardo Cansino. Margarita passed as Eduardo's wife in the raucous off-shore gambling ships and Mexican casinos where she worked from the age of 12.

Eduardo Cansino and his elder sister Elisa had been vaudeville headliners. 'They have swept American audiences off their feet,' declared the *Houston Post* in 1915.

Above Baby Margarita was born in Brooklyn in 1918.

Right Volga Cansino with her children in Los Angeles in 1928. The children euphemistically referred to Volga's debilitating alcoholism as her 'illness'.

Below The Cansino children in New York City. Margarita (3 years and 8 months), Vernon (8 months), and Eduardo, Jr. (2 years and 8 months).

los angeles - calif
april 1928.

To Aunt Eliza
to be as wonderful a
dancer as you are
is my heart's desire
Dearest Love
Margarita
1931.

Above Margarita at 12, the year her
father made her his
dancing partner.

Right Margarita (aged 9) in
costume for a Japanese dance.

Above left Margarita and
Eduardo, the Dancing Cansinos.
Her brothers revealed to
classmates that their parents
had lied about Margarita's age
to keep her out of school.

Above Rita Cansino during her
first film contract at Fox, before
she underwent electrolysis
treatments to alter her hairline.

Left Rita and her first husband
Eddie Judson shortly after they
eloped in 1937. He pressed her
to sleep with other men if it
would help her career.

Above Rita Hayworth at the time of *Blood and Sand*.

Left Rita and Eddie Judson in 1941. Rita was now a fully-fledged star. When she brought up the possibility of leaving him, Eddie threatened to disfigure her.

Above Orson Welles and Rita at the Stork Club in New York.

Right Orson Welles and Rita at their wedding in September 1943. Years later she called him 'the great love of my life'.

Above Rita and her mother Volga Cansino.

Above Rita singing 'Put the Blame on Mame' in *Gilda*.

Right Hounded by New York reporters seeking information about her scandalous affair with Aly Khan, Rita boards a ship headed for Europe – and her new life as a princess. Behind her is Rebecca Welles and Shifra Haran (partially obscured) who holds Becky's doll.

Below Rita holds hands with the Aga Khan III shortly after he approved her marriage to his son Aly.

Top Aly and a pregnant Rita marry in May 1949 on the French Riviera.

Right Aly holds Princess Yasmin soon after Rita gave birth to her second daughter in Lausanne, Switzerland in December 1949.

Rita and 3-year-old
Princess Yasmin
leave the court in
Reno, Nevada the day
Rita divorced
Aly Khan.

Crooner Dick Haymes and Princess Yasmin in Las
Vegas shortly before he married her mother.

Above Rita marries husband number four Dick Haymes in Las Vegas as her daughters Yasmin and Rebecca look on.

Armed guards assigned to protect Rita in Las Vegas after she and Princess Yasmin received a series of anonymous death threats.

Above Rebecca Welles (aged 9) is led out of the Westchester court after being questioned by the judge about the circumstances in which Rita had left her and Yasmin while travelling with Dick Haymes.

Left After a prolonged custody battle with Rita, an exultant Aly has finally won the right to have his daughter spend time with him in Europe.

Right Princess Yasmin reunited with her grandfather, the Aga, and his wife, the Begum, in Paris in 1955. The ailing Aga had feared that he would never see his only granddaughter again.

No one yet knew that Rita was suffering from Alzheimer's disease when these photographs were taken at London's Heathrow Airport in 1976 as attendants helped her off a plane. Although she was often frightened and disoriented, and sometimes violent, she continued to make public appearances around the world.

Above Rita dances with her dear friend Hermes Pan in 1978.

Rita and Mac Krim in 1979. Krim frequently escorted Rita in her final years in public.

Devastated by Alzheimer's disease, 62-year-old Rita Hayworth makes one of her last public appearances with film director Rouben Mamoulian in 1980.

Rita with Yasmin who cared for her in the final years before Rita's death in 1987 at the age of 68.

Another unsettling brush with the criminal element came shortly thereafter, but this time the target was Rita's daughter, Becky Welles. Although the child was no stranger to the threat of kidnapping, in this incident a man actually grabbed her on the beach at Deauville while she played with another child. Luckily her nanny observed the attempted abduction and screamed for help, whereupon Williams appeared with a pistol and scared off the assailant.

Life so constantly in the public eye was one of the very things Rita had longed to escape, but she struggled to adjust as best she could to the incessant exposure that her role as Aly's princess entailed. One aspect of his life to which Rita would never be able to adjust, however, was his penchant for extramarital affairs. ('I couldn't stand his playboy habits,' she would later say). For someone as jealous and insecure as Rita, the womanizing in which he indulged in Deauville was not easy to handle, especially since she could never be sure whether it was really happening or whether it was her imagination. Aly typically kept his three-storey oceanfront Villa Gorizia filled with an array of guests, and Rita never quite knew which among them were her husband's mistress of the moment. The fatigue of her pregnancy caused Rita to go to bed early most nights, and it was no secret that as soon as she was asleep Aly would usually slip out of the house to play the ladies' man about Deauville. 'Aly liked to chase girls, he was *proud* of that,' explained Orson Welles.

Still, at this point, Aly did seem to have loved Rita, albeit in his own rather peculiar fashion. Unfaithful to her as he may often have been, the prince also knew how to be incredibly tender and romantic, to win back her heart just when she was most exasperated with him. On one such occasion during her pregnancy, after dancing with an assortment of other women while his wife sat and watched, suddenly the prince signaled the butler to turn down the lights and have the orchestra play the fox-trot 'Night and Day.' Aly dramatically crossed the dance floor, extended his hand to Rita, and danced only with her for the rest of the evening, as if everyone else there had disappeared.

Although her public fainting fits and the baggy clothes that she increasingly favored had already aroused widespread suspicion that Rita was pregnant, she refrained from making a public announcement until August. Even then, although Rita was really five months pregnant, to forestall scandalous speculation she insisted that she wasn't due to give birth until February (Later, as the actual birth date in December approached, Aly and the Aga would make much public ado of there being a tradition of premature babies in the family.) The little deception about the date notwithstanding, Rita's announcement allowed her finally to stop trying to hide her pregnancy and to appear in public in couturier maternity-dresses. In private, however, she almost invariably preferred an extra-large blouse worn over loose-fitting blue jeans.

In November, when Rita and Aly repaired to Switzerland to await the birth of the baby, a more solicitous expectant father than the prince could scarcely be imagined. Rita's medical history – her earlier Caesarean, the bleeding and the other complications following her abortion, and her curettage – suggested the need for extra caution; indeed, much as feared, she nearly miscarried twice. Meanwhile, Aly and his princess were installed in a four-room suite at the Lausanne-Palace Hotel. The Aga Khan's extensive business interests in Lausanne guaranteed special treatment by the local police and others. Nearby was Rita's personal doctor, Professor Rudolph Rochat, the eminent head of the Montchoisi Clinic, long a favorite of European royalty. Since Rita was still claiming that she wasn't due to give birth until February, the press vigil outside the hotel was a source of immense agitation to her – the last thing she needed in her exceedingly delicate condition.

Lest any overzealous photographers try to burst into Rita's room, as they had at the time of her curettage, Tutti stood guard at her door. And the prince firmly warned journalists not to disturb or harass his wife. Whenever she stepped out, should any flashbulbs go off in her face, the police would be summoned immediately.

Most mornings the prince emerged alone from the hotel in quest of chocolates, roses, perfume, and other gifts for Rita. In the afternoon she would often bundle up in her mink coat for a drive through Lausanne in Aly's Cadillac convertible, where observers noted that she appeared 'drawn and shaky.' At other times, when they weren't playing cards in their suite to pass the time, the prince and princess discussed possible names for the new baby, and finally settled on Yasmin if it should be a girl, and Aladdin if a boy.

Aly was particularly irked when reports began to circulate that the baby was going to be baptized. Although he had certainly never insisted that Rita abandon the Catholic faith, from the first he had been adamant that their children be raised as Muslims. Thus baptism was entirely out of the question and he dismissed any such speculation as 'completely false rumors.'

Although the original plan had been for a police motor-cade to escort Rita to the Montchoisi Clinic, things didn't work out that way. At three A.M. on 28 December 1949, Rita awoke Aly to say that the time had come. In his panic he forgot all about the plan to summon the waiting police and drove her to the clinic himself, at top speed – terrified every second of the way that she suddenly might give birth in the car. Rita's labour dragged on for seven hours, but contrary to expectations, a Caesarean wasn't necessary to give the Khan dynasty its new five-and-a-half-pound Princess Yasmin.

Meanwhile, Aly had filled Rita's room with lilacs and posted Tutti on guard at the door. Rita was still asleep when she was brought back from the recovery room, and at length Aly, too, dozed off in a rocking chair beside her. He wanted to be there when she woke up to tell her the glorious news.

If ever Rita found what she was looking for with Aly, it was in the joyous period immediately following the birth of Yasmin, when for three months they lived relatively quietly in a chalet that the prince had rented for them in Gstaad. There Aly seemed to refrain from the assignations with other women that had tormented Rita in Deauville. He did make occasional forays to Paris, ostensibly on business, but mostly he stayed with her in Gstaad, where he played winter sports and spent time with the baby and Becky, as well as his two sons, who had come for a visit. This was the warm family life that Rita had hoped for – but all too quickly an accident brought it to an end.

Aly broke his leg skiing, yet instead of allowing Rita to pamper and indulge him, as it would have given her great pleasure to do, the prince quickly grew restless and bored with confinement and decided that the time had come to move on to the Château de l'Horizon, where a broader range of entertainments and distractions would be available.

Rita as yet had no idea that the move to the Riviera meant the end of the contentment she had enjoyed in Gstaad. As far as she was concerned, these past three months suggested that things were finally going to work out with her husband in exactly the way that she wanted. It seemed possible, as it had not in the past, to make the final break with America. Thus, in a significant gesture of confidence, she instructed her business manager back in Los Angeles to put her Brentwood house up for sale for $55,000 – her home was in Europe now, with Aly.

Sadly, however, the fleeting happiness they had known in Gstaad was gone by the time they had settled in the Château de l'Horizon, where all their old problems instantly resumed. Suddenly Rita and Aly weren't leading a quiet family life anymore and, in spite of his leg injury, his attentions quickly strayed elsewhere – frequently to the beautiful women he loved to pursue. According to Emrys Williams: 'the rows between Rita and her husband started afresh as soon as they returned to Cannes.'

Once again the château was invaded by people with whom Rita seemed constitutionally unable to play the gracious hostess. In this difficult period Rita was known to have a few drinks and shut herself in her bedroom, where she spent lonely hours dancing to the Spanish records she collected. When she appeared at the dinner table, she would often sit silently throughout the meal, uttering not a word to the gentlemen seated on either side of her. Indeed, on the occasions when Elsa Maxwell was invited to dinner, she noted that, 'More than once, I thought she looked scared, as if she did not know where to turn or what to do.'

If Rita frequently seemed withdrawn in public, alone with her husband she could be fiery and explosive. As Miss Haran had already recognized only too clearly in Mexico before they were married, Rita's wild rages had the peculiar effect of stimulating Aly, of turning him on. Thus, when the prince demanded that Rita accompany him to the races at Ascot, a particularly violent quarrel ensued. 'Never before or since have I seen such fury in a human being,' reported Emrys Williams of Rita's angry refusal to go.

When she declared that she was sick of life with Aly and wanted to go back to America, the prince calmly accused her of having been drinking. Infuriated by the suggestion, Rita began throwing things at Aly: picture frames, books – and then, having dramatically summoned one of the household staff to fetch her a glass of orange juice, she flung the contents in Aly's face. Much to her distress, however, Aly steadfastly maintained his composure throughout, and finally it was Rita who broke down in tears of frustration. 'Darling! My darling!' he was heard to console her afterward, as prelude to what Williams described as 'a tender reconciliation.'

This was how it was with Rita and Aly: repeatedly, violent discord alternated with great tenderness. Years before, Rita had heard the story of Marlene Dietrich's troubles with Jean Gabin, who longed for the exciting star he had seen on screen, not the simple, devoted hausfrau Marlene wanted to be with the man she loved. Aly, too, seemed happiest with Rita not when she was herself, but when in a fit of temper she enacted his fantasy of the fiery Gilda.

Of course, in the end Rita went to Ascot – and to most of the other social and sporting events in Aly's restless itinerary. At least one of their evenings out, however, was entirely of Rita's design. In June 1950, shortly after Rita and

Aly celebrated their first wedding anniversary watching the horses at the Epsom Downs, Orson Welles was scheduled to open a new theatrical production to be performed in English in Paris, and Rita was anxious to surprise him by attending with the prince. The evening Welles had staged at the tiny Théâtre Edouard VII consisted of two parts: a little play he had written about Hollywood titled *The Unthinking Lobster*; and an adaptation of Marlowe's *Dr Faustus* called *Time Runs*. Welles's co-star was the fabulous Eartha Kitt, whom Aly's father, the Aga Khan, had enthusiastically declared the most exciting woman in Europe, on the basis of her nightclub act in Paris.

All heads in the compact auditorium spun around when Rita and Aly made their surprise entrance. Rita wore a chic black lace gown, and her long hair was caught up with diamond combs, while more diamonds glittered on her ears and wrists. The prince, in black tie, escorted his wife to their seats in the third row. Rita, however, found herself positioned directly behind a woman wearing a hat gaudily decorated with immense ostrich plumes, so that during the first part of the show, *The Unthinking Lobster*, Orson failed to see his ex-wife out in the audience. Nor did anyone back-stage mention her presence to him during the intermission. When he went on stage again to do *Time Runs*, the lady in ostrich feathers was gone, affording him a clear view of Rita smiling up at him from behind the empty second-row seat.

Orson had not seen Rita since the strange night in Cap d'Antibes when she had summoned him to propose that they remarry. So intensely did Orson stare at her now that the other spectators strained to see the object of his gaze. That evening the audience of *Time Runs* enjoyed two shows for the price of one. From the moment he spotted Rita, Welles did not take his eyes off her. 'Dr John Faustus,' Eartha Kitt (as Helen) addressed him, 'who then is this Margarita with whom you are so in love?'

'Margarita, Margarita,' said Orson, still gazing into Rita's eyes. 'Ah, yes, a girl that I have known.'

Rita laughed loudly and appreciatively at this, but her

current husband was understandably not amused and ended the evening in a pout.

The couple's troubles had become an open secret in Aly's European social set, but tensions did not really come to a head until Rita accompanied the prince on a visit to his and the Aga Khan's Ismaili followers in Africa. Sensitive to her enormous trepidation about functioning in this entirely unfamiliar new role as the wife of a Muslim religious leader, Aly tried to put her at ease by inviting two old friends from her Hollywood days, Welles's former business manager, Jackson Leighter, and his wife, Lola, to join them in Cairo. Becky and Yasmin, however, would have to be left behind in Cannes, where the baby would celebrate her first birthday with both parents absent.

Aly announced that as soon as he had fulfilled his obligations meeting with devotees in various Ismaili communities, he would take Rita on a romantic safari. But the prospect hardly appealed to Rita, who was miserable on the trip from start to finish. It was the same old story, only somehow worse this time: wherever they went in Africa Aly seemed to pay attention to everyone but her. Already, in Cairo, Rita angrily stormed out of a New Year's Eve Party after Aly neglected her and she was left to sit alone and forlorn for much of the evening. Her agonies of loneliness were even more extreme in Nairobi, where Aly was routinely gone much of the day, meeting with followers, while at night he unwound by playing bridge for hours on end with three Egyptians who traveled with him expressly for this purpose.

When she complained of her unhappiness, Aly suggested that perhaps after the safari she ought to consider accepting an occasional acting role back in Hollywood. Nor did he seem willing to drop the subject. After she declared to an interviewer in Nairobi that she didn't want to go back to work in film, Aly wasted no time in telling another interviewer in Zanzibar that both he and the Aga felt that Rita should indeed return to film acting if the right part were to come up. Having seen her marriage to Aly as the way out of Hollywood she had long been hoping for, Rita was appalled by his suddenly telling her – and the public! – that she really ought to return to work.

On the one hand, Aly may have genuinely thought that doing a film now and then would alleviate some of the general malaise that had plagued Rita since coming to Europe. But there also is a more cynical view: in pushing her to go back to work, he had his eye on the large sums of money Rita was capable of earning in Hollywood. Despite the atmosphere of enormous wealth in which the prince had lived from day to day, his father's basic control of the fortune had been known to leave Aly with what Elsa Maxwell would describe as a 'lack of money in the purse' – only when the Aga Khan died, it seemed, would Aly's perpetual money woes (exacerbated by gambling and a spendthrift mentality) come to an end.

Although, of course, the general perception was that Rita had married a very, very rich man – as indeed she had – a dear friend of hers like Hermes Pan would also note Aly's evident lack of compunction about spending *Rita's* money: 'Aly Khan spent her money like water,' Pan recalled. 'He spent practically a fortune of hers.'

Rita's dissatisfaction with Aly had been building for a long time. Finally, in Nairobi, she decided to walk out – much as she had walked out of the New Year's Eve party in Cairo – except that this time it was a good deal more serious. What she would bitterly call 'his playboy habits' had made it obvious that the sort of life she had hoped for with Aly was simply never going to materialize. He was off hunting when Rita sent him a note to say she was returning to the children in Cannes. Whereupon the prince suddenly appeared in Nairobi to talk it over. She claimed to be fatigued and to miss her girls after three months in Africa, but it was obvious that more was involved in her decision to go back early. Aly would later say that she told him she wanted to go to New York with the girls for two months and that he had agreed, but with two important stipulations: she was to wait until he returned from Africa, and she was *not* to take their baby daughter.

Whatever assurances Rita had given her husband in

Nairobi were soon forgotten in Cannes, where she packed up both daughters and fled the Château de l'Horizon on the very day that Aly's father, the Aga Khan, was due to arrive from Pakistan for a family reunion. Her timing had been no accident. 'Miss Hayworth somehow got it into her head that either Aly or I might try to take her daughter away from her, indeed, kidnap the child,' the Aga Khan would recall. Fearful that once the Aga Khan was on the scene she would never be allowed to take Yasmin with her to New York, Rita cloaked her departure in the utmost secrecy. She and girls quietly boarded a train for Paris, then made their way to Le Havre, where, on 25 March 1951, they set sail for New York.

Chapter Nineteen

Unbeknownst to Rita, the Aga Khan had her closely monitored from the second he learned that she and his grandchild Yasmin had left the Château de l'Horizon. Only much later would Rita learn from the prince's lawyer that the French authorities had secretly informed both Aly and the Aga Khan of her every move. Had Aly decided to stop Rita from taking Yasmin to New York against his wishes, the Aga Khan's influence with the French police would have made it simple to delay Rita's departure long enough for Aly to retrieve his daughter. As she fled Europe, Rita believed that Aly had no idea what she was doing. But the truth was that if he hadn't moved against her now it was entirely by choice. Long before the press phoned him in Cairo to 'inform' him that his wife and child were en route to America, Aly had been fully apprised of the situation. But he also knew that the Aga Khan wanted, above all, to avoid further scandal. Aly might be able to take Yasmin legally, but there would undoubtedly be more embarrassing headlines. And why bother risking all the bad publicity when it seemed most likely that in New York Rita would cool down soon enough and bring the child back on her own?

Besides, after the marital difficulties they had been experiencing, Aly plainly wanted some time to himself as much as Rita did. If she expected him to follow her to the United States in order to lure her back to the château – as, after all, he had done once before – Rita had badly misjudged. To the press, Aly pretended that Rita's abrupt departure was nothing out of the ordinary. Asked whether he would be joining her soon, he blithely replied that he might, but only after the racing season. For all his attempts to cover up, the press correctly detected trouble in the marriage, and even as Rita was on her way to America the papers there were filled with the news that the Love Goddess might be coming home for good.

To Harry Cohn, Rita's return was very good news indeed. Even before her boat had docked in New York harbor, Columbia was signaling its willingness to take her back. 'Columbia is ready to sit down and negotiate with Miss Hayworth, or Princess Rita, at any time,' the studio announced. 'Naturally, we have several properties in mind for her, but it's been hard to talk business when she's been seven thousand miles away.' Columbia could say no more than that, for Harry Cohn didn't know as yet whether Rita was really leaving the prince or just visiting New York. (At this point, she wasn't entirely certain herself.)

Later, when Cohn saw that Rita definitely had decided to end her marriage and that she was in dire financial straits, he would move quickly to take advantage of her desperation. But for the moment all he could do was wait and see – knowing all the while that the daily speculation about Rita in the press was drumming up immense new public interest in her. If he had set out to publicize Rita's impending return to Columbia, Harry Cohn could not have bought exposure of this magnitude.

On 2 April 1952, when Rita arrived in New York, the press was anxiously awaiting her at the gangplank (much as they had seen her off when she fled with Aly two years before). But this time she didn't try to dodge them. Although she denied that she was leaving Aly and returning to Hollywood, her obvious effort to make amends with the American press suggested otherwise. Asked whether she expected people in America to call her 'princess,' Rita shot back: 'I just want to be known as *Rita Hayworth*.' And then, to reassure everyone that she really was still just an all-American girl, she added: 'The first thing I'm going to do is have a hot dog.'

For all her efforts to win them over, however, some of the reporters made vicious fun of the faint English accent she appeared to have picked up in Europe. And although Rita adamantly refused to allow photographs to be taken of her two daughters, pictures of both Yasmin and Becky somehow appeared in the papers the next day.

Still, Rita's first meeting with reporters since returning to America had been successful on the whole. Whether or not Rita's marriage to Aly would make people forget the damaging scandals that had preceded it – and whether or not a divorce might simply tarnish her image anew – to judge by the extent to which her desire for a hot dog was reported in newspapers across the country, the impromptu press conference had been a good first step in winning back the sympathy of the American people.

Rita was hardly anxious at this point to go back to her old life in Hollywood. Had Aly come after her now, almost certainly she would have gone back to Europe with him. But Aly didn't even give the appearance of being upset. When he returned from Africa, it wasn't long before he was publicly living it up at the Cannes Film Festival. The Aga Khan may have wanted to avoid scandal, but that didn't stop Aly from being seen in public with an array of beautiful women. It was definitely not the response for which Rita would have hoped. In particular, Rita was nettled by pictures that began to appear in the papers of her husband with actress Joan Fontaine, who had earlier played Jane Eyre to Orson Welles's Mr Rochester. Finally, Rita could stand it no more. On 28 April 1951, Rita's lawyer Bartley Crum made the first move in what would be one of the most sensational, long-running divorce cases in Hollywood history. Rather than give Aly the usual courtesy of communicating with him privately through his attorneys, Rita's lawyer first made her intentions known to the press.

Aly could not have been pleased to learn through the European newspapers that his wife was filing for a legal separation. Reporters caught up with him the next day in Cannes, where he was attending a lunch for members of the French Legion of Honor at the Hôtel Martinez. Asked what he planned to do about Yasmin, he replied, 'I have nothing to say.' But that same day, 29 April 1951, he wrote to Rita from the Château de l'Horizon a conciliatory letter that, when she finally read it, would only enrage her all the more: the very opposite of what he had hoped.

My Darling One:

I must say I was not only surprised but very much grieved and unhappy, first by your decision to leave me, and secondly by the fact that you did not inform me before placing the matter in the hands of lawyers and that I heard about it first through the press.

All this is very unlike you, and I do not know what evil influences have been working on you – they can have no interest in your happiness or mine. I will never know why you let them break something that was so true and lasting . . .

Really you could not imagine that I was capable of doing anything to annoy you or to try and interfere with Yasmin, or otherwise, to make matters in any way disagreeable to you, however painful it is for myself.

I am terribly sad for two reasons: first, your decision, and secondly, your want of confidence in me and the way you have carried it out.

Now, of course, I will do as you wish.

If you want a legal separation, with the time wasted, etc., etc., you can have it. I certainly do not want to remarry or have any woman in my heart except yourself, so I do not want a divorce from my side.

Apparently, you yourself do not want to remarry, according to what the press says, so why not just be separated without any legal separation?

You will have the same freedom and you will have the same advantages. Even after a legal separation, you will not be able to marry without going through a divorce, and whenever you want to remarry, whether the separation is legal or friendly, I will let you have the divorce. As I have said already, I do not want to marry again, so a divorce does not interest me.

About our darling Yasmin, needless to say, whether it is

friendly or legal, I take the responsibility for all the expenses of her upbringing.

My only desire, which I do hope you will fulfill, in her interest as well as for the sake of the arrangements entered into at the time of her birth, is that you will bring her up in the Muslim religion, and that when she is seven years of age, and goes to school, you will allow her to spend part of her holidays with me.

As to her financial affairs, you are well aware that we are Muslims, and your lawyers will tell you that we are governed by Muslim law. Under Muslim law, a man cannot disinherit any of his heirs, nor can he give more to one son or daughter over another heir.

According to that law, whether I like it or not, Yasmin will inherit one-fifth of my property whatever happens and whatever that property may be.

However, in these days of Communism and world revolution, all property may disappear, but unless that comes to pass, she will inherit her part of whatever I may leave after my death. From every point of view I do not see the advantage to you of a legal separation, when your wishes are for me and will be for me in this connection, my law.

Please think it over and send me a telegram if you wish for a private and friendly separation. Your lawyer and my lawyer could make the arrangements by mutual consent and by a private deed with a gentleman's agreement that if you want a divorce later on, you can have it.

While this letter may read to you cold and businesslike, you can hardly imagine how terribly I feel your loss, and as long as there is a particle of hope, I for my part will not wish to lose it.

If in time your thoughts ever turn to me and the love I have always had and have for you, my arms are then open; should such a happy change come over your wishes, then the private separation, or for that matter the legal separation, could not prevent your light returning to my life. Aly.

By the time Aly's letter reached New York, however, Rita had already decamped for Nevada. Yasmin and Becky had been sent on ahead with a nanny to the eight-room house Rita had rented in Glenbrook, at Lake Tahoe, for the standard six-week residence period required to file for divorce in that state. To give herself plenty of time to think about what she was doing, on 1 May Rita and the Leighters set out from New York in a blue Packard convertible for a long, leisurely drive to Nevada.

Meanwhile, in France, the newspaper *L'Espoir* published a report that Aly was about to begin legal action to retrieve Princess Yasmin. The prince immediately demanded a retraction. Rita was already angry enough and he did not want to make her feel threatened with regard to their daughter.

Much as the Aga Khan was anxious to keep Aly's latest mess out of the public eye, even he felt compelled to speak out publicly to calm Rita down lest she take any rash steps concerning his granddaughter. The Aga Khan knew that Rita was actually quite fond of him personally, but greatly feared his power. Thus, his reassurance that she had nothing to fear from him might carry a good deal of weight. As he prepared to leave Geneva for the Egyptian wedding of King Farouk to Narriman Sadek, the Aga Khan issued a public statement that he hoped would reach his daughter-in-law, then en route to Lake Tahoe. He reassured her that they all still loved her very much and that he, for one, hoped that a divorce could be avoided.

'I very much hope there will be no divorce,' said the Aga Khan. 'Aly is very fond of Rita, and he would very much regret losing her. But his love for her is one reason why he would do anything he can to please her – even agree to a divorce.' And if there were a divorce, he continued, the only condition would be that Rita bring up Princess Yasmin as a Muslim. Here, then, was the key issue – the one that required the greatest delicacy. 'If Rita settles in California,' the Aga Khan explained, 'there should be no difficulty about that, because there are many Muslim missions there. Rita is a very sensible girl. I am sure she will have no objections to bringing her daughter up in the Muslim faith.' To which the Aga Khan added that Aly would also want Yasmin to be permitted to visit him now and then. Clearly, the wise old man realized that in her fear

231

of losing her daughter Rita might in turn try to keep Yasmin from Aly and his family. Hence the need for him to speak out in his most diplomatic tone.

Meanwhile, the object of such great fears on both sides, Princess Yasmin, was already in Lake Tahoe, where a French maid would watch the baby in her carriage as Becky Welles played alone on the beach. 'I'll be happy when Mother arrives,' the elder child was heard to say. But, anxious to sort things out before actually filing for divorce, Rita was taking her time.

Although she registered in hotels along the way as 'Mrs A. Khan,' she went mostly unrecognized. On the few occasions when people inquired if she was Rita Hayworth, she denied it. At one point, in Nevada, a police car pulled her over in the desert and she was certain that she was about to get a ticket, but in fact the officers had recognized the woman they remembered as the Love Goddess and just wanted to say hello.

Finally, on 10 May, Rita and the Leighters pulled up in front of her new house, overlooking Lake Tahoe. 'Mommy! Mommy!' cried Becky, as she ran across the lawn to greet her. Rita hugged her eldest daughter, then picked up Yasmin and held her in her arms. She had mulled over a great many things on the way there. For the moment she had decided that she would go along with the Aga Khan's wishes to raise Yasmin as a Muslim. But neither the Aga nor Aly would be pleased with her other decision. Four days later, on 14 May, her lawyer Bartley Crum announced in New York that Rita would file for divorce and asked Aly to set up a $3,000,000 trust fund for Yasmin.

The conciliatory letter Aly had written to Rita had been published in its entirety in the French press – and the day after Crum announced that Rita would indeed be filing for divorce, Aly's letter appeared in the American papers as well. When Rita had refused to respond to his letter, Aly himself had leaked it to the French press in hopes that it would put to rest any fears about his intentions regarding Rita or the child. Rita, however, found the letter self-serving. It seemed to her that Aly was merely trying to avoid antagonizing the Aga Khan with the scandal of a noisy divorce case played out in the press. As far as Rita was concerned, it wasn't really a reconciliation that Aly seemed to want, but a quiet separation that would allow him to safely carry on his womanizing, as he had done in his first marriage. Rita was determined not to condone such an arrangement. Thus, following Crum's announcement, Rita settled in for the required six weeks of residence in Nevada.

For their second wedding anniversary, on 27 May 1951, Aly sent her two dozen roses with a note saying 'Remember me?' But Rita held her ground – she remembered him only too well! However brave and determined a front she put on in public, she was terribly upset and confused about her future. Now that she had decided to end her marriage to Aly, what would she do? The time she had spent with him in Europe had left her virtually penniless, so that she had to borrow $25,000 from her agent to tide her over.

Bob Schiffer, her longtime devoted friend, came to keep her company in Nevada, where he rented a cabin just down the road from her house. Schiffer found her confused, frightened, unsure. 'Rita was pretty lonely then,' he recalled, 'and tremendously lost. She didn't know what to do with her life or what direction to go in. She didn't know whether to resume her career, or whether she *had* a career.' Her memories of Europe were not happy ones. 'She told me that she had been like a frightened little girl at L'Horizon. She just wanted to be with her old friends now.'

Early in June Rita's lawyer Bartley Crum flew to Paris to open negotiations with Aly and his lawyer Charles Torem. At the first meeting of the opposing attorneys at Coudert Brothers in Paris, it soon became evident that the $3,000,000 trust fund that Rita wanted for Yasmin was out of the question – and that in fact Aly wasn't there to discuss a divorce at all but to press for the reconciliation that would be more acceptable to his father. Rita was not asking for alimony, but she did insist on a substantial settlement for her daughter.

After the meeting, Aly's lawyer Torem said that the $3,000,000 demand must be a 'mistake' and called the amount 'silly,' while for his part Crum announced that despite Aly's desire for a reconciliation Rita fully intended to go through with the divorce. 'We want a financial settlement for the little one that will be the same as the settlements Aly Khan made on his two sons by a former marriage,' Crum insisted. Rita, he said (with an eye toward American public opinion), was 'only insisting on "equal rights for women" in that she wants her daughter to have the same settlement as Aly Khan's sons had.' As to the issue of Yasmin's religious training, Crum declared that Rita would comply with her husband's wishes that Yasmin be raised as a Muslim – but already there appeared the first small sign of resistance: the suggestion that Rita didn't really want to. 'Miss Hayworth promised this when she was married,' Crum went on. 'She will not go back on her word. She may be reluctant to keep it in this case, but she will keep it.' Finally Crum announced that meetings would continue in Paris the following week after he had taken care of other business in Israel.

Before Crum left Paris for Israel he caught Aly in compromising circumstances that seriously undermined the prince's claim that he genuinely wanted to reconcile with Rita. It was the kind of ridiculous and self-destructive indiscretion that the prince committed all too frequently (almost as if he were torn between a desire to please his demanding father and another simply to attract his attention any way he could). Thus, only a few hours after Aly had expressed the wish to reconcile with his wife and implored Crum to see if Rita would possibly meet him in the Caribbean to talk face to face, he turned up at Club Florence, a fashionable Montmartre night spot, in the company of his lady friend of the moment, Joan Fontaine. And who should he see already seated with friends at a table there but Bartley Crum. There was considerable discomfort on both sides, with the prince desperately pretending that he wasn't really with the beautiful actress. But the most unfortunate result was that Rita grew enraged when the stories of the embarrassing encounter appeared in the papers. Once more she felt that Aly had publicly humiliated her. As far as she was concerned, nothing he said was to be believed anymore. When she received word of Aly's proposal to meet in the Caribbean, she angrily cabled her lawyer to refuse on her behalf and to press on with the divorce.

A day later Rita was plunged into a new crisis when the local district attorney, the sheriff, and deputy sheriff arrived unexpectedly at her door to inform her that from this moment on seven policemen were being assigned to protect her household from a kidnapping gang that had targeted Becky and Princess Yasmin. Already the armed guards were on duty at Rita's private beach since the kidnappers were rumored to be planning to arrive suddenly by boat, snatch the children, and flee across the lake.

Rita burst into tears at the sight of the guards. By taking the children to America, had she suddenly exposed them to new dangers? Would she be able to protect them on her own? Although the police were there to guard her and the children, even their presence seemed like an invasion to her. The district attorney, Jack Streeter, explained that he had just been in Florida, where at Miami's McAllister Hotel he had encountered local criminals who seemed far too interested in Rita's much-publicized presence in Lake Tahoe. Without knowing that Streeter was himself a district attorney, they went on to demonstrate suspiciously intimate knowledge of precisely where Rita and the children would be staying in Lake Tahoe. One of the hoods even remarked that 'Little Yasmin would be worth a lot of money.' Hence the immediate assignment of the seven policemen, who also patrolled the forest behind the house lest the kidnappers try to emerge from there. It had been widely reported that Rita was traveling with $250,000 worth of jewelry, so to protect herself against thieves she had the jewels deposited in a vault.

As if all this were not enough, Rita had yet another

major pressure with which to contend: Harry Cohn. For the moment, she was alone and vulnerable – just the way he liked her. Knowing the confusion and anxiety that she must be experiencing, Cohn shrewdly used her fears about how the American public would receive her to pressure Rita to give up the right to script approval, specified in her Beckworth contract, that had been such a sore point between them before. Anxious as Cohn may have been for her to get back to work, when they talked on the telephone he seemed pessimistic about the effect all the publicity surrounding her divorce would have on her film career. He wanted it to seem almost as if he were doing her a favor by taking her back.

Despite the cache of jewelry with which she had arrived at Tahoe, Rita found herself swiftly running out of funds. Money was so short that, toward the end of her stay in Nevada, she moved her little family to a smaller, less expensive house near the Glenbrook Inn. With bills piling up it was evident that, much as she dreaded it, she would soon have to return to Hollywood.

Although the sole purpose of making herself a Nevada resident had been to file for divorce in that state, she suddenly hesitated to go through with the legal proceedings against Aly. The reality of actually going back to work had finally hit her. What would it be like returning to a life – and an image – that she thought she had escaped forever when she married Aly? By not filing for divorce immediately, Rita was leaving her options open as she headed for her first face-to-face confrontation with Harry Cohn on his turf since she ran off in 1948.

Chapter Twenty

*O*n the afternoon of 5 July 1951, Rita and the girls pulled up the driveway of the Beverly Hills Hotel, where she had reserved a three-bedroom bungalow under an assumed name. The hotel switchboard operator was instructed to tell anyone who inquired that Rita Hayworth was not a guest there. But as Rita slept deeply one movieland reporter located her at the hotel and tricked a maid into letting her into the Love Goddess's bungalow. Before long, without Rita's knowledge, the reporter had taken Becky and Yasmin out of the bungalow to get some good photos of them. When Rita woke up and realized what had happened she went wild – understandably so. What if, instead of the reporter, it had been the kidnappers who had come into the bungalow and taken the children? Only a month before, the threat of kidnapping had been deemed so serious that the authorities in Lake Tahoe had surrounded Rita's house with armed guards. Suddenly a total stranger had stolen into her home and taken the children while Rita slept, entirely unaware that anything was wrong.

Beverly Hills Chief of Police C.H. Anderson arrived at the bungalow not long afterward to offer to post guards similar to those who had protected the children in Lake Tahoe, but Rita declined the offer. Instead, the hotel put a single armed guard at her door, while a motor-cycle cop was stationed behind her bungalow.

But the men who faithfully guarded her residence were no protection against what Rita perceived as the major threat against her youngest daughter – that somehow the Aga Khan would manage to spirit her away and keep her in Europe. More and more Rita began to feel threatened even by the demand that Yasmin be raised as a Muslim. Before this her lawyer had registered no objection to Aly's stipulations about his daughter's religious education, but suddenly Crum was saying publicly that it remained to be determined 'whether Yasmin can grow up as an ordinary American girl, drinking ice-cream sodas, or whether she has to have the special upbringing of a Muslim princess.' In part, of course, this was a tactic aimed at gaining public sympathy in America for Rita: surely most Americans would favor the child's being brought up as 'an ordinary American girl', as opposed to the dark and unnamed mysteries of what they might imagine a Muslim upbringing to be like.

The change in Rita's position on Yasmin's religious upbringing also represented her growing fears of somehow losing her own child, and would eventually develop into a full-fledged obsession with keeping her away from Aly and his family. As the subsequent behavior of both Aly and the Aga Khan would clearly demonstrate, there was no question that either of them planned in any way to take the child from her mother. Still, this was Rita's greatest fear: the single most important motive for much of her often peculiar and mercurial behavior in the divorce negotiations that followed.

When Aly sent his Paris lawyer, Charles Torem, to California to propose that Rita put off taking any legal action for six months, she said that she would do so only if he in turn agreed that, should she finally go through with the divorce, he would appear in the Nevada court. Her request was dictated by her fears about Yasmin. Only if Aly (or a representative) appeared in the Nevada court would the divorce automatically be recognized in Europe. With Aly's presence, any agreement concerning the child's custody reached in the Nevada court would subsequently be binding in Europe as well. Should Aly decide *not* to appear, or to send an emissary, however, the divorce Rita won in Nevada might well not be recognized in Europe. And should his daughter set foot on European soil, Aly would be within his legal rights to assert that Rita had never been legally awarded custody of Yasmin. Again, there is no evidence whatsoever that Aly ever even considered doing something like this, but Rita feared that he or his father would take the child from her if the opportunity presented itself, and throughout the divorce and custody proceedings she acted accordingly.

Before long Rita decided to reject Aly's proposal to put off filing for divorce for six months. By mid-August it became obvious that he simply wouldn't hear of the $3,000,000 settlement she was asking for Yasmin. Speaking on Rita's behalf, Bartley Crum once again sought to attract the sympathy of the American public by charging that Aly didn't want to give Yasmin the money because he had 'an old Eastern idea that girls aren't so valuable as boys.' According to her lawyer, in asking for $3,000,000 for Yasmin, Rita was actually 'battling for women's rights' by demanding equal treatment for their daughter.

It did not help Aly's cause that, in mid-August, the talk of Europe was the black eye he had received in Deauville from the Belgian industrialist husband of a beautiful woman with whom he'd been flirting. Later, when Aly turned up in South America, ostensibly to persuade Rita to allow him to fly up to the U.S. for a visit with his daughter, the reports of his romance with a young actress in Rio de Janeiro were most unlikely to win back his wife's sympathy or trust.

As the summer drew to a close Rita finally decided to head for the divorce court in Reno, where on 1 September 1951, she charged the prince with 'extreme cruelty, entirely mental in character.' In addition to a divorce she requested that the court grant her custody of Yasmin, with proper visiting privileges to be accorded to the prince. On the same day that she filed her suit, the Nevada court issued a summons to Prince Aly Khan in France. The prince was ordered to appear in Nevada within thirty days from the date that he received the summons. If the prince failed to come to Nevada, the court would consider him in default and Rita would have only to come back to Reno once more and to make her divorce final.

Eventually, much as she had feared, Aly did indeed fail to respond to the summons that had been served to him in Cannes. Although Rita could have made her divorce final at any time, she waited a year and a half to do so. With neither the $3,000,000 she was asking for, nor the legal assurance that Aly could not snatch her daughter from her in Europe, Rita viewed the Nevada divorce decree as a hollow victory.

Rita's messy divorce negotiations with Aly were much in the American press when she returned to work at Columbia for the first time in three years, and only naturally there was a great deal of curiosity about her at the studio. Her co-workers were anxious to see if life as a princess had changed her at all. But according to Earl Bellamy, before long everyone agreed that she was much the same Rita they remembered. She may have arrived back in New York with a faint English accent, but by the time she returned to work at Columbia there was virtually no trace left of her glamorous life abroad – except of course, that she had two daughters now, instead of one.

Eager to cash in on the immense publicity that her return to Hollywood was attracting, Cohn wanted to get Rita in front of the cameras immediately. When he assigned her to appear in a new film to be directed by Vincent Sherman, *Affair in Trinidad*, Cohn didn't even have a finished script in hand. Even as the first day of shooting approached, Cohn had only sixty pages of a rough draft to show her. Justifiably suspicious that all was not well with the project, Rita refused to begin shooting until there was a finished script for her to read. Whereupon Cohn promptly suspended her – which he had every right to do, since, as he correctly pointed out, she had just signed away her right to script approval. It was her responsibility to do any project he assigned her, no matter how objectionable. In fact, even Cohn admitted that the story idea the studio had for *Affair in Trinidad* was absolutely awful, but his business sense told him that even a bad film could make money for Columbia as long as the public interest in Princess Rita remained high.

After he suspended her, Rita decided that perhaps she would drop her objection to doing the picture if in exchange Cohn would free her from her Columbia contract. Although at first he seemed to agree to this, Cohn quickly changed his mind. Why negotiate with Rita when he knew that if he kept her on suspension long enough she would sooner or later run out of cash and have to come back to work for him anyway?

It was the *Lona Hanson* battle all over again (the script that had driven Rita to run off to Europe with Aly) – except this time Cohn had her renegotiated contract on his side. To put still more pressure on Rita, Cohn gleefully took the matter to the press. Once again she found herself painted as frivolously wasting the studio's money by refusing to report for work. Citing both *Lona Hanson* and *Affair in Trinidad*, the studio publicly complained that it had 'more than $800,000 invested in properties in which she has failed to appear.' After this Rita feared that if she continued to protest, the industry might rise against her again, as it had at the time of *Lona Hanson*. With two children to support she could ill afford to be branded recalcitrant. Even if she did eventually get out of her Columbia contract, the other studios might hesitate to hire her. What else could she do but return to work and take her chances on *Affair in Trinidad*?

During this period Rita began to date again. 'She seemed to drift in and out of men,' recalled Bob Schiffer. 'It was a *need*.'

Although she publicly denied it when they were photographed dining at Ciro's, Rita had a brief romance with Kirk Douglas, but he quickly broke things off between them. 'I felt something deep within her that I couldn't help – loneliness, sadness – something that would pull me down. I had to get away,' said Douglas.

And there was an intense love affair with the urbane

agent-producer Charles Feldman. Still, her most meaningful relationship was doubtless the long-term bond she
shared with Schiffer himself, who remained mostly in the
shadows. Tall, athletic, and ruggedly handsome, Schiffer
was far more to Rita than just the casual companion people
often presumed him to be. No matter what was happening
in her life, or with whom she was ostensibly having a
romance, Bob was always there for her when she needed
him.

One day, during her affair with Charles Feldman,
Schiffer was having a few drinks with Rita when her boy-
friend of the moment came calling at her house on North
Alpine Drive, in Beverly Hills. When the doorbell rang
Rita wondered how she was going to explain Bob's
presence. 'What am I going to do with you?' she asked
Schiffer in a panic.

'Tell him I'm Thor Heyerdahl of Norway,' Schiffer
laughed, referring to the author of the new and popular
book *Kon Tiki*, which he had just been reading. 'And tell
him that I don't speak English.'

'Oh, that's crazy!' Rita answered, also laughing.

'Speak to me in Spanish,' Schiffer went on.

The doorbell rang again and Rita went to answer it.

'Remember,' Schiffer reminded her, 'I don't speak *any*
English at all. That's all you have to tell him.'

Rita greeted Feldman and precisely as Bob had coached
her, explained that he didn't speak English and that his
name was 'Thor Something-or-other.' 'Heyerdahl!
Heyerdahl!' Schiffer chimed in.

'Thor Heyerdahl!' the agent exclaimed. Then to Rita:
'Don't you know who he is?'

'No,' said Rita, trying to keep a straight face. 'I don't
know the guy. I just met him.'

'Jesus Christ! Come in here,' said Feldman, ushering
Rita into the next room. 'I want to sign that guy! You've
got to help me talk to him!'

Meanwhile, Schiffer remembered the one bit of Norwegian he had ever heard, a curse word, and when Feldman and Rita came back, he kept repeating the word over

and over, but of course the agent had no idea what he was saying.

As the agent proceeded to try to sign up 'Thor Heyerdahl', Rita spoke to Bob in Spanish, and he in turn explained that the Norwegian word he kept repeating was an expletive. Rita could barely keep a straight face and finally rushed off into the next room to dissolve into hysterical laughter. But Bob kept up the masquerade throughout, and the agent never guessed who he had really met and how very well Rita knew him.

Bob Schiffer was one of the few people in her life with whom Rita could always be herself and not pretend that she was someone else. 'She was game to do anything except fly,' recalled Schiffer, with whom Rita spent many an idyllic hour sailing, just to get away from it all. When Harry Cohn decided to put her back to work immediately after she finished shooting *Affair in Trinidad*, she secretly turned to Schiffer to help her escape – he would understand.

Work had already begun on her next picture, *Salome*, a dreadful Technicolor extravaganza, but all Rita wanted to do was to get away. 'Screw this,' she suddenly told Bob, during preparations for *Salome*, and he instantly knew what she meant.

'I feel the same way as you do,' he replied.

'Let's get the hell out of here,' said Rita. 'Who wants to make movies?'

They drove a station wagon all the way to Acapulco and weren't heard from for days. Needless to say, Cohn was furious about his star's sudden disappearance in the middle of work.

Rita's unhappiness in Hollywood was exacerbated by a new and disturbing factor. Like a great many other people in the film industry at the time, Rita was suddenly being closely scrutinized on account of prior political activity. This of course was the period of the full-fledged Hollywood Red scare, of the reopened House Un-American Activities Committee, of informers and blacklists: a time of widespread fear, distrust, and betrayal in the movie business.

On 28 May 1951, shortly after Rita returned to

America, the FBI prepared a list of all current contract players at Columbia Pictures, with an 'X' placed next to those names for which FBI indexes disclosed prior political activity of a suspect nature. A copy of this list would appear in Rita Hayworth's FBI file, with the damning 'X' marked beside her name. Whereupon the FBI assembled a detailed dossier on Rita's political associations dating back to the time of her marriage to Orson Welles. At length, Columbia Vice-President B.B. Kahane would ask Rita for a statement 'under oath' to account for why she had lent her name to a variety of left-wing groups and causes. Wrote Kahane: 'The statement should set forth the fact (if, as I assume, it is a fact) that she is not and never has been a member of the Communist Party. It should also contain a positive, forthright affirmation of her loyalty to the United States and I hope, a strong condemnation of Communistic subversive groups and ideologies.'

Eventually, at the behest of her attorneys, the studio would settle for a written 'statement' from her, in lieu of 'a private loyalty oath.' Nonetheless Rita felt under siege again (as indeed she was), and once more she dreamed of escape, whether to Mexico for a few days with Bob, or back to Europe . . .

For some time she had been steadfastly refusing Aly's overtures toward reconciliation, but now the news from Europe caused her to reconsider. The Aga Khan had suffered a heart attack while visiting his devotees in India and had been swiftly flown back to France for medical treatment. Meanwhile, Aly had been carousing in South America, where a particularly wild party he had thrown in Argentina had scandalized local Ismailis. But when he heard about his father, the prince rushed to his side.

Hitherto Rita hadn't even wanted to talk to Aly, but now she found herself telephoning him to see if he was all right. Rita knew only too well how complicated Aly's feelings about his father were. Too often in the past Aly had failed to live up to the Aga Khan's expectations. Aly's breakup with Rita, his ill-concealed womanizing, and most recently his irresponsible behavior in Argentina had embarrassed his father. Now it was of the utmost importance for Aly to serve his seriously ailing father well in the East, where the Aga Khan had asked him to take his place touring Ismaili communities.

Once more Aly proposed to Rita that she come back to him. More than ever her calling off the divorce action would put the Aga Khan's mind at rest. The prince dispatched his lawyer to meet with Rita, but, as in the past, she resisted Aly's overtures. Still her desire not to make things any more dificult for him after the Aga Khan's heart attack kept Rita from making the divorce final just then. Elated by the good news, the prince began regularly telephoning Rita in Los Angeles. Before long she had agreed to his flying to the States for a brief visit with Yasmin. The prince was thrilled. Even if Aly couldn't persuade her to call off the divorce altogether, at least the Aga Khan would see him earnestly trying to bring about a reconciliation.

Chapter Twenty-one

*I*f Aly were as anxious as he claimed to win Rita back, his actions upon arriving in New York were peculiar, to say the least. He and his valet, Tutti, had sailed from Europe on the liner *United States*. Before going on to Los Angeles he told Rita that he would be spending a few days in Saratoga Springs, New York, where twenty of the Aga Khan's horses were being offered at the annual yearling sales. What he didn't tell her was that while in New York, he also had arranged to spend several nights with the beautiful actress Yvonne De Carlo, with whom he had begun an affair in France, after Rita's departure. The French press had even run photos of them together captioned 'Watch Out, Rita – I've Got Your Man,' that, as De Carlo noted, Aly 'seemed to enjoy.'

Fortunately for Aly, no member of the press stumbled upon him with De Carlo in New York; but several hundred curiosity-seekers showed up when he arrived at the airport in Los Angeles to watch Aly and his 175 pounds of luggage (including five immense packages of toys) being driven away to the home of producer Jack Warner. There Aly quickly showered and shaved, then dashed off for his long-awaited reunion with his two-and-a-half-year-old daughter – whom he had last seen more than a year and a half ago.

Both Yasmin and Becky had lately been suffering from whooping cough, but neither had a fever. Rita allowed them to stay up later than usual to see the prince. Evidently he was quite nervous as he approached the house on North

Alpine Drive because he told the chauffeur that he'd be back in a few minutes. Although Rita had agreed to the visit, there was no telling how long she would let him stay. Aly hadn't yet knocked on the front door when Rita's secretary opened it and showed him into the sitting room, where his estranged wife was waiting. Whatever anxiety both of them may have felt before seeing each other again, the reunion went smoothly enough that Aly stayed for more than five hours.

By two A.M. it looked as if Aly might be allowed to spend the night. Rita sent her houseboy outside to tell the prince's driver not to wait. But just half an hour later Aly drove himself home in a car borrowed from Rita's servant. At the last minute Rita had changed her mind and pulled back. After he left she didn't get to bed until three in the morning and slept late the following day, when Aly came back for lunch with her and the children.

That evening Aly had arranged to dine with a friend (Rita had failed to invite him back for dinner), but the prince had not yet gone out when he received a frantic call from Rita. He had not expected to hear from her and could tell at once that something terrible had happened. At about eight P.M. the governess had gone in to check on Becky and Yasmin, who had been sent to bed. On the floor near Yasmin's bed lay an empty box of sleeping pills. The doctor had prescribed them to help her sleep until she got over the whooping cough. To the governess's horror the box was empty and neither she nor Rita knew how many tablets were missing. According to Rita, when Yasmin found the box in her bedroom she thought they were peppermint candies. Rita told Aly that she was going to rush the child to Santa Monica Receiving Hospital. Could he meet them there?

Aly got to the hospital first. Only a few hours before, he had been overjoyed to be spending time with his beautiful little daughter, and suddenly he feared for her life. When Rita and the governess rushed in with Yasmin, the little girl was the only one who didn't seem distraught. She sucked on a red lollipop and coughed occasionally; otherwise, she seemed fine. By contrast, both Aly and Rita looked anxious and overwrought. Not knowing how many pills the child had swallowed had thrown them into a panic.

Aly was a bit short-tempered with a nurse about getting the child treated immediately, but his impatience was understandable under the circumstances. Before long the doctor in attendance lowered a rubber tube into her throat to wash Yasmin's stomach. Meanwhile Rita was much too anxious and upset to stay inside the building. In an alleyway near the hospital entrance she nervously paced back and forth until the stomach pumping was completed. For about twenty minutes Aly dashed between his wife and his daughter. Although Yasmin cried a bit when the rubber tube was inserted, she appeared basically in good spirits. But Rita required substantial help from Aly to soothe her agitated nerves. Although he was tense and anxious himself, he quickly pulled himself together to convince Rita that everything would be all right. For the first time in a long time there was suddenly a spark of love and understanding between them. He was plainly trying to give her the kind of concern and attention that she needed.

The crisis had dissolved their old animosities, and suddenly they were a couple again. An hour and fifteen minutes after the governess had discovered the empty pillbox, the doctor informed Rita and Aly that Yasmin was in no danger. She seemed to have ingested only a few of the tablets. Presently they would be able to take her home.

For Rita and Aly the crisis was over, but the bond that had been forged between them remained. He had been there for her when Rita needed him and she was very grateful. What if she had had to deal with the crisis alone? Hours before she had seemed keen to keep Aly at a distance, but now all that had changed. Suddenly she was every bit as anxious for a reconciliation as he.

After attending the races in Del Mar, Aly came for a roast chicken dinner with Rita and the children on Sunday night. The prince had told Rita that he was on a diet, so she instructed the cook not to serve the hot biscuits that she made most Sundays. It was obvious that they were behaving as a family again. Rita had always gotten along better with Aly on her own turf, far away from the outside social pressures that had driven them apart in Europe. There were no other guests at Rita's, as there almost always were at the Château de l'Horizon or at Aly's other homes; it was just the four of them – Aly, Rita, and the girls. That was the way Rita liked it best.

On 20 August Rita and Aly had a quiet farewell lunch at the Naples Café, an Italian restaurant near Columbia where Rita was still working on *Salome*. Later that day Aly and Tutti were to fly to Chicago, then on to Kentucky to see a number of horses he and the Aga Khan owned. Rita and the prince had an understanding that in September, as soon as she was finished at the studio, she would join him in Europe to see if they were still getting along as well as they had in Los Angeles. Beyond agreeing to go to France, Rita made no other promises.

Aly wanted to see his daughter again, but still Rita wouldn't bring her. That she insisted on going to France alone suggested that she wasn't entirely certain that the reconciliation attempt would be successful. If the old troubles erupted between them again, Rita wanted to avoid the risk of not being able to bring her daughter back to the States afterward. Her fears that the Aga Khan would try to keep the child were clearly still as strong as ever. Once before she had had to sneak the child out of France – or believed she had to – and she didn't want to go through all that again.

Planning to tell Aly that she had decided to drop the divorce proceedings for the time being, Rita set sail for France in mid-September on the liner *United States*. When the ship docked at Le Havre on 24 September 1952, she was immensely disappointed to discover that instead of coming himself to meet her, Aly had sent Tutti to pick her up. If he were all that anxious for her arrival, wouldn't he have come personally to greet her? This was hardly the warmth and kindness that had won her heart back in Los Angeles. Nor, to her utter amazement, was Aly waiting to greet her when they reached his house in Neuilly, the chic

Paris suburb. He had left word with the servants that business had detained him in Cannes. To make matters worse, the house was already filled with the customary assortment of guests who had always so terribly irritated Rita in the past: the very opposite of the intimate, romantic homecoming she expected. If Aly really wanted to reconcile, wouldn't it have been more sensible to spend some time alone together? The presence in the house of all the other people, coupled with Aly's rather mysterious absence, did not bode well.

Rita spent her first night in Europe in bed alone. The next morning she instructed the servants to tell anyone who inquired that she was resting and could not be disturbed. Finally, late that evening, the prince arrived from Cannes, and although they did indeed spend the night together, the next morning Rita was said to be indisposed again, and Aly went off alone to have lunch with friends. He explained her absence by saying that she had a cold.

Although the reunion was by no means going as she had hoped, Rita agreed to announce publicly that she wasn't proceeding with the divorce for now. In the past Aly had always sought to protect her from the press as much as possible, but this time he seemed suspiciously anxious to invite reporters and photographers into the house for Rita's big announcement. She later said that she felt as if he had set her up: from the first, the entire reconciliation had been staged for the press, so that the Aga Khan would read it in the papers and feel satisfied that for once Aly had handled himself well.

After Rita made the announcement, Aly proceeded to carry on socially much as he would have if she hadn't been there. On the day of Europe's premier horse race, the Prix de l'Arc de Triomphe, Rita said she wasn't in the mood to go, but Aly went anyway. Asked where his wife was, Aly explained that he and Rita each had their own business and way of life, and had decided not to interfere with each other. They might be husband and wife, but if Rita didn't want to attend the races, why shouldn't Aly go alone? And so, he seemed to suggest, it would be in all things.

In all this Aly had evidently hoped to please his father, but even now he failed miserably. Soon the Aga Khan had heard all about how desperately unhappy Rita was with Aly's behavior. While her husband made a great point of accepting invitations that he must have known Rita would decline, she moped dejectedly at home. The Aga Khan was particularly dismayed to learn that Rita had frequently been observed crying while Aly was out unabashedly carousing with other women. If Rita was gravely disappointed with this travesty of a reconciliation, so was the Aga Khan, who angrily asked Elsa Maxwell what she thought the matter was with his son. 'Can't he at least keep away from the blondes and the brunettes while Rita is here?' he lamented.

Much as he may have wanted to, the Aga Khan had no way of placating Rita, who steadfastly refused to go and see him. As she explained to her lawyer, Bartley Crum, she was, quite simply, 'scared' to pay a visit to the Aga Khan. Unlike his son, he was such a powerful, awe-inspiring figure. Face to face, how would she find it in herself to refuse him if he implored her to go back to his son or to send Yasmin to Europe for a visit? The last time, rather than face the Aga Khan, she had fled in secret on the very day he and the Begum had returned to Cannes from Pakistan. At all costs she was determined to avoid him this time as well.

Things came to a head the night Aly gave a small dinner party in honor of Rita's homecoming. By then, however, she was enraged by the all-too-public humiliation to which he had subjected her and decided to pay him back by failing to show up at the dinner. Her husband waited an hour before ordering the food to be served, even though Rita was nowhere to be found. After dinner an excursion to the chic Parisian nightclub Jimmie's had been planned. When Aly's party arrived there they encountered Rita, who had gone nightclubbing with two strange men whom the prince had never seen before. If Aly was going to proceed independently with his life, so would she. Not only had Rita embarrassed him by failing to show up for her own dinner party, but for the rest of the tense evening she and her male companions steered clear of Aly's group in the nightclub.

It had become all too clear to Rita that Aly wanted a public reconciliation, not a genuine one: a marriage in name only. She had been lured to Paris merely to put on a good show for the Aga Khan. Public appearances such as the meeting with reporters in Neuilly and even that night's outing at Jimmie's were designed to give the press an opportunity to see and photograph Rita and Aly together. At Jimmie's, however, by publicly and unabashedly spending the evening with two mystery men, rather than with her husband and his guests, Rita had offered the press quite a different view from the one Aly had planned for them to see.

On Friday, 3 October 1952, less than a week after Rita had told the press that she planned to drop the divorce action against Aly, Rita moved out of his house in Neuilly and into the Hôtel Lancaster, in Paris. Evidently embarrassing Aly in the nightclub hadn't been sufficient revenge for her. She wanted to be certain that the Aga Khan heard that the reconciliation was off and that her statements of the previous week were canceled. Thus, she summoned her Paris attorney, Suzanne Blum, for lunch at the Lancaster. Through the lawyer, Rita would make her side of the story public. She said that although Aly had asked her not to divorce him 'for family reasons,' she had decided to proceed with the Reno suit nonetheless. 'He is a playboy, while I work all year round in Hollywood,' Rita explained. 'What's more, Aly spends too much, while I have to work for the two of us.' Rita also expressed her sense of having been used during her unhappy week in France: 'When I come to Paris, it isn't to live in a house where there are eighty friends of all kinds coming and going, and it is not to dine at Maxim's,' she told the attorney. 'I don't leave Hollywood to be photographed in the salons of Paris or at dinner in big restaurants.' Next, Rita touched on the issue that would occupy her and her ex-husband for many months to come: Yasmin. 'The main thing I'm worried about is Yasmin,' Rita told the attorney. 'I don't want any of his money in order to provide for her upkeep. I'll renounce all such claims just so long as I can keep her.'

This last statement was extremely significant, for although Rita would indeed seek a proper financial settlement for their daughter, money would never be the main point of contention. Throughout the protracted struggle that followed, Rita's principal concern would always be keeping Aly and the Aga Khan from somehow wresting Yasmin away from her.

On Monday, 6 October, when Blum made public what Rita had told her, Aly could harbor no more illusions about the success of his sham reconciliation. It was no secret in Paris that the Aga Khan soon told Aly that he was merely making himself look foolish again, and that he should get off the front pages as soon as possible by expediting the divorce.

In the meantime, after Rita had summoned Bartley Crum to fly to Paris to confer with Aly's legal representatives, she impulsively took a train to Madrid. Paris had been the scene of too much unhappiness during the past week, and she wanted to unwind. No sooner had she arrived in Madrid, however, than she was confronted by a demonstration of Catholic Actionists who angrily demanded that she leave town at once on account of her 'immoral conduct' with the prince. Police were called in to curb the anti-Rita demonstrators. All in all it was hardly an auspicious beginning for what was to have been a vacation away from the problems that had besieged her in France.

For someone who had been greeted with a demonstration protesting her presence in Madrid, Rita made little attempt to conceal her love life there. After the pain and rejection to which Aly had just exposed her, Rita seemed to crave attention and reassurance from other men – principal among them Aly's friend, the dashing Count José-Maria ('Pepe') Villapadierna. Before long it was the talk of Madrid that Rita was turning down all other invitations in order to spend her time entirely with Pepe. On 5 November Crum called Rita in Madrid to warn her to be more discreet. The lawyer feared a public backlash against

253

Rita if she continued to flaunt her love life. It was imperative for the divorce negotiations that Rita maintain her image as the wronged wife. Despite the attorney's warning, however, Rita continued to attract news coverage by openly traveling about Spain with Pepe – and subsequently she even appeared with him in Paris, where she postponed returning to the States so that they could be together a while longer.

This was certainly no time for Rita to be doing anything whatsoever to jeopardize the negotiations between Crum and Aly's lawyer Charles Torem. Rita had reconsidered her hasty remark that she didn't want any money from Aly as long as she could keep Yasmin. In Paris it was being said that the Aga Khan had told Aly to agree to a generous settlement for the child and be done with all the damaging publicity that his battle with Rita was attracting. The sum being mentioned was $50,000 yearly – generous, but hardly the $3,000,000 for which Rita had been asking. On 6 November, Crum and Torem announced that they had almost reached an agreement and that they hoped to make it final within a matter of days.

The Aga Khan, however, continued to insist that Yasmin be raised as a Muslim, and when Crum proposed that Rita sit down to discuss Yasmin's religious upbringing with Aly and the Aga Khan, she said no.

Finally, on 10 November, Torem informed Crum that, although Aly would not oppose Rita's divorce action, the prince refused to be represented in Nevada as she had demanded. Rita returned to the United States intending to go through with the divorce in any case.

In January 1952, while Aly remained in Cannes with his current *amour*, actress Gene Tierney, Rita and Yasmin left Los Angeles in a chauffeur-driven black Cadillac headed for Reno, Nevada. The night before District Judge A.J. Maestretti was scheduled to award her a decree by default, Rita was so overwrought that she managed to get only an hour's sleep.

Since the custody of Yasmin was one of the issues under consideration, the judge asked that the little girl appear in court with her mother. In court the three-year-old seemed oblivious that anything very important was going on. She happily chewed gum and at one point was admonished by her mother to stop running around and sit still.

Seventeen minutes was all it took for Rita to get her decree. She was only thirty-four years old and her divorce from Aly marked her third marital failure.

As expected, she was awarded full custody of her daughter, with Aly given the right to visit. Nonetheless, the prince's failure to answer the court papers that had been served to him personally in Cannes remained a source of considerable bitterness and anxiety. As far as Rita was concerned, since default decrees were not necessarily recognized everywhere, given the right circumstances Aly or the Aga Khan might still strike at any time to take the child from her.

Chapter Twenty-two

'After Aly, Rita was on a downward path, a steep, steep toboggan slide,' said Orson Welles.

Following all that she had been subjected to, first (and most significantly) by her father, Eduardo Cansino, and then by her first husband, Edward Judson, Rita's experience of failure in her marriages both to Welles and Aly Khan seemed only to confirm her worst fears about intimate relationships – and about herself. Whatever their obvious shortcomings, the marriages to Orson and Aly had afforded rare periods of hope in Rita's personal life – but they, too, had ended in betrayal.

The failure of her reconciliation with Aly, the deception and humiliation to which she perceived him to have subjected her when she came to him in Neuilly, had triggered a new emotional crisis. Like many incest victims, who vent their rage at others principally through self-destructive acts, Rita's all-too-public fling with Count José-Maria Villapadierna (despite her lawyer's warning that such publicity could be damaging to her own interests in the divorce negotiations) had been the cry of an embittered woman whose last hopes for domestic happiness had just been dashed. After finding herself greeted in Madrid by protests angrily assailing her morality (when it was a good wife and mother she so desperately wanted to be), now it was as if she were carrying on with Pepe in public merely to confirm all that her detractors were saying about her, to show that, yes, she was unworthy of the stable marriage she had sought – and failed – to achieve with Aly.

Quite often the incest victim tragically blames herself for the abuse to which her father – and those who follow him – subjected her. Having been robbed in childhood of a normal and healthy degree of self-esteem, she regards each new assault through the years as confirmation of the low opinion she already has of herself: the bad, unworthy person she secretly knows herself to be.

All of which is essential to comprehend the terrifying 'downward path' that Rita would very publicly take now, as she threw herself into an otherwise inexplicably self-destructive relationship with the deeply troubled singer and film actor Dick Haymes: a figure every bit as loathsome and insidious in his manipulation of her as Eddie Judson had once been.

The Argentine-born, thirty-five-year-old Dick Haymes had achieved popularity during the Big Band Era of the forties as a creamy-voiced soloist with the legendary likes of Tommy Dorsey, Harry James, and Benny Goodman. By the fifties, however, the high-living crooner was reported to have squandered as much as $4,000,000 in earnings from records, nightclub appearances, and film work. 'He blew it all so quickly,' recalled Jonie Taps. 'He was a dipsomaniac, that was his problem.' When Rita met him in 1953, Dick already had the well-earned reputation of a loser, a man on the way down, a deadbeat – 'Mr Evil,' as he was called in Hollywood. And it was no secret that by that time he was in deep financial trouble, with an ex-wife, actress Joanne Dru, and three children to support, a current wife, Nora Eddington Flynn, from whom he was separated and with whom some financial arrangements would have to be made, and the nearly $100,000 he owed the government in back taxes.

In Rita Hayworth, Dick Haymes seemed to perceive his financial and professional salvation.

Haymes first hooked up with Rita while she was filming her new picture at Columbia, *Miss Sadie Thompson*, Somerset Maugham's story of a woman with a shady past who finds herself stranded on a tropical island where a hypocritical minister rapes her. 'Rita liked to have a martini at lunch, and you couldn't get it in the executive dining room,' recalled Jonie Taps, who introduced her to Haymes. 'So I took her out to lunch and on the way we ran into Dick Haymes, who had just finished a picture for me called *Cruisin' Down the River*. I said, "Come on, Dick, have lunch with us."'

At lunch, when Rita mentioned that she was about to take a train to New York for the premiere of *Salome*, Dick immediately saw his opening. Afterward, he wasted no time in securing a ticket on the same train, where he could seem to run into Rita as if by accident. Ostensibly he was on a personal appearance tour for the film *All Ashore*, but his real reason was to get close to Rita. Before they had reached Manhattan, Haymes had charmed his way into an invitation to Rita's premiere and to the party afterward at the Stork Club.

Rita appeared at the premiere on the arm of a Columbia publicity man, while Haymes came alone. He was biding his time. He waited until the party to make his move. There, he asked Rita to dance. Then again. And again. All eyes in the Stork Club seemed to be on Rita as she danced with Haymes almost the entire evening. Later, Dick, not the publicity man, escorted her to her hotel.

Even after Rita startled the other partygoers by leaving with Dick Haymes, given his abominable reputation, it seemed almost impossible to believe that the evening would lead to anything serious between them. But no sooner did she get back to Hollywood than she began meeting him for intimate dinners and long, soulful discussions at the Naples Café and the Bel-Air Hotel. Debt-ridden as he may have been, Dick shrewdly spared no expense wining and dining Rita – she was much too good an investment. Being seen regularly in public with Columbia's top star could diminish his image as a loser. And while other women might perceive Dick's broken marriages as a drawback to getting involved with him, Rita saw his marital woes as something that she and Dick had in common. Their messy troubles with ex-spouses gave them much about which to talk.

Indeed, by then Rita had a major new grievance in her

divorce dealings with Aly. While the previous January the judge in Reno had proposed that Rita and Aly settle privately the matter of Yasmin's financial support, since that time the prince had been most unresponsive to Rita's monetary demands. Thus, in April, Rita's attorneys had filed a petition requesting the Nevada court to order Aly to cough up $48,000 a year for Princess Yasmin. Within days the court had issued the order but could not enforce it since Aly had neither attended nor been represented during the Reno divorce proceedings. To add insult to injury, Rita knew only too well that Gene Tierney already seemed to have replaced her in Aly's life. (What Rita didn't know was that when the prince asked Gene to marry him, his father simply wouldn't hear of it; after the scandalous publicity that had plagued Aly's liaison with Rita from the start, the Aga Khan ruled against his marrying another movie star.)

Haymes's own abundant complaints about his ex-wives made him appear to understand Rita's painful plight as no one else did. They shared a sense of being wronged, beleaguered, under attack – the more they talked, the more he had her convinced that, somehow, it was them against the world. It seems never to have occurred to Rita that, ironically, for all the wonderful sympathy he expressed for her battle with Aly, Dick was himself constantly being pursued by his own ex-wife for the child support he kept failing to pay her.

In May 1953 Dick's budding relationship with Rita was cut short when the filming of *Miss Sadie Thompson* moved to Hawaii for location work. Rita, who had had enough of flying during her marriage to Aly, asked to travel by boat. But Harry Cohn said there wasn't enough time. Because she suddenly seemed so genuinely frightened, Cohn assigned a doctor to accompany her during the flight, to give her an injection to calm her down. Having heard that Rita seemed fond of Bob Schiffer, Cohn also asked the makeup man to travel with her. (Cohn had no idea that it was Bob with whom she had run off to Mexico during *Salome*.)

Recalled Schiffer: 'They asked me to get her on the airplane and pacify her, to help her handle the situation. In those days I drank a little, and of course she did. We had a separate cabin in the back of the airplane, just a small group of us: the doctor, his wife, Rita, and myself. And we sipped from the cup of happiness all the way to Honolulu. I did it purposely to relax her because she was frightened to death of flying. And I must say she *was* terribly relaxed. Unfortunately, they took a photo of her getting off the plane in Honolulu which was rather widely publicized and she looked like hell. What a terrible thing: I was just trying to oil her up enough so she wouldn't even know she was on an airplane.'

Much as it looked to Schiffer as if his rival Haymes, was at least temporarily out of the picture, Bob wasn't about to have Rita all to himself in Hawaii.

'I was pretty well smashed – so was she,' recalled Schiffer of their arrival in Honolulu. By contrast, for once in his life, Dick Haymes was a good deal more clear-headed at the time. Although Rita had been anxious to keep their love affair quiet, and although Dick had seemed to co-operate in this regard, he was really most eager to attract as much publicity as possible – he felt sure that it wouldn't be long before his career picked up again on account of his relationship with the Love Goddess.

Clearly it was not in his best interests to let Rita out of his grasp, even for a short while. So Dick Haymes decided to follow Rita to Hawaii, where he quickly arranged a brief singing engagement as a pretext for the trip. But Hawaii was still a United States territory, not a state; as a citizen of Argentina, Dick would need the proper documents to go there. He had lost his alien registration card, so on 21 May 1953 (a date that both Dick and Rita would have much occasion to remember), he applied for a temporary replacement at the Los Angeles office of the Immigration and Naturalization Service. Was there anything else he needed to go to Hawaii? he inquired. No, he was told at the immigration office, the temporary alien registration card was all that was necessary. Within days Dick Haymes was heading for Honolulu – and Rita.

While Rita seemed touched that Dick was coming all the way to Hawaii to be with her, understandably Bob Schiffer wasn't exactly thrilled by the news. 'I went through all these romances with her,' recalled Schiffer of the other men he had had to contend with, from Welles on. 'I don't know how I did it because I was crazy about her myself. I just suffered through a lot of these things. When she said, "Dick's coming over," I said, "Well, that's nice." But it aggravated me because we were having fun and going out and doing things.'

Soon Haymes had taken over with Rita again. The two romantic weeks Haymes spent with Rita in Hawaii would solidify their relationship. Of course, Harry Cohn would instantly be apprised of Haymes's presence during the filming of *Miss Sadie Thompson*. And if Cohn had been dismayed by her liaisons with Orson Welles and Aly Khan, he would undoubtedly be livid about Dick Haymes. Just when Cohn had retrieved his biggest star, the last thing he needed was for her to get involved with a lowlife like Haymes.

But Cohn's inevitable opposition didn't stop Dick. By now Haymes had correctly sized up Rita's psychology. Hadn't he listened to her talking about her troubles for hours? Rita's intense long-term hatred of Harry Cohn played right into Dick's hands. As Dick saw only too clearly, the mogul's opposition to their relationship was likely to drive them closer together. Anything Harry Cohn said against him would only plead Dick's cause with Rita all the more.

For the time being Dick was on his best behavior with Rita. He tried not to drink too much and to restrain his more violent impulses with her. And much as he longed for a bit of publicity, he seemed to respect her desire to keep their affair out of the papers. Thus, whatever nasty things Harry Cohn might say about Dick, Rita would probably regard them merely as ugly lies. Dick was so utterly sweet and charming – how could anyone possibly have anything bad to say about him?

On 7 June, when Dick boarded a Pan Am flight to Los

Angeles, he and Rita vowed to spend some time alone together as soon as she finished shooting *Miss Sadie Thompson*. But first, upon his return, Dick had to take care of the seemingly perfunctory matter of surrendering his temporary alien registration card and securing a new one. Nothing tricky about that. All he had to do was report back to the local office of the Immigration and Naturalization Service when he was notified that the new card was ready. Or so he thought.

Little did he suspect the profound and far-reaching effect this simple transaction was soon to have on his *and* Rita's lives – as well as on the lives of her children, and even of Prince Aly Khan.

On 8 July 1953, when Dick Haymes returned to the same office where he had applied for a temporary card in May, it was immediately evident that something was wrong. Richard Cody, the officer to whom he had spoken previously, asked him to wait, while he conferred with his superior. After some time, Cody returned and escorted Haymes to the department's investigating unit.

Suddenly Dick's every word was being taken down by a stenographer as Thomas McDermott, the examining inspector, hurled questions at him. 'I desire to take a statement from you under oath concerning your immigration status,' said McDermott. 'Any statements you make may be used by the government as evidence in any deportation or criminal proceedings. Are you willing to make such a statement freely and voluntarily under oath?'

'Certainly,' replied a baffled Haymes, who soon found himself being sworn to tell the truth. Haymes still had no idea what all this was about, and the first few routine questions provided no clue: name, birthplace, citizenship, family background, marital status.

But then: 'When and where did you last enter the United States?' asked McDermott.

Enter the United States? Dick hadn't been out of the United States recently, so how could he possibly have entered it? When he applied for the temporary alien registration card in May, he had explicitly asked whether there was anything else he needed to go to Hawaii and had been told no. 'Well, may I ask a question?' inquired Dick. 'I didn't know that I was out of the United States. I entered the United States at Los Angeles from Hawaii about six or seven weeks ago.'

'I now show you DSS Form 301 which is dated 25 January 1944, which is an application by alien for relief from military service,' said McDermott, 'and ask whether you did execute such form?'

'Yes, I did,' admitted Haymes. He had indeed signed the form during the war to exempt him from military service on the grounds that he held citizenship in a foreign country.

'Were you informed at the time you submitted this application that it would make you ineligible to become naturalized in the United States?' asked McDermott. 'The present law which became effective 24 December 1952, does contain express provision that any person ineligible to citizenship because of having applied for relief from military service is excludable from the United States.'

Haymes was thunderstuck by all this. Not only had the authorities taken the trouble to dig up a form he had signed nine years ago, but now they were spouting obscure rules and regulations at him. Obviously they had been ready for him – but why? For someone like Dick Haymes, who already suffered from paranoid tendencies, the experience would have been sheer torture.

Finally the investigator came to the point. 'Apparently,' said McDermott, 'your departure from the United States to Hawaii and your reentry at Los Angeles would place you in the category of a person subject to deportation, and under the present law there is no avenue of relief for you and there is no way by which your deportation could be stayed.'

'You mean I am going to be deported?' asked an obviously stunned Haymes. 'Excuse me.'

What was the investigator talking about? How was this possible? Just when things seemed to be looking up for a change, he was suddenly being thrown out of the country!

263

'How about a private bill?' Haymes asked McDermott, referring to the sort of bill introduced by either a senator or congressman to give citizenship to an individual who was otherwise ineligible. But it was a ludicrous question: where would a notorious drunk and deadbeat like Haymes possibly find a senator or congressman to take *him* on as a cause? Still, this was at least a technical possibility and the investigator duly admitted it.

'It is possible that your status in the United States could be legalized,' said McDermott. 'For that purpose the Immigration and Naturalization Service will withhold any further action for a period of sixty days. If during the sixty days you are successful in having a private bill introduced on your behalf, it is probable that further proceedings may be held in abeyance pending the outcome of such legislation. Do you understand?'

'I do,' Haymes replied, and left within minutes.

All his energy lately had been directed toward getting closer to Rita. Suddenly he had sixty days after which he'd be kicked out of the country. But why? Why would the government go to so much trouble to make a case against him? And why back in May didn't anyone tell him that as an alien he wasn't allowed to go to Hawaii, then return to California? He'd specifically inquired if he needed any other documents and he'd explicitly been told no. More and more Dick smelled a setup. It seemed to him that someone powerful must be behind his latest troubles – but who? Who would want him out of the country just now? What had he done lately that would cause someone powerful to plot against him? Whom had he offended or interfered with?

Who else but Harry Cohn?

The more he went over it, the clearer it seemed to him. Harry Cohn had somehow engineered Haymes's troubles with the government. He was the only one whose interests would be served if Haymes were deported, thereby removing him from Rita's life. The details were still hazy, but Haymes felt certain he knew exactly who his enemy was.

With sixty days to do something about his situation. Haymes had to act quickly. He knew perfectly well that no senator or congressman was likely to take his side, but there *was* one person of power and influence who would. More than ever he needed Rita Hayworth – she was the key to attracting national attention to his case. And, if at worst, he had to leave the country, it would obviously be far better to have her with him, especially if she were his wife. Given this unexpected new turn in his fate, it was of the utmost importance to end his current marriage immediately and persuade Rita to marry him at once.

Again, his acute understanding of Rita would come in handy. If she didn't want the press and public to know that they were lovers, how was Dick possibly going to rush her to the altar? Having closely observed the way her mind worked, he saw that if only he could persuade her that his troubles had arisen because of his great love for her, she was likely to do anything for him. So it was that Rita would become obsessed with the idea that somehow *she* was responsible for his difficulties. Hadn't he rushed to Hawaii only because he was so much in love with her that he couldn't bear for them to be apart? And now he was threatened with deportation because of it. As for Dick's suspicions that Harry Cohn was out to get him, this, too, made Rita feel that her boyfriend's terrible plight was somehow all her fault. Cohn wouldn't be after Dick if it weren't for her. In these feelings of guilt, of believing oneself responsible for another's problems, Rita recapitulated the child-victim's all-too-common belief that it is up to her to hold her father together, to *save* him; otherwise, his dire fate will be *her* fault.

Chapter Twenty-three

Dreadful as the threat of deportation may have been to Dick Haymes, nonetheless it quickly bound Rita closer to him than ever. As long as she felt guilty for his present plight, she was essentially his to command. By mid-July, with shooting on *Miss Sadie Thompson* finished, Rita headed for a vacation in New York City until post-production work on the film was to begin. Dick drove her to the Pasadena station, but because he was casually dressed and seemed not to have any luggage, the people who spotted them assumed he was merely seeing her off. But no, Dick had discreetly packed his belongings in Rita's suitcase. They were headed for the Plaza Hotel, where they had booked separate accommodations on different floors. It was all part of Rita's struggle to keep their relationship quiet. But by the time they got to Manhattan all that would change. Dick had decided that now was the time to let everyone know that he was going with her. And by now she was feeling so much guilt over his predicament that she was unlikely to resist.

Even before Dick's troubles with the Immigration and Naturalization Service, he and Rita had been planning to spend some time together like this. His unexpected troubles had greatly increased the speed with which he had to move with her. By the time they got back from New York their relationship *had* to be public knowledge. Although it may have seemed absurd to go off on a holiday with Rita when he had only sixty days to seek support in Washington on his behalf, in fact Haymes had carefully calculated the

New York trip to help with his plight. Talk of his involvement with Rita had already paid off for Dick – as a result he had lined up a singing engagement at the Sands Hotel in Las Vegas beginning on 12 August. He felt certain it was only the start of his big comeback. If he could make his affair with the Love Goddess public, the likelihood that she would be there at the ringside to cheer him on was sure to attract a substantial audience of curiosity-seekers to his show.

When Rita had been at the Plaza with Aly in 1948, he struggled to protect her from publicity. Dick Haymes had a different agenda. Like Eddie Judson, Dick knew how to attract attention by being seen in the right places. The jazz scene was Haymes's turf, and he knew all the hot clubs of the moment, like The Embers, the Spanish-flavored La Zambra, and the Bandbox, where he and Rita were likely to be spotted by columnists.

When word spread along Broadway that Rita Hayworth had gone to Duke Ellington's late show at the Bandbox, the nightclub was quickly swarming with fans anxious to glimpse the Love Goddess. Before long she also attracted the attention of a local columnist who rushed up to her table at 1.30 in the morning to ask if she and Dick were planning marriage. 'Please, please,' she replied. 'Don't, don't, I'm getting nervous. Please don't ask me those things.' This was everything Dick could have hoped for. He could make a grand show of not wanting publicity, but would benefit from it nonetheless. They had been gazing into each other's eyes all evening. And it did not go unnoticed now that Rita grabbed Dick's hand for support as she pleaded with the columnist, 'I'm just on my vacation and in my own country, so let me live a little.'

While Rita stubbornly wouldn't talk about her affair with Haymes, Duke Ellington evidently had no such qualms. 'It looks very respectable,' said Ellington of what he'd observed of Dick and Rita out in the audience. 'It's one of those respectable-type romances that are different than when people are just playing and hiding. Yeah, it looks real real.'

Precisely as Haymes had calculated, henceforth he was constantly being linked with Rita in the columns. The couple may have discreetly taken rooms on separate floors at the Plaza, but after several strategic evenings out on the town all New York seemed aware that their relationship was 'real real.'

The columnists weren't the only ones tracking Dick and Rita in Manhattan. It had been three weeks since the Immigration and Naturalization Service had given Dick sixty days to seek the support of a senator or congressman. Suddenly, with Dick making quite a splash with Rita in the nightclubs of New York, the agency changed its mind and issued orders to arrest him immediately for deportation.

On 30 July 1953, the New York office was instructed to pick up Dick before five P.M. that day. Arresting him at night was likely to attract too much attention. If the officers couldn't find him before nightfall, they were to wait until the next day. As it happened, however, before Dick could be arrested he and Rita had slipped out of town and returned to California.

Scarcely had Dick and Rita left New York than Prince Aly Khan arrived there. He planned to attend the horse sales at Saratoga, then to fly west to see Yasmin. Many months of negotiation had failed to result in a custody agreement because of Rita's perpetual fear that Aly or the Aga Khan might snatch the child from her. It had been a year since the prince had seen Yasmin, and because Rita would not agree to send her to Europe, Aly hoped to spend some time with his daughter in Los Angeles. Before he got there, however, he couldn't have helped hearing the rumor that Rita and Dick were going to be married soon, which meant that Aly's daughter was about to have a new step-father. And if the prince didn't yet know much about Dick Haymes, he found out soon enough.

The very day after Aly's arrival in America, Dick's car was stopped on Sunset Boulevard by federal agents armed with a warrant for his arrest. The Immigration and Naturalization Service had caught up with him. The agents hauled Dick downtown to their office, where he summoned his lawyer Robert Eaton to post a $500 bond. A formal hearing would take place in two weeks. Meanwhile, the agency's district director announced that Dick was subject to deportation to his native Argentina under the McCarran–Walter Immigration Act.

Suddenly, in addition to all the other names that people called him, he was tagged a wartime draft dodger as well. Dick was terrified that the charge might not sit well with the American public. The last thing he needed was for anything to interfere with his all-important comeback in Las Vegas.

And what would Rita think of the charges? Aly Khan, after all, had a distinguished war record. How would Dick look beside him? Haymes frantically explained to Rita that he'd briefly evaded military service in order to be with his pregnant first wife. He declared that once the baby had been born, he'd withdrawn his request for an exemption, but that the military had twice turned him down on account of his high blood pressure. Despite all his agitation, Dick quickly discovered that with Rita these explanations were strangely unnecessary. His increasingly beleaguered circumstances brought out her nurturing instincts. The more trouble he got into, the more she wanted to help.

Dick went on ahead to Las Vegas, with Rita scheduled to join him on opening night. Meanwhile, she was talking regularly on the phone with Aly, who agreed to provide an immediate $8,000 for Yasmin's expenses. He had been due in Los Angeles any day, but at the last minute news that the Aga Khan had been taken ill again required Aly to rush home.

Since her return from New York, Rita had been finishing up post-production chores on *Miss Sadie Thompson*. As Dick's opening night approached, a combination of acute stress and simple exhaustion landed her in bed. Much to Dick's chagrin, in the end ill health precluded her turning up for his big night. If she couldn't go to him, Dick decided to go to her. In a gesture sure to endear him further to Rita, and to add an important touch of drama to his Vegas opening, hours before he was sched-

uled to go on at the Sands Haymes flew to Los Angeles to
see how she was.

That night onstage in Vegas, Dick's eyes welled with
tears at the enthusiastic response he received for his
opening number, 'There'll Be a Great Day.' It certainly
appeared that this was going to be the successful comeback
of which he had dreamed. Still, there was no denying that
after all the press items about his love affair with Rita,
people were interested in more than just his singing. Back-
stage, reporters asked about the latest flurry of rumors that
he and Rita Hayworth were engaged. 'I'm in no position to
confirm any stories as to my marriage,' Dick replied. 'I'm
not even divorced from my present wife.'

And indeed, his exceedingly inconvenient status as a
married man was much on Dick's mind at the moment. He
had wanted a quick Nevada divorce, but now Nora seemed
inclined against it. A California divorce would make it
easier to hold Dick to his financial commitments – not a
small consideration, since his previous wife, Joanne, was
already having trouble collecting monies due her. But a
California divorce required a year's waiting period to
become final, and by then Dick might have been deported
to Argentina. Negotiations were under way to try somehow
to speed up the divorce. Perhaps Nora could get her
divorce in California, while Dick got his in Nevada.
Nothing had been agreed as yet, so Dick was still by no
means free to take a new bride.

While Dick was in Las Vegas, the Immigration and
Naturalization Service was preparing its deportation case
against him. An official memo dated 14 August declared
that Haymes was 'persona non grata at Columbia Studios'
– one of several such indications in his deportation file that
from the first the government was curiously well informed
on Columbia's negative attitude toward him.

On 26 August 1953, Dick appeared in Los Angeles for
his hearing. Questioned by the examiner about his past and
family background, Dick seemed cloudy on details. He said
he didn't know in what country his father held citizenship
or when he had died. As to his own marital history, at first

Dick claimed to have been married twice (the story he'd told Rita and others), but with some prompting he suddenly 'remembered' an additional earlier marriage, which had lasted only two or three weeks. This made it apparent that the agency had dug up information about him that he didn't care to admit. What else had the service found?

When, with obvious reference to Rita, Dick was asked if he planned to marry again now, his attorney promptly objected and the objection was sustained.

Next the examiner came to what would be the heart of the matter: Had Dick ever claimed United States citizenship? Although the examiner did not disclose where his line of questioning was leading, Dick's hesitant answer suggested that the authorities had indeed hit upon something that might cause immense problems for him later. 'I don't know how to answer that question,' he replied. 'Sometimes – I will answer the question this way, sometimes to avoid confusion I have said I came from Santa Barbara, but not officially have I claimed to be a citizen of the United States.'

'What do you mean "to avoid confusion"?' inquired the examiner, still not tipping his hand.

'In magazine stories, for example,' Haymes replied. 'I did live in Santa Barbara for quite a while, knew some people up there and called it my home, but officially I have never claimed to be a citizen of the United States.'

The examiner then moved on to Dick's wartime application to be exempted from the draft as a citizen of a neutral country, and Dick repeated publicly that he had considered it a 'temporary deferment' that he'd requested, 'because my wife was pregnant at the time and she was feeling pretty badly and it wouldn't have been very long.'

But now it seemed as if Dick was simply being given plenty of rope to hang himself. His attorney requested and was granted a continuance. But when Dick complained that he would be in the East presently and might not get back in time for the next hearing, scheduled for 28 September, his protest was overridden. Evidently the agency was anxious to get on with its case to deport him.

However, now Dick Haymes was no longer standing alone against the government. Much as he had hoped she would, Rita publicly aligned herself with his case. In anticipation of divorcing Nora, Dick had returned to Nevada to wait out the six-week residence requirement (whereas his wife would be divorcing him in California). The day after Rita finished some additional scenes for *Miss Sadie Thompson* she drove to Vegas to be by Dick's side. 'I'm one hundred percent behind Dick in all his troubles,' she announced. 'I love him and I will marry him here as soon as possible.' Haymes went so far as to specify where the wedding would take place: the Sands Hotel. But it seemed that even if Rita had agreed to marry him the moment his Vegas divorce came through, they would not be able to live together legally as man and wife in California until Nora's final decree was granted there a year later.

After Rita told reporters that she believed marrying Dick was the best way to help him through his deportation troubles, Columbia – the studio that had declared him 'persona non grata' – promptly summoned her back to Los Angeles for publicity pictures. Rita regarded the assignment as a trick to lure her away from Haymes. 'I'm not leaving Las Vegas until Dick and I are married,' she declared stubbornly. Let Harry Cohn suspend her if he liked – she wasn't going to leave Dick Haymes's side. But a Columbia suspension was by no means the gravest threat Rita faced now.

Chapter Twenty-four

*T*he month before Dick Haymes's deportation hearing, an anonymous letter postmarked 'New Rochelle, New York, 24 August 1953' was sent to Louella Parsons at the International News Service in Hollywood. 'Please not let Rita Haywood [sic] marry Dick Haymes,' it said. 'Advised Princess Yasmin be returned to Aly Khan or child would be killed.' Upon receipt of the unsigned, undated letter, Parsons had notified Rita, Columbia Pictures, and the Los Angeles Police Department of its disturbing contents.

Then, on 9 September, two days after Rita had publicly declared that she loved Dick and intended to marry him, she received a second, more detailed warning (again postmarked 'New Rochelle, New York'), but this time addressed to her directly at the Sands Hotel in Las Vegas, and threatening bodily harm to her as well as death to Yasmin.

RITA:
  But think that this won't happne because it truely will if you marry dick Haymes your litlee girl YASMIN will be kill and if you dont want this to happen then you had better go back to Aly Khan. and else for you your rotten and there will be some one that will beat you so that you will have to go to the hospital and your career as move star will be over.'

Although the threats had obviously not come from her

273

ex-husband or from anyone directly connected with him nonetheless the letters seemed to exacerbate Rita's fears about Aly and the Aga Khan's intentions regarding the child – which would explain her peculiar overreaction to a reporter's question about the latest negotiations with the prince.

In Paris, Rita's lawyer Bartley Crum had just announced the results of his latest round of negotiations with the prince's attorney. Crum was to fly to Las Vegas to discuss the terms that had been tentatively agreed upon. First, Aly had agreed to establish a $1,000,000 trust fund for three-year-old Yasmin, whom Rita was free to raise as a Christian. And while neither Aly nor the Aga Khan insisted any longer on a Muslim upbringing for the little princess, they did request that at the age of seven (which Muslims regarded as the age of reason) she be exposed to Ismaili teachings.

Before the attorney could present these utterly reason-able requests to Rita, newsmen in Las Vegas asked her how she felt about being required to raise Yasmin as a Muslim (which in fact she *wasn't* being required to do anymore at all). What the reporters didn't know was that she had received an anonymous threat that very day, and the experience had left her distinctly on edge. 'All the money in the world can't buy my child's right to be raised as an American,' she exploded. 'Whatever religion I choose for Yasmin is my own business. I don't have to specify any particular religion. Millions of dollars or not, Yasmin is now being reared as a normal Christian American child and will continue to be – and all the money in the world can't buy that right from us.'

All in all, it was a most unfortunate outburst, especially in view of the actual position Aly had taken, and of which Rita had evidently not yet been properly apprised. Nor did Rita's increasingly strident assertions about wanting to raise her daughter as 'a normal Christian American child' quite ring so true anymore, coming as they did two days after she announced plans to marry the notoriously dissolute Dick Haymes, whose latest woes and imbroglios were being played out daily in the press. Whatever one might say about or against Aly, there was no denying that he was a loving and devoted parent – but what would life with 'Mr Evil' as a stepfather possibly be like?

Rita's attorney arrived in Nevada to discuss the negotiations he had just concluded with Aly, but when he learned of the death threats to Yasmin, he instantly reported them to the FBI and ordered twenty-four-hour armed guards for Rita in Las Vegas, and for Becky and Yasmin back in Los Angeles, where Rita had left them to be with Dick. Only naturally Aly and his father would be gravely concerned by press reports of the threatening letters, but Bartley Crum cabled the Aga Khan.

As spiritual leader of millions of people in the world today, you are hereby advised that threats against the life of your grandchild Yasmin and Rita Hayworth have been received. We appeal to you as the spiritual director of the Muslim world to use your influence and appeal to guarantee their safety and well-being.

Rita's recent public outburst against Aly had been bad enough, but Crum's appeal to the Aga Khan was offensive in the extreme – as if the Aga Khan or his followers would ever possibly sanction any harm whatsoever being done to Aly's daughter. As always, the Aga Khan was most anxious that his sect be pictured in the most favorable public light, so it could only have been infuriating to discover Crum's cable reprinted in its entirety in the press the next day. Crum's suggestion to reporters that the threats might have 'originated with some followers of the Muslim faith' was the latest move in a public-relations campaign to alarm Americans about Rita's Muslim adversaries in the custody dispute. But in view of the actual death threats that had been received, publishing the cable to the Aga Khan and making inflammatory statements to the press plainly and dangerously risked further arousing the ire of whoever had written the anonymous letters, or even of provoking other unbalanced individuals to take action.

'Afford matter continuous investigative attention until

brought to logical conclusion,' wrote FBI Director J. Edgar Hoover in a memo to agents in Salt Lake City and Los Angeles. The seriousness with which the FBI took the death threats to Yasmin is suggested by the full-scale investigation Hoover promptly launched. In the FBI laboratory the letters were inspected for fingerprints, which were then compared with prints already on file at headquarters. After tracing the manufacturers of the paper on which the threats had been written, FBI agents determined where in the New Rochelle area such paper was sold and interviewed the proprietors of those outlets for possible leads. Employees of the New Rochelle Post Office and Police Department were similarly questioned. The FBI Washington field office contacted the State Department for names of 'Muslim exchange students in the New York area,' and these were furnished to the New York office, where agents were assigned to interview possible suspects, as well as obtain 'hand printing and handwriting specimens for submission to the FBI Laboratory.' ('It is requested that this lead be given expeditious attention,' came the directive from headquarters.) Further, FBI agents contacted the registrars at New York-area colleges to determine 'whether any students registered there from Muslim countries might reside in New Rochelle, New York.'

Meanwhile, on the West Coast, FBI agents interviewed Louella Parsons and officials at Columbia Pictures, and a watch was duly placed on incoming mail – not just for new threatening letters, but for any correspondence postmarked 'New Rochelle, New York.'

Interviewed by FBI agents in Las Vegas, Dick and Rita said that they did not recognize the hand in which both death threats had been written; nor did they know anyone in New Rochelle, New York, where the envelopes had been postmarked. Then, according to the FBI report of the interview, Rita 'further advised that she had received numerous crank letters in the past but that none of them had ever been of a threatening nature to her or her children' – a curious statement when one recalls (as Rita apparently did) the threats to her and Rebecca by James Gibson, for which

276

crime he had been sentenced to a prison term in Tennessee.

In the meantime, determined to remain by Dick's side no matter why ('I'll follow Dick anywhere on earth,' she vowed), Rita sent for Becky and Yasmin. Private detectives escorted the children to the Los Angeles airport, while on the other end, in Nevada, Rita and three security guards from the Sands Hotel would meet their plane.

By now Las Vegas was crawling with journalists eager for the latest developments in the Haymes–Hayworth saga. When one considers that Yasmin had just received two death threats, bringing her into the center of a vast media circus was not the best idea. Although the FBI had explicitly cautioned the actress not to allow Yasmin to be photographed, Rita was soon blithely posing for pictures with both daughters. In the wake of the death threats, it violated simple parental common sense to permit photographs in the press showing exactly what Yasmin looked like, but Dick's perpetual quest for publicity seemed to have affected Rita's better judgment. These weren't candid shots, either. Rita invited photographers into her suite at the Sands, where she posed with the children on the sofa. In another picture the girls were in their nightclothes being prepared for bed: Rita brushed Yasmin's hair while Becky seemed absorbed in a comic book. And, of course, Dick Haymes was frequently shown with them as well.

On Friday, 18 September, a United Press photograph of Yasmin as she 'displays her affection for her prospective stepfather, crooner Dick Haymes' was juxtaposed with the news that Haymes's wife, Nora, had been granted an interlocutory decree of divorce on the basis of 'testimony that he was cruel to her, insulted their guests, and drank too much.'

But nothing that Nora or anyone else said against Dick Haymes seemed to give Rita the slightest pause about marrying him. All that remained was for Nora to sign a waiver allowing him to proceed in Nevada; the $8,000 lump sum she'd been awarded in addition to $100 weekly alimony was yet another debt with which Dick would henceforth have to contend. His Nevada divorce was scheduled to come through on 23 September, and, wasting no time, he and Rita planned to marry the very next day at the Sands Hotel. Meanwhile, there was more posing with the children for photographers and frequent evenings out in Las Vegas. For Rita it was a throwback to her early days with Eddie Judson, when making herself visible was all – except that now it was Dick who sought visibility for himself and used Rita to get it.

Still Dick made much ado of showing the world that he wasn't exploiting her. When he and Rita signed a prenuptial agreement, of course the press was invited to attend. 'I love this girl so much that I will do anything to protect her,' Dick asserted. 'I intend to stand on my own two feet and take care of all my own troubles. I only thank God that I have her and her love to inspire me to work and fight my own battles.'

Since Rita was the big earner in the family, one would have expected a prenuptial agreement to protect her against Dick. Instead, the agreement's chief concern seemed to be protecting her against his creditors. Sid Luft's ex-wife had recently claimed in court that the earnings of his current wife, Judy Garland, were community property, and as such ought to be considered when determining alimony payments. Dick Haymes certainly didn't want anything like that happening to him! Dick may have publicly emphasized his desire to protect Rita, but in fact the prenuptial agreement didn't prevent her from handing over virtually every cent she had to him – which at length was precisely what she would do. Quite simply, Dick didn't want anyone else, especially not his ex-wives, getting at her money first.

As it turned out, the wedding ceremony also principally served *Dick*'s needs. From the first it was carefully cal-culated to attract as much media attention as possible. Rita's statements prior to the big day would never have led anyone to expect what actually occurred. 'We want a simple wedding,' she insisted, apparently hoping to contrast it with her wedding to Prince Aly Khan. 'This one is too important to me to clutter up with a lot of unnecessary frills. It's enough that we love each other, and we're finally getting married after so many difficulties.'

The advance word from the Sands's publicist painted a distinctly different picture. He announced that the wedding would occur in the hotel's Gold Room, where celebrity press conferences were held. Newsreel and television cameras would record every minute of the ceremony, after which Dick and Rita would host a celebratory lunch *for the press*. Ironically, the last time Rita got married, Aly devoted enormous effort to shutting out reporters and photographers, but now at her wedding to Dick virtually the only 'guests' would be the press!

Three days before the by-now abundantly publicized wedding ceremony was scheduled to take place, Rita received a third threatening letter at the Sands Hotel, this one postmarked 'Brooklyn, New York':

> Miss Hayworth,
>
> You should've taken my advice.
> Yasmine will die unless her
> father is permitted to raise her as
> a Muslim.
> You will suffer too!! Praise Allah.
>
> Mohammed and His Followers

It is a measure of how entirely Rita had submitted to Dick's control that, even now, she went through with the media extravaganza he had planned, however much it may have placed her two daughters in serious jeopardy. Both girls were paraded before journalists at a pre-wedding press conference at the Sands, where the hotel's publicist proudly proclaimed: 'Yasmin is the only granddaughter of the Aga Khan, and that makes her the only female direct descendant of Mohammed.' The little princess, whose life had just been threatened three times, should hardly have been put on display in rooms full of jostling strangers, but this was precisely what Rita found herself doing because of Dick's belief that the more sympathetic attention their wedding attracted, the harder it would be for the authorities to deport him.

From the moment the press corps arrived at the Sands, the hotel's publicist was with them every step of the way. Little that occurred during this most curious forty-eight hours was spontaneous, unselfconscious. In effect, the 'festivities' began with Dick's divorce from Nora the day before the wedding. The official 'Outline of Events – Hayworth–Haymes Wedding' distributed by the hotel promised that Dick would make himself available to journalists for 'pictures and comment' outside the Las Vegas court.

But first, when he appeared before Judge Frank Gregory, Haymes charged that Nora had committed mental cruelty when she refused to go on the road with him on his nightclub engagements. 'As a result I could not handle my work, lost weight, and could not sleep well,' Dick complained. In California his wife had charged him with drinking and abusive behavior, but in Las Vegas her apparent dislike of travel was all it took to secure a divorce in seven minutes.

'Is everybody happy?' called out the Sands's publicist as photographers took pictures of Dick posing with his decree. Afterward reporters were also on hand in abundance as Dick and Rita applied for their marriage license.

Four years before, as Rita was driven to her previous wedding in France, crowds of well-wishers lined the picturesque winding roads from Aly's Château de l'Horizon to Vallauris. Now, on the morning of 24 September 1953, curious fellow guests at the Sands perched on the pool's diving board or rushed out of the barbershop and beauty parlor to catch a glimpse of the wedding procession, from Rita's outlying bungalow to the casino. To help photographers focus their cameras, the hotel publicist dutifully marched several feet in front of Dick and Rita. Then suddenly, unexpectedly, the couple slipped out of sight. Where had they gone? Had the media circus finally gotten to Rita? Had she come to her senses and run off?

No. Haymes and writer Jim Bacon, who was covering

the wedding for the Associated Press, were with her when she disappeared into a private office at the hotel. 'She apparently had her period,' Bacon recalled. 'So the wedding was delayed while a secretary had to run out and get Tampax or whatever.'

In the meantime, the couple quietly sipped bourbon to steady their nerves.

Before long the wedding procession resumed through the perpetual night of the gambling casino, where Bacon noticed something exceedingly odd: 'Here was one of the great screen beauties, a great sex symbol, but the gamblers didn't even look up,' he recalled. 'That's the way gamblers are. Especially those guys that are playing in the daytime. They're the *real* gamblers.'

The hoopla that awaited in the Gold Room more than compensated for the gamblers' lack of curiosity. Flashbulbs started popping and TV cameras began grinding the moment Dick and Rita appeared. Rita's two little girls were prominently positioned up front on a sofa. Eight-year-old Becky sat quietly, but three-year-old Yasmin chattered sweetly throughout. 'Mommy, what are you doing?' she kept asking Rita. 'Are you getting married, Mommy?'

At the publicist's signal, District Judge MacNamee got things started, although his voice would barely be audible above the din of the TV cameras. Since both bride and groom had been thrice married and divorced, this time their vows did not commit them to a life together. Instead: 'Will you love, honor, and cherish each other throughout your married life?' seemed the more realistic question.

As Dick slipped the ring on Rita's finger, Princess Yasmin was heard to cry out, 'I want a ring, too.' Where-upon the hotel manager, who was serving as Dick's best man, promptly gave the child his own diamond ring. 'Have you got two of these? asked Yasmin.

'I'll try to get you another one,' replied the hotel man.

The lunch reception that followed was yet another giant photo opportunity. But of all the innumerable images of Rita's wedding, one photograph, later published in *Life*,

quite exactly captured its flavor. There was Dick kissing
Rita for the cameras, while a few feet away stood the hotel
publicist, lips pursed, unabashedly cuing the embrace. And
stranded between the newlyweds and the publicist were
Rita's two little daughters: Yasmin, watching her mother
with apparent fascination; and Becky, staring forlornly at
the floor.

Chapter Twenty-five

Dick and Rita spent their wedding night at the Sands. Then, after apprising the FBI of their itinerary and promising to check in regularly, they flew to New York with Becky and Yasmin. From there Dick headed for a ten-day singing engagement at Philadelphia's Latin Casino, and Rita took the girls to the fourteen-room Tudor house Dick's mother had rented for them in Greenwich, Connecticut.

For Dick, the afterglow of the wedding publicity didn't last long. Putting Becky in school and breaking in a new baby-sitter kept Rita from joining him at the Latin Casino, where business immediately fell off when word got around that the Love Goddess wasn't there. In a humiliating blow, Dick found himself advised by the Latin Casino's management to summon Rita to Philadelphia. Only then was business likely to pick up. It had become painfully obvious that Dick needed Rita at ringside to draw a substantial audience. His comeback had been a sham. To make matters worse, before he could collect his $5,000 weekly salary ($7,200 total), the Internal Revenue Service attached it to help pay off his nearly $100,000 in back taxes. Suddenly not only was Dick working for free, but he couldn't even pay his pianist – a brand-new debt was all he needed.

By the end of the week Dick had reached his breaking point and failed to appear as scheduled. Initially, he phoned from Connecticut to say that his plane had broken down, but then he canceled the engagement altogether. He'd already had words with the management, arguing that Rita's ringside presence hadn't been part of his contract. But now that he wasn't even getting paid, there seemed little reason to go on. The embarrassingly poor business he'd been doing in Philadelphia made it obvious he wouldn't be missed.

If Dick wanted to draw the big crowds he needed on his comeback tour, it was evident that he'd better have his wife along. Thus, a few days after Haymes had walked out at the Latin Casino, Rita left the children with the new baby-sitter in Connecticut and dutifully accompanied her husband to gigs in Alabama, Indiana, and Texas.

As much as Rita clearly loved her children, she seemed almost to reenact her own mother's role with them: the mother who puts her husband's needs first, no matter what the cost; who fails to protect her children as she should. Soon after her younger daughter had been subjected to three anonymous death threats, not only was Rita leaving the girls behind to travel with her husband (much as Volga had guiltily left her boys to go off with Eduardo), but – incredibly – she was leaving them a short drive away from the Westchester town where the first two of the anonymous letters had been mailed.

In adulthood, victims of childhood abuse may long to be the perfect mothers they were denied as children (remember Rita's vow to Orson that she would be a more responsible parent than Volga had been), but often there is also another part of them that despairs of living up to this image, so that such women secretly believe themselves doomed to fail, much as their own mothers did. Worst of all, perhaps, they fear that when their parental inade-quacies are made public, 'their children will be taken away from them.' These two aspects of a single self, the good mother and bad mother they alternately see themselves as, are locked in perpetual battle, each struggling to be mani-fested in actual parental decisions.

Hence, one suspects, the strange, contradictory behavior that Rita so often publicly exhibited with regard to her children. On the one hand she was the 'good mother,' the protector, struggling desperately against what even the Aga Khan recognized she genuinely believed to be the threat that he or Aly would take Yasmin; on the other, she was the 'neglectful mother,' mysteriously seeming to disregard the repeated death threats that had been made against her child.

After Birmingham, Alabama, and Indianapolis, Indiana, Dick and Rita moved on to the Shamrock Hotel in Houston, Texas, where the Internal Revenue Service was waiting for him. When IRS agents moved to attach his $6,000 weekly salary, they were surprised to discover that the Shamrock had paid him in advance. This time there was nothing for them to take. Still, it was evident that Uncle Sam would be hounding him for cash at every step. Rita and Dick summoned their attorneys to Houston to discuss their mounting financial difficulties.

In the meantime, something had to be done to stop the government from taking Haymes's paychecks. Thus, on 15 October, Rita went before reporters in Houston to proclaim herself 'flat broke' and to announce that Dick 'has to support me and my family and household out of his earnings as a singer.' Rita continued: 'Contrary to popular belief that I'm a wealthy woman, I don't have any money at all. As a woman in love with her husband, I can tell you that you have no idea how horrible it is for me to see Dick spending sleepless nights over his bills, penalties, and income-tax problems without being able to do anything about it. I feel so helpless.' And what about Aly? This was a question that would have been much on people's minds. 'I've only received $8,000 support from him,' she declared in Houston. 'I've supported Yasmin and Rebecca on my own ever since the divorce.'

Whatever the potential embarrassment to her, by openly pleading poverty Rita hoped to convince the IRS not to attach Dick's entire salary at every nightclub where he appeared.

'There's no use beating around the bush,' said Rita. 'We need the money to keep going.'

Not everyone found Rita's plea convincing, however. A spokesman at Columbia pointed out that since returning to work Rita had been earning more than $250,000 yearly, with twenty-five percent profits still to come from *Affair in Trinidad*. But given Dick and Rita's serpentine legal entanglements (lawyers flying to Houston didn't come cheap), those monies would come in handy for their ever-increasing attorneys' fees.

A few days after Rita had publicly swallowed her pride for him, Dick repaid her devotion by slapping her in the Shamrock Hotel's cocktail lounge, the Cork Club, where they were drinking after his show. When Rita wanted to go upstairs before he was ready, Dick lashed out at her. In response to patrons who complained afterward that they'd seen him strike Rita, Dick insisted that he'd merely been reaching for her arm, and downplayed the incident as a 'honeymoon spat.' But for Rita, who had often been beaten by her father in youth, the pattern of violence was clearly beginning again. 'I could hardly believe I could be a princess one minute and be treated like that the next,' she later told actress June Allyson of the physical violence to which Dick Haymes had subjected her.

From Texas, Dick and Rita returned to Las Vegas, where she received what seemed like good news from Bartley Crum. In New York the lawyer had located the physician who had declared Haymes physically unfit for military service on the basis of chronic hypertension. Dick hoped that this would bear out his claim that he had temporarily sought a deferment as an Argentinian citizen, and had subsequently offered himself for military service, only to be declared 4F. Thus, it would be argued, his initial hasty declaration never to seek American citizenship shouldn't be held against him.

What Dick wasn't admitting to anyone was that he hadn't exactly given up his original deferment voluntarily, but had lost it when Argentina ceased to be a neutral country. Only then had he been granted a medical exemption. Nonetheless on 28 October 1953, he entered his latest deportation hearing confident that the discovery of the doctor who had declared him 4F would turn everything around. But as he quickly discovered, the immigration authorities were anxious to press other matters.

At the previous hearing, when the examiner asked whether he'd ever claimed to be an American citizen, Dick had denied it. Perhaps in magazine interviews, he admitted, but never *officially*. Now the examiner returned to this line of questioning. 'Did you represent yourself to be a citizen of the United States to the Actors' Equity Association?' he asked.

'I may have possibly,' replied Dick, clearly aware that he *had*. According to Actors' Equity rules, being a US citizen was financially advantageous. There was no mistaking that on his application for membership Dick had falsely claimed to have been born in Santa Barbara, California, and to be a US citizen.

The evidence was damning: Haymes had claimed Argentinian citizenship when it suited him (his draft exemption), and American citizenship when that was preferable (Actors' Equity). Dick's credibility was being seriously undermined, and hence his all-important claim not to have fully understood what he was doing when he waived any future right to apply for American citizenship. The hearing ended on this sour note, and another was scheduled for November.

Back in Las Vegas after the disastrous proceedings, again it was Rita who spoke out publicly on Dick's behalf (although prior to her statement the couple had been observed furiously quarreling at the hotel). Increasingly her tone was one of desperation as she suggested to the American people that as yet unidentified powers were secretly behind Dick's deportation troubles: 'It seems awfully peculiar that the whole weight of the Justice Department, with all the problems confronting the country today, suddenly is thrown against one lone man for an incident that happened ten years ago,' Rita declared. 'Dick has never been accused of anything except a violation of the McCarran Act, which I understand was meant to keep crooks, cranks, and commies out of the country. Why don't they consider the fact that he withdrew his request for deferment and that twice he was turned down for service in the army – even the doctor who had to turn him down in New York for his physical examination ten years ago telegraphed us he would like to testify and help Dick with his case. There's a lot of taxpayers' money being spent on this case. It seems that the public and the press are willing to give Dick fair play, but I think there's something behind all this and I am appealing to my lawyer to demand a congressional investigation. Dick has been torn apart and crucified. His career has been ruined. He has been financially hurt. For two months I have watched all this and suffered with him. I can't keep quiet any longer as Dick has asked me to. I am appealing to Congress, the public, and the press for fair American justice to Dick, and God help anything that is responsible for unfair play in this case.'

For the first time now, in Paris, Prince Aly Khan overtly moved to take Yasmin away from Rita. From the press accounts of Dick and Rita it was clear that things had gotten entirely out of hand. Shortly after she had publicly called for a congressional investigation into her present husband's problems, Rita received a cable from Aly asking that she send Yasmin to him for safekeeping in Paris. It was what any concerned parent probably would have done.

According to Bartley Crum, who had joined Rita in Las Vegas, Aly asked for the child on the grounds that the FBI wasn't adequate to protect her. After the recent unsolved death threats, Aly understandably feared for the child's safety. Despite the unambiguous gravity of the threats, the little girl had been much photographed and exposed to potential danger. And clearly Rita's extensively publicized troubles since marrying Dick Haymes didn't help matters.

Instead of pointing an accusing finger at Rita, as well he might have, Aly diplomatically shifted the blame to the FBI.

But – although Rita did not have her children with her anyway, and should have had no reason to balk at Aly's request – she responded angrily: 'The function of the FBI is to investigate – not to protect – as you and your attorneys should know,' she cabled him immediately.

Once again Crum went before the press to announce that Rita had no intention of surrendering Yasmin to Aly. Again the religious issue was raised: Rita planned to bring up the child as a Christian, he declared, and would 'resist to the limit' all efforts to remove Yasmin from her custody. In this context, invoking the 'Muslim' issue yet again was more than a little disingenuous. With each new tawdry story about Dick and Rita in the press, her strident assertions about giving the princess a Christian upbringing were becoming increasingly absurd. But the air of persecution and paranoia that she was daily breathing with Haymes made it impossible for Rita even to consider that Aly simply and honestly had their daughter's well-being at heart.

After an appearance in Toledo, Ohio, Dick and Rita headed for Pittsburgh, where Dick was set to open at the Carousel Theater. As they changed trains in Chicago, in an apparent attempt to downplay the concerns Aly had recently expressed, Rita told reporters that she no longer feared for Yasmin's safety (despite the fact that the FBI was still actively investigating the case). Rita also announced that after Pittsburgh she would continue to accompany her husband to subsequent singing engagements in Buffalo and Boston. However, although they were observed to board the train, they never arrived in Pittsburgh.

Instead, they slipped off in New York City, and on the evening of 2 November, even as Dick was scheduled to be opening in Pittsburgh, he checked into Park East Hospital, in Manhattan, where he was sedated for hypertension, and a 'No Visitors' sign was hung on his door. The hospital predicted that he would likely be there for 'quite a while.'

'I don't know what to do,' he told his lawyer, David Marcus, when he called him in Los Angeles. 'I'm going insane. My nerves are shot. I don't know where to turn. I want to work. I'm trying to work, but they won't let me.'

It seemed to Marcus that Haymes was 'on the verge of a breakdown.'

The day after Dick had entered the hospital in what Rita described as 'a state of collapse,' Dick checked himself out again to join his wife and the girls in Connecticut. His doctor promptly ordered him back to Park East for a week of rest, but no amount of medical attention could cure what really ailed Dick: ceaseless conflicts with the Immigration and Naturalization Service and the IRS, not to speak of pressing financial claims on him by two ex-wives.

As soon as he was out of bed, he and Rita were on the road again, or – between out-of-town engagements – at the fashionable Hotel Madison in New York City. Meanwhile, Rita's daughters remained with their baby-sitter in nearby Greenwich – until the owner moved to evict them because Dick had fallen behind with the rent. At the last minute he managed to pay the owner in full and agreed to have his family and possessions out of the house by 15 February.

It was at the Hotel Madison that Dick and Rita soon publicly demonstrated how very close to the edge they had come. At eight P.M. on 1 February, they were ensconced in their twelfth-floor suite when they heard a knock on the door. Dick called out to ask who was there. Whereupon two men identifying themselves as sheriff's deputies informed Haymes that they intended to arrest him. Dick and Rita listened in horror as the lawmen explained that earlier in the day Supreme Court Judge James B.M. McNally had signed a civil arrest warrant for him.

This had nothing to do with Dick's troubles with the immigration service or the IRS. Instead, his ex-wife Joanne Dru was after him now for sums owed her in excess of $33,323.49. Apparently he had earlier agreed in court to give her ten percent of his gross earnings until the debt was paid off. Now the ex-wife charged that Dick had been arranging with nightclubs to pay him in advance, so that she couldn't collect her fair share. Lest Dick be deported soon and end up beyond her legal reach, Joanne had decided to move against him immediately.

The news plunged Dick into a fit of hysteria. He still hadn't opened the door, and now he adamantly refused to do so. When the deputies demanded to be let in, Dick shouted that the door would remain locked until he'd conferred with his attorney. While Rita placed a frantic call to Bartley Crum, the two armed lawmen prepared themselves in case Dick and Rita made a run for the elevator or one of the two stairways on the floor.

Bartley Crum wasn't alone in rushing to the hotel to see what was going on. Joanne Dru's lawyer, Lewis Greenbaum, joined him there, as did a crowd of reporters who had heard about the 'siege' at the Hotel Madison. The hallway outside Dick and Rita's suite was soon packed to capacity. Still Dick wouldn't open the door. It was a measure of Dick's overwrought state of mind that, although he had summoned his own lawyer to the hotel, he even refused to allow him inside. As the others watched in amazement, Crum soon found himself communicating with Dick and Rita through the keyhole, presumably so that they could confer in hushed tones.

Dick told him that he'd locked himself and his wife in because he feared going to jail. From then on it was a stalemate. Nothing anyone shouted to him through the door seemed to change Dick's mind. He appeared to have lost touch with reality; by not opening the door he apparently hoped that somehow he could make this latest problem just go away.

Eventually the lawyers and reporters went home to bed. As for the deputies, short of breaking down the door there was little they could do under the circumstances except to spend the night in the corridor on two overstuffed chairs. Dick and Rita had to come out eventually, and the two lawmen would be there to arrest him when they did.

By morning Dick and Rita's latest imbroglio was all over the papers. If Aly had been acutely alarmed by previous reports of Rita's strange life with Dick, what would he think of this?

Dick and Rita remained locked in their suite while Bartley Crum conferred with Under-Sheriff W. William Cahill. At this point the authorities were willing to humor Dick. If he didn't want to open the door, he didn't have to. They would be willing not to arrest him for now if he agreed to slip a check for $26,000 under the door immediately. Although Dick owed his ex-wife a good deal more than that, the sum would at least cover his share of the California property tax that she had paid in its entirety during their marriage. When Dick and Rita eventually came out he could get his check back as soon as he posted a bond for the same amount.

To this proposal Crum responded that if indeed Dick wrote them a check for $26,000 it wouldn't be any good since he didn't have any money in the bank. Nor did he have the collateral necessary to post a bond. No, some other arrangement would have to be worked out with Joanne's lawyer.

At length Dick agreed to open the door briefly so that Bartley Crum could slip inside. Despite the maelstrom in the hallway, Dick and Rita were sitting quietly, dressed in lounging clothes. Rita, of course, could have left at any time, it was Dick they were after. But she vowed to stay with her husband until the end. It was evident to the lawyer that the past few hours had caused Rita considerable 'mental anguish.' There was no food in the suite and they hadn't had anything to eat since the previous day. When, at Crum's urging, the authorities offered to send in some breakfast, Dick shot back that he wasn't hungry. By two P.M., however, Dick had changed his mind and he and Rita ordered eggs Benedict, grapefruit juice, and coffee. Thus, in addition to Crum, soon a hotel waiter was allowed into the besieged suite.

Too many reporters had been trying to push their way into the chaotic twelfth-floor corridor, so the hotel management eventually confined them to a press room at the north end of the lobby. There they waited until Crum announced that he had reached an agreement with Joanne's attorney.

Twenty-four hours after Dick and Rita had panicked and locked themselves in their hotel suite, the armed guards were removed from in front of their door, and the couple were free again to come and go as they pleased.

Dick and Rita were by no means finished with deputy sheriffs. Ten days later, Haymes and Hayworth were still living at the Hotel Madison when they learned that another deputy sheriff had appeared at their house in Greenwich, Connecticut. This time the charges were completely different. Dick had agreed to move his family out by mid-month, but in the aftermath of all the curious news coverage Dick and Rita had been receiving lately, the owner feared that they planned to skip out without paying. Further, the owner claimed that in the short time the Haymes family had inhabited the premises, there had been $4,000 worth of damage. Thus, the deputy sheriff announced that henceforth one of his men would be stationed inside to assure that Dick and Rita did not remove their personal belongings until after paying the owner for all back rent and damages.

However, instead of finding the parents there, the deputy sheriff discovered only Becky, Yasmin, the babysitter Mrs Dorothy Chambers, and a housekeeper. Rita's daughters were reportedly 'quite bewildered by all the strange goings-on' – as indeed any child would be, confronted with a strange man standing vigil in the family living room.

Chapter Twenty-six

*I*n the aftermath of Dick and Rita's latest run-ins with the law, Aly dispatched his attorney Charles Torem to New York. Given Haymes's apparent instability, something obviously had to be done at once. Although Rita's personal life was clearly in crisis, and although by now it was common knowledge that she didn't even have the children with her much of the time, she persisted in her refusal to send Yasmin to Aly for safekeeping. Rita seemed to have put her own destiny in the hands of Dick Haymes, and as a result there was no telling what she might do or where she might turn up next. A newspaper in Buenos Aires had reported recently that Dick would soon be returning to Argentina for good. Of course he publicly denied the report; to acknowledge that it might be true would be to concede that he was about to lose his deportation case. Still, when he moved his family's possessions from the house in Greenwich, he instructed the storage company to pack them 'for overseas shipment.'

In New York there followed four weeks of urgent negotiations with Aly's lawyer, who was at pains to reach an equitable agreement on Princess Yasmin's custody. Although one might have expected Rita's latest embarrassments to have put her on the defensive, this was by no means the case. As would become increasingly clear, in the battle for Princess Yasmin Aly was no longer dealing only with Rita; now Dick Haymes was in the thick of it, and was most anxious to assert himself with the prince.

In addition to demanding that Aly or a representative appear in Nevada to 'validate' Rita's sole custody of the child, she also stipulated that until Yasmin was twelve Aly could visit his daughter only in the United States, and, further, that his visits be limited to two-week periods with a three-month gap in between. Such terms were predictably offensive and unacceptable to Aly. By limiting his visits to two weeks each, Rita was denying him the right to spend significant and substantial periods of time with his daughter while she was still young. Perhaps even worse, by keeping Yasmin in America until she was twelve, Rita was in all likelihood preventing the ailing Aga Khan from ever seeing his beloved grandchild again.

Unfortunately, Rita was so caught up in her obsessive fear of the Aga Khan's power that she failed to perceive the very real dangers that imperiled her children even as the custody negotiations were going on. The day the family's possessions were moved out of the house in Greenwich, Rita had brought Becky and Yasmin to stay in the suite at the Hotel Madison. But soon she sent the girls to stay with Mrs Chambers in White Plains in a neighborhood of motels and rooming houses – in the very county, Westchester, from which the recent death threats had emanated. By contrast with Rita's luxurious quarters in Manhattan, photographs show that Mrs Chambers's house was shabby and untidy. Far worse, the girls went surprisingly unsupervised and unprotected. Strangers could easily enter the establishment and do whatever they wished with Rita's daughters – which was precisely what occurred on 18 and 19 March, as the latest round of Princess Yasmin's custody negotiations drew to a close.

On 18 March a strange man knocked on Mrs Chambers's door to say that he was interested in renting her house and wanted to look around. Mrs Chambers planned to rent out the premises while she traveled with Dick and Rita as the children's governess. She promptly invited the stranger into the kitchen, where she pointed out the window to identify Rita Hayworth's daughters. There the stranger could see Princess Yasmin Aga Khan 'in a trash-littered backyard, playing among an assortment of loaded ash cans.' Rebecca Welles 'was sitting on a back porch heaped with trash, reading a book.'

Mrs Chambers had no idea who her visitor really was. He could have been a kidnapper or assassin: possibly the crank who had mailed death threats to Princess Yasmin from nearby New Rochelle. In fact, he was a reporter from *Confidential*, a notorious scandal sheet of the day. Indignant neighbors had apparently alerted *Confidential* to the conditions inside the Chambers house.

Soon the reporter was out back chatting with Becky Welles. 'I'm not as good as I should be,' she reportedly said of her reading. 'But I'd read better if I could go to school, like the other kids.' Whereupon it became clear that since boarding her out in White Plains, Rita had failed to register her elder daughter in school.

Mrs Chambers remained inside as little Yasmin accompanied the reporter, presumably to inspect the furnace in the basement. Thus, at a moment when Rita was still adamantly refusing Aly Khan's offer to take Yasmin for safekeeping, a stranger was being left entirely alone with the princess. Had he wanted to, he could easily have made off with the child or done her other harm.

Princess Yasmin was no better guarded the next day, 19 March, when the reporter returned to the house. While he diverted Mrs Chambers's attention, a photographer took a series of pictures. One might have been skeptical about what the reporter claimed to have witnessed inside the Chambers house, but there was no denying the evidence of the photographs. The princess was shown digging in a bushel basket of trash, 'sweeping' the floor with a broom, or playing in a sink stacked with unwashed dishes, pots, and pans. In another shot Becky and Yasmin posed on a trash-strewn porch. Another showed a dilapidated bathroom with peeling walls.

Photographing the little girls like this was in itself a cruel form of exploitation. They could have had no idea of what was being done to them as the photographer asked them to pose. Nonetheless, far more alarming than the living conditions the pictures disclosed was the very fact that it had been possible to take them. Exploitative as the photographs may have been, they demonstrated vividly the little girls' absolute vulnerability. But it would be a while before Rita was forced to come to terms with the conditions in which Becky and Yasmin had been placed in White Plains. For now quite different matters preoccupied her.

Just then, on 22 March 1954, the immigration authorities ruled for Dick's deportation. Much as Dick and Rita may have been expecting the worst, nothing had prepared them for the shock of the actual decision. While Dick and Rita huddled inside their suite at the Madison, planning an appeal to the immigration authorities, their lawyers in Los Angeles and New York publicly blamed Haymes's enemies for the cruel fate that had befallen him.

Without mentioning the name of Harry Cohn (although who else could they have meant?), Dick's side went so far as to suggest that the deportation case had been 'inspired by a person or persons in the movie industry.' 'They are designing to break up the marriage of Rita and Dick,' Bartley Crum asserted. And lest anyone get the impression that the decision to deport Dick Haymes had been fairly arrived at, Crum argued otherwise: 'It is apparent to any lawyer that the decision was reached that Haymes was deportable before the hearing was held,' he said. 'The decision was reached in Washington.'

But if the original motivation for having Dick Haymes deported had been to end Rita's involvement with him, the plan had badly backfired. Since running off with Dick, not only had Rita been generally unavailable to work in films, but she had exposed herself to a good deal of ugly publicity that could prove detrimental to her future value as a star. To make matters worse, now that Dick was finally being kicked out of the country, she vowed to go with him.

Rita temporarily brought her daughters into Manhattan from Mrs Chambers's house. The morning after Haymes had received the bad news about his deportation, he accompanied Rita and Becky to the US Passport Office in Rockefeller Center. He obviously hadn't shaved and appeared anxious and exhausted behind dark glasses. Dressed in a mink coat, Rita appeared similarly tense. A frightened Becky Welles clutched tightly at her mother's hand as once again the photographers' flashbulbs popped and reporters shouted questions at them. This was the way it had been for Becky all too many times in her brief life thus far. Instead of having grown accustomed to the cameras, it was evident from the pained look on her face that the child loathed them more than ever. When Rita made her dramatic appearance at ten A.M. there was already a long line of approximately one hundred passport applicants. Rita wanted to be taken first, but a clerk informed her that she would have to wait in line like everyone else, and she swept out of the office with Dick and Becky trailing behind.

By the time they returned two hours later, it had been arranged for her to go directly to the front of the line. Renewing the passports of Rita and the girls took about fifteen minutes. The still unshaven Haymes answered a clerk's routine questions on Rita's behalf as she stared straight ahead and Becky, in silence, stroked her mother's fur coat.

Initially it may have seemed gallant of Dick to take care of things like this, but more and more he would be assuming the old Eddie Judson role: doing all the talking for a wife who remained disturbingly silent. Much as she often did on film sets, Rita seemed somehow to withdraw into herself. Observed at the Hotel Madison, she was described as 'coldly calm' and 'a martyrlike figure.'

'I feel like a Japanese fisherman,' she told Leonard Lyons apropos the deportation order when she and Dick met him at three A.M. at El Morocco. It was an exceedingly odd thing to say. But comparing herself to the victims of radioactive fallout during a recent H-bomb explosion reflected the strong sense of being under attack that she and Dick shared.

In fact, on the deportation front, new evidence had emerged that might help Dick's case. Dick's lawyer, David Marcus, happened to meet Richard Cody – the officer who had cleared Dick Haymes's trip to Hawaii back in May

1953 – in a restaurant. Now no longer with the Immigration and Naturalization Service, Cody disclosed to Marcus that his department had explicitly told him *not* to warn Haymes that he might be subject to deportation if he made the Hawaiian trip. Presently he gave Marcus a formal statement to that effect, so that on 26 March Haymes was confidently claiming that he had been entrapped. Marcus announced that he was sending a copy of Cody's statement to the Senate Judiciary Committee and would call for a congressional investigation into the Haymes case.

But if things looked brighter for Dick, Rita's custody battle with Aly seemed far from over. It had been a year and a half since Aly had been allowed even a brief visit with Yasmin. All he asked was to settle things with Rita as quickly as possible so that he could be with his little girl. Unfortunately, however, Dick's latest victory seemed to have spurred him to assert himself with Aly as well. The results were disastrous all around.

Aly's lawyer was working on an agreement that would allow Aly to visit the United States without Rita's serving him with court papers for unpaid child support. (Aly's dissatisfaction with the custody arrangements had led him to refuse to pay.) Once in the States Aly hoped to talk with Rita in person to settle their differences over Yasmin. In a typically self-destructive gesture, however, he made the mistake of arranging to spend time with Gene Tierney in Mexico until he received the okay to go to the United States.

Although he had earnestly hoped to avoid publicity, experience should have told him that it was inevitable that the press would find them there, and that within days Rita would be reading all about how he was reprising their Mexican sojourn of several years past, but with another woman. And he should have known that the news would not sit well with her – nor with the Aga Khan, who didn't object to Aly's relentless womanizing so much as to the embarrassing publicity he seemed incapable of avoiding. As the Aga Khan himself was the first to admit, in his day he had done plenty of womanizing of his own. 'But I didn't attract the publicity my son's behavior is getting,' he complained to Elsa Maxwell. 'Communication is universal today, my followers can read – what do you think their reactions are when they hear that my son has married one movie star, been divorced by her, and now is involved with another?'

If Aly was upset that the press had so quickly discovered his little rendezvous in Mexico, he soon grew furious when Dick Haymes, of all people, began phoning him there. Aly intended to go to America to have a serious talk with Rita. Now Haymes had stepped in, instructing Rita that it would be best if *he* dealt with Aly. Thus, he began to place person-to-person calls to the prince in Mexico. Understandably, Aly was enraged at the idea of having to negotiate matters pertaining to the custody of his own child with Dick Haymes. The prince persisted in refusing to deal with him. Hadn't Rita's erratic new husband already done enough harm? The last thing Aly needed was to let Haymes into the middle of what was already a terrible situation.

By 6 April lawyers for Aly and Rita had worked out the agreement for him to enter the United States without being summoned to court. He and Gene promptly left for Los Angeles. From there he would fly to New York to settle the custody dispute with Rita and to see his daughter at last. To this end the prince's lawyer Charles Torem had already arrived in New York from Paris. But no sooner had Bartley Crum publicly announced Aly's imminent arrival than Dick and Rita abruptly decamped for a vacation in Florida. Becky and Yasmin were left behind with Mrs Chambers.

It was evident that Dick and Rita had timed their unexpected departure to short-circuit Aly's plans. Dick seemed oddly anxious to keep Rita from settling Yasmin's custody with Aly. At the Casa Marina Hotel, in Key West, asked if the site of Rita's previously announced meeting with Aly had been shifted from New York to Florida, Dick shot back: 'This is the first thing I've heard about it. I just came here to rest and fish. That's the only reason we are down here.' By now the press had begun to notice that Dick was consistently doing all the talking for Rita, who typically remained silent as he pontificated on Yasmin's custody.

Thus, the *New York Herald Tribune* reported: ' "If any kind of settlement is made it's up to Aly,'' said Mr Haymes. Miss Hayworth said nothing.'

For his part, Aly was determined to put a stop to this nonsense. He hadn't come to America only to be denied access to his little girl again. And he certainly didn't intend to return to Europe without having first talked things over with Rita. Repeatedly he called Rita person-to-person in Florida, but Dick always answered, and refused to put him through. If the prince wanted to discuss Yasmin, he'd have to do it with Dick Haymes.

While Aly refused to accept Dick's self-appointed role in the custody dispute, he was powerless to alter the situation. As if to taunt his adversary, Dick bragged to the press that Rita had been refusing Aly's calls. For the first time in years Dick Haymes seemed totally in control – he was calling the shots and loving it.

Chapter Twenty-seven

When Dick and Rita left Key West it wasn't to return to New York, as Aly might have hoped. Instead, they turned up in Miami Beach, where they took rooms at the Roney Plaza. The hotel would have held bittersweet memories for Rita, who had lovingly nursed an ailing Orson Welles there only ten years before. How immensely her life had changed in those ten intervening years! Back then with Welles, it appeared as if she had finally put her miserable past behind her. Now, all too often, it seemed that the worst was yet to come.

And so it did on 21 April, when the Westchester Society for the Prevention of Cruelty to Children received a complaint from two of Dorothy Chambers's neighbors in White Plains about the conditions in which Rita Hayworth's daughters were living. The society immediately dispatched two caseworkers to the Chambers house to assess the merit of the complaint. The disturbing photos taken inside the house had not yet appeared in print, so there was no telling what the caseworkers might find. After two days of intense scrutiny of the circumstances in which Becky Welles and Princess Yasmin Aga Khan were then living, the caseworkers turned in a report that prompted William J. Bennett, the society's Director of Child Protection, to file a formal neglect petition at once. Becky, it seemed, had not been registered in school, and both girls were said to go without proper supervision.

Only a short while ago the children had been perplexed

when a deputy sheriff arrived at their door in Greenwich. Now, in White Plains, another deputy sheriff came to announce that they were being placed in the protective custody of the Children's Court. Before the girls could actually be taken away, however, a lawyer representing Mrs Chambers petitioned the court to leave Becky and Yasmin with her until the neglect hearing, scheduled for the following week. Although the authorities let the children stay with Mrs Chambers for the weekend, still Becky and Yasmin remained technically in the court's protective custody.

A day passed before Rita learned about the neglect charges. She and Dick had been driving a borrowed Jaguar en route from Florida to Washington, D.C., when the children had been placed in protective custody, so there had been no way to reach her immediately with the devastating news. For many women who have suffered incestuous abuse in youth, this is perhaps the greatest secret fear – that they will be revealed as bad mothers like their own, and that they will lose their children. It was precisely the nightmare that appeared to be happening now as the court took the girls into protective custody and a neglect hearing was scheduled. That Rita could have allowed herself and her children to be placed in such a position suggests how wildly out of control her life with Dick had spun.

Bartley Crum had gone to Washington, D.C., to press the appeal in Dick's deportation case. Word of the neglect charges reached the lawyer there first, and he publicly suggested that they, too, might be part of the larger plot against Dick Haymes. According to Crum, too much had been happening to Dick and his family to be entirely coincidental.

On the West Coast, Aly and Gene Tierney were out looking at horses when reporters called Tierney's home to get the prince's reaction to Yasmin's having been placed in protective custody. Gene's mother, Belle, had been there to hear the startling news instead. When Aly found out, he perceived at once that this changed everything. Given the

303

seriousness of the allegations, Rita would hardly be able any longer to refuse to talk to him about Yasmin. Was this the normal American life that Rita had been arguing was so much better for the child than what Aly had to offer?

His lawyer Charles Torem was soon on the case in New York, and Aly left immediately to join him there. This time, no matter what Haymes said, there would be no keeping Aly away from his daughter. The neglect charges clearly gave him new leverage in the custody dispute. Still, whatever his anxieties about Yasmin's well-being, he couldn't legally just storm into Mrs Chambers's house and remove her. If he did that, Rita would be able to charge him with kidnapping.

That weekend Becky and Yasmin remained locked inside as Mrs Chambers's house became a local tourist attraction. By then news of the neglect charges had been widely published, and carloads of curiosity-seekers arrived en masse in White Plains. The ongoing custody dispute over Princess Yasmin had been much in the press lately, so the neglect charges only naturally caused a good deal of excitement. Anxious to keep the girls out of sight, Mrs Chambers drew all the shades. For her part, she indignantly blamed the scandal on a malevolent neighbor. 'It must be somebody who's vicious and seeking publicity,' she declared. 'Anyone who would seek to exploit the misfortunes of children should drop dead.'

The denials of Crum and Mrs Chambers notwithstanding, the Westchester Society for the Prevention of Cruelty to Children stood firm in its allegations of neglect. 'We sent two caseworkers out to investigate,' retorted Walter W. Westall, the society's president for the past eighteen years. 'They were experienced workers and we don't make mistakes.'

Orson Welles was in Europe struggling to finish the troubled film *Mr Arkadin* when he heard about the neglect charges. Although he had certainly never paid much attention to her, Becky Welles was, after all, his daughter, so, like it or not, the case had a very direct bearing on him. Orson immediately instructed his New York attorney,

Arnold Grant, to do whatever he could to support Rita, which included informing the judge of Welles's opinion that Rita had always been a good mother. Should the girls be removed from Rita's physical custody during the hearing, Grant (who by chance lived in Westchester County) was to offer to take them into his own home.

In addition to so instructing his attorney, Orson wired United Press to state publicly of the neglect charges that 'whatever the truth may be, Rita is not herself to blame, since she has always been a most devoted mother to both girls.' What Orson didn't say, however, was that he privately feared that, in the wake of the neglect charges, Aly would move to take custody not just of Yasmin, but also of Becky. As Orson would admit years later, he had always felt intense guilt about his own blatant failure as a parent, but as long as Rebecca was with her mother he could tell himself that everything was all right. Letting Aly take Becky from Rita (although, again, there was no indication that the prince ever intended to do so) would have been too much for Orson's ego to bear: a confession that both he and Rita had been inadequate to the responsibilities of parenthood.

By contrast with Welles, Aly initially refrained from commenting publicly on the charges. Although as she may have feared he would, Aly did not speak out against Rita, he did not attest to her being a good mother, either. His strategy was to minimize the scandal as much as possible. Although he had no control whatsoever over his daughter's circumstances, Aly also came under implicit criticism in the press now, when more than one account noted that both parents had been enjoying expensive vacations while their daughter was being housed in conditions so unsuitable as to have prompted neglect charges. Clearly this episode would not play well with the Aga's religious followers, who would be appalled to learn that their little princess had been neglected. Aly would send his lawyers in with Rita to help her regain custody of the girls. Meanwhile, he would be working quietly behind the scenes to come to terms with her about Yasmin. Under the circumstances it seemed more than likely that Rita would finally be amenable to granting him significant time with his daughter, which was all he had really been seeking all along.

Aly arrived in New York by plane early Monday morning, 26 April. The neglect hearing was scheduled for two P.M. that day. Rita and Dick had checked into the Roger Smith Hotel in White Plains at two A.M. in the morning, and by eight A.M. they pulled up in their borrowed Jaguar in front of Mrs Chambers's house, where Rita quickly ducked inside to avoid the humiliation of facing reporters. Despite her deep Florida tan she appeared haggard and distraught. Dick's seemingly interminable problems had subjected her to far too much pressure of late, and she was evidently not holding up well after this latest blow. According to Mrs Chambers, when she arrived to fetch her daughters, Rita had been 'so upset she was ill.'

Two hours later, Rita faced a battery of cameras head on as she emerged from the Chambers house. Dick carried a small suitcase of the girls' things in his right hand and held Yasmin with his left. Becky followed close behind. Both girls were impeccably well groomed now. They looked as if they were on their way to a fancy children's party, rather than to Rita's hotel to prepare for the ordeal of a courtroom appearance.

At about noon that day Aly and his lawyer pulled up at the Roger Smith Hotel in a chauffeur-driven limousine. There he would be reunited with his daughter for the first time in a year and a half. Clearly these were not the circumstances in which Haymes had envisioned having his first meeting with Aly. The scandal of the neglect charges had left Dick and Rita in a considerably weakened bargaining position. But whatever his resentment against Haymes, Aly was never one to make a scene. And now, as always, he was the soul of courtesy. Having waited so long for this moment, he was overjoyed to see Yasmin. Ever concerned for the well-being of both girls, he would not have wanted them to be further upset by an unpleasant exchange with Dick. The room-service waiter who delivered a lunch of chicken sandwiches was surprised to see that everyone seemed so happy.

Nevertheless, Aly was also there to have a serious talk with Rita as she braced herself to appear in court. Now was the time to press his appeal for an equitable custody agreement. He would provide whatever guarantees to return the child that Rita might require, but he must be allowed to have Yasmin with him in Europe, and for a decent length of time. It was imperative that Yasmin visit with her grandfather the Aga Khan, whose extremely poor health precluded his traveling to America to see her. If too much time elapsed before the princess came to France, the Aga Khan might well be dead. A great deal had changed since the unsatisfactory custody negotiations in March. If ever Rita was likely to come to terms, it was now.

Charles Torem later recalled Rita's statement to Aly on 26 April 'that she did not wish to deny him the love and affection of their daughter' and 'that she would cooperate in making possible the visitations.' Had the terrible events of the past few days made her temporarily come to her senses? Or was she willing to promise anything as long as Aly did not oppose the return of the children to her custody? Whether or not she spoke sincerely, for the moment it appeared as if the protracted battle over Yasmin was finally coming to an end. At least that bit of good would have come out of the otherwise painful scandal.

Yasmin remained in the hotel with Aly, who got down on his knees to play with her, while Rita, Dick, and Becky left for the White Plains County Office Building, where the neglect hearing was about to start. As they approached the main entrance they could see several hundred newsmen and curiosity-seekers waiting anxiously for Rita's arrival. In hopes of avoiding them Dick found a rear entrance, but no sooner had they slipped quietly inside than cries from those waiting in the lobby caused a virtual stampede toward Rita. Fortunately, the Haymeses quickly spotted an available elevator and before long they were safely up on the court floor.

For the next two hours behind closed doors, Judge

George W. Smyth interviewed all concerned, including young Becky, whom he later described as 'a very sweet little girl.' At length, however, although Rita herself was not charged with willful neglect or improper guardianship, the judge declared that the Westchester Society for the Prevention of Cruelty to Children had been 'fully justified' in bringing Becky and Yasmin under the court's care and protection.

The court ruled that within a reasonable amount of time Rita would have to rectify such unacceptable conditions as Becky's not having been enrolled in school – in this case it was agreed that Rita would hire a private tutor until such time as regular schooling could begin. Finally, Judge Smyth returned the care and custody of her children to Rita. But in an important stipulation, the case would remain under the court's jurisdiction for three months, so that the judge could keep an eye on what became of Becky and Yasmin. Accordingly, Rita indicated that, for at least the period of the court's continuing jurisdiction, she and the girls would remain in the state of New York.

Then came the moment when Rita had to face the press and public after this latest ordeal. The *New York Herald Tribune* reported that Rita 'appeared hysterical as she left the judge's chambers.' She nervously clutched Dick's hand as they tried to make their way through the surging crowd outside. Becky was turned over to Bartley Crum and a policeman, who each took a hand and virtually carried her down the steps into the waiting throng.

Rita finally broke down as the mob pressed in around her. Tears could be seen pouring down from behind her dark glasses. 'Please, please!' she begged. 'Please go away. Leave me alone!'

That evening at eight P.M. a smiling Aly Khan emerged from his reunion with Yasmin. He and Rita had further discussed the custody settlement and he left confident that they would reach a final agreement the next day. After signing autographs for several teenage girls outside the Roger Smith Hotel, the prince headed for the Carlton House, in New York, four blocks north of Dick and Rita's suite at the Hotel Madison. An hour later, in White Plains, the police cleared the way for the Haymeses. Dick carried the sleepy Yasmin in his arms and Rita led Becky by the hand to a limousine they had hired for the trip to Manhattan.

Although Rita had regained custody of her two daughters, she knew only too well that the painful words *fully justified* would be endlessly repeated in the press tomorrow and for many days thereafter. And how humiliating that the court had retained jurisdiction over her daughters for three months! It was hardly the atmosphere in which to negotiate with Aly about Yasmin. No matter how outwardly agreeable she had seemed to him that day, she persisted in her obsession that, given the chance, he would steal their daughter away from her forever. Had she regained custody only to lose Yasmin all over again?

The next day attorneys for Rita and Aly bustled up and down Madison Avenue carrying messages between them. The prince desperately wanted to make the custody arrangement final before he boarded a six P.M. flight to London. To judge by the battalion of reporters that pursued the lawyers back and forth, the entire country was eagerly awaiting the latest news on Princess Yasmin. Following the custody dispute had become something of a national pastime.

Dick and Rita remained in seclusion all that day. But at two P.M. the tiny object of all the commotion, Princess Yasmin, emerged from the Hotel Madison, accompanied by Bartley Crum, who warned photographers not to take pictures of her. He reminded them that less than a year ago the FBI had urged that she not be photographed. The lawyer's sudden concern seemed rather absurd at this point, when in fact Rita had allowed Yasmin to be photographed a great many times in the interim. At Rita's wedding alone the little princess had been readily available for all too many a photo opportunity. Why all the caution now? Until only a few days ago Yasmin had been so entirely unguarded that even a *Confidential* photographer had enjoyed easy access to her. Suddenly Crum had gone so far as to hire two private detectives to accompany Yasmin for the four-block trip to see Aly at the Carlton House.

The day after the neglect hearing it was important that Rita publicly demonstrate her motherly concern for the child's safety. That much was understandable. But that afternoon as Aly enjoyed a second visit with Yasmin, little did he suspect that, once again, Rita was gearing up to invoke him as a potential threat to their daughter's well-being! The private detectives and the prohibition of photographs were to establish a climate of fear in which Rita's trepidation about sending her daughter to Europe might seem perfectly reasonable. After visiting with her father, when Yasmin returned to the Madison Crum picked her up and rushed into the lobby. As they passed the waiting photographers he held the child against him so that no pictures could be taken of her face.

Meanwhile, Rita had been meeting with Charles Torem, with whom she finally appeared to have reached an agreement whereby Aly would have his daughter with him in any country he liked for three months every year. As the time approached for Aly to leave for London, Rita assured Torem that he need only get Aly's signature on the papers and that within thirty minutes she would sign as well. Fair enough.

Thus, when Aly left the Carlton House on his way to Idlewild Airport, he could calmly announce that, having just signed the agreement himself, he was sending it over to the Hotel Madison for Rita's signature. He seemed to anticipate no problems. But no sooner had Aly departed than Rita declared that she had had second thoughts. When Aly's lawyer arrived with the signed agreement, he was informed that she couldn't sign now. Rita needed time to talk the whole thing over with Dick. Could she have until eleven the next morning?

This was by no means what Torem or Aly had been led to expect. But they simply had not counted on Dick Haymes's continued involvement. Surely by now he should have backed down. On the contrary, Dick seemed to envision the custody dispute as a personal duel between Aly and himself. Wherever possible Dick sabotaged the proceedings, sarcastically referring to one of Aly's attorneys as the 'Prince of Darkness.'

Suddenly Rita's lawyer was going before the press to announce: 'Mrs Haymes wants to make sure that she is given sufficient power to invoke police action if the father should attempt to hold Yasmin.'

Although Rita had not signed the papers as expected, the subject of Yasmin's projected inheritance was soon much in the news. Wrote the *New York Times*: 'A fortune of $1,500,000 was offered yesterday to four-year-old Yasmin Khan, who had been adjudged a neglected child only the day before.' Rita, however, would later claim through her attorney Bartley Crum that Torem had repeatedly told her that if Yasmin did not visit with her father, her inheritance might be jeopardized.

Rita had indicated that, with Dick Haymes's consultation, she would have made up her mind by eleven A.M. Wednesday. But when the time came still she procrastinated. She and Dick spent most of the day conferring with lawyers, but by nightfall she said she required additional time. Nor the next day did she sign the agreement. By then it was evident that Dick had had his way, and that Rita had no intention whatsoever of coming to terms with Aly.

Having left New York confident that his troubles with Rita over Yasmin had drawn to a close at last, now Aly would have to pursue a very different avenue with her. Thus, Aly's next step would be to try to put pressure on Rita through the White Plains court that had retained jurisdiction over both daughters for three months to come.

Chapter Twenty-eight

*I*n the months that followed, Dick led Rita deeper and deeper into a Kafkaesque maze of lawyers and lawsuits. If they weren't initiating legal action, they seemed to be defending themselves against accusations of one sort or another. There were always new lawyers to be consulted and fees to be paid.

Early in May Dick's latest attorney, Welburn Maycock, urged the Board of Immigration Appeals in Washington, D.C., to reverse Dick's deportation order on the grounds that he had been entrapped. Finally the Cody affidavit convinced the appeals board at least to reopen Haymes's case. A new hearing was scheduled for June in Los Angeles.

At Dick's instigation Rita was soon launching legal action of her own. On 12 May at Federal Court in New York City Rita filed suit against Columbia Pictures to end her Beckworth agreement of 1947. Given the excellent terms that Johnny Hyde had secured for Rita's Beckworth contract, trying to break it now seemed a rather peculiar move. By contract, twenty-five percent of her films' net profits went to Rita, so that if she had worked more regularly between 1947 and 1954, she probably would have been a very wealthy woman by now. Of course, film studios are notorious for endlessly putting off the recording of profits when someone on the picture receives a percentage. The expenses keep piling up somehow, while the profits never seem to begin. But Rita's suit was more than just a matter of demanding a full financial accounting from

Columbia. Retrieving profits that Rita claimed were right-fully due to her from past films would take time, as would waiting for profits from *Miss Sadie Thompson*. Dick Haymes needed money now. Hence, Rita's curious attempt to get Columbia to buy out her 450 Beckworth shares (Columbia already owned 500 shares, and her agency, William Morris, 50).

Not only would this provide a much-needed influx of cash, but henceforth it would also give Dick complete control of Rita's movie career. No longer under contract to Columbia, the Love Goddess would be his to use entirely as he wished. Her name on the marquee would work wonders to bolster his own faltering career. Before long Dick was declaring his intention to use the $700,000 he hoped to get from the sale of Rita's Beckworth shares to form a film-production company with her in Europe. 'We want to do some mood things that could be better done there,' Dick told Earl Wilson. 'Hollywood's such an assembly line with such a habit pattern, it's hard to do anything different, even if you have your own company.'

Of Dick's relationship with Rita, Wilson did not fail to point out that Haymes was 'now captain of both their destinies.'

Dick plainly did all the thinking and talking for her.

Meanwhile, Dick and Rita's finances were dwindling rapidly. Dick's big singing comeback had fizzled, and Rita hadn't been drawing a salary at the studio since she ran off after *Miss Sadie Thompson*. So while Dick waited to cash in on the sale of her Beckworth shares, he and Rita launched themselves on a strange new fantasy: the simple life. They would put fashionable spots like the Hotel Madison and El Morocco behind them and repair to a peaceful, Bohemian existence in Nevada. Although in April Rita had assured Judge Smyth that she planned to remain with the girls in New York for at least three months, in June Dick's mother, Marguerita Haymes, accompanied Becky and Yasmin, as well as a tutor and a nursemaid, on a train trip west. Dick and Rita followed by car. Bartley Crum appealed to the White Plains court for an early end to its continuing jurisdiction over Rita's daughters, but no decision would be forthcoming until July.

On 18 June Dick and Rita pulled up at the Sands Hotel, where they had been married nine turbulent months before; they planned to stay until they could find a simple, secluded house to rent in the woods at Lake Tahoe. Almost as soon as they arrived, word came from Los Angeles that Rita's grandfather, Padre Cansino, had died. Padre had long been Rita's special favorite, but – although she was due to go to Los Angeles anyway for Dick's latest deportation hearing – she did not attend the funeral, explaining to the press that she would have to miss it because she couldn't leave her children. Since she and Dick had just traveled cross-country without them, a more plausible explanation might have been that Dick wanted her with him, as he huddled with attorneys in anticipation of his appeal.

At the deportation hearing in Los Angeles, the government denied Dick's lawyers' request that the charges against him be dropped without further ado. By law, in order to grant Dick Haymes such 'discretionary relief,' the government would first have to be persuaded that 'Mr Evil' was of good moral character – and a confidential memo in Dick's deportation file expressed the government's confidence 'that the alien cannot make a showing of good moral character, but, on the contrary, a showing can be made conclusively that he is not a person of good moral character.'

Nor were the immigration authorities alone in taking a dim view of Dick Haymes. While he and Rita were in Los Angeles, Dick unexpectedly found himself summoned to appear in court on 2 July on charges that he had not made the agreed-upon payments to Joanne Dru. (Dick was also already in default of his alimony payments to Nora.) His presence in California for the deportation hearing made it all the easier for Joanne to serve him with court papers. The last time Joanne had gone after him, the previous February, Dick and Rita had locked themselves in their suite at the Hotel Madison. This time, however, Dick ignored the summons, and by the time of the court date he was safely back in Nevada. Accordingly, the judge issued a bench warrant for his arrest. Should Dick return to Los Angeles henceforth, he faced five days in jail for contempt of court.

For the time being Dick and Rita had no intention of going anywhere near Los Angeles. Back in Nevada Dick signed a year's lease on a modest, secluded two-bedroom bungalow 6,200 feet up in the mountains, at Crystal Bay in Lake Tahoe. There Rita hoped to do some painting and Dick planned to take up furniture refinishing. Newspapers and magazines were strictly banned from the premises. Only music played on the radio – when the news came on it was swiftly turned off. Even the curious costumes Dick and Rita wore bespoke their desire to escape. 'They were both walking around with these long brown monks' robes on!' recalled Bob Schiffer, who brought his new wife to stay with Dick and Rita in Crystal Bay. 'They were just kind of wandering around up there – it was the weirdest! We stayed in a cabin next to them and when we went over for dinner there was not really much to eat. They looked like they were having some sort of communion. I didn't know what the hell was going on. My wife said, "Let's get out of here – it's too far out for me." '

Living as they were in almost complete isolation, more than ever Rita's only source of information and advice was Dick. With no one else around to suggest other possibilities, he exerted total mind-control over her. She saw everyone and everything through his eyes. Still, no matter how much he tried, he could not entirely shut out reality. Thus it had been when they locked themselves in their Manhattan hotel suite, and so it was in Crystal Bay.

Aly had no intention of giving up his battle for Yasmin, who was now sharing the bungalow's second bedroom with her sister. When he learned that Bartley Crum had appealed for an early end to the White Plains court's juris- diction over the girls, Aly objected vehemently to Judge Smyth. The prince held out hope of pressuring Rita to come back to New York by the end of July, so that he might take Yasmin with him for a visit to the Château de l'Horizon. In view of Aly's objections, on 8 July Judge Smyth rejected Rita's plea. Dick and Rita may have decided not to look at newspapers anymore, but there she was in the headlines again. 'COURT REFUSES TO END CUSTODY OF RITA'S 2 CHILDREN'; ALY BARS RITA'S TRY FOR GIRLS' FULL CUSTODY NOW.'

Four days after Judge Smyth's decision, Dick spoke out on Rita's behalf: 'All we want is complete worldwide custody of Yasmin and eight thousand dollars a year support for her,' he declared. 'I say "we" because I love that child like my own. You know who supported Yasmin until I came along – Rita!' It could not have been easy for Aly to read words like these in the papers.

As the three-month period of the court's jurisdiction drew to a close, Aly suddenly made a move that took Dick and Rita entirely by surprise. His attorneys asked the court to extend its jurisdiction over Becky and Yasmin. Originally scheduled to end on 26 July, the court's jurisdiction was thereby extended for one week, until 2 August. Aly's surprise move substantially heated up the battle for Princess Yasmin. If in extending the period of its jurisdiction over her daughters the court was implying a lack of confidence in Rita, then she in turn would have to air some of Aly's dirty linen in public. Bartley Crum was in Israel when he learned of the court's unexpected ruling. Rushing back to New York to deal with the situation, he threatened to expose details of Aly's many love affairs: 'We shall show the court what kind of homelife Aly Khan has, and no doubt shall subpoena his current girlfriends, including some of Hollywood's most famous stars,' Crum warned. 'It's about time we had a showdown.'

As if in answer to his challenge, Aly and Charles Torem immediately flew from Paris to New York, where there was already much excited speculation about which of the women in Aly's life might find themselves testifying in court. Would it be Gene Tierney, Yvonne De Carlo, or Joan Fontaine? Other, less well-known names were also mentioned.

'If they want a fight, we'll fight,' Bartley Crum warned.

But shortly thereafter, at New York's Idlewild Airport, when Crum's counterpart, Charles Torem, was asked whether he, too, anticipated a fight, he replied in a dignified manner, 'I hope not.'

Still, a fight was inevitable. Crum had announced that Yasmin would be permitted to go to Europe only if Rita went along 'to make certain of her return.' Aly knew perfectly well that Dick Haymes wasn't about to let Rita out of his sight. She was allowed to go nowhere without him. For the time being, at least, Dick's immigration woes precluded foreign travel, so naturally Rita wouldn't be going abroad either. And by the terms that Crum had set, if Rita didn't accompany Yasmin to Europe, the child must remain in America.

There followed a closed hearing in the White Plains court on 2 August, where Aly sought a court order that would permit him to have more time with Yasmin. After listening to arguments from both Aly's and Rita's attorneys, Judge Smyth reserved decision for four days. On 6 August, the word from White Plains came as a new blow to Rita. Not only was the court continuing its jurisdiction over the case, but Judge Smyth had decided to expand his study of Rita's custody of her daughters and requested new briefs and affidavits from lawyers for both sides within ten days. Clearly Aly had won a major victory in the battle for his daughter.

On a different front Rita was just then suffering an even worse setback – the government had moved again to deport Dick Haymes. On 29 July, his claim of entrapment had been rejected. But Dick and Rita didn't actually learn about the disastrous decision until 2 August, the day Aly went to court in White Plains. Instantly Dick and Rita launched a new appeal in the deportation case and vowed to go to the US Supreme Court.

As the couple sank ever more deeply into the legal mire, it occurred to Dick that this might actually be the moment to negotiate with his enemies: Harry Cohn (whom he believed to be the author of so many of his troubles of late) and Aly Khan.

As for the Columbia mogul, Dick knew that he had in his possession something Cohn badly wanted: Rita Hayworth. Her involvement with Dick Haymes had already cost Harry Cohn a great deal of money. When she should have been making movies at Columbia, instead Rita had been making a public spectacle of herself with Dick. To Harry Cohn the immense public interest in Rita represented money in the bank for Columbia. But lately, the name Rita Hayworth had been selling newspapers, not movie tickets, and Harry Cohn didn't profit from that one bit. By now Cohn had to have seen and accepted that his initial attempts at getting rid of Dick had badly backfired. As a businessman, he would be ready to cut his losses and listen to what Haymes had to say. Thus, even as Rita's lawsuit against the studio was under way, Dick prepared a peace offering to Columbia that was designed less to serve Rita's interests than his own.

'Harry Cohn and I were up in Vegas at the Sands,' recalled Columbia Vice-President Jonie Taps. 'The telephone rings and it's Dick Haymes. He's over at the Desert Inn with Rita Hayworth. So he says, "You or the Boss can come over if you want." "Come *over*?" I said. "How'd you like to go and fuck yourself?" And I hung up. So Harry Cohn said, "Who'd you say that to?" I said, "Dick Haymes." He said, "You did the right thing." Fifteen minutes later there's a knock on the door. It was Rita Hayworth with Dick Haymes. And we finally made a settlement with her.'

But from the first it was Dick Haymes who figured most prominently in that settlement. Rita simply would not return to work until four major conditions were met: each of them having to do with Dick. That August Rita's agent, William Morris, presented her unusual stipulations to Columbia Vice-President B.B. Kahane. First, Columbia was to lend Dick Haymes $50,000 so that he could immediately pay off the back alimony and other debts he owed his ex-wives. The loan was crucial because, on account of those debts, Dick was currently subject to arrest in California. Since Rita did not go anywhere without

Dick, she certainly could not return to work in Hollywood until Dick was free to travel there without being thrown in jail. Dick agreed to repay Columbia's loan at a rate of $10,000 yearly.

Rita's second condition was that Dick Haymes (whose deportation file noted that he was persona non grata at Columbia) be afforded full access to the studio. Since Dick was now doing all the talking for Rita (as usual, at the preliminary contract discussions she sat quietly while Dick spoke), there was no question of her setting foot on a movie set without his being fully welcome there as well.

And since Dick and Rita suspected that Harry Cohn had been behind his deportation troubles all along, her third condition for returning to work was that the studio do whatever it could to help him reverse the deportation order. If indeed Cohn had instigated the government to act against Dick in the first place, the mogul's help and support could be invaluable now.

Fourth and final, if at length the United States government successfully deported Dick Haymes, Rita insisted on being allowed to fulfill her obligations to Columbia by making movies in whichever country she and Dick might choose.

In short, Columbia was being presented with a package deal: to get Rita back they had to accept Dick as well. And they *had* to buy out Beckworth. Dick still had his eye on the $700,000 she could get for her shares.

While negotiations with Columbia dragged on that fall, Dick and Rita also seemed anxious to come to terms with Aly. The continuing involvement of the White Plains court hung like the sword of Damocles over Rita's head. It seemed that only by negotiating with Aly might she get the court finally to abandon its jurisdiction. Not surprisingly, in September, when the long-awaited announcement came that Yasmin's parents had agreed 'in principle' on her custody and support, it was neither Rita nor Aly who made it, but Dick Haymes. However conciliatory Dick and Rita might appear at the moment, Aly knew only too well that promises and apparently good intentions were worthless

319

without Rita's signature on a solid custody agreement – and *that* he still had not been able to secure.

Now, however, both sides hammered out a complex nineteen-page agreement that Rita would indeed sign that November, after two drafts and numerous revisions. It seemed like everything for which Aly had hoped. Three and a half years had passed since Rita had fled the Château de l'Horizon with Yasmin, who was now nearly five. The Aga Khan had not glimpsed the child since then. Now at long last Yasmin would be spending substantial periods of time with her father and his family so that they might develop a meaningful relationship.

In 1955 Yasmin was to visit Aly in Europe for eleven weeks beginning 1 July. On this first visit Rita would have the right to accompany the child. Visits to her father in Europe were also scheduled for subsequent years, until Yasmin reached the age of twenty-one. If, as anticipated, she attended boarding school in either Switzerland or France, Aly was to have her for four weeks during vacation and for school holidays of less than one week.

In exchange for all this, Aly had to assuage Rita's fears about his or the Aga Khan's refusing to return Yasmin. Thus, whenever Yasmin visited Aly, he would be required to deposit $100,000 in a bank of Rita's choice. Should Aly try to keep Yasmin in Europe, Rita could use the money for the legal costs of getting her back. If, however, Aly did indeed return Yasmin to Rita, the money would grow into a trust fund of approximately $1,000,000 that would go to Yasmin in a lump sum when she turned twenty-five. Further, before Yasmin left to visit Aly, his father, the Aga Khan, would be required to give Rita his personal written guarantee that the child would be returned as promised. It did not exactly befit the Aga Khan's dignity to admit the possibility that the child might not otherwise be returned, but seeing his granddaughter and normalizing her situation were clearly worth catering to Rita's embarrassing demands.

As if all this were not enough, Rita sought – and received – two other important forms of protection. She required

Aly to recognize officially her American divorce decree by filing an Entry of General Appearance in the Nevada court. In addition, in each European country where Yasmin visited him, Aly would be expected to apply for an exequatur decree, thereby assuring full local recognition of the terms of the American divorce.

There were also significant changes in the financial settlement. In April 1953 Aly had been ordered to pay $48,000 yearly child support for Yasmin. The figure was now diminished to $8,000 yearly, as long as Yasmin was living at home and until she reached the age of twenty-one. But if at ten or twelve Yasmin were enrolled in a Swiss boarding school, Rita would receive $1,000 monthly, while Aly paid all of Yasmin's school expenses. Besides her secular education, it was agreed that Aly would provide his daughter with a Muslim tutor for two hours of religious instruction every week.

In her dealings with Aly of late, more than once Rita had seemed to change her mind about what she wanted. In the new agreement she formally waived her right to apply for future changes in the support provisions for Yasmin. In other words, this was it.

But would she sign?

On 8 November in White Plains Judge Smyth declared that he had found no reason to continue the inquiry into Rita's care of her children. Still the court's jurisdiction over Becky and Yasmin was to continue until 24 December. In the meantime, in Paris Aly anxiously signed the new agreement and waited to see if, as promised, Rita would do the same.

On 20 November, in Nevada, Rita finally signed the agreement Aly had sought for so long. Throughout, she was conspicuously, mysteriously silent. But when she lifted pen from paper she smiled with apparent satisfaction.

A month later, on 28 December, she also compliantly signed a new contract with Columbia. The meeting at the Riverside Hotel, in Reno, lasted for nine hours and signatures were required on more than thirty documents. This would be Rita's final contract with the studio that had made her a star. It had been seventeen years since, under the auspices of Eddie Judson, she first signed with Columbia. But for all the fame and success that she had enjoyed in the intervening years, Rita was *still* playing Trilby – to Dick Haymes's Svengali. As Rita herself would say later in court, it was Dick who had been behind her signing this new contract. Even Harry Cohn acknowledged that giving up the profit-sharing Beckworth contract for a straight salary had been a dumb mistake on her part. But for a change Cohn wasn't ramming these new, unfavorable terms down Rita's neck, her husband was.

As usual, Rita allowed Dick to speak for her. Perhaps if she had considered that Dick had made and foolishly lost a fortune of his own, she would have thought twice about turning over her business affairs to him. But by now Rita was so entirely under his spell that it simply would never have occurred to her to question anything he said or did.

Much as it must have galled Harry Cohn to do so, Columbia accepted all of Rita's stipulations regarding Dick Haymes. Cohn was anxious for Rita to start work on filming Clifford Odets's script *Joseph and His Brethren*: a biblical epic that Cohn believed could do as well at the box office as Rita's *Salome*. Speed was of the essence, however. Rita was thirty-six and her days as a sex symbol were obviously numbered. Cohn needed to get at least two more pictures out of her before she reached thirty-eight or thirty-nine. After that, if she tried to escape him again, she would be well past her prime anyway, and he really wouldn't need her anymore.

Thus, her new contract committed Rita to make two films for Columbia at a fee of $150,000 each. Since Aly expected Yasmin's first visit to begin 1 July, and since Rita planned to accompany the child, Columbia promised that shooting on *Joseph and His Brethren* would begin on 8 March and that Rita would be all finished filming by 25 June. Meanwhile, to tide her over until her $12,500 weekly salary began, Rita received a loan of $17,844 and a $75,000 advance against salary.

In addition, as Rita signed her new contract, Columbia

322

presented Dick Haymes with the $50,000 loan he had demanded. Even as Dick and Rita were meeting with Columbia representatives in Reno, his attorney was at the Beverly Wilshire Hotel in Los Angeles, negotiating a financial settlement with lawyers for two of his ex-wives that would enable him to accompany Rita to California without facing imminent arrest.

Still Columbia was worried about whether Rita would ever actually show up to make the two films in her contract. The cause of the studio's anxiety was the approximately $700,000 Rita would receive for her Beckworth shares upon dropping her stockholder's suit against Columbia. With all that cash suddenly in hand, there was no telling what the mercurial Haymes might advise Rita to do next. He had, after all, made himself an officer in her new company, Crystal Bay Productions, and had been sounding off lately about making movies with her in Europe. A Columbia interoffice memo indicated that the studio didn't put it past Dick and Rita to take the money and run. To assuage these fears Rita was required to place $100,000 of the Beckworth money in escrow in a Reno, Nevada, bank as a guarantee that she would indeed make the two films she owed the movie studio.

Also, Columbia took an option on Dick's services as a screen writer (!), presumably to give him some role that would justify his presence at the studio henceforth. Although he didn't mention it as yet, Dick already had in mind a far more grandiose role for himself. In anticipation of co-starring as Joseph in Rita's new film, he had begun to cultivate a beard.

Certainly no one at Columbia had offered him the part, but Dick figured that once he and Rita got to Hollywood, it would be only a matter of time before he was cast. Still, that he hadn't included the role of Joseph in the original demands suggests that even he was not so deluded as to think that Columbia would be overjoyed by the idea. He would have to wait until the studio executives saw for themselves how entirely indispensable he had become to Rita's proper day-to-day functioning.

Chapter Twenty-nine

*F*rom the moment Dick and Rita arrived in Hollywood, leaving the girls behind with a nursemaid in Crystal Bay, it was abundantly clear that Haymes was calling all the shots. Even Rita's press conference on her first day back at the studio co-starred Dick Haymes, ranting about his myriad personal problems. *His* tax debts. *His* ex-wives. *His* worries about being deported. And again, at Rita's February story conference with writer Clifford Odets, it seemed to the producer, Jerry Wald, that Dick Haymes 'did ninety-eight percent of the talking.' While Rita listened quietly, Dick said that *he* was happy that Columbia had hired Odets to do the screenplay and that *he* approved of the changes Odets had made to render Rita's role as Zuleika more sympathetic. What did *Rita* think? Rita agreed with everything her husband said.

In addition to attending story conferences, Dick also accompanied Rita to wardrobe fittings and even to the studio hairdresser. Before long Dick was answering for Rita when she wasn't even there, as when B.B. Kahane mentioned to him that Columbia was considering Orson Welles for the role of Potiphar in the film. Since Welles was Rita's ex-husband, Kahane suggested that Haymes ask Rita if casting Orson was all right with her. But Dick cut it short right there. 'She wouldn't even consider it,' Dick promptly told the studio vice-president. 'Forget it.' And Kahane did.

Afterward Dick never mentioned the proposal to Rita. He certainly would not have wanted anyone like Welles around who might be able to break through the emotional wall Dick had built around Rita. Just as Dick had sought to keep Rita constantly at odds with Aly Khan, so now he was careful to keep the possibly even more threatening Orson Welles away.

In the course of her film career until now, everyone would have agreed that Rita was almost invariably easy to work with. She may have been volatile and explosive in her personal life, but never on a film set – there she methodically did as she was told, without protest. But with Dick speaking for her at all times, almost everything suddenly seemed a cause for complaint – *his* complaint, although ostensibly on her behalf. At such times her desire to please him seemed to have overcome her innate professionalism. Later, when Dick was out of her life, she would say that much of what he had done at Columbia in this period was without her knowledge and consent, and that was undoubtedly so. But it was also often the case that Rita appeared simply to tune out what he said and did – much as she had always had the mysterious ability to blank out, to withdraw into herself, when unpleasant things were happening.

By now it was apparent that they were both drinking heavily. When Dick had too much to drink he could be verbally and physically abusive. He claimed to be protecting Rita, but he thought nothing of humiliating her by berating her loudly in public.

Meanwhile, he worked diligently to bind her to him for a long time to come. Indeed, he was already quietly negotiating for the pictures Rita would co-produce with him once she had fulfilled her obligations at Columbia. Shooting had not yet begun on *Joseph and His Brethren* when United Artists announced that it would finance and distribute two Rita Hayworth pictures to be made by Crystal Bay Productions. The surprise announcement did not endear Haymes to Harry Cohn, who had been anxious to reap the full publicity benefit of Rita's return to the screen.

Still Dick clung to the hope that the part of Joseph in Rita's new picture would soon be his. As it happened, the

325

start of production, originally scheduled for 8 March, had been delayed because of Columbia's inability to decide upon the right actor for the role. The studio reassured Rita that as long as it started shooting by 11 April it could film her scenes in the first five or six weeks of production, so she would be finished in time to accompany Yasmin to Europe to see Aly. For his part, Dick tried to exploit the delay to force the studio to lend him an additional $25,000, but he didn't get far with this scheme, nor did he succeed with his bid to play Joseph.

On 5 April Dick was enraged to learn that Kerwin Matthews, a young Columbia contract player, had landed the part of Joseph. Although not the slightest indication had ever been given to Dick that he would play Joseph, he genuinely believed himself to have suffered a massive betrayal. As usual that day, the ubiquitous Dick was hovering about Rita at a reading with the director, William Dieterle. By this time the producer, Jerry Wald, was apparently fed up with Haymes and asked him to leave. One of Rita's main conditions for returning to work at Columbia had been Dick's enjoying full access to the studio. To his immense consternation, he suddenly found himself being kicked out. Already seething over his failure to be cast as Joseph, Dick made his exit, vowing revenge.

Later, when they finished for the afternoon, the director, Dieterle, asked Rita to return that evening at eight-thirty to resume work. But she never showed up. Instead, she sat quietly at Dick's side in the Polo Lounge at the Beverly Hills Hotel as he called Jerry Wald to say that she was ''too tired' to return that night. Then Dick placed a call to Dieterle to announce that Rita was ill.

At midnight Dick and Rita were still at the Polo Lounge, both of them very drunk, when Dick thought of one other person to call. 'Mr Haymes was in a very angry mood,' recalled Clifford Odets of the bizarre midnight call he received from Dick and Rita. 'He talked forty or forty-five minutes and kept telling me he was very annoyed. He wasn't talking very coherently and it was difficult for me to follow him.' When Odets protested that he'd wasted the evening at the studio waiting for Rita to show up, Haymes said that she'd been with him at the Polo Lounge.

'You'd better get over here or I'll be in the Bahamas or Jamaica tomorrow,' Dick warned Odets, before suddenly accusing him of not having properly discussed the 'psychology' of Rita's part with her.

Then, Odets recalled, 'Mrs Haymes got on the phone and discussed conditions of the world and how difficult it was to function as an artist.' Further, Odets remembered that Rita 'showed an air of general discontent. She generally backed up and seconded what her husband had said. Then Miss Hayworth told me, "I'd better put my husband back on the phone."'

Dick seemed even angrier than before. 'I think you're on their side,' he accused the playwright. There followed more of the same: drunken, paranoid, irrational. All of it clearly masked what Dick couldn't bring himself to say: he was pulling Rita out of the picture because he hadn't won a co-starring role.

The next day, 6 April, after Dick called to say that Rita wouldn't be in for work, Columbia dispatched a telegram ordering her to report to the studio in twenty-four hours. Instead, on 7 April, Rita wired the studio to declare that their not having started shooting *Joseph and His Brethren* by 8 March constituted a breach of contract that entitled her to terminate her two-picture deal with Columbia. In addition, Rita's lawyers filed suit to compel the studio to pay her $150,000 fee, as well as to release the $100,000 that she had been required to place in escrow in Nevada.

Columbia wasn't going to let her out of her contract that easily. By 9 April the studio had brought a countersuit against Rita. Lest Dick get any idea about Rita's going to work for United Artists, as previously announced, Columbia declared that Rita had been placed on suspension and that 'under her contract she cannot work elsewhere until she makes two films for Columbia.'

On 1 May Rita was scheduled to repay the studio's $17,844 loan. When she didn't, Columbia filed yet another lawsuit against her.

Although Rita certainly couldn't say it openly in her lawsuit against Columbia, it was soon no secret around Hollywood that Dick had pulled her out of the film because he hadn't been cast as Joseph and was anxious to terminate her Columbia contract so that they could get started at United Artists as quickly as possible. The official reason Rita had given for walking out was that *Joseph and His Brethren* wouldn't be finished in time for her to accompany Yasmin to Europe. But before this latest contretemps with the studio, Rita had already given disturbing indications that she didn't really plan to live up to her November agreement with Aly after all.

Now that the pressure of the White Plains court's jurisdiction over the girls' welfare had been lifted, Rita would become increasingly less cooperative with Aly's plans for Yasmin's long-awaited visit on 1 July. That spring the prince flew to Los Angeles in hopes of making final the details of the visit. But Rita continued to drag her heels in a seemingly picayune legal matter that, if not promptly resolved, could end up spoiling everything.

Rita had insisted that Aly secure the French court's recognition of their divorce (a decree of exequatur), but she inexplicably failed to sign the necessary papers on time, even though she had had them in her possession for two weeks. In addition, she entered into a financial dispute with her Paris lawyer that would undoubtedly further stall the proceedings. Despite Aly's mounting fears, none of this was as yet proof that Rita actually intended to sabotage the November agreement. Then came the startling news that Haymes had been booked for a three-week singing engagement at the Dunes Hotel in Las Vegas, from 18 June to 8 July – and that Rita had no intention whatsoever of bringing Yasmin to Europe as promised on 1 July. How could she if she was going to be in Las Vegas at the time? What Aly didn't know, although he must have suspected, was that, as she later admitted, Dick had simply forbidden Rita to go. All the rest were excuses so that she might obey a despotic husband.

Yet even as Rita continued unquestioningly to obey

Dick, two significant changes occurred in her life that would eventually help make it possible for her to break free of his domination. First, with the money from the sale of her Beckworth shares, they rented a house on the beach at Malibu. The bungalow in Crystal Bay was abandoned with a month still to go on the lease, and Rita's daughters joined her in California. Until then most of their marriage had been spent shuttling from one hotel to another, so that, other than their cadre of lawyers, Dick was really the only person she was seeing and talking to regularly. His view of the world became her principal point of reference. He was on the run – and so was she. She became increasingly dependent on him to do the thinking for the two of them. Then when they went into seclusion at Crystal Bay her life became even more tightly constrained. There was virtually no one else around to put Haymes's ceaseless anxiety in perspective. The move to Malibu allowed Rita to see some other people again. Simple pleasures like the dinner party for Noël Coward that she attended at the home of her old friends from the Welles days, Lenore and Joseph Cotten, allowed her to rediscover that there was still a sane, rational world out there beyond the mental bunker into which she had so entirely retreated with Dick Haymes.

The other significant change in Rita's life involved Dick's deportation case. She had never gotten over the intense sense of guilt she felt for having caused him to face deportation after his romantic visit with her in Hawaii had given the government the excuse to move against him. And, of course, if, as they both suspected, it had been Harry Cohn who had secretly instigated the deportation proceedings against Dick, Rita was responsible for that as well. Dick's knowledge of her guilty feelings gave him an important hold over her. No matter how awful the abuse, both verbal and physical, to which he subjected her, hadn't she been responsible for this terrible thing that had happened to him? Hadn't he gotten into trouble in the first place because he loved her and couldn't bear to be away from her? Accordingly, wasn't it her duty to stand by him now?

Although one of Rita's major conditions for returning to Columbia had been its helping Dick in any way it could with his deportation case, at first things had not looked very bright that spring. There was even the embarrassing public announcement from one of Dick's lawyers that he was so fed up with Dick that he was giving up the case. 'Mr Haymes's attitude is such that I cannot continue as his attorney,' declared David Marcus. 'I do not wish anymore to try to keep the Argentine-born singer in this country.'

Then, in May, came the dramatic turnaround for which Dick and Rita had been waiting. The US District Court ruled that Dick was *not* deportable because, contrary to the arguments of the Immigration and Naturalization Service, when Dick went to Hawaii to see Rita he had *not* left the United States. According to this new ruling, although it was not a state at the time, Hawaii was 'a geographical part of the United States.' Therefore, when he returned to California, Dick had not reentered the United States from a foreign port, as the Immigration and Naturalization Service had claimed.

This ruling did not, however, settle the question of whether Dick's draft exemption during World War II had rendered him permanently ineligible for US citizenship. Thus, if he left the country now, he might well find himself unable to get back in again. But for Rita, the essential thing about the ruling was that it slowly began to lift the terrible burden of guilt that had been hanging over her since the trouble began.

Soon, much as Aly had feared, instead of accompanying Yasmin to Europe, Rita went with Dick to Las Vegas. On 27 June, as stipulated in the custody settlement, the Aga Khan sent Rita his written promise that Yasmin would be returned to her. But once again the old man would be gravely disappointed when his granddaughter did not arrive on 1 July.

Meanwhile, in Las Vegas, Rita was enjoying the urbane company of Noël Coward and his companion, Cole Lesley. While Dick was busy singing at the Dunes, and Coward was at the rival Desert Inn, Rita did the town with Cole

Lesley. After seeing a show at one of the other hotels and dancing for a while at the Golden Nugget, they would head back to the Desert Inn 'just in time to catch Noël singing "Nina," which,' Lesley recalled, 'because Rita had made her dancing debut in Tijuana, he used to sing very pointedly at her.'

Although Dick's Las Vegas engagement ended 8 July, it had become evident that Rita would not be bringing Yasmin to Europe later in the month either. Because of the way she had deliberately dragged her heels in the matter of securing a decree of exequatur, Aly would be unable to make final the necessary legal arrangements before the French court's judicial holiday began on 15 July. He would have to wait until the court reconvened on 15 September. That winter Aly faced his annual religious trip to the East, so it was imperative that Yasmin's visit be arranged as soon as possible. But how? At Dick's instigation, Rita was blocking Aly at every turn.

There followed a series of telephone calls and wires between Charles Torem and Bartley Crum. Aly's lawyer suggested that since July was almost over, perhaps Yasmin could be brought to Europe in August. Although the decree of exequatur had not been obtained in time, still Rita had guarantees from Aly, the Aga Khan, and Torem that Yasmin would be returned, as well as the $100,000 bond that Aly would secure in New York. And if Haymes's circumstances made it difficult for Rita herself to leave the country, why not send Bartley Crum in her place? Crum seemed amenable to the proposal, but of course he would have to confer with Rita, whose final decision it must be.

Meanwhile, on 25 July the government announced that it was dropping its move to deport Dick Haymes. Aly's side was thrilled. With Haymes no longer threatened by deportation, it looked as if Rita would finally feel free to go to Europe. Little did anyone expect that, even now, Haymes would forbid her to go since he still could not accompany her.

Shortly thereafter, when her lawyer advised her to accept Aly's latest proposal, although Rita declined to make the

331

trip to France herself, she authorized Bartley Crum to deliver Yasmin to the prince. That night Aly received the cable for which he had been waiting:

> RITA AGREEABLE . . .
> CRUM

In response he wired Rita excitedly:

> DELIGHTED YASMIN ARRIVING
> CAN'T WAIT TO SEE HER
> STOP PLEASE CABLE ME
> DATE AND TIME
> ARRIVAL LOVE ALY

A week passed as Aly made all the necessary arrangements in anticipation of Yasmin's long-awaited arrival.

Then it happened again. As she had so many times in the past, Rita suddenly changed her mind. The cable said it all:

> RITA INSISTS COMPLETION
> EXEQUATUR – CRUM

It was, as Charles Torem later described it, a 'crushing denouement.'

This time Dick and Rita had finally pushed Aly to the limits of his patience. Hitherto he had done everything he could to avoid initiating court proceedings against Rita. But on 10 August 1955, he filed a 'Motion for Order for Child Visitation' in the court at Reno, Nevada.

In addition to undermining his own right to see and spend time with his daughter, Aly claimed, Rita's decision not to cooperate with the custody agreement had resulted in 'a deprivation of the rights of the child, who should have her real father's love.'

After the child-neglect scandal of the previous year, being told now that she was depriving her daughter of her rights could not have been easy for Rita to bear. With her court date with Columbia scheduled for 31 August, to be followed by a custody hearing on 14 September, she was understandably anxious.

When she first heard that Aly was taking legal action against her, she and Dick went into seclusion at the Malibu beach house. But the couple's relationship had changed dramatically. For Rita, the government's decision to drop its deportation case against Dick had been the psychic trigger that enabled her to see her personal circumstances with new clarity. And she definitely didn't like what she saw. Before long the discord between them exploded in public.

On 23 August Dick opened a two-week singing engagement in Los Angeles at the Cocoanut Grove in the Ambassador Hotel. The Haymeses planned to stay in the hotel on the nights he was performing, while the children were left with a nurse in Malibu. The first night Dick and Rita quarreled openly. Between shows customers witnessed them yelling at each other, and after that Rita wasn't seen again in the nightclub for several evenings. Her conspicuous absence notwithstanding, at each show Dick made much ado of dedicating his version of 'Come Rain or Come Shine' to 'my wife, Rita.'

Much as he struggled to cover up, the mounting tensions with Rita were having a visible effect on his work. 'Patrons of the Cocoanut Grove have reported that, in his nightly appearances there, Haymes has seemed distraught, faltering, unsure of himself, far from the poised entertainer he once was,' noted the *Los Angeles Times*.

No sooner did Rita return to the nightclub than their quarreling escalated to physical violence. Saturday night, when she arrived at the Cocoanut Grove, Rita looked a good deal older than her thirty-six years. Her face was etched with strain and anxiety. Again she and Dick began arguing, but this time, as customers watched in horror, he struck a blow to her face, blackening her eye. Before the government's decision to discontinue its efforts to deport him, Rita had all too frequently allowed Dick to hit her. Now that she was free of the guilt that had bound her so tightly to him, she awakened from the passive, submissive state of mind that had allowed her to tolerate her husband's persistent abuse.

Rita dashed out of the Ambassador and drove back to Malibu, where she spent the night without Dick. Sunday morning she packed Becky and Yasmin into a station wagon and left Dick forever.

Chapter Thirty

At the Cocoanut Grove there was no Monday show, so after Dick finished his act Sunday night he headed home to Malibu. To his surprise Rita and the girls weren't there, but he had no idea that she had left him. He found out soon enough.

At six A.M. Monday morning a reporter called to ask Dick if the rumors about his and Rita's separation were true. By now all of Hollywood was talking about how he had punched her Saturday night. 'For God's sake!' Dick responded. 'There's nothing to it. Nothing at all. Why, Rita is right here with me now.'

He hung up and went back to sleep for two hours, when another call came from the press.

This time Dick was evasive. When the reporter inquired about the separation rumors, Dick replied, 'Why do you ask?'

Next the reporter suggested that he prove that Rita was there by putting her on the phone, but of course Dick said no.

The next time the press called, Dick had a new story: Rita was at her attorney's office to discuss the impending legal battle with Columbia. Although he admitted to having had an argument with Rita at the Ambassador, he claimed not to remember the details: 'It was that unimportant.'

By eight A.M. reporters had gathered outside Dick and Rita's beach house to see what they could find out. The only person who got inside, however, was Rita's maid. Scarcely had the maid arrived, when she was mysteriously leaving again. 'I am leaving because there is no work for me here today,' she explained. 'Only Mr Haymes is in the house and he is sleeping.'

When, however, a reporter for the *Los Angeles Times* peeked inside Dick's window, the view belied what the maid had said about there being nothing to do: 'The living room was in a state of disarray with ashtrays overturned on the floor.'

Clearly Dick was in turmoil in there, which was further suggested by his steadfast refusal to open the door.

Much as he and Rita had done in a similar fit of panic in New York, now Dick locked himself inside the beach house. Even when his physician arrived to see him, Dick wouldn't open the door. Instead, the press watched in wonder as Dick helped the doctor climb in through the bedroom window. Once inside, the doctor ascertained that Dick was 'in no condition to see anyone.'

By contrast, Rita seemed a good deal more clear-headed that morning when, accompanied by her brother Vernon, she went straight to her lawyer to prepare a public statement confirming the rumors that she had walked out on her husband. Throughout the brief meeting with reporters that followed, Rita wore dark glasses that concealed the physical evidence of her brawl with Dick. When photographers called out to Rita to remove the glasses, her lawyer abruptly cut off the proceedings, swiftly ushering her back inside his office.

There was much to discuss. Her court date with Columbia was scheduled for the following day, but Rita didn't feel up to it. After meeting the press she became so overwrought that a doctor was called in to sedate her. The physician prepared an affidavit stating that Rita had suffered a 'severe emotional shock' and that he had confined her to bed. Presently, when the studio's attorney raised no objection, Judge Benjamin Harrison ordered Rita's court date with Columbia postponed until 15 November.

'I don't believe it,' Dick told a reporter who called to tell him about Rita's announcement that she had left him. Yet when he finally absorbed that Rita was gone, Dick typically blamed everyone but himself. His rambling public statements were tinged with paranoia. The breakup, he said, had been caused by 'the same people who tried to throw me out of the country. This is exploitation. They're using Rita again. This is what they've been waiting for.'

But hadn't he hit her? Wouldn't he at least admit that? What about all the witnesses? Or her black eye?

'He may have cuffed her around a little, that's all,' said one of Dick's Hollywood chums.

No matter what people had seen, Dick steadfastly denied striking his wife: 'I never touched her. I love her. We did have an argument just as all married people do, and we discussed our careers, our previous marriages, and many things. It got pretty bad.'

Before long Dick couldn't resist inviting photographers in, so he could pose unshaven, exhausted, and clutching a telephone to show Rita he was waiting for her call.

Dick spent the next day, Tuesday, publicly debating whether he would go on that night at the Cocoanut Grove. In case he canceled at the last minute, the nightclub had Vic Damone waiting to replace him. But Dick had no intention of missing out on the massive publicity value of his latest crisis. Indeed, his performance began while he was still in Malibu that afternoon, sobbing for the benefit of reporters: 'If she doesn't come back, I can't go on!'

By the time he arrived at the Cocoanut Grove it was ten P.M. Dick vowed to sing in a little while, 'if I live that long.' Despite the bad word of mouth about Dick's show, that night the house was packed. The news stories and photos depicting his public nervous breakdown the day before had attracted a crowd of about six hundred, anxious to see if the distraught crooner would make it through the show. Upstairs, in his and Rita's suite at the Ambassador, Dick chain-smoked in a yellow terry-cloth robe and fretted, 'I hope I don't collapse.'

Minutes later, when he walked out onstage, the audience

gave him a standing ovation as he sang 'Something's Gotta Give.' One observer described him as looking like 'a tuxedoed Pagliacci.' If people had come to see Dick Haymes collapse onstage, they would be disappointed. By all accounts he actually sang better that night than he had in years, as if exhilarated by all the personal attention he was getting.

Afterward, in his hotel suite, the show continued for reporters as a newly confident Dick proclaimed: 'I think everything is going to be absolutely okay. I think Rita and I have been as close as any two people in the whole world. I know she loves me and I love her. This whole thing came about when we sort of got a lot of pressures. It has nothing to do with our marriage.'

Much as Dick struggled to minimize what had happened, Rita seemed determined to put substantial physical distance between her violent, abusive husband and herself. Although he repeatedly claimed only to have argued with her, the fact remained that Dick had physically assaulted Rita. Nor was it the first time he had done so. On 10 September, Rita quietly slipped out of town, escaping detection by using an alias, Mrs Philsbury. With Becky, Yasmin, and a nurse, Rita boarded the *Super Chief*, headed for New York. Their twenty pieces of luggage suggested that Rita planned to be away for some time.

And indeed, on 28 September, when Dick Haymes was scheduled to come to New York for a singing engagement, Rita and the girls sailed for Europe on the *Queen Elizabeth*. Rita had finally dropped her stipulation that the French courts officially recognize her and Aly's divorce before she would permit Yasmin to visit her father. Whatever fears she still may have had about the Aga Khan, her desire to get away from Dick was clearly stronger.

Her own fears aside, she noted with pleasure how excited Yasmin was about seeing her father again. At the end of the voyage, when the *Queen Elizabeth* arrived in Cherbourg, Rita's longtime legal adversary Charles Torem was waiting at the dock in Aly's limousine to take her and the girls to Paris. A station wagon followed with their luggage.

If Rita had wondered how Aly would greet her after all these years of acrimony, she soon discovered that there was nothing to fear. As she was shown into her six-room suite at the Hôtel Le Bristol she saw his flowers everywhere. By the time Aly himself pulled up at the Bristol in his cream-colored Alfa Romeo, Yasmin had already been put to bed. Nonetheless, Rita took him in for a glimpse of their sleeping daughter.

'She's terrific, simply wonderful!' cried Aly. Bursting with excitement, he said he could hardly wait for Yasmin to wake up and play with him. Meanwhile, things had gone so smoothly between Rita and her ex-husband that she invited him to join her for a late supper and champagne. He stayed for four hours. Then, at about one A.M., he left the hotel by a side entrance.

The next morning great numbers of well-wishers lined the Champs-Elysées in hopes of seeing Princess Yasmin. Overnight the little girl with the big brown eyes seemed to have conquered Paris. 'The "City of Light," the most sophisticated capital in the world, gave its heart Tuesday to a five-year-old girl and to her father's love for her,' reported the *Daily Mirror*. However benevolent they may have been, the crowds were too large to ensure safety and police had to be summoned to escort Yasmin, wearing a frilly dotted dress and clutching a white toy poodle and a teddy bear, into her father's automobile for the drive to Neuilly.

Waiting there with Aly were the Aga Khan and the Begum, who had brought two trunkloads of toys with them from the Riviera. For his part, Aly fretted that he didn't know exactly what kinds of playthings Yasmin favored, so he had filled her nursery with an immense variety of dolls and toys. Two vast crates had been ordered from German and Swiss toymakers alone. The opulence of Aly's house in Neuilly was a far cry indeed from the shabby surroundings in which Yasmin had been left – and photographed – only a year before. No one was ever again going to say that Aly Khan's daughter had been neglected.

When the car carrying the little princess finally arrived,

there were so many reporters outside that police had to clear a path for her to get into the house. Now at last came the happy ending for which Aly and his father had been fighting.

If, as would be only natural, they did resent all Rita had done to keep Yasmin from them, they made every effort to smooth things over. The afternoon after Yasmin arrived at Neuilly, Rita was invited for tea with the Aga Khan. His poor health notwithstanding, photographs show that the reunion with Yasmin had put the old man in exceedingly high spirits. This was hardly the terrifying figure Rita had conjured up in her thoughts, but a benevolent, loving grandfather who was quite simply ecstatic to see his only granddaughter again. For Rita it must have been like awakening from a terrible nightmare. Obviously the Aga Khan was hardly about to kidnap Yasmin, as Rita had long feared.

The little princess fit so harmoniously into these happy new surroundings, with a father and grandfather who clearly adored her. Could this joyous reunion possibly be what Rita had been struggling so fiercely to keep from happening? With his consummate charm and diplomacy, the Aga Khan instantly put Rita at ease. It was not in his interest to alienate her in any way. Nothing must occur to upset her or cause her to change her mind. After many months of Dick Haymes's incessant abuse, Rita finally found herself being treated with courtesy and respect again.

Her afternoon with the Aga Khan went so well that she agreed to dine with Aly that evening at Maxim's. When people glimpsed them enjoying dinner together behind red-velvet draping in a secluded alcove at Maxim's, it was widely rumored about Paris that Aly wanted Rita to marry him again as soon as she divorced Dick Haymes. But far from playing matchmaker, the Aga Khan had merely begun to win back Rita's trust that afternoon, and Aly diligently followed suit. Only if Rita could learn to have faith in them again would the custody agreement continue to work.

And it appeared that it *might* work. The trip to France

had had a distinctly therapeutic effect on Rita. Putting the ocean between her and Dick Haymes afforded her a new perspective. No wonder Dick had persistently struggled to keep her with him at all times. Much as he had always feared, the moment Rita was safely beyond his reach she was lost to him forever.

Before October was over she instructed her attorney to move for divorce. After the public incidents of verbal and physical abuse, there was really nothing Dick could do to stop the divorce, which would be further expedited by Rita's already having established legal residence in Nevada at the time of her divorce from Aly. Because of the pre-nuptial agreement no property was involved. And Rita obviously had no intention of asking Dick for alimony.

When through an attorney she filed for divorce in Reno, Nevada, on 4 November 1955, she asked only to give up the name 'Haymes' and to become Rita Hayworth again. The charge was 'extreme cruelty,' which Rita asserted had 'injured her mental health.' Rita gave her testimony at the American embassy in Paris on 6 December. 'My husband used vile and abusive language to me and called me a "goddamned motion-picture star," was quarrelsome with me, and used vile and abusive language in front of my children and my servants,' she declared. 'I felt if I continued to live with him as his wife, my health would be permanently injured.' Six days later, with neither Dick nor Rita in attendance, the Nevada court granted her fourth divorce, at the age of thirty-seven.

Meanwhile, Aly had taken Becky and Yasmin for a visit to the Château de l'Horizon. The prince had always shown great kindness to Becky Welles, whose own father had little time for her. Just then Orson was launching a comeback on the New York stage with a new production of *King Lear*. And he was about to become a father for the third time, with his third wife, the beautiful Italian Countess di Girfalco, who acted under the name Paola Mori. As it turned out, his third daughter, Beatrice Welles, would see a good deal more of Orson throughout her childhood than her half-sister Becky ever did.

Allowing Aly to take both girls to the Riviera while she remained in Paris was a big step for Rita. Still Aly was clearly anxious to dispel any lingering doubts she might have. When she took a train to Nice to see how Becky and Yasmin were doing, Aly and the girls appeared at the Hotel Negresco within thirty minutes of her arrival, and they were soon sharing a happy family lunch together, as if the long years of acrimony and separation had really never taken place. But Rita and Aly were definitely friends now, rather than lovers. In Rita's absence another woman of great beauty was often seen making a similar foursome with Aly and the girls. This was Bettina, a former Jacques Fath model and Aly's principal romantic interest of the moment. As chance would have it, Bettina had modeled Rita's wedding gown prior to Rita's marriage to Aly in 1949.

As for Rita, by this time, she, too, already had a new boyfriend. Scarcely had she gotten rid of Dick Haymes than she entered into yet another liaison with a man whose interest in her was professional as well as amorous: the Egyptian-born producer Raymond Hakim wanted to star Rita in a film based on the life of Isadora Duncan. Both Raymond and his elder brother, Robert, were significant figures in the international film scene. After getting their start with Paramount in Paris, in 1934 they had formed a French production company that was responsible for such important films as *Pépé le Moko* and *La Bête Humaine*. In the forties they branched out to producing in America, but by the fifties they were back in France again.

Before Raymond Hakim could use Rita in a picture, however, she would have to get out of her Columbia contract, and it was soon agreed that Hakim should accompany her to Los Angeles for her impending court date with the studio. After all, the prospect of having Rita Hayworth under contract to him gave Hakim a major stake in the outcome of the 27 December legal proceedings.

Rita decided that while she and Hakim were off in California, Aly could take care of Becky and Yasmin. Only a short while ago she had been fighting desperately not to send Yasmin to Europe, but now she was happy to leave both daughters with the prince. The old obsessive fears about him and his father were gone, and in their place Rita seemed mostly preoccupied with terminating her Columbia contract so that she could appear in Hakim's film.

On 13 December 1955, just one day after she was officially granted a Reno divorce from Dick Haymes, Rita and Hakim sailed from Le Havre on the *Île de France*, bound for New York – having neglected to inform her Paris lawyer of her departure. Although Rita seemed to have lost interest in the matter, the long-awaited hearing in the French courts to validate her divorce from Aly was scheduled for the next day and the attorney reportedly 'boiled with anger' at the news that, without a word, she had suddenly slipped off to America.

Chapter Thirty-one

Raymond Hakim watched from the spectator's section of Federal Court in Los Angeles as Rita nervously took the stand on 27 December 1955. Although at first she claimed that she had walked out at Columbia because delays in the filming of *Joseph and His Brethren* would have kept her from taking Yasmin to Europe on time, it was soon evident that Dick Haymes had been the real reason for her actions. Under questioning by Columbia attorney Macklin Fleming, Rita was forced to admit publicly that Dick had been calling all the shots.

By the end of the week Judge Benjamin Harrison urged both Rita and Columbia to settle the dispute between themselves, before he delivered his own ruling. 'From the testimony it was my impression that Mr Haymes was obviously the source of the trouble between Miss Hayworth and her studio,' said Judge Harrison. 'The testimony has Mr Haymes woven throughout the whole picture, and I wish that attorneys for both sides would research the right of a husband to speak for his wife.'

The judge's entreaty to settle notwithstanding, Rita insisted on being allowed to make *Isadora* in Europe for Raymond Hakim before fulfilling her contractual obligations to Columbia. This, of course, Harry Cohn could not possibly accept. In court Rita had all too obviously been unable to justify walking out on her Columbia contract, so that the judge was almost certain to rule in the studio's favor. Why possibly buckle under to Rita's absurd demands? As Cohn's star property, Rita Hayworth should be earning money for him, not for Raymond Hakim. All Harry Cohn had to do was wait and he'd have her back soon enough.

Nothing had been settled when Rita left for Europe on the *Queen Mary* on 19 January. Hakim remained behind in the States but promised to join her soon. Rita had decided that even if the court forced her to go back to work at Columbia, which seemed likely, she preferred to live in Paris, where she could send Becky and Yasmin to the American Community School. Los Angeles wasn't someplace she wanted to go again in the near future.

Meanwhile, as she waited for the judge's decision, she took her daughters for a skiing vacation at Megeve. There they were joined by Aly, who was about to embark on his annual Eastern tour but wanted to see them one last time. A new tranquillity suffused his once turbulent relations with Rita. By day he took the children skiing, and after dark he and Rita were observed dancing cheek to cheek and talking and laughing into the early morning hours. Still he remained passionately involved with Bettina, whom he frequently phoned in Paris, and Rita eagerly awaited the arrival of Raymond Hakim, whom she wired in New York:

Good morning, darling. Hurry up. Margarita.

Shortly thereafter, Hakim did indeed join her in France, but it soon became evident that his dream of Rita's playing Isadora was not to be. By mid-March 1956, much as she had feared, Judge Harrison had ruled against Rita in her suit against Columbia. 'I find that the plaintiff repudiated her contract with the defendant without justification,' he declared.

In other words, Rita had better go back to work – or else. The matter of Columbia's countersuit against her remained to be resolved. If at length Judge Harrison ruled in favor of Columbia, Rita could find herself owing the studio a great deal of money – which put substantial pressure on her to reach some accommodation with Columbia as quickly as possible.

Her disinclination to return to America just now made the offer that came presently from director Robert Parrish seem like an ideal solution. He offered her a starring role in *Fire Down Below*, to be shot on location in the West Indies and at the studios in London. Since Columbia was financing and distributing the film, *Fire Down Below* afforded Rita the opportunity to go back to work for Harry Cohn without having to do it in Los Angeles. Rita's final contract with Columbia, which she signed in Paris on 13 April, committed her to make this and one additional film – and then she would be finished with Harry Cohn forever.

On 15 May 1956, Rita arrived in New York on the *Queen Elizabeth*, en route to Tobago, in the British West Indies, to begin work on *Fire Down Below*. By now it was nearly three years since she had finished *Miss Sadie Thompson*. Slim-figured and ever so carefully attired in a dark tailored dress and a double strand of pearls, she was well prepared for the inevitable clicking cameras at dockside. Yet despite the artfully applied makeup and shoulder-length red hair, there was no concealing the ravages of drink and stress. Deep lines had crept around her eyes and mouth, and she appeared worn, exhausted – older than her thirty-eight years.

New legal woes awaited her in New York, where Bartley Crum announced that she had signed an affidavit in anticipation of suing Orson Welles for back child support. In 1947, Orson had been ordered to pay $50 a week for his daughter Becky, but, according to Rita, Welles had 'not paid a penny,' which left him owing her $22,450 so far. As long as Orson was kicking around Europe (and reinvesting virtually all of his acting fees into his own independent film work), there had been scant hope of collecting from him, but now he was back in the States, where it looked briefly as if he was about to launch a successful television series, and Rita's lawyer hoped to scare him into settling out of court before the TV money started rolling in (which of course it never did).

These lawsuits and countersuits were upsetting Rita's always fragile equilibrium. On location in the Caribbean, co-workers were soon to observe a strange sight: according to *Fire Down Below*'s director, Robert Parrish, when Rita received her first bundle of mail since leaving New York, the letters remained unopened as she tore them to pieces that she scattered in the sea. Reminded that there might be a check in one of the envelopes, she replied that they were likely to contain 'more trouble than money.'

She could tear up envelopes that she feared contained bad news, but there was no avoiding another kind of pain: in London when it took too long to light one of Rita's shots in *Fire Down Below*, a voice was heard to complain that they should hurry up, no amount of time was going to make her look any younger. Although the cruel remark apparently had not been meant for Rita's ears, she heard it anyway and began to cry.

Worst of all, there had been some truth to it. Co-starring Jack Lemmon and Robert Mitchum as a pair of rough-and-tumble sailors vying for the affections of an aging beauty who had seen better days, *Fire Down Below* would reveal an unprecedentedly lifeless and haggard Rita Hayworth. Nor was Rita merely playing a part. In *Gilda*, although she is supposed to seem drunk in the 'Put the Blame on Mame' nightclub sequence, Rita is able to invest her every movement with ineffable grace; not so in *Fire Down Below*, where her big dance number, set in a Caribbean night spot, is startlingly graceless, clumsy, and embarrassing – suggesting how very great a toll the past few years had taken, and how little in shape she was to return to the screen now.

During the shooting of *Fire Down Below*, Becky and Yasmin had been with Aly in France. When the production moved to London after nearly two months in the Caribbean, Aly arrived with the girls for a visit, then took them back to the Château de l'Horizon.

Not long afterward, Rita joined them all in Deauville, where she accepted the prince's invitation to move into his house there, even though his girlfriend Bettina was also in residence. The night of Rita's arrival, Aly escorted her *and* Bettina to dinner at the casino in Deauville. Curious eyes watched the threesome's every expression for discomfort, jealousy, perhaps even the makings of a cat fight – but there was none of that. After a quiet dinner, Aly and his two ladies paraded through the gambling rooms of the casino, where they were observed to play roulette and baccarat.

Rita and her daughters remained in France through the fall as she worked on losing fifteen pounds in anticipation of the inevitable return to Hollywood that faced her in December. For the last film she owed him, Harry Cohn had a prestige picture in mind: John O'Hara's *Pal Joey*, with music by Rodgers and Hart. Cohn had owned the film rights to the smash Broadway musical for some time, and had initially planned to pair its original star, Gene Kelly, with Rita, as a follow-up to *Cover Girl*. At that point she would have played the *younger* woman in the tale's triangle – but now that part went to Kim Novak, and Joey was to be played by Frank Sinatra. For Rita there remained the role of the wealthy *older* woman with the tawdry past.

'There was another girl who was anxious for the part and whom Harry and I liked very much,' recalled *Pal Joey* director George Sidney. 'We went out with her a few times in New York and visited with her – her name was Marlene Dietrich. Marlene wanted the part, and we thought about it and decided to stick with Rita – it was the right part for her at the moment.'

Casting Rita opposite Kim Novak possessed a built-in public-relations bonus since it was common knowledge that Harry Cohn had anointed Kim to replace Rita at Columbia. 'When you came here you were a nothing, a nobody,' Cohn was supposed to have blasted Rita when she walked out on *Joseph and His Brethren*. 'All you had were those two big things and Harry Cohn. Now you just got those two big things.'

Shortly thereafter, the creation of Kim Novak as Columbia's next 'big star' was widely thought to be Harry Cohn's revenge on Rita, so that putting the two actresses together made the press and public expect fireworks. Still, according to George Sidney, on the set 'there was no friction between Rita and Kim.' Although Rita did lament that she was actually *younger* than Frank Sinatra, she was really just anxious to fulfill her final obligations to the studio as quickly and smoothly as possible. 'She comes in, you tell her what to do, she does it,' as George Sidney would characterize her consummate professionalism during *Pal Joey*. 'We were shooting on location in San Francisco and it was bloody cold. I had on three overcoats. Rita had a little chiffon dress on. The wind was howling. I said, "Come on, we'll shoot it in the studio." She said, "No, please, stay with it." I said, "Come here." I grabbed her and she was absolutely purple. The pigment had changed, it was *that* cold.'

The bitter cold wasn't the only trial Rita had to contend with in San Francisco. Again (although this time she had worked hard to get into shape for the part) there were hurtful remarks about her loss of youth. Rita's stand-in, Grace Godino, recalled one such painful incident: 'It was at night. We were shooting outside and the crowds had gathered around for autographs. Frank had gone somewhere else. But Rita and Kim were there, and a crowd of people came up to get Kim's autograph. Then as they started toward Rita, somebody said in one of those inimitable rude fan voices, "Oh, she looks *so old!*" Rita just blanked out. She acted like it didn't bother her, but it must have hurt.'

There were also moments when Rita seemed quite content to pass the torch (and all that went with it) to the younger actress. Thus, Grace Godino would recall the day back in Hollywood when 'Kim Novak's costume split at the dress rehearsal and there was a big hullabaloo. Kim got hysterical and of course the wardrobe lady was in tears. Harry Cohn came on the set and the whole production stopped while they all went on about this. But Rita was at that period of life when it just wasn't important to her. She walked over to her chair and sat there with that cute smile of hers. She didn't have to say it but you could just sense the thought, "Let them have their fun. Here's the new sexpot they're going to have to worry about. *I* don't have to worry about that anymore." '

Anxious as she may have been to be done with her obligations in Hollywood, once more now there appeared a new man in her life who wanted to get her in front of the cameras again. James Hill was a partner in the Hecht-Hill-Lancaster independent production team (*Vera Cruz, Trapeze*) when Rita was introduced to him by Bob Schiffer at a New Year's Eve party. After Rita's divorce from Haymes, the Schiffers had been concerned about her and thought that their offbeat forty-one-year-old bachelor friend Jim Hill might be good for her. Indeed, in the beginning of their romance Hill gave Rita the opportunity to indulge her longing to hide from people, to spend idyllic periods of time alone with a man. She and Jim would hole up in his apartment in Los Angeles with enough Dom Pérignon to last a month. Once Rita had satisfied her commitments to Columbia by making *Pal Joey*, they would get away from the demands of the movie business so that she could devote herself to painting, and Jim to writing.

Years later Hill would recall the 'sad, faraway look in her eyes' that made him want to 'rescue' Rita; instead, by his own account, he 'wound up as anxious to use her as all the rest.' Soon he became caught up in big plans for transforming her Love Goddess image. Once he had found the right comic role for Rita, *he* would direct her in a film that he assured his mother would be 'the fulfillment of *both* our careers.' Even Jim's mother could plainly see that Rita was anxious to be finished with filmmaking. But now the old pattern repeated itself as Rita put herself in a lover's hands and basically did what he wanted her to do.

Meanwhile, that spring Aly had sent word from Europe that the Aga Khan was seriously ill and wanted to see his granddaughter. The Muslim leader had suffered a recurrence of pulmonary bronchitis and was being attended on a twenty-four-hour basis by a team of four doctors. Although Rita and Aly had mended fences of late, she cabled him now declining to send the child who, she said, had just gotten used to California and her new school. Rita told the prince that by summer she would be finished at Columbia, and only then would she be able to accompany

Yasmin for a visit. When July came, however, Rita had changed her plans and sent Yasmin to Europe with a nanny on the liner *Île de France*.

Shortly before the little princess was expected, the Aga Khan suffered a heart attack at his Villa Barakat, on Lake Leman, outside Geneva, where he had recently been moved from Paris to escape the stifling heat. When Aly heard the news he rushed to his father's side, then flew back to Paris to fetch Yasmin for a visit to her grandfather's deathbed. They scarcely arrived in time, however. On 11 July 1957, the day after his beloved granddaughter arrived, the Aga Khan III died in Switzerland at the age of seventy-nine.

After virtually a lifetime of conflict with his emotionally distant father, it seemed that Aly was about to succeed him as the next Imam, although it was certainly no secret that the Aga Khan had long harbored serious doubts about the prince's fitness to lead the Ismailis. The scandals with Rita had been but one of many lapses in judgment that had gravely disturbed the Aga Khan, who was widely rumored to have been considering passing over Aly in favor of his younger half-brother, Sadruddin. Still, Aly was immensely popular with the Ismailis, and when, on the occasion of the seventieth anniversary of the Aga Khan's installation as the forty-eighth Imam, Aly had been designated his ailing father's 'lieutenant,' it certainly looked as if the Aga Khan had relented and decided to name Aly his successor after all.

Immediately after the Aga Khan's death, all those who came to pay condolence calls at Barakat were greeted by Aly, whose name – it was generally noted – preceded Sadruddin's in the official announcement of death. But no, when the Aga Khan's will was read at last, both Aly and Sadruddin failed to be named Aga Khan IV. Instead, the Aga Khan startled everyone by designating Aly's twenty-year-old son Karim as his successor. If ever in death a father struck a devastating blow at his surviving son, this was it. It was the Aga Khan's last word, his final – and very public – comment on a son who had always somehow failed

351

to please him. All the old animosities between father and son had found expression here.

If the world expected Aly to bristle in his humiliation, that was by no means what they saw. Indeed, to many observers, it looked like the finest moment of Aly's life. As if suddenly liberated by the death of his father, Aly handled the situation with matchless style. Unlike the Aga Khan, Aly was unreserved in his affection for his children, and whatever terrible hurt his own parent may just have caused him, he showed no sign of it and gave Karim his full and unambiguous support.

Although in America there had been much speculation about whether the Aga Khan had left any of his great fortune to Rita, she was not named in his will – nor had she expected to be. For her part, Rita was preoccupied just now with her decision to appear in the film version of Terence Rattigan's stage hit *Separate Tables*, which her boyfriend Hill's company was set to produce. Jim saw it as 'the first big step toward changing her image, which meant the first big step for me and my dream of directing her.' Under the sensitive direction of Delbert Mann, Rita would play another fading beauty, but this time in a serious and artistic drama that would give her an opportunity to show the public that she wasn't just a movie star, but an actress.

Could she bring it off? Or would she be absurdly out of her element working with eminent actresses like Deborah Kerr, Wendy Hiller, Cathleen Nesbitt, and Gladys Cooper? 'I was concerned because I had never seen Rita do anything remotely resembling this,' recalled Delbert Mann. 'The pressure would constantly be there because of the cast she was surrounded with.' And indeed, at his first meeting with Rita in her home on Roxbury Drive, the Academy Award-winning director could see that he was not alone in his hesitation. 'Rita was apprehensive and really quite insecure about it,' Mann recalled. 'It was clear she would need help. And my task, as is so often the case with a director, was to be a father figure and assure her that she could do it. Rita put herself in my hands in a strange and rather complete way that was almost childlike. There was no sense of resistance or questioning of any kind.'

The three weeks of rehearsal in which, as Mann recalled, 'we simply did it as a play' were 'frightening for Rita because she'd never done that kind of thing before.' It seemed to Mann that, throughout, 'she gave the best she had to offer.' But he also found that, with Rita, he was 'never able to go to the depths of the character' as he was with a highly skilled actress like Deborah Kerr.

Later, when the actual filming began, a new pressure was added: 'Rita was quite conscious of her looks,' said Delbert Mann. 'And one understood why and wanted to protect her and make her look as good as we possibly could. We lit *very* carefully. There is a little scene in her room at the hotel where she invites Burt [Lancaster] up to her room; she changes into a kimono and he gets her face up into the light and sees the lines there. I remember it was a problem for the cameraman and me: how to make Rita look in that light. You could make it look very harsh, which is what the scene is about. Or you could try to cheat it. I think we tried very hard to compromise, to give the sense of a harsh light and age lines showing, without being *brutal* about it.'

Finally, it seemed to the director that, whatever Rita's lack of training, skills, and serious acting experience, portraying a lonely lady of a certain age allowed her to bring some of her own recent loneliness and pain to the role. 'The role was a good one for her to play because of the character's age and the fact that she was still a glamorous woman, a very chic and sophisticated woman, but terribly lonely and frightened,' said Mann. 'These were things in the character that Rita could latch on to and relate to, very much so. She could comprehend the character and invest some of herself in it. With Rita, I had a sense of someone who was obviously seeking things that, after a number of unhappy, unfulfilled marriages, were not happening in her personal life. I think that there were a lot of things in Rita's heart and mind and soul that were working for us in *Separate Tables*. The character is frightened of being alone and needs someone to cling to, and I had a great sense that a lot of the truth of that performance came from Rita herself.'

Indeed, just before shooting of *Separate Tables* began, Rita had decided to try her luck at marriage yet again when Jim Hill proposed to her during a flight to Palm Springs for dinner. Although she clung to her hope of going off with him to paint and write, by now he was clearly much more interested in guiding her career and determined to make her see things his way. This total – and persistent – disparity in their aspirations seems to have doomed the marriage from the start. 'RITA TAKES THE FIFTH' read the headline when she and Hill tied the knot at a small ceremony in her rented Roxbury Drive home on Sunday, 2 February 1958.

According to Hill, they wanted to buy a house behind the Beverly Hills Hotel but didn't have the necessary cash, which meant that Rita would have to sign up for a new film after *Separate Tables*. While Rita had not been keen to accept a role in *They Came to Cordura* when Hill had suggested it in the past, she agreed to do it now to earn the money to pay for their new house. 'In retrospect,' Hill would explain, 'I'd like to believe that – remembering her earlier reluctance about the project – I didn't put pressure on her, but I know better.'

Nor did the pressure end there: time and again in the marriage, Rita would indicate in one way or another that she wanted to give up film acting, but Jim would always maneuver to 'bring her around.' Besides *Separate Tables* and Robert Rossen's *They Came to Cordura*, in keeping with her husband's program for launching her as a serious actress, Rita accepted roles in Clifford Odets's *The Story on Page One* and George Marshall's *The Happy Thieves*. As a result, the public image of her relationship with Hill projected a new seriousness and stability – but their turbulent private life was a very different matter.

There was abundant drinking on both sides – and Rita sometimes grew violent. On one occasion Rita bloodied her husband's forehead by hitting him with a telephone receiver. Another time, after they both had been drinking, a gun went off mysteriously in their hotel suite. Questioned by the police, who had come to investigate the gunshot, neither husband nor wife could remember where the gun had come from, who had fired it, or why. When the Hills entertained at their new Beverly Hills home (which more than once Rita declared she wanted to blow up), she would repeatedly disappear into the kitchen to drink in solitude. And even with guests present, sudden, alarming violence might erupt, as it did on an evening when Hermes Pan had been invited to dinner. 'There was a candelabra on the table,' Pan recalled. 'And she just took the candelabra and threw it at Hill! It just missed his forehead. He said, "Oh, you shouldn't have done that." But Rita didn't say a word. She just sat there.'

Rita also suddenly resumed the old hostilities with Aly, who appeared to have flourished since his father's death. In a surprise move, Pakistan had named Aly its United Nations representative. Although the appointment had been greeted with skepticism in diplomatic and journalistic circles, Aly finally seemed to find himself and come into his own in this important new role, and before long he had impressed the other UN delegates with his commitment, diligence, and personal warmth. When in the midst of all this Rita moved to take him to court for more than $18,000 in legal expenses, which he had refused to pay on the grounds that the bill was too high, Aly's new position in the UN allowed him to claim diplomatic immunity.

Once again it looked as if Rita was about to retaliate by keeping Aly from seeing Yasmin. Fortunately, however, unlike Dick Haymes, who had actively worked to *increase* the tensions between Rita and Aly, Jim Hill talked her into sitting down face to face with the prince to settle their differences without litigation. 'The only one hurt by this was the child,' Rita admitted after she and Aly had made peace anew in New York. 'She has her whole life ahead of her. Why should we complicate it?'

The decision never again to let anything keep father and daughter apart had come none too soon.

355

In April 1960, Aly flew to Los Angeles for a visit with Yasmin before returning to France. As soon as school was out for the summer she was set to join her father there. But that visit was not to be. On the night of 12 May 1960, en route to a dinner party, Aly was at the wheel of his Lancia sports car, with Bettina beside him and his chauffeur in back, when he collided head on with another automobile. Both his passengers and the other driver escaped with minor injuries, but shortly before midnight Prince Aly Salomone Khan died in a Paris hospital at the age of forty-eight.

Chapter Thirty-two

Rita sought her fifth and last divorce on 7 September 1961, before Santa Monica Superior Court Judge Orlando Rhodes (who on that very day eighteen years before had married her to Orson Welles). The forty-two-year-old actress's hoarse voice was so low it was barely audible in the courtroom.

The stormy marriage to Hill had repeated a pattern familiar from Rita's earlier failed love relationships. But it was complicated by the fact that (unbeknownst to anyone, including herself) she had begun to succumb to a mysterious degenerative disease involving changes in the brain's structure and the progressive loss of mental functions.

In retrospect, it sometimes seems a relatively simple matter to pinpoint that an individual was in the initial stages of the intellectual decline or dementia known as Alzheimer's disease (after the German neurologist Alois Alzheimer), but at the time they occurred those early warnings may have been quite imperceptible – all the more so in Rita Hayworth's singular case, where a good many of the standard symptoms, such as mood swings, violent outbursts, temper tantrums, and other losses of emotional control were actually exaggerated versions of psychological damage she had already long exhibited as a consequence of childhood trauma. Still, to an old friend like Hermes Pan, who had known Rita to exhibit mood swings as early as her twenties, it had become evident now that something else was involved – but what?

'I saw this whole thing coming on just gradually,' Pan recalled. When he observed her suddenly hurl the candelabra at Jim Hill and then just sit there in silence afterward as if nothing had happened, it seemed to Pan that 'something was *very* strange because Rita was not like herself' – although of course at the time he had no idea why. More and more his dear friend's often entirely un-provoked 'fits of temper,' as he described them, would come to perplex and alarm him. 'She would scream and holler at someone for no good reason,' Pan explained. 'And then she wouldn't remember.'

Similarly, her daughter Yasmin would describe her mother's abrupt mood swings and subsequent forgetful-ness, also dating back to Rita's marriage to Hill: 'She would suddenly be in a bad mood and I'd never know why. As a child, I just had to learn to deal with it. We would be sitting at the dinner table, and suddenly she'd become furious about the food, or about something she thought the maid had done wrong. Then she would go off to her room and come back several minutes later as if nothing had happened. I always thought it was because of her drinking, but I never really saw her drink that much. I just assumed that she had a very low tolerance for alcohol.'

Indeed, angry outbursts that erupt without substantial – or *any* – cause and are forgotten just as suddenly are common warning signs to family members and close friends that something may be seriously amiss with the as yet undiagnosed victim of dementia. The key is that the anger (or other violent and excessive upset) is totally out of proportion – a *catastrophic* reaction – to what appears to have triggered it. As for the often puzzling forgetfulness that demented persons exhibit, it is generally the most *recent* events that tend to be forgotten, rather than memories of the more distant past.

Although Rita had been known to imitate her mother's excessive drinking as early as the marriage to Orson Welles, by the time of her fifth, and final, marriage, alcohol was clearly becoming a serious problem. Researchers differ over whether drink can cause dementia, but there is no denying that it can make things substantially worse for someone afflicted with a dementing disease. Indeed, dementia is known to make its victims so susceptible to the influence of drink that, as those around Rita were to discover, even small quantities of alcohol can have a disastrous impact. 'She'd tell anybody off in a minute after about two drinks,' Ann Miller explained. 'She was really like a dual personality. Basically Rita was a very shy person. But when she drank, out would come this spittin' gypsy! If somebody said something she didn't like, off with the head!'

Until now, however, Rita's gradual deterioration had manifested itself mainly in private and seemed to be the result of drinking. Then, after her divorce from Hill, something happened that perhaps could not be so easily explained away by alcoholism – at least not by anyone who had ever worked closely with Rita and witnessed her lifelong professionalism and capacity for hard work, whatever personal problems she might be experiencing. For the first time her as yet undiagnosed brain disease would undermine her ability to function as an actress. Both daughters were away in boarding school at this point, Becky in northern California and Yasmin in Switzerland; and Rita had a new boyfriend, actor Gary Merrill, whose tempestuous marriage to Bette Davis had broken up. When Merrill was offered a starring role in the Broadway play *Step on a Crack*, he suggested to the producer that Rita be cast to play opposite him as a former vaudevillian whose marriage to a small-town doctor is falling apart. It was January 1962. Rehearsals were set to begin in August, which left her plenty of time to work with a speech coach in anticipation of the challenging new experience of theatrical acting. 'Miss Hayworth will work tirelessly on her role,' her publicist declared. 'She is a perfectionist.'

But when she got to New York City that summer, it quickly became obvious that something was wrong. She struck others as somehow 'distraught' and 'increasingly nervous over the prospect of acting on the stage.' As serious and eager to work hard as she appeared, just reading the play with the director and other company members seemed to overwhelm her and made her excessively anxious. The schedule called for Rita to rehearse in New York for three and a half weeks; after that, the play would go on the road, first to Torono, then Cleveland and Detroit, before finally returning to Broadway, for an October opening.

By the end of the first week of rehearsals, however, Rita had had it. Saturday night she complained that something she had eaten had made her 'ill,' and by Monday, instead of returning to work, she checked into Flower-Fifth Avenue Hospital, where she was variously said to be suffering from anaemia, nervous exhaustion, and low metabolism. 'I just want to rest,' she told reporters when, several days later, she left the hospital on the arm of her doctor – and mysteriously pulled out of the play.

At the time, of course, no one knew that she had fallen victim to a dementing disease that sooner or later inevitably interferes with job performance. Significantly, the mental deficits associated with Alzheimer's disease often make it especially hard for the afflicted person to adjust to new and strange situations, such as acting in a stage play would have been for Rita. When the unfamiliar routines and expectations seem too complicated and difficult to handle, the victim may panic and – as Rita did – withdraw. Various explanations were subsequently offered for why Rita left *Step on a Crack*: that the heat and humidity in the un-air-conditioned Ethel Barrymore Theater had proven too much for her; that she suddenly decided she just didn't like the play; and, undoubtedly much closer to the truth, that she had simply found herself unable to make the transition to stage acting – a transition that, one might add, would have been rendered all the more terrifying by the as yet undiagnosed dementia with which she was afflicted.

Before long she had returned to the familiar, hence more manageable, ground of film acting (between 1963 and 1971 she made seven films), but still the slow deterioration of Rita's mind grew increasingly evident. The trouble started in Spain, where she played Claudia Cardinale's mother in the film *Circus World*. Much to Rita's perplexity and frustration, she experienced her first obvious difficulty remembering dialogue. And problems related to her disease arose off the set as well. As her daughter Yasmin would subsequently point out, 'Not everyone always reacts the same way, but when the mental capabilities diminish, when there is memory loss or disorientation, the victim sometimes turns to alcohol out of sheer frustration.' Out on the town in Madrid, it became clear that Rita needed only a drink or two to set her off. In one of several such incidents, for no apparent reason she obscenely tongue-lashed a female American tourist.

Although some of her tirades seemed to have been triggered by almost nothing at all, others were caused by irritation with something at work. She might refrain from exploding on the set, but as her agent Bud Moss recalled, 'That little piece of sand would start to develop there, and it would start grinding on her. Then at the end of the day we'd be going over the script at dinner and she might have a drink and, all of a sudden, *blow*.' According to Moss, who was with Rita in Madrid to shoot another picture, *Sons of Satan*, 'Looking back at it now, the one thing which was very sad was that when the word "drinking" came up, nobody realized that this was all Alzheimer's. Nobody had any idea. Whenever she would go into her lapses or what people used to think were drunken stupors, it was Alzheimer's setting in.'

It has been said that for the victim of a dementing disease the boundary between normal and abnormal mental ability is not a clear-cut 'line,' but rather a 'zone.' Thus, despite memory lapses, violent mood swings, and other alarming symptoms, Rita continued to function professionally as best she could until a series of major career crises called into question once and for all her ability to go on working as an actress. By then the boundaries of normality had all too clearly been crossed.

The first of these crises occurred when Rita was hired to replace Lauren Bacall in the Broadway hit *Applause*. After some years of making increasingly obscure films that by and large were barely even screened in the United States, the offer to do a prestige production like *Applause* seemed like the turnaround her career desperately needed now. She had been cast at the suggestion of her friend from the early days at Columbia, Ann Miller, now herself a major Broadway star. 'But when they sent Rita the script, she had a very hard time learning the lines,' Miller recalled. 'She came over one day and said, "Annie, I don't know whether I can do this." Now, I thought this was *very* peculiar because when Rita was at Columbia she was *never* like that. Learning lines was no problem for her at all. She was very professional, a lady who really knew her craft.'

Although, understandably, Rita did not want the public to find out about it, in private she admitted her memory problem to her friend.

'She was very conscious something was wrong,' said Miller. 'I sat with her with a script and tried to throw lines at her, and she did it pretty good with me. But then she'd get up in front of those people in New York and just couldn't remember. They worked with her trying very hard to get her to learn her lines, but finally she just said, "No, I can't do it."'

Rita was upset, however, when word about her troubles got out to the press, and she vehemently denied that she'd had any difficulty committing the part to memory. Instead, she insisted that she'd had to pull out of *Applause* after the flu caused her to miss a week of rehearsals. Conscious as she may have become that something strange had been happening to her, still Rita hesitated to consult a doctor about her ever worsening plight. 'She didn't go to doctors,' said her friend, producer Curtis Roberts. 'I know why, of course. They would have told her to stop drinking. She didn't want to hear that.'

According to Roberts, simply to suggest that Rita should refrain from having a drink would result in getting 'the bottle thrown at you.' Like many Alzheimer's victims, Rita often reacted angrily at even the most tactful suggestion that something might be wrong. When a publicist who worked with Rita in this period made the mistake of broaching the subject of her apparent alcohol problem, Rita launched into a furious screaming fit and threw him out of the house.

Another big chance came her way when Robert Mitchum suggested Rita to co-star with him in the most important film she'd been offered in years: Ralph Nelson's *Wrath of God*, for MGM. At this point financial woes had forced her to rent out her house behind the Beverly Hills Hotel and to retreat to a more modest furnished place in Brentwood, where director Nelson (*Lilies of the Field, Charly*) found her sitting in total darkness. 'The room was very dark,' Nelson said, recalling his visit with Rita to discuss the script. 'There were no lights.'

'Rita was real upset about having to work,' explained her hairstylist on the picture, Lynn Del Kail, 'but she didn't have much money. It was so pathetic. One day she started crying and said that it was a shame she had this beautiful house and couldn't live in it.'

Still, as long as Rita *had* to go on working, *Wrath of God* – an action-adventure film set in South America in the 1920s – was exactly the kind of major project she needed to revive her career, and she was most anxious to do well in it, especially after the disaster of *Applause*. While she hadn't been able to learn the script for *Applause*, that had been a stage play, in which the actor must memorize the *entire* text. By contrast, because a movie is shot in fragments, the actor need remember only a small portion of the script at a time, which should have made things easier for Rita. But what no one had quite realized was that by the time she went to Taxco, Mexico, to shoot *Wrath of God* in November 1971, Rita's intellectual impairment at the age of fifty-three had progressed to the point where remembering even tiny bits of dialogue proved impossibly difficult.

'Her memory had just *gone*,' said Lynn Del Kail. 'And finally she came to me and asked me if I'd help her to remember her dialogue. I'd take her into her room and I'd teach her *one* line. Then she'd go out and they'd shoot the one line. And then we'd go back into the room and do another line.'

According to Ralph Nelson, even when Rita had the

script on her lap, she would experience 'total memory lapses' that required him to shoot 'line by line.'

Nor were these lapses confined to her acting. In casual conversation as well she would suddenly forget the topic. 'You'd be talking to her about a subject and all of a sudden she was talking about something else,' said Lynn Del Kail. 'At first I thought, "Oh, my God, it's me." Then I finally realized it was her attention span.'

Because Lynn Del Kail seemed to get along so well with Rita, she was assigned to keep an eye on her to make certain she wasn't drinking or using drugs, which her persistently odd behaviour suggested might be the case.

'Rita had so many different problems,' said Del Kail. 'She was afraid of so many things.'

Transportation to and from the location posed special difficulties. In the car she would insist that the driver was speeding when in fact the pace was perfectly normal. 'She would make the driver crawl along, very slow,' explained Rita's makeup man, Del Armstrong.

And according to Ralph Nelson, 'One driver quit on her when we moved from Taxco up to Cuernavaca because she insisted he drive about ten miles an hour.'

Even when a driver dutifully followed her orders and crawled along to the location, Rita's agitation persisted. 'Rita just was very, very nervous and uncomfortable in a car,' said Lynn Del Kail, who usually rode to work with her in the morning. 'It took the crew twenty or thirty minutes to get to the location. It took us an hour and a half. And the whole time she'd be talking because she was so nervous. She talked *the whole time* we were in there and moved around and used her hands a lot.'

Another source of trouble was what Del Armstrong characterized as her 'claustrophobia' or 'fear of confined spaces.' At the simple prospect of entering an elevator Rita grew strangely anxious and upset.

'She had a big phobia about elevators,' said Lynn Del Kail. 'When we were in Mexico City a group of us always drank in a bar at the top of the hotel. I remember Rita wanted to have a drink with us but she was terrified to go up in the elevator. Finally she did it, but she was very nervous the whole time. When the elevator stopped at one floor and three or four people wanted to get in, I asked them not to because she was so scared. Later, we had to get her down the same way. We all just felt real bad for her.'

Rita's 'fear of confined spaces' also posed problems during filming when, perhaps for the first time in thirty-seven years of always doing whatever was asked of her on a film set, Rita suddenly found herself unable to follow the director's instructions – in this case, to walk into a cave for a scene that was being shot. 'She just flat out wouldn't go in,' Del Armstrong recalled. 'She was afraid to step in there.' Although (as is often the case with victims of Alzheimer's disease) her fear seemed quite irrational, it was evidently very real to Rita.

Nothing anyone said would convince her that stepping into the cave was perfectly safe. 'She only had to walk in a few feet,' said Lynn Del Kail, 'but she just couldn't do it. She was too scared.' When it became evident that there was no possibility Rita would change her mind, Lynn Del Kail put on a wig and did the scene instead, with the camera shooting her from the back. Fortunately no one in the company expressed the slightest irritation with Rita for her failure to do as instructed. But in the career of an actress long known and admired for her consummate professional-ism, the moment was a particularly sad one.

In social situations as well Rita's intellectual impairment might cause her to seem entirely out of touch with reality, as when she misinterpreted things people said and did, and took grave offense where, plainly, none had been intended. Thus, on the evening when she was the dinner guest of producer William Gilmore's warm and charming wife, Polly, Rita was consistently – and quite inexplicably – hostile toward her hostess, who was clearly going out of her way to make the actress comfortable. From the moment she arrived Rita looked a big strange because, despite the sweltering heat, she was wearing a long wool skirt and a wool sweater. 'The evening was just disastrous,' Polly Gilmore recalled. 'I'd never had an experience like that before. It started when we went in to dinner and she began to sing something. Just to make her happy, I asked, "Oh, do you like to sing?" And she looked at me and snapped, "Am I supposed to *perform* for dinner?" As victims of Alzheimer's disease will often do, Rita had evidently misinterpreted and grown incensed at her hostess's quite innocent remark. From then on, no matter what Mrs Gilmore said, Rita responded with the most peculiar hostility, whereas she was characteristically charming with the two men at the table, Polly's husband, Bill, and director Ralph Nelson. 'She was like Jekyll and Hyde,' Polly Gilmore recalled. 'Now, with hindsight, we all know what she was going through. But back then, well, it was a very trying evening for me. I just didn't know *what* to do.'

Although Rita finally managed to finish filming *Wrath of God*, it was only because her co-workers helped her get through it. Back in the States, however, she was mostly on her own again. Yasmin attended Bennington College, in Vermont. And Rita's relations with her elder daughter, Rebecca, were not the best. 'She's had a hard time,' said Hermes Pan, speaking of Rebecca Welles. 'Rita, I'm sorry to say, showed a little favoritism to Yasmin and Rebecca felt it.'

And, said Curtis Roberts: 'Rita couldn't communicate too well with Rebecca. But, you know, Yassy was always her favorite.'

Rebecca herself would declare that sometimes she was 'real bitter' about her childhood. 'I'm not saying I'd rather not be the child of my parents,' she explained. 'I just wish some things had been different.' Indeed, left alone so much of the time, lonely little Becky had felt like what she called 'a part-time child': 'It was hard to compete for attention when everybody in the world was seeking Mother and Father, or Aly,' she would say. 'I know I resented the demands that everybody else made on their time.' Later, after she had graduated from the University of Puget Sound, in Washington, Becky had married a young aspiring artist in Tacoma, although neither Rita nor Orson attended the wedding.

And so it was now that, although Rita had finally moved back into her own house in Beverly Hills, as she had longed to do, it seemed to a number of her friends that living all alone in such a large establishment only made things worse for her. 'Rita was very lonely and had nobody really to talk to,' recalled Lynn Del Kail of the period following *Wrath of God*. 'She would call me and say, "I'm sorry I didn't call you back, I got your message." And half the time I *hadn't* called her!'

Ralph Nelson was another of the people whom she took to calling in fits of loneliness. 'She would call me in the middle of the night,' said Nelson. 'Twelve or one o'clock in the morning. She wanted me to come over. I'm a widower now, but at the time I was happily married. So I said, "Rita, I can't come over. What would my wife think?" Something like this had happened to me once before with a story editor I had at one time. She committed suicide and I finally realized that when she started calling me in the middle of the night it had been a cry for help. And now that was probably what Rita was doing.'

Still another regular recipient of Rita's late-night phone calls was Hermes Pan, whom she often roused from bed. 'She'd call me at one or two in the morning,' Pan remembered. 'I'd be asleep, but I would never tell her she woke me up. And I knew well enough not to ask what the matter was because she would resent it and scream *"Eeee!! Shut up!!"* '

During these last, terrible years Rita was fortunate to have an understanding and affectionate next-door neighbor like her old co-star Glenn Ford, who would often come by when she needed somebody. But not everyone Rita turned to in moments of desperation was as benevolent. Thus, her friend from the Welles days, Libby Sloane, caught a sad and depressing glimpse of Rita in a Hollywood nightclub: 'As we were walking to our table, we had to pass the bar,' Sloane recalled. 'All these people were standing at the bar drinking it up. And there was Rita. She was quite tight. It was a very, very sad thing to see because a terrible, terrible thing happened. She dropped something and her *escort* said

367

to her, ''Pick that up!'' I wanted to kill him! It was one of the worst things I've ever seen. It was just horrifying. At that point I knew she was a goner: that she would be at the level of having to take that kind of thing from some beast.'

Chapter Thirty-three

*T*he practical difficulties Rita had experienced during the shooting of *Wrath of God* suggested that by and large she was probably no longer in any condition to work in films. But her as yet mysterious problems on that picture had been kept quiet enough that, within months, the offer of a new role came from England. Initially she hesitated to accept, but when her friend Curtis Roberts said he would accompany her, Rita signed on to appear in *Tales That Witness Madness*, a 'psycho thriller' to be directed by Freddie Francis at Shepperton Studios.

As they departed for London that November 1972, fifty-four-year-old Rita certainly *looked* well enough to do the film. Frightened by all that had been happening lately, Rita seemed finally to have sworn off the bottle – although, as would soon become abundantly clear, even without alcohol Rita's mental powers kept slowly, relentlessly diminishing.

At first she seemed perfectly all right as she settled in at the Dorchester. But scarcely had they left the hotel on the way to Shepperton than she was plunged into a fit of agitation at the prospect of appearing on camera again. 'It started on the way to the studio,' Roberts recalled. 'She had a moment of *utter* panic. Then it grew and grew. By the time we had arrived at the studio she had *really* worked herself up.' Rita swiftly composed herself to make her appearance at the studio. 'She was *trained* to do that,' Roberts explained. But it wasn't long before she fell apart again.

'I don't think she could face that camera,' said Roberts, who stayed with her every step of the way. 'We went into the dressing room to go over her lines and she had no problem. She figured I was there and we were confident about it. But then suddenly the panic set in. Something snapped and it all went.'

Once again Rita exhibited the same strange inability to follow simple orders that had plagued her during her previous film. In Mexico, she had found herself unable to step into a cave when the director asked her to do so. Now it was the need to descend a flight of stairs that precipitated a catastrophic reaction.

'Rita was blind as a bat without her glasses,' Roberts recalled. 'She kept staring and bending over to look at those stairs. That was one of the big problems they had with shooting her, just coming down those stairs. It was so odd. She wouldn't trust it. I said, "Rita, why can't you just walk down the stairs?"'

What seemed like a perfectly simple, everyday task to others filled Rita with inexplicable dread.

'That was the disease,' Roberts explained. 'They kept saying she was drunk. But I had spent every minute with her and she had not *touched* a drink. No, she was not drinking at that time.' As is often the case with dementia victims, her quite normal physical appearance – 'Actually, she looked absolutely marvelous,' said Roberts – made the emotional outbursts that followed seem all the more perplexing to those around her.

'It's all shit!' Rita exploded, when things had completely overwhelmed her. 'It's cold! I think I'm getting pneumonia!'

Then came the sort of baseless – and often bizarre – accusations against others that are frequently heard from those afflicted with Alzheimer's disease. As Curtis Roberts recalled, 'She complained that it was thirty below zero and that we were freezing her to death.' A doctor was summoned and agreed to give Rita some time off from the picture. But when he examined her again he declared that she was well enough to go back to work. This precipitated what Roberts described as 'a violent outburst at the doctor. She called him a quack and threw ashtrays and other things at him. "Get out! Get out! He doesn't know what he's talking about!" '

Faced with an order to return to work the next morning, Rita turned to a man she had met in London, whom Roberts facetiously tagged the 'Armenian rug peddler.' 'She was always with the most peculiar people in the later years,' said Roberts of Rita's latest suitor. 'I swear he used to stand there like a comic figure, with the flowers in one hand, and the box of candy in the other. She would tell me how rich he was, and I said, "The only oil he has is on his shoes." ' When the Shepperton Studios driver arrived at the Dorchester at 6.30 the following morning to take Rita to the set, it was discovered that she and the 'rug peddler' had fled to America.

This time a flurry of rumors about what had gone on at Shepperton Studios followed Rita to Hollywood. Her ability to function on a film set had pretty much broken down by the time she made *Wrath of God*, but it was her peculiar behavior during *Tales That Witness Madness* – and especially her much-talked about 'disappearance' in the middle of shooting – that would keep her from ever appearing in a film again. (Ironically, her replacement on the picture was Kim Novak, whom Harry Cohn had once groomed to take over for her back at Columbia.)

When Curtis Roberts caught up with Rita in Hollywood, much to his chagrin he discovered that she had 'started drinking again.' He tried to talk to her about what had happened back in London, but all she would say was, 'It was a piece of junk and I didn't wanna do it!'

As to what had really caused Rita suddenly to disappear like that: 'She didn't remember,' Roberts explained. 'It was so sad!'

For all intents and purposes her screen career had ended with the flight from the Dorchester Hotel in 1972, but – sad to say – it would still be nearly eight years before Rita's disease was actually diagnosed. In the meantime, she would live a life of pure hell that was made all the worse by the fact that no one understood quite what was happening to her. Terrified, often violent, increasingly confused and disoriented, beset by hallucinations and suspicions, Rita was a source of immense pain, frustration, and heartache to those who knew and loved her, but had no idea of how they could help.

Like a great many others afflicted with Alzheimer's disease, Rita often exhibited hostile and aggressive behavior that alienated friends who couldn't figure out why she was possibly acting that way. 'It was terrible,' said Hermes Pan, 'because her friends began to desert her. They were afraid, you know. One woman said to me, "I just hate to go over there because I never know what Rita's going to say or do."'

And, as her daughter Yasmin would explain, 'Because of her volatility, some people got tired of being around her.'

At a dinner party to which Hermes Pan had invited Rita, Fred Astaire, and his sister, Adele, Pan recalled that 'we were sitting at dinner and Adele said, "Oh, I hear Yasmin is studying voice." And Rita said, "Yes." Then, Adele – which was *only natural* – said, "I wonder where she gets that talent from?"' Adele Astaire plainly intended the remark by way of casual conversation, but, as Alzheimer's victims are known to do, Rita completely misinterpreted it as a grave insult. 'Rita sort of rose up,' Pan explained. 'You know, the *Spanish* coming out. But she didn't say anything. Later on, we were sitting around talking – although Rita hadn't said much all evening. Adele was sitting next to Rita, who had a drink in her hand. And suddenly, Rita took the drink and threw it right in Adele's face! Adele didn't say a word at first. Then she looked at Fred – who always hated incidents – and said, "Fred, I think we'd better leave. This lady is crazy." Fred said good-night politely and they walked out. Rita didn't say a word. Not a word. So after they left, I said, "What happened?" She just shrugged, as if to say, "Isn't it fun?" When she called me the next day she didn't remember. Didn't say a word about it. Just "Hello honey, how are you?" – as if nothing had happened.'

Another of Rita's strange outbursts cut short a dinner party of her own, but this time the cause of her agitation could not be ascertained.

'Ann Miller and I had gone to her house for dinner,' Hermes Pan recalled. 'We had just finished eating when suddenly she said, "I want you all to get out! Just get out!" And *nothing* had happened! Ann said, "Oh, what's the matter?" But Rita didn't answer. "Just get out!" she kept saying. "Leave me alone." '

Nor, on another such occasion, could Pan comprehend why, within minutes, Rita abruptly changed her mind about going out for the evening. One moment she was all set to leave for a glamorous Hollywood preview, and the next she was violently, inexplicably opposed to the very idea of it.

'The limousine came by to pick me up,' Pan explained, 'so I called Rita and said, "I'm leaving now. I'll be over in ten minutes." And she said, "Fine." Just ten minutes later, when I rang her doorbell and she came to the door, she was dressed beautifully and *looked* wonderful. But then she said, "I'm not going to this blankety-blank party!" and slammed the door in my face. I had *just* talked to her!'

But the worst of these perplexing incidents occurred one evening when Rita inexplicably threatened her friends with a butcher knife. 'Rita had invited Hermes and myself over for dinner at her house,' recalled Ann Miller. 'We rang the doorbell and a Spanish woman came to the door. I said, "We're invited for dinner. Is Miss Hayworth home?" And she said, "Yes, one moment please. I'll get her" – and left us standing outside. "Why don't they let us in?" I asked Hermes. When Rita came to the door, she had a butcher knife in her hand and said, "I'm not signing any autographs today! Who are you?" She didn't know who we were!' Agnosia, or the ability to recognize otherwise familiar people or things, is a common symptom of Alzheimer's disease. It wasn't that Rita didn't remember her friends Ann Miller and Hermes Pan, just that the brain damage had made her unable to identify who was at the door just then. 'We were terrified,' Miller continued. 'She chased us out with the butcher knife. As we got in the car she was still screaming, "How dare you invade my private property! I don't see autograph seekers! How dare you! Get out! Get out!" She had no idea who she was screaming at. Then the next day she called me and said, "Why didn't you come for dinner?" I just didn't know what to make of it. I said to Hermes, "Hermes, something is terribly wrong. Is she an alcoholic?" And Hermes said, "I don't think so, Annie. I don't think she drinks that much." We were *very* puzzled.'

Even when she wasn't hostile or threatening, Rita gave signs of being strangely out of control. Once while Rita was visiting Hermes Pan the conversation turned to the fashionable primal-scream therapy, which involved purging one's aggressions by screaming. 'She had heard about it and she said, "Oh, I think it's wonderful!" ' Pan recalled. 'And then she started to scream, "*Yeeeee!*" I said, "Rita, not so loud!" And she said, "*Whaaaaa!*" I took her home shortly afterward. And on the way down through Beverly Hills she was *still* screaming. If a cop came along he would have thought I was kidnapping her or something, so I said, "Rita, quiet! Please don't do that!" But she wouldn't stop. "I'll do what I want to do!" she said, and just kept screaming like that: "*Yeeeee! Whaaaaa!*" '

'Some nights she'd be up all night screaming,' said Curtis Roberts of Rita's often nightmarish existence during this period. Rita's drinking problem had been common knowledge in Hollywood for some time now, but the full extent of her disintegration did not become public until January 1976, when a disturbing series of photographs afforded a glimpse into Rita's private hell. There she was being carried off an airplane in London, wild-eyed, disheveled, and disoriented: a woman in torment.

The trip hadn't started out that way, however, as she and her agent Bud Moss left California on Super Bowl Sunday, headed for England, where Rita was set to appear on a TV talk show. By now there was no longer really any question of finding new film work for Rita, since even her agent realized that she wouldn't be able to handle it. 'If someone would say, ''Please sign this picture to Bob or to Nancy'' or something like that, she would just write ''Rita Hayworth'',' Moss explained. 'That's *all* she could do.' But while actual film roles were ruled out, Rita continued to make sometimes zombielike public appearances, whose purpose her agent would describe as an attempt to 'try and keep *the image* of Rita as alive as we possibly could without embarrassing her in public.'

But despite everyone's best efforts, on account of Rita's condition the flight to London proved very embarrassing indeed. The problem started prior to boarding, when Rita's lifelong fear of flying caused her to have a vodka on the rocks, which did not mix well with the tranquilizer she had also taken. By the time she got to the first-class section of the TWA 747 she was already extremely 'uptight', as Moss described her. During dinner she repeatedly lashed out at one of the stewardesses for no rational reason. 'She doesn't like me!' Rita insisted to her agent, who did his best to soothe her. Eventually Rita seemed to calm down a bit and went into the rest room, where she changed into her pajamas. Covered by her fur coat, she made her way back to her seat.

'I sat with her for a couple of hours,' Moss recalled. 'She fell asleep in my arms.' But when Moss and an associate went to the first-class lounge to chat, some other passengers, a couple on their honeymoon, quite innocently woke Rita up to offer her the glass of celebratory champagne that, in her already confused state of mind, triggered a massive new emotional outlet. Witnesses reported that Rita began to shout and throw her arms about and that she looked 'very ill.' And according to Moss, she suddenly 'hauled off and slapped' a stewardess who was only trying to assist her. 'She doesn't like me!' Rita told Moss. 'She's an evil person!'

Word of the unruly celebrity passenger had reached Heathrow Airport, in London, even before they landed, so that a crowd of photographers and reporters was waiting there to see what it was all about. A TWA representative boarded the plane to warn Rita's agent of what faced her:

'Mr Moss, I'm sorry to inform you that there's about thirty press waiting outside in the lobby for Rita.' Since Rita was obviously in no condition to be photographed at the moment, she was left behind on the plane as her agent went out to try to avert further trouble.

'When is she getting off the plane?' the press people demanded to know.

'Well, shortly,' Moss replied. 'But I must tell you that she doesn't feel good. She has no makeup on and she has not done her hair.' If only they would agree to leave her alone now, Moss offered to have them all up to Rita's suite at the Savoy later the same day. 'We're going to have a cocktail party for you gentlemen this afternoon, and you guys can all meet Rita then,' Moss promised.

'We want Rita as she is!' one photographer called out, and the others agreed. Whereupon Moss went back into the plane to try something else.

About half an hour later, a decoy put on Rita's hat and coat in an attempt to divert the press's attention as Moss and the TWA representative struggled to get Rita down a ramp that had been brought around to the back of the plane. 'She was rubber-legged,' said Moss of Rita's inability to stand up by herself. 'We held her up, carried her down the steps.'

The photographers hadn't been fooled, however – within seconds they swarmed around and got their pictures of Rita, who looked like a poor, frightened doe, rendered helpless by a hunter's blinding lights.

At the hotel Moss had the telephone shut off so that the press couldn't get through to them. To one reporter who slipped a note under the door that said 'Either Rita comes out or we're going to print the pictures,' Moss replied, 'Go screw yourself! Print the pictures!' The agent knew only too well that the photos would be published no matter what. Meanwhile, Rita had gone to bed, oblivious to all that had just happened to her. When she woke up later, she was fed soup and eggs, and then she dozed off again. 'The next morning, it was as if nothing had happened,' Moss recalled Rita's attitude and appearance when she got up. 'She said,

''Okay, let's get to work!'' ' – by which she meant preparing for the TV talk show.

Although by now Rita's horrific display at Heathrow was all over the international press, she was not shown any of the newspapers in which the appalling photos appeared. In an attempt to downplay the horrors that the press had just glimpsed, London photographers were soon invited to snap pictures of Rita at a well-supervised golf outing. While she definitely looked much better, the photo session also had its disturbing moments, such as Rita's answer to a newsman's question about what had happened to her at Heathrow: 'I don't know what you're talking about,' she replied, apparently in all honesty.

When at length Rita appeared on TV in London, she struck the talk-show host, Russell Harty, as 'drained, tired and bewildered.' Amazingly, however, given all that had happened on the trip thus far, Rita and company pressed on to Spain, where other TV engagements were scheduled.

Rita also turned up on a number of 'celebrity cruises' in this period. The films of the stars on board were screened, and afterward they answered questions posed by the other passengers. 'That was one of the sad moments of my life,' said Ann Miller of the cruise she took with Rita. 'I was just heartbroken about Rita. She got so bad she couldn't make her face up or roll her hair up and comb it out properly.' Thus, Rita was accompanied by a woman who, as Miller observed, 'helped put her makeup on and helped to dress her.' As for the question-and-answer sessions, 'Rita was fine as long as she didn't have to remember lines,' Miller recalled. 'She spoke in a shy, almost little-girl voice and handled herself pretty well. But I did think she was drinking heavily because sometimes her words were slurred and she would get very disheveled.'

With hindsight it seems obvious that at this point Rita was hardly in any condition to go on making public appearances, but still she dragged from one such event to another, a mere shell of her former self. It is a grotesque commentary on the Hollywood star system that, although she was no longer even remotely functional as a performer, Rita

Hayworth remained an attraction, a marketable commodity. By now, as Hermes Pan recalled sadly, 'She had almost a *glazed* look, like she was very bored – or had just given up. Well, that's Hollywood publicity, you know. They'll squeeze the blood out of you if they can.'

In October 1976 Rita left for Argentina on what Bud Moss would describe as 'probably the hairiest of our trips.' Rita had accepted an invitation to appear on a televised homage to her career, but little did anyone quite expect the extent of the violent political unrest that would greet her there. Worst of all, according to a confidential telegram sent from the American embassy in Buenos Aires to the Secretary of State in Washington, D.C., local terrorists evidently hoped to use Rita's much-publicized visit to attract international attention to themselves by staging a 'grenade attack' as she emerged from her hotel.

Rita's plane landed in Buenos Aires in the midst of a torrential rainstorm. It was about five in the morning and the flight was three hours late, yet, some fifty fans were there to meet her. Many of them clutched signs – 'GILDA HAS RETURNED!' and 'WELCOME, RITA!' – whose ink had started to run in the downpour. Suddenly a voice was heard to declare, 'We are here to protect you,' and Rita looked up to see the armed agents assigned to keep her from harm.

'As we got off the plane we were surrounded by five guys and a girl who looked like Diana Rigg, with a leather jacket, the tightest slacks I've ever seen, and a German Luger under her breast,' Moss recalled. 'They became our team for five days. Wherever we went, they went with us in two cars. Rita and I got in one of the cars with three of the agents who kept their guns on the dashboard or on their laps in case they needed them in a hurry.' On the way to the hotel through the pouring rain, Rita 'just kept humming and singing along,' said Moss. 'I'm sweating bullets. And Rita's the calmest, the coolest. She's oblivious to everything.'

At the hotel two additional security people guarded the door to Rita's suite.

378

'The sun is now coming up over this little square where our hotel is,' Moss recalled. 'Rita goes to the window, opens the shades, says, "God, what a beautiful morning!" and *a bomb* explodes in the park in front of us! The security threw Rita back from the window and jumped on her.' Still, she seemed not to grasp any of what was happening. '*Nothing*,' said Moss to describe her reaction to the terrible explosion. 'She was the calmest of all of us.' As the American embassy would subsequently report to Washington, these were the grenades that the terrorists planned to use as Rita left the hotel; they had been discovered in advance, however, and were being deactivated when one exploded.

Repeatedly, in the strange days that followed, Rita appeared never really to register the violence and unrest all around her. Even when an office building suddenly exploded some ten feet from the automobile carrying Rita and her agent ('We were seconds from having blown up!' Moss recalled), and debris was falling on all sides, she hardly seemed to comprehend the peril.

Which made it all the more frightening when, on the next stop of their South American trip, in Rio de Janeiro, Rita disappeared by herself for several hours. 'Everybody panicked,' said Moss. Indeed, oblivious as she had just been to exploding grenades and crumbling buildings, how was she possibly going to protect herself now all alone in a strange city? Fortunately, however, Rita had meanwhile fallen into quite innocent company. 'All of a sudden we got a call,' said Moss. 'About a mile up the road, on the beach, there was a group of kids, ten- to fifteen-year-old kids, flying these beautiful kites. And there was Rita just sitting there on the beach with these little kids, flying the kites with them.'

Chapter Thirty-four

*N*ot long afterward, back in California, Rita's ability to take care of herself would publicly and officially be called into question when the situation became so out of hand that the Orange County Public Guardian's Office moved to take charge of her. Her alarming condition had come to the attention of the authorities when a boyfriend of the period, an artist named Bill Gilpin, brought her to Hoag Memorial Hospital, in Newport Beach, to try to find out what was wrong with her.

In the course of their relationship, Gilpin (who had first picked up Rita on a golf course where she was playing alone) had witnessed various symptoms of her mental deterioration: memory loss, confusion, and occasional urinary incontinence. By now, however, the magnitude of her losses had made the need for professional help abundantly obvious. 'Sweetheart,' he said before taking her to Hoag Memorial, 'we're going to put you in a hospital for a few days so you can have some tests.'

There, Dr James Miner examined Rita and found her 'gravely disabled as a result of mental disorder or impairment by chronic alcoholism and . . . unwilling to accept, or incapable of accepting, treatment voluntarily.' Based on Dr Miner's addidavit 'recommending temporary conservatorship,' Warren W. Morse, the Supervising Deputy Public Guardian, filed a court petition to assume control of Rita's 'person and estate.'

Accordingly, on 9 March 1977, the Orange County Superior Court appointed the Public Guardian, James E.

Heim, Rita's temporary conservator. At a later date a court hearing would assess the need for the state to oversee Rita on a more permanent basis. Until then, the court stipulated that, whatever opposition she might express, Rita could be 'detained in a facility providing intensive treatment' (a medical, psychiatric, or nursing institution, a state hospital, or county alcoholic treatment center), where she would have no choice but to undergo any procedures (excluding surgery) that the temporary conservator deemed necessary.

In response, Rita's attorney Leonard Monroe acted on her behalf to retrieve control of her affairs from the Public Guardian's Office and to get her out of Hoag Memorial. Meanwhile, her clothes were removed from Bill Gilpin's Newport Beach apartment, where she had been staying lately; and, much to his chagrin, the boyfriend who had taken her to the hospital in the first place suddenly found himself barred from seeing her.

When her old and loyal friend Bob Schiffer rushed to Newport Beach to see Rita at Hoag Memorial, at first, he, too, was denied visiting privileges. But, devoted to Rita as always, Schiffer wasn't about to give up, and eventually he did indeed gain access to her bedside, where he was relieved to discover that at least she recognized him and seemed 'fairly well with it,' under the circumstances. And soon, he observed Rita's spirits pick up appreciably when her daughter Yasmin called. 'Thank God for Yassy!' said Schiffer. 'She called while I was there and talked to Rita about getting her outfitted to come to New York. Rita was so happy! She hung up the phone and said, "Yassy's going to get me a dress!" '

But when, in turn, the princess appeared at the hospital, she was upset to find that Rita did not know the month, the current president, or even the names of friends. 'She had become very closed, very silent,' Yasmin would recall. 'But you could see the despair in her face. I knew by then that I had to take control.'

Twenty-three years before this, Rita had rushed to White Plains with Dick Haymes when a court had taken her daughters into protective custody, but now it was Rita herself of whom the state had taken charge, and Yasmin who had come for her.

By mid-April Rita's attorney had struck a deal with the Orange County Superior Court in Santa Ana to remove her from the control of the Public Guardian's Office, so that she could be taken east for treatment of what was still presumed to be her alcoholism at the posh Silver Hill drying-out clinic, in Connecticut.

Once before, however, at the time of *Tales That Witness Madness*, Rita had stopped drinking but failed to return to normal, and so it was again. She may have abandoned the bottle at Silver Hill, yet her disintegration plainly continued. Back in Hollywood that summer, following her stay at the drying-out clinic, Rita appeared considerably more 'together' – her hair was lighter and more fashionably cut, and her clothing a good deal more elegant. Although she resumed making carefully orchestrated public appearances, and collecting awards, statues, and tributes throughout America and Europe, an old friend like Bob Schiffer could clearly see that, in private, Rita only seemed to be getting much worse. When he had visited her in the hospital in Newport Beach only a few months earlier, Rita had had no difficulty in recognizing Bob. But by the time he saw her again that Christmas everything had changed. 'I spent Christmas with her and we sat on a couch and looked through an old album,' Schiffer recalled with deep emotion. 'There were photographs of her and of myself, but she didn't really seem to recognize us. I had a feeling she didn't even know who I was! She just sort of sat there.'

Still, even at this point there was a man in Rita's life, Kim Novak's former beau Mac Krim, who regularly squired her about town and to certain of her public appearances. Krim would recall with particular fondness the evening when, in anticipation of his arrival, Rita had put on an old recording of 'Put the Blame on Mame.' Much to Mac's delight, she greeted him at the door with a rendition of the famous dance from *Gilda*, in which she drunkenly, sensuously peels off her long black gloves.

Although Rita successfully continued to avoid alcohol (according to Krim, she drank only 7-Up), based on her behavior people still often assumed she was drunk. Writer Jim Bacon would remember one such occasion in the Polo Lounge, at the Beverly Hills Hotel, where Rita started screaming for no apparent reason. 'When she began to scream she was in a back booth with two guys,' said Bacon. 'I don't know who the hell they were. They just got up and left.' Only naturally, Bacon 'figured she was drunk,' but when he went back to offer to take Rita home, she stopped screaming and was suddenly '*very* coherent,' saying, 'Jim, how are you dear?'

In the past, friends had worried about her living alone in the big house in Beverly Hills, but as her condition worsened, the situation became even more disturbing. She already had a history of insisting she heard intruders in the house when there were none, and needlessly summoning the police. And neighbors reported that on many a night Rita would deliberately let out her dogs and pretend that they were lost, in hopes of finding someone to talk to as she called for them. In her desperate search for companionship, she indiscriminately allowed into her home people whom she didn't even know. 'All the freeloaders in town were there on Sundays,' Curtis Roberts recalled. 'She always had a bunch of people and I don't think she knew who half of them were. I think she had no idea of what she was doing anymore.'

In 1979 Rita's house was put up for sale and she moved into an apartment in the same building in Beverly Hills where Mac Krim lived, and which he had recommended to her for its excellent security. But as Krim would recall, Rita was never left alone now. An attendant looked after her around the clock, and there was a constant stream of associates to handle her ongoing public appearances and other business.

Henry Rogers, who had launched Rita's first major publicity campaign when she was married to Eddie Judson, and who had run into her on various occasions in the intervening years, encountered her at a public-relations event in

Los Angeles, where the diminished responsiveness that psychologists call a 'flattening of effect' was much in evidence. Many years before this, Rogers had observed Rita's strange ability to blank out at photo sessions where she typically 'just went through the motions, almost *robot-like*' – but that was nothing compared with what he witnessed now as she posed with him for a photo. 'She was really out of it,' Rogers recalled. 'She was sitting on a chair and I was kind of kneeling next to her. But her eyes looked unfocused and I don't think she knew who I was.'

When Rita's old friend Roz Rogers (who also had seen her on various occasions over the years) approached, Rita responded just as blankly to her. 'I said hello to her and tried to talk to her for about five minutes before there was any recognition in her eyes,' Mrs Rogers recalled. 'Suddenly she said, "Roz, Roz, it's you!" Oh, I tell you, my heart sank.'

But perhaps the most poignant of these late encounters would occur the evening when Orson Welles spotted Rita at a hotel and went over to kiss her and chat about old times. Rita may once have called Orson 'the great love of my life,' but 'My blood ran cold,' said Welles of the terrible moment when his lips touched her cheek and he realized that she clearly had no idea who he was.

By 1980, after consulting various physicians about her mother's perplexing condition, Yasmin was finally told by one doctor that its cause might not be alcoholism, as others had hitherto presumed, but the then little-known brain disorder Alzheimer's disease, which remains incurable to this day. For Yasmin, although it was extremely painful to learn that her mother had fallen victim to illness, there was also what she called 'a sense of relief' in finally knowing the source of Rita's recent problems. 'So much embarrassment and heartache could have been saved,' Yasmin declared, 'if at that time it had been known that Rita Hayworth was ill and not guilty of any misconduct.'

But the world did not learn of Rita's incurable brain disease until 1981, when Yasmin moved to be legally appointed her mother's conservator, since, at the age of sixty-two, Rita was plainly no longer able to care for herself. By now, according to Mac Krim, Rita had ceased even to take short walks outside with her attendant. As happens with other Alzheimer's victims, Rita's intellectual ability had declined to the point where she simply would not survive without constant care.

In June 1981, a month after Yasmin returned to New York City from Munich, where she had been studying voice, Rita's attorney filed a petition in Los Angeles Superior Court that publicly identified for the first time the progressive brain disorder with which Rita was afflicted. At length the court determined that she was indeed entirely unable to attend to her most basic physical needs. Health, food, clothing, shelter: in each of these areas Rita required personal assistance. Maintaining her own bank account and personal records was also impossible now, as was clearly answering an investigator's questions and making explanations.

Robert Gary, an attorney whom the court had appointed to represent Rita's interests in the case, concurred that she could no longer handle her own affairs and would be best off with Yasmin. When Los Angeles Superior Court Judge Ronald E. Swearinger asked the attorney how Rita would react to Yasmin's plan to move her to New York City, Gary replied, 'I don't think she has the capacity to decide one way or another. I think her best interest is with her daughter.'

Thus, on 23 July 1981, Judge Swearinger officially named Princess Yasmin Aga Khan Rita's conservator. Until the move to New York could be arranged, Rita would continue to be cared for by the medical staff Yasmin was already providing in her mother's Beverly Hills apartment.

'Yasmin was just marvelous to Rita,' said Ann Miller of the final years in New York. 'She always had somebody come in to set her hair, do her makeup, and dress her. She kept her just like a big French doll. I really admire that little girl.' Indeed, prior to Rita's death, on 14 May 1987, at the age of sixty-eight, she inhabited an apartment adjoining Yasmin's in the elegant old San Remo, overlooking New

York City's Central Park. (Meanwhile, Rebecca, whose marriage had broken up, continued to live far from the public eye in the state of Washington.)

Until she became bedridden, Rita spent a good deal of time seated in an armchair, gazing straight ahead, much as she used to do on her parents' porch in Chula Vista a half century before, as she waited to be driven to Mexico to dance. While dancing was obviously beyond her now, she would still respond a little to the music she had always so passionately adored. Whenever music was played for her, her shoulders and feet might briefly come alive in her chair, or she might even clap her hands a bit. Her daughter speculated that perhaps this might be Rita's memory of life as a dancer coming back.

With the passage of time, however, even minimal responses such as these dwindled noticeably as Rita underwent the final stages of the total loss of self associated with irreversible dementia. Eventually it became too much for her even to walk into the room and lower herself in her chair. Instead, as her daughter watched in horror, 'She fearfully clung to the doorframe, her eyes darted back and forth from chair to door, door to chair.' Until she was finally assisted to her place, Rita just hovered there like that: terrified, helpless, bewildered.

To care for Rita, Yasmin put aside her aspirations to a singing career and soon the princess had established herself as an important international spokesperson for the Alzheimer's Disease and Related Disorders Association, for which she organized yearly fund-raising galas in honor of her mother.

In May 1985, the thirty-five-year-old Princess Yasmin married Basil Embiricos, of the prominent Greek shipping family, in a ceremony at the San Remo. Their son, Andrew, was born that December. But the marriage was soon over, and Yasmin and the baby lived on in the apartment next to Rita, who showed no sign of comprehending that Yasmin had a new son. 'I put him in Mother's lap, but there was no reaction,' Yasmin reported in 1986. 'She is unable to understand.'

Eventually, those afflicted with Alzheimer's disease become unable to learn and retain new information, such as the news of a new grandchild's arrival. Since the present seems no longer to exist for them, many demented persons retreat into the past, where the people and events seem a good deal more vivid – more *real* – than anything actually happening now: an especially chilling prospect in the case of someone like Rita, whose past held all too much pain and unhappiness. For, even with the revelatory 1980 Alzheimer's diagnosis, an essential part of the puzzle of Rita's behavior remained missing: the memories of incestuous abuse that had secretly, insidiously shaped the turbulent events of her personal life and determined so much of the scandalous, self-destructive, and seemingly irresponsible and irrational behavior that Rita had exhibited long before the onset of brain disease.

In 1968, Eduardo Cansino had died in Florida, where he lived with a second wife, but there could be no undoing the lifetime of inner torment to which he had condemned his daughter. Given the hatred and resentment that she had long felt toward him, Rita was unlikely to put him out of her thoughts now.

'It's so hard to know what she's feeling, what's going on inside,' said Yasmin of her mother in later years. Still, there were fleeting hints, indications. Although Rita was silent most of the time (and eventually would altogether lose the capacity for speech), suddenly for no apparent reason that anyone in the room could discern, she would utter one or two odd, enigmatic sentences. Could they be a clue to what she was thinking, to the images and memories flickering in her mind as she sat in her armchair, gazing straight ahead?

'He used to do that,' Rita would say. 'He told me how to do that.'

But no one knew what she meant.

Acknowledgments

I would like to thank all the many people who helped in so many different and important ways to make this book possible.

Above all, I am fortunate to have Amanda Vaill as my editor at Viking Penguin. Once again Amanda's intelligence, sensitivity, and style made working with her an immense pleasure. At Viking Penguin I would also like to acknowledge the particular kindness of Francesca Belanger, Victoria Meyer, Neal Stuart, and Anne Tergesen.

At Weidenfeld and Nicolson in London, it was George Weidenfeld who first suggested that I undertake this biography of Rita Hayworth. I am grateful to him for initiating the project. Also at Weidenfeld, my editor Allegra Huston provided much enthusiasm and made many invaluable suggestions. Further important help came from David Roberts and, in the early stages of research and writing, Juliet Gardiner.

Beatriz de Moura at Tusquets Editores in Barcelona also provided early support for the project; as did my agents Lois Wallace of the Wallace Literary Agency in New York and Anthony Sheil of Anthony Sheil Associates in London, whose tireless efforts on my behalf are much appreciated.

Special thanks are also due to all the people who so generously shared their memories of Rita Hayworth with me, and to the endlessly helpful and patient staffs of the numerous governmental agencies, courts, archives, and libraries listed in the source notes. And I must thank each of the following for special help and services along the way: Michael Bicknell, Jo-Ann Cassler, Elsa Feminella, Timothy Mawson, Ricky Lynn Moskowitz, Walter Neville, Harry Packman, Sylvia Packman, Muriel Tecoz, Renato Tonelli, and Lisa Valkenier.

Finally, for everything – and more – my husband, David.

Notes and Sources

*I*n my research for this book, I made extensive use of the Freedom of Information Act. As a result, quantities of United States government documents pertaining to Rita Hayworth's life were released. In addition, I consulted many other governmental agencies, courts, archives, and libraries. Among the more important sources were:

Academy of Motion Picture Arts and Sciences, Beverly Hills, California.
Archives, County Records Center, Los Angeles, California.
Circuit Court of Cook County, Chicago, Illinois.
Clerk of Superior Court, Yuma, Arizona.
County Clerk, California Superior Court, Los Angeles, California.
County Clerk, Vital Records, Waukegan, Illinois.
County Clerk's Office, Reno, Nevada.
County Recorder, Clark County, Las Vegas, Nevada.
County Recorder, San Jose, California.
Department of State, U.S.A., Washington, D.C.
The Diplomatic Branch, National Archives and Records, Administration, Washington, D.C.
Hunter College of C.U.N.Y. Library, New York, New York.
Jackson Heights Library, Jackson Heights, New York.
Lilly Library, Orson Welles Papers, Indiana University, Bloomington, Indiana.
Lincoln Center Library Dance Collection, New York, New York.
Lincoln Center Library Theater Collection, New York, New York.
Long Island Room, Jamaica Library, Jamaica, New York.
Los Angeles Superior Court, Civil Division, Los Angeles, California.

Marriage Records, City Hall, Philadelphia, Pennsylvania.
Museum of Modern Art Film Department, New York, New York.
National Archives, Eastpoint, Georgia.
National Archives and Records Administration, Washington, D.C.
New York City Public Library, New York, New York.
Office of Vital Statistics, Jacksonville, Florida.
Orange County Clerk, Santa Ana, California.
Selective Service System, National Headquarters, Washington, D.C.
U.S. Department of Justice, Federal Bureau of Investigation, Los Angeles, California.
U.S. Department of Justice, Federal Bureau of Investigation, New York, New York.
U.S. Department of Justice, Federal Bureau of Investigation, Washington, D.C.
U.S. Department of Justice, Immigration and Naturalization Service, Los Angeles, California.
U.S. District Court, Clerk's Office, Chattanooga, Tennessee.
University of California at Los Angeles, Los Angeles, California.
Vital Records Section, D.C. Department of Human Services, Washington, D.C.
Vital Statistics Branch, Sacramento, California.
Washoe County Clerk's Office, Reno, Nevada.

Notes and Sources

In the notes that follow, 'to BL' denotes interview with author.

CHAPTER ONE

Page

9   '*to them but . . .* ': *Duluth Herald*, 14 February 1917.
9   '*rather a lonely . . .* ': Ibid.
10   '*that American audiences . . .* ': Ibid.
10   Joaquin and Avecillo and Rosario Montero: Antonio Cansino's Death Certificate, Los Angeles, California, 20 June 1954.
10   Gabriel Cansino: Gabriel J. Cansino Death Certificate, San Francisco, California, 2 March 1963. Elisa Cansino and Nathaniel A. Jackolo Marriage License Application, Philadelphia, Pennsylvania, 14 January 1918. Cansino-Jackolo Marriage Certificate, 14 January 1918.
11   U.S. arrival of Eduardo and Elisa Cansino: 'Alien Passengers' Manifest for U.S. Immigration,' S.S. *Prinz Friedrich Wilhelm*, 12 January 1913.
12   Of many general works on vaudeville consulted, two were especially helpful: Charles W. Stein, ed., *American Vaudeville as Seen by Its Contemporaries*; and John C. DiMeglio, *Vaudeville USA*.
12   '*the most dreaded . . .* ': Fred Astaire in *American Vaudeville*.
12   '*For an opening . . .* ': *New York Star*, 15 November 1914.
13   '*a world renowned . . .* ': *San Antonio Light*, 25 April 1916.
13   '*champion axmen . . .* ': Ibid.
13   '*They offer . . .* ': *Houston Post*, 19 April 1915.
13   '*both have . . .* ': *Los Angeles Examiner*, 28 December 1915.
13   '*The pair . . .* ': *Toldeo Blade*, 14 September 1915.
13   '*the most glamorous . . .* ': DiMeglio.
13   '*only a minor . . .* ': Fred Astaire, *Steps in Time*.
14   '*Dancers to the Spanish Court*': Program for *Follow Me*, 29 November, 1916.
14   Volga's birth and family background: Volga Hayworth Birth Certificate, Washington, D.C., 25 August 1897. Volga Cansino Death Certificate, Los Angeles, California, 25 January 1945.
15   Adoption: *New York Telegraph*, 4 August 1917.
16   '*I had wanted . . .* ': Eduardo Cansino, quoted in Janet Rae Mills, 'The Love Goddess', *Photoplay*, February 1958.

18 Eduardo's U.S. Citizenship: 'Declaration of Intention,' 13 January 1923. 'Petition for Naturalization,' 23 July 1926. 'Certificate of Naturalization,' 16 November 1926.

19 Woodside: Brooklyn–Queens Telephone Directories, 6 May 1925, 7 October 1925, Summer, 1926, Winter, 1927. Also, Eduardo Cansino's 'Certificate of Naturalization.'

20 *'She was always . . .'*: Audio tape of the late Vernon Cansino, courtesy Mrs Vernon Cansino.

CHAPTER TWO

21 *'he was the . . .'*: Vernon Cansino, audio tape.
22 *'It got very . . .'*: Ibid.
23 *'A roly-poly . . .'*: Laura Hollingshead-Meyer, quoted by Bob Thomas, *Associated Press,* 17 May 1949.
23 *'All of a sudden . . .'*: Eduardo Cansino, quoted in *Life,* 10 November 1947.
23 *'start her off'*: Eduardo Cansino, quoted in *Time,* 10 November 1941.
24 *'one of the kindest . . .'*: Laura Hollingshead-Meyer.
24 Catch fish: Shifra Haran to BL.
25 Tijuana: Memo in Rita Hayworth's FBI file, 23 May 1952, 'General Investigation Intelligence file, San Diego Division,' no. 94–27.
25 Margarita's age: Loretta Parkin to BL.
25 Thirteenth birthday: Rita Hayworth, quoted in *W.,* 4 October 1974.
26 Her own father: Orson Welles to BL.
26 Orson Welles: Ibid.
26 Among the many works on incest consulted, three proved particularly useful: John Crewdson, *By Silence Betrayed*; Judith Lewis Herman, *Father–Daughter Incest*; Eleanore Hill, *The Family Secret.*
26 *'narcissists'*: Crewdson.
26 *'perfect patriarch'*: Herman.
27 *'incest mother'*: Crewdson.
27 *'the preferred child'*: Natalie Shainess, M.D., 'Foreword' to Hill.
27 *'freer to be children'*: Herman.
27 *'the ultimate betrayal'*: Crewdson.
29 *'She was so . . .'*: Loretta Parkin to BL.
29 *'Why doesn't she . . .'* Ibid.
29 *'We talked to . . .'*: Ibid.

29 *'they'd both sit . . . '*: Ibid.
29 *'Sometimes in the . . . '*: Ibid.
30 *'a little petty . . . '*: Ibid.
30 *'high heels . . . '*: Ibid.
30 *'You could tell . . . '*: Ibid.
31 *'The boys would . . . '*: Ibid.
31 *'That was another . . . '*: Ibid.
32 *'intuitively'*: Shainess.
32 *'holding the family . . . '*: Herman.
32 *'the family income'*: Loretta Parkin to BL.
35 *'an extension of . . . '*: Crewdson.
36 *'painfully shy'*: Louella Parsons, *Tell it to Louella.*
36 *'the spiritual dimension . . . '*: Bela Balazs, *Theory of the Film.*
37 *'decidedly sensuous'*: William K. Everson, Program notes for
    The New School Film Series 18, 12 October 1973.

CHAPTER THREE

38 *'terrified'*: Rita Hayworth, quoted in *Hollywood Reporter*, 2
    November 1972.
38 *'couldn't stop stuttering'*: Ibid.
38 *'beautiful sixteen year . . . '*: Fox press release.
39 *'Such bewilderment I . . . '*: Gelal Talata, 'Dancing Feet Lead to
    Stardom,' *The Milwaukee Journal*, 1935.
39 *'He's closely watching . . . '*: Ibid.
39 *'He and Rita . . . '*: Vernon Cansino, audio tape.
40 *'normal adult mechanisms . . . '*: Herman.
40 *'repetition compulsion'*: Herman.
40 *'He was always . . . '*: Henry Rogers to BL.
40 *'Nobody ever really knew . . . '*: Roz Rogers to BL.
41 Four hundred dollars: Margarita C. Judson's 'Amended
    Complaint for Divorce and Appointment of a Receiver,' Los
    Angeles Superior Court, 20 March 1942.
41 *'A very successful . . . '*: Adela Rogers St Johns, *American Weekly*,
    19 April, 1942.
41 Judson's birth: Record of Birth for Edward Charles Judson,
    County of Santa Clara, California, 4 May 1896.
41 Marriage to Dorothy Oliver: Marriage License and Marriage
    Certificate, Lake County, Illinois, 8 March 1921.
41 Desertion and divorce: 'Decree of Divorce, Dorothy Oliver
    Judson vs. Edward Charles Judson.' Circuit Court of Cook
    County, Illinois, 9 December 1926.

41 Marriage to Hazel Forbes: 'Record of Marriage,' Town of Mamaroneck, Westchester County, New York, 4 January 1929.

41 *Whoopee*: Program for the Ziegfeld Production, 1928.

43 '*Nobody in the . . .* ': Henry Rogers to BL.

44 '*I couldn't understand . . .* ': Roz Rogers to BL.

44 '*Eddie Judson was . . .* ': Helen Hunt to BL.

44 '*traumatic*': Vernon Cansino, audio tape.

46 '*A group of . . .* ': Helen Hunt to BL.

46 '*an awful picture*': Ibid.

46 '*didn't want to . . .* ': Ibid.

47 '*specialness*': Herman.

47 Rita's marriage to Judson: Marriage License and Marriage Certificate, Yuma County, Arizona, 29 May, 1937.

CHAPTER FOUR

48 Important information on the Hayworth–Judson marriage and divorce came from: Case No. D217773: Margarita C. Judson, Plaintiff, vs. Edward Charles Judson, Defendant, Superior Court of the State of California, Los Angeles County. Also, Case No. 485908: Edward Charles Judson, Plaintiff, vs. Margarita C. Judson, also known as Rita Hayworth, Defendant, Superior Court of the State of California, Los Angeles County. Also: FBI File No. 911718: Rita Hayworth.

48 '*a real blow*': Vernon Cansino, audo tape.

48 '*upset*': *Citizen*, 1 June 1937.

48 '*She slapped him . . .* ': Vernon Cansino, audio tape.

48 '*come over just . . .* ': Ibid.

49 '*He didn't work . . .* ': Henry Rogers to BL.

49 '*she was Trilby . . .* ': Ibid.

49 '*She reflected what . . .* ': Bob Schiffer to BL.

50 '*I didn't think she . . .* ': Helen Hunt to BL.

50 '*She looked just . . .* ': Ibid.

50 '*terrible*': Ibid.

50 '*There was something . . .* ': Henry Rogers to BL.

51 '*She'll never do . . .* ': Helen Hunt to BL.

51 '*skinned straight back*': Ibid.

51 '*She hated to . . .* ': Ibid.

51 '*We'd turn her . . .* ': Ibid.

51 '*He would go . . .* ': Ibid.

53 'Harry Cohn would . . . ': Ibid.
53 'He hadn't even . . . ': Ibid.

CHAPTER FIVE

55 'Only Angels Have Wings, that . . . ': Henry Rogers to BL.
56 'The reason why . . . ': Joseph McBride, Hawks on Hawks.
56 'She got quite . . . ': Ibid.
56 'Once Harry Cohn . . . ': Henry Rogers to BL.
57 'She didn't know . . . ': Ibid.
57 'I said to . . . ': Roz Rogers to BL.
58 'I don't remember . . . ': Henry Rogers to BL.
58 'In a movie . . . ': Loretta Parkin to BL.
59 'He never let . . . ': Roz Rogers to BL.
59 'Let her make . . . ': Ibid.
59 'Here was a . . . ': Henry Rogers to BL.
59 'She was open . . . ': Roz Rogers to BL.
59 'She was much . . . ': Ibid.
61 'Once the ball . . . ': Henry Rogers to BL.
61 'She was basically . . . ': Roz Rogers to BL.
61 'just went through . . . ': Henry Rogers to BL.
61 'I owe everything . . . ': Rita Hayworth, quoted in 'A Husband
     Can Help,' by May Mann, in The San Diego Union, 1941.
62 'He told her . . . ': Jonie Taps to BL.
62 'a monster': Roz Rogers to BL.
62 'He was trying . . . ': Ibid.
62 'It seemed to . . . ': Henry Rogers, Walking the Tightrope.
63 'repeated victimization': Herman.
63 'It's the saddest . . . ': Orson Welles to BL.
66 'She was so . . . ': Hermes Pan to BL.
67 'She always reminded . . . ': Ibid.
67 'She would never . . . ': Ibid.
67 'she didn't like . . . ': Ibid.
67 'I have seen . . . ': Ibid.
68 'the most beautiful . . . ': Ibid.
68 'That picture is . . . ': Ibid.
69 'A whole different . . . ': Ibid.
69 'She always reminded . . . ': Ibid.
69 'She didn't want . . . ': Roz Rogers to BL.
69 'It was almost . . . ': Ibid.

CHAPTER SIX

70 'a tremendous proprietary . . . ': Orson Welles to BL.
70 'pimp': Ibid.
70 'All Harry Cohn . . . ': Bob Schiffer to BL.
71 'Harry Cohn always . . . ': Ann Miller to BL.
71 'He had spies . . . ': Shifra Haran to BL.
71 'She was stronger . . . ': Roz Rogers to BL.
71 'They were always . . . ' Bob Schiffer to BL.
72 'He gave her . . . ': Ann Miller to BL.
72 Disciplined labor: Herman.
73 'born dancer': Fred Astaire, quoted in New York Herald Tribune, 2 November 1941.
73 'I'd see Fred . . . ': Hermes Pan to BL.
73 'In rehearsal she . . . ': Ibid.
73 'She was nervous . . . ': Earl Bellamy to BL.
74 'Fred used to . . . ': Orson Welles to BL.
74 'terrific lover': Los Angeles Times, 24 September 1942.
75 'I know the . . . '. Roz Rogers to BL.
75 Acid: Shifra Haran to BL.
76 Threats of disfigurement: Margarita C. Judson's 'Amended Complaint for divorce,' 20 March 1942.
76 'an old man . . . ': Ibid.
76 Married her for an investment: Ibid.
76 Number of previous wives: Ibid.
76 'In the beginning . . . ': Bob Schiffer to BL.
77 'only comes out . . . ': The New York Times, 2 November 1941.
77 'Sometimes you are . . . ': Rita Hayworth, quoted in New York Sunday News, 2 November 1941.
78 'more poised': Ruth Waterbury, 'Round-Up of Romances,' Photoplay, 19 November 1941.
78 'He it is . . . ': Ibid.
78 'Personally I think . . . ': Ibid.
79 'They went a . . . ': Orson Welles to BL.
80 'He was sort . . . ': Hermes Pan to BL.
80 'He's very funny . . . ': Orson Welles to BL.

CHAPTER SEVEN

81 Hiding assets: 'Affidavit of Margarita C. Judson Persuant to Court Rule 26, 20 March 1942. Also, 'Margarita C. Judson's "Amended Complaint for Divorce and for Appointment of a

Receiver,'' 20 March 1942. Also 'Restraining Order,' 24
February 1942.

81   $25,000. 'Affidavit of Patricia Biddle,' Los Angeles Superior
Court, 20 March 1942.

81   Secretary heard threats: Ibid.

81   '*She needed help . . .*': Roz Rogers to BL.

82   Threats: Margarita C. Judson's 'Amended Complaint for
Divorce,' 20 March 1942. Also, Margarita C. Judson's
'Answer,' Los Angeles Superior Court, 2 July 1943.

82   '*obscene letter written . . .*': FBI memo – 'Judson, Rita Hayworth,
Victim. Character of Case: Miscellaneous Extortion,' Los
Angeles Bureau, File No. 62-2475, 17 May 1944.

82   '*set out various . . .*': Ibid.

82   Self-destructive action: Herman.

83   '*great and grievous . . .*': Margarita C. Judson's 'Complaint for
Divorce,' 24 February 1942.

83   '*injured and undermined . . .*': Ibid.

83   '*threatened plaintiff with . . .*': 'Affidavit for Temporary Restraining Order,' 24 February 1942.

83   Court action: 'Restraining Order,' Los Angeles Superior
Court, 24 February 1942.

85   '*I can only say . . .*': Edward C. Judson, quoted in *Los Angeles
Examiner*, 25 February 1942.

85   '*She has been . . .*'. Ibid.

85   '*She didn't have . . .*': Hermes Pan to BL.

85   Charles Beardsley: 'Demurrer,' Los Angeles Superior Court,
17 March 1942.

86   '*into public contempt . . .*': Margarita C. Judson's 'Affidavit,'
20 March 1942.

88   '*fair and just*': Rita's testimony, quoted in 'Affidavit of Harry
G. Sadicoff,' Los Angeles Superior Court, 9 September 1943.

88   '*She wasn't sure . . .*': Roz Rogers to BL.

88   '*the great love . . .*': Rita Hayworth, quoted by James Bacon to
BL.

CHAPTER EIGHT

90   '*I saw that . . .*': Orson Welles to BL.

90   '*He said that . . .*': Jackson Leighter to BL.

91   '*he arranged a . . .*': Shifra Haran to BL.

91   '*The whole wicked . . .*': Orson Welles to BL.

91   '*She wouldn't answer . . .*': Ibid.

91 '*I am like . . .* ': Ibid.
92 '*She had been . . .* ': Ibid.
93 '*She wanted to . . .* ': Ibid.
93 '*She didn't wear . . .* ': Ibid.
93 '*Miss Hayworth was . . .* ': Shifra Haran to BL.
94 '*Orson, too, was . . .* ': Roger Hill, *Time and Chance*.
94 '*Welles was a . . .* ': Hermes Pan to BL.
94 '*She respected Orson . . .* ': Bob Schiffer to BL.
94 '*When she was . . .* ': Shifra Haran to BL.
94 '*She had just . . .* ': Ibid.
95 '*She was very . . .* ': Ibid.
95 '*I don't think . . .* ': Elisabeth Rubino to BL.
96 '*When it came . . .* ': Ibid.
96 '*She was terribly . . .* ': Orson Welles to BL.
96 '*I didn't know . . .* ': Ibid.
96 '*I sat in . . .* ': Ibid.
97 '*It started because . . .* ': Shifra Haran to BL.
97 '*I felt guilty . . .* ': Orson Welles to BL.
98 Excuse to stall Judson: Letters of Don Marlin to Harry Sadicoff, quoted in 'Affidavit of Harry G. Sadicoff,' Los Angeles Superior Court, 9 September 1943.
98 Judson lawsuit: 'Complaint for Money on Contract,' Los Angeles Superior Court, Case No. 485908, Edward Charles Judson, Plaintiff, vs. Margarita C. Judson, also known as Rita Hayworth, Defendant.
99 Decree: 'Final Judgment of Divorce,' 24 May 1943.
99 Afraid of Judson: 'Answer,' filed by Don Marlin on behalf of Margarita C. Judson, Los Angeles Superior Court, 2 July 1943.
99 Rita's move to overturn property settlement: Ibid.
99 '*He didn't like . . .* ': Shifra Haran to BL.
100 '*fragile*': Orson Welles to BL.
100 '*That's why I . . .* ': Ibid.
100 '*She had this . . .* ': Shifra Haran to BL.
101 Abandonment and betrayal: Herman.
101 '*I replaced her . . .* ': Marlene Dietrich to BL.
101 '*Come teach me . . .* ': Orson Welles to BL.
101 '*Those guys practically . . .* ': Shifra Haran to BL.
101 '*She was so . . .* '. Orson Welles to BL.
101 '*Marlene was the . . .* ': Ibid.

CHAPTER NINE

103 *'Harry Cohn didn't . . .'*: Shifra Haran to BL.
104 *'I dreaded it . . .'*: Orson Welles to BL.
104 Hayworth–Welles Marriage: Certificate of Marriage, County of Los Angeles, California, 7 September 1943.
105 *'I never saw . . .'*: Shifra Haran to BL.
105 *'Goodness, I wish . . .'*: Volga Cansino, quoted in *Philadelphia Inquirer,* 8 September 1943.
106 *'believes that because . . .'*: Affidavit of Harry G. Sadicoff,' 9 September 1943.
106 Court sided with Rita: 'Order Continuing Deposition,' 14 September 1943.
106 *'the combination of . . .'*: Beatrice Straight to BL.
107 *'Imagine the great . . .'*: Louis Dolivet to BL.
107 *'I didn't want . . .'*: Orson Welles to BL.
108 *'Miss Hayworth was . . .'*: Shifra Haran to BL.
108 *'She loved to . . .'*: Ibid.
108 *'frustrating dichotomy'*: Roger Hill to BL.
108 *'glamour image'*: Ibig.
108 *'face and form'*: Ibid.
108 *'reality: a sweet . . .'*: Ibid.
108 *'the role of . . .'*: Ibid.
109 *'Until that time . . .'*: Ibid.
109 *'Orson's finest hour . . .'*: Ibid.
109 *'Until she met . . .'*: Orson Welles to BL.
109 *'mother figure'*: Roger Hill to BL.
109 *'the weeks would . . .'*: Hill, *Time and Chance.*
110 *'An unfortunate impulse . . .'*: Ibid.
110 *'Our efforts at . . .'*: Ibid.
110 Passport for Rita: Cable from Orson Welles to Sir Alexander Korda, 25 October 1943.
111 *'very, very upset'*: Beatrice Straight to BL.
111 Fraud: Crewdson.
112 *'particularly important'*: Beatrice Straight to BL.
112 *'very nervous'*: Ibid.
112 *'When she didn't . . .'*: Libby Sloane to BL.
113 *'sweet, shy, undemanding . . .'*: Beatrice Straight to BL.
113 *'that was the . . .'*: Ibid.*f*
113 *'drove the staff . . .'*: Ibid.
113 *'If he believed . . .'*: Shifra Haran to BL.
114 *'It was so . . .'*: Ibid.
114 *'well thought of . . .'*: Orson Welles to BL.

115 '*bought her former* . . . ': Florabel Muir, 'To Silence Judson on Marital Fight,' *New York Daily News*, 18 November 1943.

115 obscene letter: FBI memo, File No. 62–2475, 17 May 1944.

116 '*particularly of the* . . . ': Ibid.

116 '*mysterious letter*': Ibid.

117 '*He was very* . . . ': Beatrice Straight to BL.

117 '*walked around on* . . . ': Ibid.

117 '*She was worried* . . . ': Elisabeth Rubino to BL.

118 '*He probably enjoyed* . . . ': Shifra Haran to BL.

118 '*I sat in* . . . '. Orson Welles to BL.

119 '*He imagined that* . . . ': Ibid.

119 '*There was a* . . . ': Ibid.

120 '*deliciously happy*': Shifra Haran to BL.

120 '*wasn't his thing* . . . ': Ibid.

120 Orson's drinking: Louis Dolivet to BL.

121 '*It was the* . . . ': Shifra Haran to BL.

121 '*Maybe I tried* . . . ': Rita Hayworth, quoted in June Allyson, *June Allyson*.

122 '*She would be* . . . ': Shifra Haran to BL.

123 '*The only way* . . . ': Ibid.

123 '*I really think* . . . ': Ibid.

124 '*Those were the* . . . ': Ibid.

124 '*Something happened when* . . . ': Gloria Vanderbilt, *Black Knight, White Knight*.

124 '*alive every second*': Ibid.

124 '*think about him* . . . ': Ibid.

CHAPTER TEN

126 '*whose reliability is* . . . ': FBI memo – 'Orson Welles, with alias: George Orson Welles. Character of Case: Security Matter-C,' File No. 100–5440, Los Angeles, 3 November 1944. Copy in Rita Hayworth's FBI file.

126 '*unable to find* . . . ': Ibid.

127 '*follow and report* . . . ': Ibid.

127 Rita's political activities are traced in: FBI File No. 100–345057: Rita Hayworth. Also: FBI Cros-refs. to Rita Hayworth in Files No. 100–29822-6; 100–138754-52; 100–2348-24; 94–43615-123; 100–0-27010; 62–75147-46-114; 100–0-29234; 100–3-83-A.

127 White House congratulations: Letter from Eleanor Roosevelt to Orson Welles, 3 January 1945.

128 'Congratulations on the . . . ': Letter from Harry S. Truman to Orson Welles. 24 February 1945.

128 'not all that . . . ': Shifra Haran to BL.

129 'Too Much': 1943 Christmas list, Orson Welles and Rita Hayworth.

129 'Somebody always wanted . . . ': Shifra Haran to BL.

129 'Is there something . . . ': Elisabeth Rubino to BL.

130 Volga's death: Death Certificate, Volga Cansino.

131 'He was a . . . ': Orson Welles to BL.

131 'Every night I . . . ': Ibid.

131 'For him to . . . ': Shifra Haran to BL.

131 'I think if . . . ': Orson Welles to BL.

132 'She was at . . . ': Shifra Haran to BL.

132 'We're such a . . . ': Orson Welles to BL.

133 'seemed so out . . . ': Ibid.

133 'If I hadn't . . . ': Ibid.

134 'Rita seemed to . . . ': Elisabeth Rubino to BL.

134 'She had her . . . ': Ibid.

CHAPTER ELEVEN

136 'Miss Hayworth herself said . . . ': Shifra Haran to BL.

137 'Rita never considered . . . ': Jonie Taps to BL.

137 Co-sign contract: Letter from Orson Welles and Rita Hayworth Welles to The Haig Corporation and International Pictures, Inc., 20 September 1945.

137 $30,000: Letter from Frank B. Belcher, of Jennings & Belcher, to Loyd Wright, 5 April 1946.

137 'He had a . . . ': Jim Pratt to BL.

138 'He impressed me . . . ': Ernest Nims to BL.

138 'She didn't like . . . ': Orson Welles to BL.

138 'Rita was very . . . ': Ibid.

139 'I could have . . . ': Ibid.

139 'Lonely tears . . . ': Shelley Winters, Shelley, Also Known as Shirley.

139 'the lonesomest time . . . ': Ibid.

139 'so lonely and . . . ': Ibid.

139 'her hair and . . . ': Ibid.

140 Financial terms: Letter from Frank B. Belcher to Loyd Wright, 5 April 1946.

141 Interest in Around the World: Telegram from I.H. Prinzmetal to Orson Welles, 17 April 1946.

142 '*The other day* . . . ': Letter from Dr Maurice Bernstein to Orson Welles, n.d.

142 '*She looked at* . . . ': Memo from Lolita Hebert to Orson Welles, 26 July 1946.

142 '*She would far* . . . ': Memo from Lolita Hebert to Orson Welles, 5 June 1946.

143 '*huge*': Wilbur Menefee to BL.

143 '*In the course* . . . ': Orson Welles to BL.

143 '*If this was* . . . ': Ibid.

144 '*Rita used to* . . . ': Ibid.

144 Application for passport: Letter from Margarita Carmen Cansino Welles to U.S. Secretary of State, 23 January 1947.

CHAPTER TWELVE

146 '*There should be* . . . ': Letter from Joseph I. Breen to Harry Cohn, Columbia Pictures Corp., 22 August 1946.

148 '*When Rita worked* . . . ': Earl Bellamy to BL.

148 '*He went mad!*': Bob Schiffer to BL.

148 '*Everybody practically had* . . . ': Earl Bellamy to BL.

149 '*The first time* . . . ': Ibid.

149 '*Makeup!*': Bob Schiffer to BL.

149 '*The more he* . . . ': Ibid.

150 '*Well, she's sleeping* . . . ': Ibid.

150 '*At that time* . . . ': Ibid.

151 '*I would have* . . . ': Ibid.

151 '*Jesus Christ, get* . . . ': Ibid.

151 Rita's party: Letter from Salvador Barragan, Assistant Manager, Hotel de Las Americas, to Richard Watson, 23 October 1946.

151 '*They were cute* . . . ': Libby Sloane to BL.

152 '*Everybody got into* . . . ': Ibid.

152 '*The monkey took* . . . ': Ibid.

153 Threat of violence: the 1947 extortion case is documented in: FBI File No. 19–12779: Rita Hayworth. Also: Case No. 9133: United States vs. James Gerston Gibson, District Court of the U.S., Eastern District of Tennessee, Southern Division at Chattanooga. Also: Case No. 9131: U.S. of America vs. James Gerston Gibson, District Court of the U.S., Eastern District of Tennessee, Southern Division.

153 Text of extortion letter: Teletype from FBI Los Angeles Office to Director SACS Atlanta and Knoxville, 10 February 1947.

153 Former naval-yard worker: Transcript of 1 March 1947,
     hearing in U.S. District Court, Chattanooga, Tennessee.
154 FBI custody in Atlanta: U.S. Government Memo from
     C.W. Evans to Mr Ladd, 8 February 1947.
154 Tennessee police: FBI Teletype from FBI Atlanta Office to
     Director, and SACS Los Angeles and Knoxville, 10 February
     1947.
155 FBI interview with Gibson: FBI report from Knoxville,
     Tennessee, File No. 9-208, 16 April 1947.

CHAPTER THIRTEEN

157 'Harry Cohn was . . . ': Bob Schiffer to BL.
158 'She hated them . . . ': Ibid.
158 'She was within . . . ': Earl Bellamy to BL.
158 'She had the . . . ': Grace Godino to BL.
158 'He would spend . . . ': Bob Schiffer to BL.
158 'It's like saying . . . ': Ibid.
158 'There was a . . . ': Earl Bellamy to BL.
158 'let down her . . . ': Ibid.
158 'After we'd finished . . . ': Ibid.
158 'All the men . . . ': Grace Godino to BL.
159 'When they photographed . . . ': Shifra Haran to BL.
159 'Miss Hayworth needed a . . . ': Ibid.
160 'The Hughes thing . . . ': Ibid.
160 'You know I . . . ': Ibid.
161 'We never went . . . ': Ibid.
161 'I never left . . . ': Ibid.
162 'They thought they . . . ': Ibid.
162 'He was just . . . ': Ibid.
162 'She had hemorrhaging . . . ': Ibid.
163 'Miss Hayworth was . . . ': Ibid.
163 'The whole hospital . . . ': Ibid.
163 'All of a . . . ': Ibid.
164 'Who told you . . . ': Countess de Faucon, 'Rita Hayworth
     Found Ill in Hospital Near Paris,' Chicago Tribune, 1948.
164 'a yellow complexion . . . ': Ibid.
164 'might get hysterical . . . ': Ibid.
164 'She doesn't want . . . ': Ibid.
164 'suffering from anemia . . . ': Ibid.
164 'They were very . . . ': Shifra Haran to BL.
165 'her thoughts were . . . ': Elsa Maxwell, Photoplay, February
     1949.

166 *'Rita, I think . . . '*: Ibid.
167 *'Rita Hayworth and Welles Rumored Wed'*: *Los Angeles Times*, 24 July 1948.
167 *'She was the . . . '*: Shifra Haran to BL.

CHAPTER FOURTEEN

169 Important information on Rita and Aly's marriage, divorce, and custody battle came from nine years of court records: 'Case No. 136772: Margarita Cansino Khan, Plaintiff, vs. Aly Salomone Khan, Defendant, Second Judicial District Court of the State of Nevada, Washoe County.
170 *'The prince was . . . '*: Shifra Haran to BL.
171 *'I don't think . . . '*: Ibid.
171 *'He was buzzing . . . '*: Ibid.
171 *'The prince was . . . '*: Ibid.
171 *'She didn't want . . . '*: Ibid.
172 *'He looked gorgeous . . . '*: Mercedes McCambridge, *The Quality of Mercy*.
172 *'Rita kept looking . . . '*: Ibid.
172 *'I had seen . . . '*: Ibid.
173 *'How the woman . . . '*: Shifra Haran to BL.
173 *'She seemed to . . . '*: Ibid.
174 *'She didn't care . . . '*: Ibid.
175 *'Those Europeans the . . . '*: Ibid.
175 *'She had a . . . '*: Ibid.
175 *'It was too . . . '*: Ibid.
176 *'Rita, in the . . . '*: Elsa Maxwell, *Photoplay*, February 1949.
178 *'I am a . . . '*: Emrys Williams, *Bodyguard*.
178 *'Pale with fright . . . '*: Ibid.
178 *'These were really . . . '*: Ibid.
178 *'She danced like . . . '*: Ibid.

CHAPTER FIFTEEN

180 *'All of a . . . '*: Shifra Haran to BL.
182 *'They just stayed . . . '*: Ibid.
183 *'I never saw . . . '*: Ibid.
183 *'In the precise . . . '*: Leonard Slater, *Aly*.
183 *'The prince was . . . '*: Shifra Haran to BL.
184 *'Nobody knew who . . . '*: Ibid.

185 *'Miss Hayworth had . . .'*: Ibid.
185 *'This was the . . .'*: Ibid.
186 *'She couldn't stand . . .'*: Ibid.
186 *'Oh, it was . . .'*: Ibid.
187 *'They were such . . .'*: Ibid.
188 *'Those were trying . . .'*: Ibid.
189 *'She didn't have . . .'*: Ibid.
191 *'in love with . . .'*: Yvonne De Carlo, *Yvonne*.

CHAPTER SIXTEEN

193 *'She was very . . .'*: Shifra Haran to BL.
193 *'There were no . . .'*: Ibid.
193 *'I could have . . .'*: Elisabeth Rubino to BL.
195 *:She didn't ride . . .'*: Shifra Haran to BL.
196 *'She would have . . .'*: Ibid.
196 *'The affair with . . .'*: Ibid.
196 *'She seemed remote . . .'*: Ibid.
196 *'I think her . . .'*: Ibid.
199 *'Same as me . . .'*: Ibid.
200 *'maddeningly beautiful'*: *New York Daily News*, 3 January 1949.

CHAPTER SEVENTEEN

206 *'freeloaders'*. Shifra Haran to BL.
207 Ellroy: Slater.
207 *'She sent for . . .'*: Orson Welles to BL.
207 *'There were candles . . .'*: Ibid.
207 *'She was marrying . . .'*: Ibid.
208 *'Aly was her . . .'*: Ibid.
209 *'Is that all . . .'*: Williams.
211 *'biggest Moslem marriage . . .'*: Si Caddour Ben Ghabrit, quoted in *Los Angeles Times*, 26 May 1949.
214 *'trying to lose . . .'*: *New York Post*, 27 May 1949.
214 *'didn't seem happy . . .'*: Louella Parsons, *International News Service*, 20 September 1953.
214 *'The Church ignores . . .'*: 'Hayworth Wedding "Illicit" to Church,' *New York Post*, 27 May 1949.
214 *'conceived in sin'*: Ibid.

CHAPTER EIGHTEEN

215   'She reflected what . . . ': Bob Schiffer to BL.
216   'Rita was quite . . . ': Williams.
217   'I couldn't stand . . . ': Rita Hayworth, quoted in Allyson.
217   'Aly liked to . . . ': Orson Welles to BL.
219   'drawn and shaky': United Press, 10 December 1949.
220   'the rows between . . . ': Williams.
221   'More than once . . . ': Elsa Maxwell, Photoplay, June 1952.
221   'Never before or . . . ': Williams.
221   'a tender reconcilation': Ibid.
224   'lack of money . . . ': Elsa Maxwell, Photoplay, August 1951.
224   'Aly Khan spent . . . ': Hermes Pan to BL.
225   'Miss Hayworth somehow . . . ': Aga Khan, quoted in Slater.

CHAPTER NINETEEN

226   French authorities: 'Affidavit' of Bartley C. Crum, Washoe
      County District Court, Nevada, 18 September 1958.
226   Aga Khan's influence: Ibid.
229   Aly's letter: Los Angeles Examiner, 15 May 1951.
231   'I very much . . . ': Aga Khan, quoted in Los Angeles Examiner,
      6 May 1951.
231   'If Rita settles . . . ': Ibid.
233   'Rita was pretty . . . ': Bob Schiffer to BL.
233   'She told me . . . ': Ibid.
233   First meeting: 'Affidavit' of Bartley C. Crum, 18 September
      1958.
233   Alimony: Ibid.

CHAPTER TWENTY

237   Movieland reporter: Fortnight, 6 August 1951. Also, New
      York Herald Tribune, 7 July 1951.
238   Aly's presence: 'Affidavit' of Bartley C. Crum, 18 September
      1958. 170 'extreme cruelty . . . ': 'Complaint', Margarita
      Cansino Khan, Plaintiff, vs. Aly Salomone Khan, Defen-
      dant, Second Judicial Court of Nevada, 1 September 1951.
239   Ordered to appear: 'Summons,' Second Judicial Court of
      Nevada, 1 September 1951.
240   Failure to respond: 'Findings of Fact and Conclusions of

Law,' A.J. Maestretti, U.S. District Judge, Washoe County, Nevada, 26 January 1953.

240 Served in Cannes: 'Affidavit of Service,' Pierre Bernard, 4 June 1952.
241 *'She seemed to . . .'*: Bob Schiffer to BL.
241 *'I felt something . . .'*: Kirk Douglas, *The Ragman's Son.*
242 *'What am I . . .'*: Bob Schiffer to BL.
243 *'She was game . . .'*: Ibid.
243 *'Screw this . . .'*: Ibid.
244 FBI list: FBI Memo from SAC Los Angeles to FBI Director, 28 May 1951.
244 Detailed dossier: Rita Hayworth's 'Confidential FBI File': File No. 94–43615-123.
244 Kahane letter: Victor Navasky, *Naming Names.*
244 *'statement'*: Ibid.

CHAPTER TWENTY-ONE

246 *'seemed to enjoy'*: De Carlo.
251 *'Can't he at least . . .'*: Aga Khan, quoted in Elsa Maxwell, *The American Weekly,* 28 December 1952.
252 Suzanne Blum account: *Los Angeles Daily News,* 6 October 1952.
254 Default decree: 'Judgment and Decree of Divorce,' 26 January 1953.
255 Custody: Ibid.

CHAPTER TWENTY-TWO

256 *'After Aly, Rita . . .'*: Orson Welles to BL.
257 Important information on the Hayworth–Haymes marriage and divorce came from: Case No. 159275: Margarita Cansino Haymes, Plaintiff, vs. Richard Benjamin Haymes, Defendant, Second Judicial District Court of the State of Nevada, Washoe County.
257 *'He blew it . . .'*: Jonie Taps to BL.
257 Haymes's debts: U.S. Department of Justice, Immigration and Naturalization Service File E 070883, Los Angeles, 22 March 1954.
257 *'Rita liked to . . .'*: Jonie Taps to BL.
259 Privately settle: 'Judgment and Decree of Divorce,' 26 January 1953.

259 Rita's petition: 'Petition for Modification of Decree,' 11 April 1953.

259 Court order: 'Order Amending Judgment and Decree of Divorce,' 14 April 1953.

259 *'They asked me . . . '*: Bob Schiffer to BL.

260 *'I was pretty . . . '*: Ibid.

260 Temporary replacement: 'Application for New Alien Registration Receipt Card,' 21 May 1953.

260 Haymes's inquiry: 'Affidavit of Richard R. Cody,' 25 March 1954. Also, 'Transcript of Sworn Statement by Richard Benjamin Haymes to Inspector Thomas D. McDermott, 8 July 1953.

261 *'I went through . . . '*: Bob Schiffer to BL.

262 Vital information on the Haymes deportation case came from the more than 1,000 pages of documents contained in: U.S. Department of Justice, Immigration and Naturalization Service File No. E-070883: Richard Benjamin Haymes. Also, File No. A5 992 057: Richard Benjamin Haymes.

262 Events of 8 July 1953: Cody Affidavit of 25 March 1954. Also, Transcript of Haymes's Statement, 8 July 1953. Also, Transcript of Deportation Hearing, Los Angeles, California, 23 June 1954

265 Hold together: Eleanore Hill, *The Family Secret.*

CHAPTER TWENTY-THREE

267 *'Please, please . . . '*: Rita Hayworth, quoted in Earl Wilson, *New York Post*, 20 July 1953.

268 Instructions to New York: 'Memorandum for File,' M.F. Fargione, Chief, Investigations Section, 30 July 1953. Also, 'Warrant for Arrest of Alien,' 30 July 1953.

268 Los Angeles arrest: 'Warrant for Arrest of Alien,' 3 August 1953. Also, 'Bond Conditioned for Delivery of an Alien,' 6 August 1953. Also, Los Angeles District Office of Immigration and Naturalization Service 'Memorandum of Facts in Deportation Case of Richard Benjamin Haymes,' 11 August 1953. Also, Letter from David C. Marcus, Attorney to Department of Justice, 22 September 1953. Also, Department of Justice Press Release, 6 August 1953.

270 *'persona non grata . . . '*: Memo from Thomas D. McDermott, Investigator, Los Angeles Immigration and Naturalization Service to District Director, Los Angeles, 14 August 1953.

270   26 August 1953 hearing: Transcript of Immigration and Naturalization Service Hearing, 26 August 1953.

CHAPTER TWENTY-FOUR

273   Information on the 1953 death threats from: FBI File No. 9-24752: Rita Hayworth.
273   24 August 1953 death threat: Teletype from FBI, Los Angeles to Director and SAC, Salt Lake City, 13 September 1953.
273   9 September 1953 death threat: Teletype from FBI Salt Lake City to Director and SACS Los Angeles and New York, 14 September 1953.
275   '*Afford matter continous . . .* ': Teletype from J. Edgar Hoover to SACS Salt Lake City, Los Angeles, 15 September 1953.
276   FBI Laboratory: FBI Memo to Mr Rosen from Mr Price, 16 September 1953.
276   Paper: FBI Air-Tel from SAC Boston to Director, 28 September 1953. Also, FBI Report, 30 November 1953.
276   Post Office and police: FBI Report, 26 October 1953.
276   '*Moslem exchange students . . .* ': FBI Memo from SAC Salt Lake City to Director, 22 September 1953.
276   '*whether any students . . .* ': FBI Report, 26 October 1953. Also, FBI Report, 23 December 1953.
276   Columbia and Parsons: FBI Report, 7 January 1954.
276   '*Further advised that . . .* ': FBI Report, 9 October 1953.
276   Prison term: 'Judgment: U.S. vs. James Gerston Gibson,' Chattanooga, Tennessee, Case No. 9133, 1 March 1947.
279   Third death threat: FBI Teletype from FBI Salt Lake City to Director and SAC New York City, 21 September 1953.
281   '*She apparently had . . .* ': James Bacon to BL.
281   Marriage: Marriage Certificate, Richard B. Haymes and Rita Hayworth, 23 September 1953.

CHAPTER TWENTY-FIVE

283   Apprise the FBI: FBI Report, 9 October 1953.
284   '*their children will . . .* ': Crewdson.
285   '*neglectful mother*': Herman.
286   '*I could hardly . . .* ': Rita Hayworth, quoted in Allyson.
286   Located physician: Telegram from Bartley Crum to Rita Hayworth, 27 October 1953.

286 Lost deferment: 'Findings and Recommendations' by General Attorney (Nationality), U.S. Department of State.

286 Deportation hearing: Transcript, 28 October 1953.

287 Actors' Equity: Haymes's 'Application' for Equity membership.

293 *'quite bewildered by . . . '*: *New York Daily News*, 13 February 1954.

CHAPTER TWENTY-SIX

295 Rita's custody stipulations: 'Affidavit' of Charles Torem, Second District Court, Nevada, 11 June 1958.

295 *Confidential* reporter: Jay Breen, 'How Rita Hayworth's Children Were Neglected!', *Confidential*, 1954.

297 Deportation ruling: Ruling by Joseph A. Dummel, Special Inquiry Officer, Immigration and Naturalization Service, 22 March 1954.

298 *'coldly calm'*: *New York Post*, 24 March 1954.

298 *'I feel like . . . '*: Leonard Lyons, *New York Post*, 25 March 1954.

298 Formal statement: 'Affidavit of Richard R. Cody,' 25 March 1954.

300 *'But I didn't . . . '*: Aga Khan, quoted in Elsa Maxwell, *The American Weekly*, 30 May 1954.

301 *'If any kind . . . '*: *New York Herald Tribune,* 9 April 1954.

CHAPTER TWENTY-SEVEN

302 Protective custody: 'Actress's Daughters in Custody of Court,' *The New York Times*, 24 April 1954. Also, 'Rita Hayworth Faces Child Neglect Charge,' *Los Angeles Times*, 24 April 1954.

304 *'We sent two . . . '*: Walter W. Westall, quoted in *New York Herald Tribune*, 27 April 1954.

304 Welles's instructions: Wolfe Charney, attorney to BL.

305 privately feared: Orson Welles to BL.

305 Aly's restraint: 'Affidavit' of Charles Torem, Second District Court, Nevada, 12 August 1955.

307 *'that she did . . . '*: Ibid.

308 *'fully justified'*: *New York Herald Tribune*, 27 April 1954.

310 Apparent agreement: 'Affidavit' of Charles Torem, Second District Court, Nevada, 11 June 1958.

310 Refusal to sign: Ibid.
311 '*A fortune of . . .* ': *The New York Times*, 28 April 1954.
311 Inheritance jeopardized: 'Affidavit' of Bartley C. Crum, Second District Court, Nevada, 18 September 1958.

CHAPTER TWENTY-EIGHT

312 Entrapment: Transcript of 'Oral Argument Before Board of Immigration Appeals,' 11 May 1954.
312 Case reopened: 'Ruling by Board of Immigration Appeals,' 25 May 1954.
313 '*now captain of . . .* ': Earl Wilson, *New York Post*, 12 July 1954.
314 June hearing: Transcript of 'Reopened Hearing in Deportation Proceedings,' 23 June 1954.
314 '*that the alien . . .* ': Memo to A.C. Devaney, Assistant Commissioner, 20 August 1954.
315 Crystal Bay: 'Deposition of Joseph Tiano,' 6 December 1955, in Divorce Records Case No. 159275, Margarita Cansino Haymes vs. Richard Benjamin Haymes.
315 '*They were both . . .* ': Bob Schiffer to BL.
316 Rejected plea: 'Hayworth Plea Denied,' *The New York Times*, 9 July 1954.
317 Expand study: 'New Briefs in Hayworth Case,' *The New York Times*, 7 August 1954.
317 Deportation decision: 'Decision of Special Inquiry Officer,' 29 July 1954.
318 '*Harry Cohn and . . .* ': Jonie Taps to BL.
319 Nov. 1954 Agreement: 'Contrat, Fait en L'Etat de Nevada, le 20 Novembre 1954, entre Prince Aly Salomone Khan et Rita Hayworth Haymes.' Also, 'Modified Decree of divorce,' 24 November 1954.
320 Officially recognize: 'Entry of General Appearance,' 24 November 1954.
320 To begin 1 July 1955: 'Affidavit' of Charles Torem, 12 August 1958.

CHAPTER TWENTY-NINE

328 Forbidden to go: 'Affidavit' of Charles Torem, 11 June 1958.
331 '*just in time . . .* ': Cole Lesley, *Remembered Laughter*.
331 Yasmin's visit: 'Affidavits' of Charles Torem: 12 August

1955, 9 September 1955, and 11 June 1958. Also, 'Affidavits' of Bartley C. Crum: 2 September 1955 and 18 September 1958. Also, 'Affidavit of Rita Hayworth Haymes,' 31 August 1955.

331 Cables: 'Affidavit' of Charles Torem, 12 August 1955.
332 *'crushing denouement'*: Ibid.
332 Aly's legal action: 'Motion of Order for Child Visitation,' 10 August 1955.
332 *'a deprivation of . . . '*: 'Affidavit' of Charles Torem, 12 August 1955.
333 *'Patrons of the . . . '*: *Los Angeles Times*, 31 August 1955.

CHAPTER THIRTY

337 *'He may have . . . '*: Quoted in Earl Wilson, *New York Post*, 30 August 1955.
338 *'a tuxedoed Pagliacci'*: *International News Service*, 31 August 1955.
338 Aga Khan's letter: Letter from Aga Khan to Mrs Richard Haymes, 19 September 1955.
339 *'The City of Light . . . '*: *Daily Mirror*, 5 October 1955.
341 Filed: 'Complaint: Margarita Cansino Haymes, Plaintiff, vs. Richard Benjamin Haymes, Plaintiff, 4 November 1955.
341 Rita's testimony: Transcript of 'Deposition of Margarita Cansino Haymes,' taken at U.S. Embassy, Paris, France, 6 December 1955.
341 Divorce granted: 'Decree of Divorce,' 12 December 1955.

CHAPTER THIRTY-ONE

347 *'more trouble than . . . '*: Robert Parrish, *Hollywood Doesn't Live*
348 *Here Anymore.*
348 *'There was another . . . '*: George Sidney to BL.
349 *'there was no . . . '*: Ibid.
349 *'She comes in . . . '*: Ibid.
349 *'It was at . . . '*: Grace Godino to BL.
350 *'Kim Novak's costume . . . '*: Ibid.
350 *'sad, faraway look . . . '*: James Hill, *Rita Hayworth: A Memoir.*
350 *'wound up as . . . '*: Ibid.
352 *'the fulfillment of . . . '*: Ibid.
352 *'the first big . . . '*: Ibid.
352 *'I was concerned . . . '*: Delbert Mann to BL.

352 *'Rita was apprehensive . . .'*: Ibid.
353 *'we simply did . . .'*: Ibid.
353 *'Rita was quite . . .'*: Ibid.
353 *'The role was . . .'*: Ibid.
354 Marriage: Marriage Certificate of James Harry Hill and Rita Margarita Hayworth, 2 February 1958.
354 *'In retrospect . . .'*: James Hill, *Rita Hayworth: A Memoir.*
354 *'bring her around'*: Ibid.
355 'There was a . . .': Hermes Pan to BL.
355 More than $18,000: 'Motion to Require Defendant to Pay Plaintiff for Certain Legal Fees Incurred,' 12 May 1958.
355 Refused to pay: 'Affidavit' of Charles Torem, 11 June 1958.
355 Diplomatic Immunity: 'Motion to Stay Proceeding,' 14 October 1958. Also, Letter from George Cochran Doub, U.S. Department of Justice, to Legal Adviser, Department of State, 3 November 1958.
355 Settle their differences: James Hill to BL.

CHAPTER THIRTY-TWO

357 Of many works on Alzheimer's disease consulted, three proved especially useful: Donna Cohen and Carl Eisdorfer, *The Loss of Self*; Nancy L. Mace and Peter V. Rabins, *The 36-Hour Day;* Barry Reisberg, *A Guide to Alzheimer's Disease.*
358 *'I saw this . . .'*: Hermes Pan to BL.
358 *'fits of temper'*: Ibid.
358 *'She would suddenly . . .'*: Princess Yasmin Aga Khan, quoted in Rosemary Santini and Katherine Barrett, 'Rita Hayworth's Tragic Decline,' *Los Angeles Herald Examiner*, 17 January 1983.
358 Catastrophic reactions: Mace and Rabins. Also, Cohen and Eisdorfer.
359 *'She'd tell anybody . . .'*: Ann Miller to BL.
359 *'distraught'*: *New York Post*, 24 August 1962.
359 *'increasingly nervous over . . .'*: *New York Post*, 22 August 1962.
361 *'Not everyone always . . .'*: Princess Yasmin Aga Khan, *People*, 1 June 1987.
361 *'That little piece . . .'*: Bud Moss to BL.
361 *'Looking back at . . .'*: Ibid.
361 *'zone'*: Cohen and Eisdorfer.
362 *'But when they . . .'*: Ann Miller to BL.
362 *'She was very . . .'*: Ibid.

361 '*No, I can't . . .* ': Ibid.

362 '*She didn't go . . .* ': Curtis Roberts to BL.

362 '*the bottle thrown . . .* ': Ibid.

363 '*The room was . . .* ': Ralph Nelson to BL.

363 '*Rita was real . . .* ': Lynn Del Kail to BL.

363 '*Her memory had . . .* ': Ibid.

364 '*total memory lapses*': Ralph Nelson to BL.

364 '*You'd be talking . . .* ': Lynn Del Kail to BL.

364 '*Rita had so . . .* ': Ibid.

364 '*She would make . . .* ': Del Armstrong to BL.

364 '*One driver quit . . .* ': Ralph Nelson to BL.

364 '*Rita just was . . .* ': Lynn Del Kail to BL.

364 '*claustrophobia*': Del Armstrong to BL.

364 '*She had a . . .* ': Lynn Del Kail to BL.

365 '*She just flat . . .* ': Del Armstrong to BL.

365 '*She only had . . .* ': Lynn Del Kail to BL.

365 '*The evening was . . .* ': Polly Gilmore to BL.

366 '*She was like . . .* ': Ibid.

366 '*She's had a . . .* ': Hermes Pan to BL.

366 '*Rita couldn't communicate . . .* ': Curtis Roberts to BL.

366 '*real bitter*': Rebecca Welles, quoted in *Chicago Tribune*, 16 January 1972.

367 '*Rita was very . . .* ': Lynn Del Kail to BL.

367 '*She would call . . .* ': Ralph Nelson to BL.

367 '*She'd call me . . .* ': Hermes Pan to BL.

367 '*As we were . . .* ': Libby Sloane to BL.

CHAPTER THIRTY-THREE

369 '*It started on . . .* ': Curtis Roberts to BL.

369 '*She was trained . . .* ': Ibid.

370 '*I don't think . . .* ': Ibid.

370 '*Rita was blind . . .* ': Ibid.

370 '*That was the . . .* ': Ibid.

370 '*Actually she looked . . .* ': Ibid.

370 '*It's all shit . . .* ': Ibid.

370 '*She complained that . . .* ': Ibid.

370 '*a violent outburst . . .* ': Ibid.

371 '*She was always . . .* ': Ibid.

371 '*started drinking again*': Ibid.

371 '*It was a . . .* ': Ibid.

371 '*She didn't remember . . .* ': Ibid.

372 'It was terrible . . . ': Hermes Pan to BL.
372 'because of her . . . ': Princess Yasmin Aga Khan, quoted in Los Angeles Herald Examiner, 17 January 1983.
372 'we were sitting . . . ': Hermes Pan to BL.
372 'Rita sort of . . . ': Ibid.
373 'Ann Miller and . . . ': Ibid.
373 'The limousine came . . . ': Ibid.
373 'Rita had invited . . . ': Ann Miller to BL.
373 Agnosia: Mace and Rabins.
373 'We were terrified . . . ': Ann Miller to BL.
374 'She had heard . . . ': Hermes Pan to BL.
374 'Some nights she'd . . . ': Curtis Roberts to BL.
374 'If someone would . . . ': Bud Moss to BL.
375 'try and keep . . . ': Ibid.
375 'uptight': Ibid.
375 'She doesn't like . . . ': Ibid.
375 'I sat with . . . ': Ibid.
375 'very ill': New York Daily News, 21 January 1976.
375 'hauled off and . . . ': Bud Moss to BL.
376 'She was rubber . . . ': Ibid.
376 'The next morning . . . ': Ibid.
377 'drained, tired, and . . . ': Russel Harty, Observer (London), 10 April 1977.
377 'That was one . . . ': Ann Miller to BL.
377 'helped put her . . . ': Ibid.
377 'Rita was fine . . . ': Ibid.
378 'she had almost . . . ': Hermes Pan to BL.
378 'probably the hairiest . . . '; Bud Moss to BL.
378 'grenade attack': Confidential Telegram from American Embassy, Buenos Aires, to Secretary of State, Washington, D.C.' 5 October 1976.
378 'As we got . . . ': Bud Moss to BL.
378 'just kept humming . . . ': Ibid.
379 'The sun is . . . ': Ibid.
379 'We were seconds . . . ': Ibid.
379 'Everybody panicked': Ibid.
379 'All of a . . . ': Ibid.

CHAPTER THIRTY-FOUR

380 Various symptoms: Bill Gilpin to BL.
380 Vital information on the 1977 conservatorship case came from: Case No. A90772: Conservatorship of the Person and

Estate of Margarita Cansino, aka Rita Hayworth, Proposed Conservatee. Superior Court of the State of California, Orange County.

380 '*gravely disabled as* . . . ': 'Petition for Appointment of Conservator of the Person and Estate', Orange County Superior Court, California, 7 March 1977.

380 '*recommending temporary conservatorship*': Ibid.

380 '*person and estate*': Ibid.

381 '*detained in a* . . . ': 'Order Appointing Temporary Conservator of the Person,' 8 March 1977.

381 Clothes removed: Bill Gilpin to BL.

381 '*fairly well with* . . . ': Bob Schiffer to BL.

381 '*Thank God for* . . . ': Ibid.

381 '*She had become* . . . ': Princess Yasmin Aga Khan, quoted in *Los Angeles Herald Examiner*, 17 January 1983.

382 Remove her from: Orange County Superior Court Report on Hearing, 15 April 1977.

382 '*I spent Christmas* . . . ': Bob Schiffer to BL.

383 '*When she began* . . . ': James Bacon to BL.

383 '*All the freeloaders* . . . ': Curtis Roberts to BL.

384 '*flattening of affect*': Reisberg.

384 '*She was really* . . . ': Henry Rogers to BL.

384 '*I said hello* . . . ': Roz Rogers to BL.

384 '*My blood ran* . . . ': Orson Welles to BL.

384 '*a sense of relief*': Princess Yasmin Aga Khan, *People*, 1 June 1987.

384 '*So much embarrassment* . . . ': Princess Yasmin Aga Khan, 'Slipping into Solitude,' *New York Daily News, Sunday*, 19 May 1985.

385 '*Yasmin was just* . . . ': Ann Miller to BL.

386 '*She fearfully clung* . . . ': Princess Yasmin Aga Khan, quoted in *New York Daily News*, 26 April 1984.

386 '*I put him* . . . ': Princess Yasmin Aga Khan, quoted in Cindy Adams, *New York Post*, 23 April 1986.

387 Death of Eduardo Cansino: Certificate of Death for Eduardo Cansino, Fort Lauderdale, Florida, 24 December 1986.

387 '*It's so hard* . . . ': Princess Yasmin Aga Khan, quoted in *Los Angeles Herald Examiner*, 17 January 1983.

387 '*He used to* . . . ': Rita Hayworth, quoted in *Los Angeles Herald Examiner*, 17 January 1983.

Selected Bibliography

Allyson, June, *June Allyson*, New York: Berkley Books, 1982.

Armstrong, Louise, *Kiss Daddy Good-night: A Speak-Out on Incest*, New York: Pocket Books, 1979.

Astaire, Fred, *Steps in Time*, New York: Perennial, 1987.

Bacon, James, *Hollywood Is a Four-Letter Town*, New York: Avon Books, 1977.

Balazs, Bela, *Theory of the Film*, New York: Dover, 1970.

Bettina, *Bettina*, Paris: Flammarion, 1964.

Cassini, Oleg, *In My Own Fashion*, New York: Simon and Schuster, 1987.

Cohen, Donna, and Carl Eisdorfer, *The Loss of Self: A Family Resource for the Care of Alzheimer's Disease and Related Disorders*, New York: New American Library, 1987.

Cook, Mary, and Kevin Howells, *Adult Sexual Interest in Children*, New York: Academic Press, 1981.

Crewdson, John, *By Silence Betrayed: Sexual Abuse of Children in America*, Boston: Little, Brown & Co., 1988.

De Carlo, Yvonne, *Yvonne*, New York: St Martin's Press, 1987.

Dieppel, Raye Lynne, and J. Thomas Hutton, *Caring for the Alzheimer's Patient*, Buffalo: Prometheus, 1988.

DiMeglio, John C., *Vaudeville USA*, Bowling Green: Bowling Green University Popular Press, 1973.

Douglas, Kirk, *The Ragman's Son*, New York: Simon and Schuster, 1988.

Dyer, Richard, *Stars*, London: British Film Institute, 1979.

Finkelhor, David, *Sexually Victimized Children*, New York: Free Press, 1979.

Fraser, Sylvia, *My Father's House: A Memoir of Incest and Healing*, New York: Ticknor and Fields, 1988.

Friedrich, Otto, *City of Nets*, New York: Perennial, 1987.

Herman, Judith Lewis, *Father–Daughter Incest*, Cambridge: Harvard University Press, 1981.

Hill, Eleanore, *The Family Secret: A Personal Account of Incest*, New York: Dell, 1985.

Hill, James, *Rita Hayworth: A Memoir*, New York: Simon and Schuster, 1983.

Hill, Roger, *Time and Chance*, Privately printed, 1977.

Kanin, Garson, *Hollywood*, New York: Limelight, 1984.

Kidd, Charles, *Debrett Goes to Hollywood*, New York: St Martin's Press, 1986.

Kleiman, Dena, *A Deadly Silence*, New York: Atlantic Monthly Press, 1988.

Kobal, John, *People will Talk*, New York: Alfred A. Knopf, 1985.
————— *Rita Hayworth: The Time, the Place, and the Woman*, York: Berkley Books, 1982.

Lesley, Cole, *Remembered Laughter: The Life of Noël Coward*, New York: Alfred A. Knopf, 1977.

Mace, Nancy L. and Peter V. Rabins, *The 36-Hour Day: A Family Guide to Caring for Persons with Alzheimer's Disease, Related Dementing Illnesses, and Memory Loss in Later Life*, New York: Warner Books, 1984.

Martin, Russell, *Matters Gray and White: A Neurologist, His Patients, and the Mysteries of the Brain*, New York: Fawcett, 1986.

McBride, Joseph, *Hawks on Hawks*, Berkley: University of California Press, 1982.

McCambridge, Mercedes, *The Quality of Mercy*, New York: Berkley Books, 1982.

Merrill, Gary, *Bette, Rita, and the Rest of My Life*, Augusta: Lance Tapley, 1988.

Morella, Joe, and Edward Z. Epstein, *Rita*, New York: Delacorte Press, 1983.

Morin, Edgar, *The Stars*, New York: Grove Press, 1960.

National Center on Child Abuse and Neglect, *Sexual Abuse of Children: Selected Readings*, Washington: U.S. Department of Health and Human Services, 1980.

Navasky, Victor, S., *Naming Names*, New York: Penguin, 1981.

Parrish, Robert, *Hollywood Doesn't Live Here Anymore*, Boston: Little, Brown & Co., 1988.

Parsons, Louella, *Tell It to Louella*, New York: G.P. Putnam's Sons, 1965.
————— *The Gay Illiterate*, Garden City, Doubleday, 1944.

Porter, Ruth, *Child Sexual Abuse Within the Family*, London: Tavistock, 1984.

Powell, Lenore S., and Katie Courtice, *Alzheimer's Disease*, Reading: Addison-Wesley, 1986.

Rasponi, Lanfranco, *The International Nomads*, New York: G.P. Putnam's Sons, 1966.

Reisberg, Barry, *A Guide to Alzheimer's Disease: For Families, Spouses and Friends*, New York: The Free Press, 1983.

Ringgold, Gene, *The Films of Rita Hayworth*, Secaucus: Citadel, 1974.

Roach, Marion, *Another Name for Madness*, New York: Pocket Books, 1985.

Rogers, Henry, *Walking the Tightrope*, New York: William Morrow, 1980.

Slater, Leonard, *Aly: A Biography*, New York: Random House, 1965.

Stein, Charles W. (ed.) *American Vaudeville as Seen by Its Contemporaries*, New York: Alfred A. Knopf, 1984.

Straight, Michael, *After Long Silence*, New York: W.W. Norton, 1983.

Thomas, Bob, *King Cohn*, New York: G.P. Putnam's Sons, 1967.

Tierney, Gene, *Self-Portrait*, New York: Wyden, 1979.

Vanderbilt, Gloria, *Black Knight, White Knight*, New York: Alfred A. Knopf, 1987.

Vander Mey, Brenda, J., and Ronald L. Neff, *Incest as Child Abuse: Research and Applications*, New York: Praeger, 1986.

Walker, Alexander, *Stardom*, New York: Stein and Day, 1970.

Ward, Elizabeth, *Father–Daughter Rape*, New York: Grove Press, 1985.

Williams, Emrys, *Bodyguard*, London: Golden Pegasus, 1960.

Winters, Shelley, *Shelley Also Known as Shirley*, New York: Ballantine Books, 1982.

Index

Affair in Trinidad (film), 240-1, 286
Affectionately Yours (film), 65
Aga Khan III, 169, 175, 201-2, 204, 205, 209-11, 212, 213-4, 216, 218, 222, 224-5, 226, 228, 231-2, 233, 237-8, 239, 244-5, 246, 249, 250, 251, 252, 253, 254, 255, 259, 268, 274, 279, 285, 295, 299-300, 305, 307, 320, 339-40, 343, 350-2; RH's fear of, 225, 231-2, 238, 253, 254, 273-4, 285, 295, 320, 340
Aga Khan III, Begum, 211, 251, 339
al-Khuri, President of Lebanon, 160
All Ashore (film), 258
Allen, Fred, 19
Allen, Gracie, 19
Allyson, June, 121, 286
Alvarez del Vayo, J., 111
Alzheimer, Alois, 357
Alzheimer's disease, dementia, 357, 358, 359, 360, 361, 362-3, 365, 366, 370, 371, 372, 373, 341-7
American Hospital, Paris, 163-4
Anders, Glen, 145-6
Anderson, C.H., 237
Angel (maid), 162, 163, 175
Angels Over Broadway (film), 63-4
Applause (play), 361-3
Armstrong, Del, 364-5
Arno, Max, 35
Arthur, Jean, 55

Astaire, Adele, 13, 71. 88. 372
Astaire, Fred, 12, 13, 21, 66, 71-4, 88, 172, 372
Australian Woodchoppers, The, 13
Avecilla, Joaquin, 10

Bacall, Lauren, 361
Back Street (film), 22
Bacon, Jim, 93, 280-1, 383
Balmain, Pierre, 165
Barrymore, John, 19
Barthelmess, Richard, 55-6
Baxter, Warner, 38
Beardsley, Charles, 85
Beck, Martin, 9, 13
Bellamy, Earl, 73, 148, 149, 158, 240
Bennett, William T., 302
Benny, Jack, 19
Bernstein, Dr Maurice ('Dadda'), 104, 118, 120, 122, 129, 130, 142, 159
Bête Humaine, La (film), 342
Bettina, 342, 345, 347-8, 356
Biddle, Patricia, 81, 85, 87
Blondie on a Budget (film), 63
Blood and Sand (film), 65, 66, 67, 68-9, 78, 91, 166, 177-8
Blum, Suzanne, 252-3, 343
Bogart, Humphrey, 142
Boussac, Marcel, 216
Boyer, Charles, 79, 166
Breen, Joseph I., 146
Bringing Up Baby (film), 55

Broadway, 14, 16, 79, 359-60, 361-2
Broken Oath, The (film), 58
Burns, George, 19
Butler, Harold, 111

Cagney, James, 21, 64, 65
Cansino, Angel, 18
Cansino, Antonio ('Padre'), 10, 18, 29, 178, 314
Cansino, Carmellia, 10
Cansino, Eduardo, 9-37, 39, 42, 43-5, 46, 47, 48-9, 69, 75, 79, 92-3, 104, 108, 128-9. 130-1, 178, 215, 256, 284, 387; and incest, 26, 27, 28, 30, 32, 148
Cansino, Eduardo, Jr ('Sonny'), 17, 28, 29, 31-2, 129
Cansino, Elisa, 9-11, 12-14, 15-16, 17, 18, 20, 22
Cansino, Gabriel, 10, 15-16, 22
Cansino, Gracia, 10
Cansino, Susan, 32
Cansino, Vernon, 17, 20, 21, 25, 26, 28-29, 31, 32-4, 38, 44, 48, 129, 336
Cansino, Volga (*née* Hayworth), 14-15, 16-17, 18-19, 21, 24, 28, 30-1, 32-4, 39, 47, 73, 104, 105, 109, 120, 128-30, 284; alcoholism, 17, 24, 27, 34, 130, 358; and incest, 27, 32-4
Cantor, Eddie, 41
Capra, Frank, 45, 55
Carberry, Jackson, 60
Cardinale, Claudia, 360
Catroux, George, 212
Chambers, Dorothy, 293, 295-97, 300, 302-3, 306
Chaney, Lon, 91
Charlie Chan in Egypt (film), 39
Charly (film), 363
Chevalier, Maurice, 216
Churchill, Winston, S., 107
Circus World (film), 360-1
Citizen Kane (film), 89, 96, 107
Clair, René, 36
Clark, Judge John Gee, 87

Cody, Richard, 262, 298, 312,
Cohn, Harry
  as head of Columbia, 45-6, 63, 64, 65, 70-2, 103, 142-4, 147, 148-9, 227, 240-1, 259, 317-9, 344-5, 348, 371
  and discovery of RH, 46, 50, 52-4, 55, 56-7, 63
  RH's refusal to sleep with, 69-72
  obsession with RH, 70-72
  spies, 71, 103, 147, 157-8, 160, 261
  control over RH and RH's hatred of, 84, 92-3, 99-101, 105, 109, 122, 155, 181, 184, 189-90, 208, 227, 235-6, 240-1, 243, 272, 317-8, 322, 346
  and Eddie Judson, 56, 57, 69, 79
  and Orson Welles, 119, 143-4
  and Dick Haymes, 261, 317, 325-6; Haymes's suspicion of over immigration troubles, 264, 297, 317-8, 329
Colbert, Claudette, 131
Columbia Pictures, 45-7, 48-9, 52, 55, 77, 88, 99, 103, 119, 136-7, 141, 144, 145, 149, 150, 152, 156, 157, 189, 244, 249, 257, 258, 273, 276, 286, 362, 371
  and RH, 50, 63-4, 69, 70-2, 74, 77, 84-5, 100, 148-9, 227, 272; contractual negotiations and disputes, 77, 141-2, 241, 312-3, 318-9, 323, 324-8, 330, 335, 336, 342, 344-5, 350
Communist Party, 126
Confidential magazine, 295-7, 309
Cooper, Gladys, 352
Cotten, Joseph, 96, 104, 329
Cotten, Lenore, 329
Council of Hollywood Guilds and Unions, 127
Cover Girl (film), 99, 100, 103, 105, 162, 348
Coward, Noël, 329, 330-1

Crescent Pictures, 45
Criminals of the Air (film), 45
Crotters, Rachel, 63
Cruisin' Down the River (film), 258
Crum, Bartley, 228, 232, 233-5,
    238, 239, 251, 253, 254, 274-5,
    286, 288-9, 291, 292, 297, 303,
    304, 308, 309-11, 313-7, 327,
    331-2, 335, 336, 341, 346
Cukor, George, 63

Damone, Vic, 337
Dancing Cansinos, The, 9-14, 15,
    16-17, 18, 19-20, 22-4, 28, 34-6,
    42
Dante's Inferno (film), 37, 38
Darnell, Linda, 68
Davis, Bette, 189, 359
De Carlo, Yvonne, 246, 316
de Havilland, Olivia, 64
Del Kail, Lynn, 363, 364, 365, 367
Del Rio, Dolores, 39, 46, 90, 93,
    95, 103, 104, 107
dementia *see* Alzheimer's disease
Dempsey, Jack, 41
Derignon, Paul, 209, 211, 212-3
Dieterle, William, 326, 327
Dietrich, Marlene, 65, 101-2, 105,
    221, 348
Dodero, Alberto, 170
Dolivet, Beatrice, *see* Straight,
    Beatrice
Dolivet, Louis, 106-7, 111, 112-4,
    117, 120, 124
Don Juan (film), 19
Dorsey, Tommy, 257
Douglas, Kirk, 241
Down to Earth (film), 155
Doyle, Judge Elmer, 189
Dreyer, Carl, 36
Dru, Joanne (first Mrs Dick
    Haymes), 257, 269, 270, 290,
    291, 314, 318, 323
Duncan, Isadora, 342, 345
Dwan, Allan, 43

Eaton, Robert, 269
Ellington, Duke, 267

Ellis, Anita, 136
Ellroy, Lee, 207
Embiricos, Andrew, 386
Embiricos, Basil, 386
Eristoff, Prince Gregory, 215

Farouk, King, of Egypt, 167, 231
Fath, Jacques, 206, 212, 342
Federal Bureau of Investigation
    (FBI), 82, 116, 126, 153-4, 155,
    243-4, 275-7, 283, 288-9, 309;
    file on RH, 82, 126, 244
Feldman, Charles, 241-3
Fire Down Below (film), 346-7
Fish, Mamie (Mrs Stuyvesant), 11
Flashing Skates see *Game That Kills,
    The*
Fleming, Macklin, 344
Flynn, Errol, 152, 155-6
Follow Me (musical comedy), 14
Fontaine, Joan, 228, 234, 316
Forbes, Hazel (second Mrs Eddie
    Judson), 41-2, 76, 77-8
Ford, Glenn, 136, 367
Fox films, 35-7, 38-9, 46, 50; *see
    also* Twentieth Century-Fox
Fox, William, 36
Francis, Freddie, 369
Freud, Sigmund, 40

Gabin, Jean, 101-2, 221
Gable, Clark, 166
Game That Kills, The (film), 47
Garbo, Greta, 65, 66
Gardner, Ava, 139-40
Garland, Judy, 132, 133, 278
Gary, Robert, 385
Ghabit, Si Caddour Ben, 211
Gibson, James ('The Scar'),
    153-4, 155, 276-7
Gilda (film), 65, 91, 135, 136-7,
    140, 141, 177, 191, 200, 221,
    347, 378, 382
Gilmore, Bill, 365-6
Gilmore, Polly, 365-6
Gilpin, Bill, 380, 381
Girls Can Play (film), 46, 50
Godino, Grace, 158, 349

Goodman, Benny, 257
Grant, Arnold, 304-5
Grant, Cary, 55, 56
Greenbaum, Lewis, 291, 292
Greenwich Village Follies (musical
    comedy), 18
Gregory, Judge Frank, 280

Hakim, Raymond, 342-3, 344-5
Hakim, Robert, 342
Happy Thieves, The (film) 354
Haran Shifra, 12, 46, 91, 93, 94-5,
    97, 99, 100-1, 103, 105, 108,
    113, 114, 118, 120, 121, 122,
    123, 124, 125, 128, 129, 130,
    131, 132, 136, 159, 160-7, 170,
    171-2, 173, 174, 175, 179, 180,
    181-3, 184, 185-9, 192, 193,
    194-5, 196-7, 198-9, 202, 221
Harrison, Judge Benjamin, 336,
    344, 345
Harty, Russell, 377
Hawks, Howard, 52, 53, 55-6
Haymes, Dick, 257-338, 341, 343,
    344, 350, 355, 381; reputation,
    257, 259, 264-5, 274-5, 313; and
    wives, 257, 258, 271-2, 290-2,
    314, 323, 324; finances, 257,
    277-8, 283-6, 290, 313-4, 318-9,
    324; immigration troubles, 260,
    262-5, 266, 263-72, 273, 286-8,
    290, 294, 297-9, 303, 312,
    314-5, 317, 324, 329-30, 333;
    paranoia, 259, 264-5, 289, 327,
    337; drinking and violence, 261,
    264, 277, 280, 286, 325, 326-7,
    329, 333-4, 335, 336, 337, 338,
    340; nervous health, 289-90,
    294, 336, 338; 'siege' in Hotel
    Madison, 291-2; and role in
    Joseph and His Brethren, 323,
    325-7; exploitation of RH,
    257-8, 278, 313, 318, 322-3
Haymes, Joanne *see* Dru, Joanne
Haymes, Marguerita, 283, 313
Haymes, Nora (*née* Eddington
    Flynn), 257, 270, 272, 277, 280,
    314, 318, 323

Hayworth, Allyn Duran, 14, 15,
    16
Hayworth, Maggie (*née* O'Hare),
    14, 16
Hayworth, Rita (*née* Margarita
    Carmen Cansino): birth 16;
    dance classes, 17-18, 22; school,
    18-19, 20, 24, 25-26, 29, 32;
    move to California, 21; first
    public performance, 23; works
    floating casinos, 24, 92; works
    Mexican clubs, 24-5, 28, 30-1,
    92; meets Hollywood producers,
    35; screen tests, 35, 36; contract
    with Fox, 37; meets Eddie
    Judson, 42; Fox contract
    dropped, 43; free-lance work,
    45, 160; Columbia contract, 45;
    changes name, 46; marries
    Eddie Judson, 47; reconciliation
    with parents, 48; undergoes
    electrolysis, 51; B-pictures at
    Columbia, 52; comes to Cohn's
    attention, 53; first big picture,
    55-6; pushed to have affairs by
    Judson, 62, 69-70, 82, 186;
    career stalls, 63; becomes a star,
    64; refuses to sleep with Cohn,
    70; Columbia contract renewed,
    71; marital difficulties with
    Judson, 72-6; files for divorce,
    77, 81-8; obscene letter, 82, 105,
    115, 116; agrees to pay off
    Judson, 87, 115-6; meets Orson
    Welles, 91; moves in with
    Welles, 94; marries Welles,
    103-4; goes east with Welles,
    111-8; returns to Hollywood,
    119; pregnant, 120; Carmelina
    Drive home, 121, 141, 196;
    birth of Rebecca, 127; mother
    dies, 130; marital difficulties
    with Welles, 131-5, 137; decides
    to divorce Welles, 138; backs off
    divorce, 140; forms Beckworth
    Corporation (*see below*), 142;
    tries for reconciliation with
    Welles and campaigns to do

Lady from Shanghai, 143; pin-up photo on atom bomb, 144; reconciliation fails, 151-4; receives threat, 153-4, 155, announces divorce, 154; trip to Europe, 155-6; files for divorce, 156; pregnancy by Howard Hughes and abortion, 159; leaves for Europe, 159-61; curettage, 162-3; meets Aly Khan, 170; visit from gypsy fortune-teller, 172-3; trip to Spain, 176-9; returns to California, 180; trip to Mexico and Cuba, 184-8; Welles divorce final, 189; suspended by Columbia, 190-1; leaves US, 191-2; announces marriage to Aly Khan, 203-4; pregnant, 205; marries Aly Khan, 212-3; health during pregnancy, 214, 216; birth of Yasmin, 219; attends Welles premiere, 222; trip to Africa, 223-5; leaves Aly Khan, 225; kidnap threat to daughters, 235; files for divorce, 239-40; returns to Columbia, 240; under suspicion from HUAC, 243-4; reconciliation with Aly Khan, 246-52; divorce final, 255; meets Dick Haymes, 257-8; guilt feelings about Haymes, 265, 266, 329, 333; threat to RH and Yasmin, 273-4, 275-7, 279, 284-5, 288; marries Dick Haymes, 281-2; custody battle over Yasmin, 259, 274-5, 288, 294-5, 299-311, 315-22, 328-38, 338-9; child neglect charges, 302-9, 317, 321, 332, 381-2; files suit against Columbia, 312-3; moves to Nevada, 314-5; agreement with Columbia, 321; forms Crystal Bay Productions, 323, 325; lawsuit against Columbia, 307-8, 349; marital troubles with Haymes, 333-4; leaves Haymes, 334; takes daughters to Europe, 338; files for divorce, 341; signs final contract with Columbia, 346; marries Jim Hill, 354; divorces Jim Hill, 357; Alzheimer's disease/dementia, 357, 358, 359, 360, 361, 362-3, 365, 366, 370, 371, 372, 373, 384-7; screen career over, 366; disastrous trip to London, 374-7; celebrity cruises, 377; Argentina trip, 378-9; ward of Orange County Public Guardian's Office, 380-1; Yasmin appointed guardian, 385

appearance, 23, 38, 44, 50, 59, 68, 76-7, 158, 346, 349, 353, 370; hair, 25, 50-1, 57, 68, 148, 155
intelligence/lack of education, 24, 91, 95, 108, 112, 121-2, 162
shyness, 20, 34-5, 52, 61, 65, 88, 92, 105, 108, 113, 114, 117, 122, 196, 215, 359, 377
silence, 25, 28-9, 31, 58-9, 65, 67, 91, 112-3, 197, 221, 298, 301, 321, 324-5, 355, 358, 381
ability to 'blank out'/withdraw/ 'mask', 26, 61, 65, 77, 112, 157, 221, 298, 323, 385, 386
submissiveness, 23, 29, 50, 59, 62, 70, 78, 112, 113, 149, 215, 279, 294, 314, 322, 324, 328, 334, 349
professionalism, 71, 111, 158, 191, 347, 358-9, 360, 362
'little girl'/simplicity, 69, 101, 107, 108, 113, 120
insecurity/ego, 57, 75, 87, 88, 91, 92-3, 94, 95, 100-1, 107, 112-3, 119, 123, 215, 256, 353
sexuality, 35, 39-40, 49, 55, 62, 64, 91-2, 94, 120, 123, 130, 136, 144, 183, 185, 241, 254
jealousy, 96-7, 132, 176, 186, 216

anxiety, 38, 72, 133, 134, 136, 152, 162, 196, 239, 359

moodiness/rages, 67, 133-4, 143, 186, 197, 220, 354-5, 357, 358, 361, 362-3, 370-1, 372-4, 387

self-destructive impulses, 82, 256, 387

drinking, 133, 159, 221, 260, 325, 346, 354-5, 358-9, 361, 362, 371, 374, 375, 377, 381, 382-3, 384

fear of flying/phobias, 152, 189, 259, 364-5, 369-70, 375, 386

loss of memory, 357, 362, 371, 373, 377, 380

and Catholicism/Christianity, 203, 214, 219, 253, 274, 289

and dancing, 29, 34, 38, 45, 66, 72, 88, 159, 180, 221, 386

and acting, 38, 144, 159; 'terrified', 38, 55-6

as sex symbol, 32, 56, 68, 135, 157, 175; pin-up photo, 65, 77, 90, 136, 144

dislike of Hollywood, 92, 100, 107, 110, 119, 131, 191, 208, 228, 236, 349, 354

publicity/relations with the press, 38, 52, 56, 60-2, 63, 65, 72, 77, 82-3, 84-5, 103, 115, 143, 150, 152, 155, 162, 175, 182, 192, 200, 203-4, 211-12, 216, 227-8, 241, 134, 277, 279-82, 298, 374

and money, 45, 56, 72, 78, 81, 82, 85, 86, 97, 114, 136, 141-2, 158, 176-7, 206-7, 225, 228, 234, 236, 253-4, 285-6, 312-3, 322-3, 354, 363

Beckworth Corporation, 142, 144, 157, 181, 189, 236, 312, 313, 319, 322, 323, 329

and father, 18-23, 26-8, 29, 30, 35, 39, 49, 69, 101, 128-9, 256, 286, 387

and incest, 26-8, 26, 27, 28, 40, 44, 47, 62-3, 72-3, 101, 111-2, 133, 256, 265, 284, 303, 357, 387

father figures, 43, 46, 62, 94, 108, 352-3,

and mother, 32-4, 39, 101, 120, 128-30, 283, 358

as mother, 120, 128-9, 200, 210, 224, 256, 284-5

Hayworth, Vinton, 73

Hearst, William Randolph, 89

Hecht, Ben, 63-4, 350

Heim, James E., 380-1

Held, Anna, 14

Heyerdahl, Thor, 242-3

Hill, Hortense, 107-10, 120, 121-2, 130, 196

Hill, Jim, 350-5, 357, 358, 359; career, 350, 352; drinking, 354-5; 'using' RH, 350, 351, 352

107-10, 121-2, 130, 196

Hiller, Wendy, 352

Hit the Saddle (film), 45

Holden, William, 160, 190

Hollywood Canteen, 97

Hoover, J. Edgar, 275-6

House Un-American Activities Committee, 243

Hughes, Howard, 159, 160, 163, 182, 210

Human Cargo (film), 43

Hunt, Helen, 44, 46, 47, 50-4

Hyde, Johnny, 141-2, 312

International Free World Association, 106, 111

International Pictures, 137

Iran, Shah of, 167

Isadora (film), 342, 344, 345

Islam, Ismaili Muslims, 169, 202, 204, 205, 210, 211, 214, 219, 223, 230, 231, 232, 234, 238, 244, 254, 274-6, 279, 289, 305, 351

It Happened One Night (film), 45

It's All True (film), 90

Jackolo, Nathaniel A., 15-16, 18

427

Jackson, Helen Heurt, 39
James, Harry, 257
Jane Eyre (film), 91
Jazz Singer, The (film), 19
Jean (waiter), 172
Jessel, George, 13
Joint Anti-Fascist Refugee
    Committee, 127
Jolson, Al, 12, 19
Joseph and His Brethren (film), 322,
    323, 325-8, 344, 348
Judson, Dorothy (*née* Oliver), 41
Judson, Eddie, 40-88, 98-9, 105,
    106, 109, 110-12, 114-17, 119,
    141, 148, 160, 215, 256, 267,
    278, 298, 322, 383; background,
    40-2; finances, 41, 75, 82, 86;
    plans for RH, 49, 52, 59, 61-2,
    81, 86-7; exploitation of RH,
    48-9, 62-3, 69, 70, 75-6, 81-2,
    86, 87, 94; pushes RH to sleep
    with other men, 62, 69, 70-1,
    82, 86; obsessive harassment of
    RH, 85, 74; infidelity, 74;
    threats, 75-6, 78, 82, 83, 84,
    111; lawsuit against RH, 98,
    106, 110-11, 114-15
Judson, Hazel *see* Forbes, Hazel

Kahane, B.B., 244, 318, 324
Keene, Tom, 45
Kelly, Gene, 99, 348
Kerr, Deborah, 352-3
Khan, Aga *see* Aga Khan III
Khan, Prince Aly, 93, 166, 168,
    169-235, 238-40, 241, 244-56,
    261, 262, 268, 269, 273-5, 278,
    280, 285, 325, 326, 328, 338-40,
    341-3, 345, 347-8, 350-2, 355-6,
    366; pursues RH, 170-1; goes
    to Spain with RH, 175-9;
    follows RH to California, 182;
    goes to Mexico and Cuba with
    RH, 184-8; marries RH, 212-3;
    trip to Africa, 223-4; letter to
    RH about divorce, 229-30;
    effects reconciliation, 247-52;
    divorce final, 255; custody battle

over Yasmin, 259, 274-5, 288-9,
    294-5, 299-311, 325-21, 328-33,
    338-40; reunited with Yasmin,
    339-40; French divorce hearing,
    343; UN representative for
    Pakistan, 355; dies, 356

    as Muslim leader, 169, 202,
        204, 205, 210, 211, 214, 219,
        223-4, 238, 244, 305, 351-3
    and money, 174, 194, 205-6,
        209-10, 224, 252-3
    as lover, 169, 183, 217
    womanizing, infidelity, 207,
        217, 220, 224, 228, 233,
        234-5, 239, 244, 246, 251,
        254, 299-300, 316
    with children, 183, 191, 194,
        199, 220, 247-9, 275, 339-40
    charm, 189, 207, 340
    and father, 169, 175, 201, 202,
        205, 209-10, 244-5, 250, 259,
        299-300, 351-2
    image of RH, 166, 179, 190,
        210, 221
Khan, Prince Amyn, 171, 199,
    204, 205, 220, 234
Khan, Princess Joan Aly (*née*
    Yarde-Buller), 171, 199, 204,
    205, 212
Khan, Prince Karim (now Aga
    Khan IV), 171, 199, 204, 205,
    220, 234, 351-2
Khan, Prince Sadruddin, 351
Khan, Princess Yasmin, 219, 220,
    225, 226, 228, 229-36, 237-9,
    240, 245, 246-9, 251, 252-5,
    259, 268, 269, 273-7, 281-2,
    283-5, 288-90, 293, 295-300,
    302-11, 313-7, 319-322, 324,
    326, 328-34, 335, 338-43, 345,
    346, 347-8, 350-1, 355-6, 358,
    359, 361, 366, 372, 381-2,
    384-7
    religious education, 204, 219,
        230, 231, 234, 238, 254, 274,
        289, 321
    kidnap threat, 235, 237; second

series of threats, 273, 275-7, 279, 284, 288, 295
custody battle, 259, 274-5, 288-9, 294-5, 299-311, 315-21, 328-33, 338-40
and press, 237, 277, 279, 295-7
child neglect charges, 302-11, 317, 321, 332
reunited with father, 339-40
RH's guardian, 384-7
marries and has child, 386
King Lear (play), 341
King, Sherwood, *If I Die Before I Wake*, 145
Kitt, Eartha, 222
Korda, Alexander, 110, 117, 119, 144, 172
Krim, Mac, 382, 383, 385

Laage, Barbara, 143
Lady from Shanghai, The (film), 65, 145, 153, 156, 172, 186
Lady in Question, The (film), 63
Lady in the Dark (play), 79
Laemmle, Carl, Jr, 35, 57-8, 60
Lahr, Bert, 19
Lancaster, Burt, 353
Landry, Bob, 77, 90
Lang, Fritz, 36
Lawrence, Florence, 57-8, 61
Lawrence, Gertrude, 79
League of Nations, 169
Leighter, Jackson, 90, 104, 119, 223, 231, 232
Leighter, Lola, 223, 231, 232
Lemmon, Jack, 347
Leon, Gary, 37
Lesley, Cole, 330-1
Life, magazine, 77
Lilies of the Field (film), 363
Lombard, Carole, 60
Lona Hanson (film), 160, 181, 184, 189, 241
Look magazine, 60-1
Louis, Jean, 137
Loves of Carmen, The (film), 157, 159, 160, 210
Luft, Sid, 278

Lyons, Leonard, 298

Macbeth (film), 156
McCambridge, Mercedes, 172
McDermott, Thomas, 262-4
McNally, Judge James B.M., 290
MacNamee, Judge, 281
Macready, George, 136
Maestretti, Judge A.J., 254
Magliano, Thérèse, 212
Magnificent Ambersons, The (film), 89, 90, 96
Mamoulian, Rouben, 66
Mann, Delbert, 352-4
Marcus, David, 289, 298-9, 323, 330
Marden, Ben, 78
Markle, Fletcher, 172
Marlin, Don, 82, 83, 87, 98, 100
Marlowe, Christopher, *Dr Faustus*, 222
Marshall, George, 43, 354
Martin, Tony, 63, 140
Maté, Rudolph, 36-7, 158
Matthews, Kerwin, 326
Mature, Victor, 79-80, 88, 91, 92, 94
Maugham, W. Somerset, 257
Maxwell, Elsa, 165, 166, 167-8, 170, 176, 202, 221, 224, 251, 300
Mayock, Welburn, 312
Meet Nero Wolfe (film), 45
Menefee, Wilbur, 143
Mercury Wonder Show, 97-101, 103, 105, 106
Merimée, Prosper, *Carmen*, 10, 157
Merrill, Gary, 359
Message to Garcia (film), 43
Meyako Sisters, The, 13
MGM, 21, 153, 363
Miller, Ann, 71, 72, 359, 362, 373-4, 377, 385
Miner, Dr James, 380
Miss Sadie Thompson (film), 257, 259, 261, 262, 266, 269, 272, 313, 346
Mitchum, Robert, 347, 363
Monroe, Leonard, 381
Monroe, Marilyn, 156

Montero, Rosario, 10
Montespan, Françoise de, 165
Montez, Maria, 66
Moorehead, Agnes, 96
Mori, Paola, Countess di Girfalco (third Mrs Orson Welles), 341
Morris, William (agency), 313, 318
Morse, Warren W., 380
Moss, Bud, 361, 374-7, 378-9
Mr Arkadin (film), 304
Music in My Heart (film), 63, 140
My Gal Sal (film), 79, 80

National Council of American-Soviet Friendship, 127
Nelson, Ralph, 363, 364, 366, 367
Nesbitt, Cathleen, 352
Nicolson, Virginia, 90
Nims, Ernest, 138
Niven, David, 154, 155
Niven, Primmie, 154
Novak, Kim, 348-9, 371, 382

Odets, Clifford, 322, 324, 326-7, 354
O'Hara, John, *Pal Joey*, 348
Old Louisiana (film), 45
Only Angels Have Wings (film), 52, 53, 55-6, 63
Orleans Braganza, Prince Jean d', 212
Otero, Carmencita and Caroline, 11
Othello (film), 166, 199

Paddy O'Day (film), 40
Pahlavi, Mahmud, 158-9
Paka, Toots, 13
Pal Joey (film), 348-9, 350
Pan, Hermes, 66-9, 73, 76, 80, 85, 94, 224, 355, 357-8, 366, 367, 372-4, 378
Paramount Pictures, 79, 190, 342
Parkin, Loretta, 28-30, 31, 38, 58-9
Parrish, Robert, 346, 347
Parsons, Louella, 35, 36, 84, 214, 273, 276
Passion of Joan of Arc, The (film), 36

Pastor, Tony, 12
Pépé le Moko (film), 342
Picasso, Pablo, 209
Poggi, Grace, 28
Porter, Cole, 138
Power, Tyrone, 68, 107, 166
Pratt, Jim, 137-8
Prohibition, 24

Queen Christina (film), 66

Ramona (film), 39, 42, 43, 44
Rattigan, Terence, *Separate Tables*, 352
Rebellion (film), 45
Reina, Carmine, 10
Republic Studios, 45, 156
Rhodes, Judge Orlando, 104, 357
Richman, Harry, 77-8
Richmond, Paul Owen, 41-2
RKO Pictures, 42, 90
Roberts, Curtis, 362-3, 366, 369-71, 374, 383
Rochat, Professor Rudolph, 218
Rodgers and Hart, 348
Rogers, Ginger, 71, 73, 88
Rogers, Henry C., 40, 43, 49, 50, 55, 56, 57, 58-62, 69, 383-4
Rogers, Roz, 40, 44, 49-50, 57, 58, 59, 60, 61-2, 69, 71, 75, 81, 88, 384
Rogers St John, Adela, 41
Roosevelt, Eleanor, 127
Roosevelt, Franklin Delano, 107, 122, 124-5, 126, 127
Rose, Billy, 120
Rossen, Robert, 354
Rosser, Frances ('Aunt Fanny'), 155, 180
Rousselet, Judge Jacques, 204
Rubino, Elisabeth, 95, 96, 117, 129, 134, 193-4
Russell, Lillian, 12

Sadek, Narriman, 231
Sadicoff, Harry, 87
Salome (film), 144, 243, 249, 258, 259, 322

Sargent, John Singer, 137
Scarface (film), 55
Schenck, Joe, 28, 34, 35, 43
Schiffer, Bob, 49, 70-2, 76, 94,
    148, 149-51, 157, 158, 183, 215,
    233, 241, 242-3, 244, 259-60,
    261, 315, 350, 381, 382
Scott, Walter, *Ivanhoe*, 121
Separate Tables (film), 352-4
Sheehan, Winfield, 35-6, 39,
    42-43, 46
Sheridan, Ann, 64
Sherman, Vincent, 240
Shorty (chauffeur), 103-4, 105,
    132, 198
Shubert Brothers, 14
Sidney, George, 348-9
Sinatra, Frank, 348-9
Slater, Leonard, 183
Sloane, Everett, 112-3, 145
Sloane, Libby, 77, 152, 367-8
Smyth, Judge George W., 307-8,
    313, 315-7, 321
Sons of Satan (film), 361
Spiegel, Sam, 79, 134, 139-40
stars, star system, 45, 57-8, 65, 77,
    377
Stauffer, Teddy, 155-6
Step on a Crack (play), 359-60
Stevenson, Robert, 91
Story on Page One, The (film), 354
Straight, Beatrice, 106, 111,
    113-4, 117, 124
Stranger, The (film), 134-5, 137,
    138, 139, 141, 142
Strawberry Blonde, The (film), 64-5,
    66, 67-8, 78, 91
Streeter, Jack, 235
Stromberg, Hunt, 35
Sunset Boulevard (film), 41
Susan and God (film), 63
Swanson, Gloria, 41
Swearinger, Ronald E., 385

Tales of Manhattan (film), 79
Tales That Witness Madness (film),
    369-71, 382
Taps, Jonie, 62, 137, 257, 258, 318

They Came to Cordura (film), 354
Three Mesquiteers, The, 45
Tierney, Belle, 303
Tierney, Gene, 254, 259, 299,
    300, 303, 316
Time Runs (play), 222
Todd, Mike, 142
Tomlin, Pinky, 40
Tomorrow Is Forever (film), 131
Tonight and Every Night (film), 119,
    120, 122
Torem, Charles, 233, 234, 238,
    254, 294, 299, 304, 306, 307,
    309-11, 316-7, 331, 332, 338
Tracy, Spencer, 37
Truman, Harry S., 127-8
Tutti (valet), 182, 202, 218, 219,
    246, 249
Twentieth Century (film), 55
Twentieth Century Films, 28, 43
Twentieth Century-Fox, 43, 45,
    65-6, 79

Under the Pampas Moon (film), 38-9
United Artists, 325, 328
United Nations, 355
Unthinking Lobster, The (play), 222
USO, 97

Vanderbilt, Gloria, 124-5
Van Upp, Virginia, 136
vaudeville, 9-10, 11-15, 17-20, 97,
    359
Vera Cruz (film), 350
Vidor, Charles, 63, 136, 157
Villapadierna, Count José-Maria
    ('Pepe'), 253-4, 256

Wald, Jerry, 326
Walsh, Raoul, 64, 66
Warner, Jack, 166, 246
Warner Bros, 19, 20, 21, 35, 43,
    64, 65
War and Peace (film), 110, 118, 119
War of the Worlds (radio broadcast,
    89
Waterbury, Ruth, 78
Wei Tao Ming, 111

431

Welles, Beatrice, 341
Welles, Dick, 87; alcoholism, 133, 147
Welles, Orson, 26, 70, 74, 79, 80, 88-156, 157, 159, 166-8, 171, 172, 181, 183, 185, 193, 196, 215, 217, 228, 244, 256, 261, 284, 302, 324, 329, 346, 357, 358, 366, 367; sees photo of RH, 90; meets RH, 91; RH moves in with, 94; *Mercury Wonder Show*, 97-101; marries RH, 103-4; falls ill, 117-18; guilt at turning away from RH, 132-3; RH countersigns *Stranger* contract, 137; *Around the World* collapses, 142; agrees with Cohn to do *Lady from Shanghai*, 142; reconciliation during filming, 143, 149-52; leaves RH, 154; leaves for Italy, 156; in Italy, 165; evening with RH in Cannes, 166-7; RH attempts to win back, 176; divorce final, 189; RH summons before marriage to Aly Khan, 207-8; Paris premiere, 222; supports RH in child neglect case, 304-5; RH sues for back child support, 346; RH doesn't recognize, 384

as film-maker, 89, 134, 145-7
care for RH, 95, 100, 108-9, 123, 139, 143
pursues political career, 106-7, 110-15, 122, 126-8, 130, 138
lack of paternal feeling, 108-9, 120, 128, 142, 183, 199, 305, 341
health, 117-9, 120, 124-5; drinking, 120
infidelity, 124, 132, 137-8, 207
psychology reflected in *The Lady from Shanghai*, 145-7

Welles, Paola *see* Mori Paola
Welles, Rebecca, 127, 128, 130, 138, 139, 140, 142, 143, 144, 152, 153, 154, 155, 159, 167, 180-1, 183, 191, 192, 193-4, 195, 197-8, 200, 201, 214, 217, 220, 225, 228, 230, 232, 235, 237, 246-7, 275, 276, 277, 281-2, 283-5, 290, 293, 295-300, 302-9, 313-6, 321, 324, 328-9, 333, 334, 335, 338, 341-3, 345, 346, 347, 348, 359, 366, 382, 386
threat, 153-4, 155, 276-7; attempted kidnap, 217; kidnap threat, 235, 237
and press, 237, 295-7
child neglect charges, 302-11, 317, 321, 332
marries, 366
Welles, Virginia (*née* Nicholson), 90
Westall, Walter W., 304
Westchester Society for the Prevention of Cruelty to Children, 302, 304, 308
Whoopee (musical comedy), 41
Williams, Emrys, 170, 175, 176, 177, 178-9, 209-10, 216, 217, 220, 221
Wilson, Earl, 313
Windsor, Duke and Duchess of, 206
Winters, Shelley, 139-40
World War II, 81
Wrath of God (film), 363, 366, 367, 369, 371
Wright and Millikan, 111

You'll Never Get Rich (film), 71, 72, 73-4, 77, 93
Young, Loretta, 43
You Were Never Lovelier (film), 73, 88

Zanuck, Darryl F., 28, 43, 65-6, 166, 167
Ziegfeld, Flo, *Ziegfeld Follies*, 14, 16, 41

432